The Good Nanny Guide is wri |
twenty years of hiring and fi |
pairs between them. They |
hundreds of employers, nan |
to produce a unique referen |
the essential information and   ...pe with the current
nanny explosion.

Charlotte Breese and Hilaire Gomer met in the maternity ward
of the West London Hospital when each was having her first
child. Now they have four apiece. Charlotte Breese is an
experienced employer of NNEB-trained nannies, maternity
nurses and temps. Hilaire Gomer is an old hand with mother's
helps and au pairs. Both have known triumph and disaster.

Charlotte Breese worked as a publisher's editor and helped
pioneer the market for information books on the Middle East.
Hilaire Gomer is a freelance journalist who has worked for
numerous national newspapers.

THE GOOD NANNY GUIDE

GUIDE

*The Complete Handbook on Nannies, Au-Pairs,
Mother's Helps and Childminders*

Charlotte Breese and Hilaire Gomer

CENTURY

LONDON SYDNEY AUCKLAND JOHANNESBURG

Reprinted 1988, 1989
Second edition 1991
First published in 1988 by Century, an imprint of
the Random Century Group Ltd,
20 Vauxhall Bridge Road, London SW1V 2SA

Random Century (Australia) Pty Ltd,
20 Alfred Street, Milsons Point, Sydney, NSW 2061
Australia

Random Century New Zealand Ltd,
18 Poland Road, Glenfield, Auckland 10,
New Zealand

Random Century South Africa (Pty) Ltd,
PO Box 337, Bergvlei, 2012 South Africa

British Library Cataloguing in Publication Data

Breese, Charlotte
    The good nanny guide.
    I. Title   II. Gomer, Hilaire
    649

    ISBN 0 7126 50660

Photoset by Deltatype Ltd, Ellesmere Port
Printed by
Mackays of Chatham, Chatham, Kent

Acknowledgements

We are indebted to all the following employers for filling in a detailed questionnaire well:

Serena Ballin, Nicky Baring, Claudia Bartosik, Kipper Bosanquet, Judith Becher, Imogen Mary Birch Reynardson, Judi Bodenham, Sarah Bolton, Victoria Borwick, Charlotte Burnaby-Atkins, Carolyn Chambers, Renu Chopra, Sarah Cottenham, Ros Caldecott, Caroline Davidson, Sarah Douglas-Pennant, Juliet Dunn, Elinor Elliott, Patricia Elliott, Damaris Fletcher, Susie Green-Armytage, Mary Hall, Siri Harris, Rachel James, Kay King, Lucy Le Fanu, Jean Letts, Penny Lucy, Philippa Lloyd, Loraine Melville, Victoria Moger, Cheryl Mowinckel, Emma Mumtaz, Bunny Murray-Willis, Katie Neilson, Jane Nerizzano, Kathy Pflaum, Fiona Peel, Laura Pym, Phyllis Rennell, Tish Seligman, Caroline Serocold, Gill Smith, Elodie Stanley, Davina Thackara, Mary-Rose Thompson, Anne Tickell, Sarah Tillie, David Toms, Bridgett Walters, Rebecca Willer, Cherry Williams, Sarah Williams, Victoria Wilson, Suzanne Woloczynska, Bobby Wylie.

A few of those listed below are nannies, but to all those nannies who returned questionnaires anonymously as we requested, very many thanks. Others to whom we are grateful for research, help or information include:

Deborah Bedford, Jean Richardson, Deirdre Davis, Dawn Watts, Jennifer Ellard, Mary Padfield, Jenny Curtis, Stephen Patrick, Tessa McCormack, Nanny Jones, Patsy Smith, Betty Parsons, Christine Hill, Lizzie Heskett, Polly Woodman, Fayleen Mun-Gavin, Denny Chambers, Helena Buxton, Caroline Dawnay, Louise Davis, Mary McRae, Pamela Townsend, Camilla

Acknowledgements

Harford, Peter Johnson, Peter Breese, Bert Myrin, James Odgers, Hilary Clarke, Angela Hovey, Sally Ann Lloyd, Sheila Bellamy, Jeanne Magagna, Hugh Thompson, Judith Hackman, Kelly Meighen, Dick Odgers, Jilly Norris, Linda Layton, Nicki Sievwright, Jessica Johnson, Barbara Nicholls, Jane Ingham, Clare Bryne, Morwenna Haig, Karen Smelt, Winifred Symonds, Julie Rhodes, Angela Orssich, Gail Seaton, Kathrin Ahrens, Nathalie Phillimore, Clare Odgers, Sabrina Duppel, Victoria Russell, Rick Pflaum, Nick Whitmey, Robert Sutton, Melissa Perkins, Jackie Baxendale, Susan Hay, Mrs Baxter, Radina Batica, Julia Bates, Clare Asquith, Jane Ingham, Nina Prentice, Ann Biddescombe, Caroline Alcock, Mrs Wasmuth of the Pre-Select Agency, Solihull, Ann Bristow of the Kensington Tax Office, Sue Owen of the NCMA, Peter Moss of the Thomas Coram Research Institute and Lucy Daniels of the Working Mothers' Association.

Special thanks to John Gomer for all his work on the word processor. Also to Sarah Wallace and Sarah Riddell of Random Century for their efficiency and kindness.

For Olivia and in memory of Georgia

Preface

A book about nannies is a book about people, as well as many issues which are not at first sight anything to do with the subject. The aspects that a nanny touches on in her employer's life are limitless – all human life is there. Throughout the book the authors have used 'he' almost always when referring to children. This was done purely because most child carers are women, so using 'he' limited the potential confusion of too many 'shes' in the text.

The effect of a nanny on a household is deep. Children make parents emotional and this colours the climate of their dealings with whoever is in their house looking after their children for them – be it nanny, mother's help or au pair. The book discusses questions of personalities, background, taste, morals, manners, standards, class, child abuse, maternity, child psychology, state-funded child care, childminders, day nurseries, sex, work-place crèches, handicapped children, holidays and travel, the Inland Revenue, suing, nannies' residential colleges, idealism, discipline, training, the role of parents and child-rearing philosophies.

When the two authors started having children there was no book that could give them a few clues about the pros and cons of childminders, the art of living with a residential nanny or an au pair, the advantages of daily nannies and whether maternity nurses were worth the cost. Day nurseries were not an option in those days, as they are for many mothers today. They had to learn from more experienced mothers, and through trial and error. They have refined their interviewing techniques and become better at dealing with nanny problems over the years. Between them they have experienced just about every variation of living-in child carer as well as daily help, temporaries, maternity nurses, a daily male mother's help and a childminder.

Contents

Contents

Contents

1

Definitions

History does not relate quite when the word 'nanny' joined the English language. Even the *Complete Oxford English Dictionary* has little to say about it or its derivation.

The appellation 'nurse' was used as early as the fifteenth century to refer to a woman who looked after children. Nurse itself sprang from 'wet nurse', a woman who was hired to suckle a child – a 'nursling'. She did this for various reasons, including the death of the child's mother in childbirth or, if she survived, because of her vanity. Bonding was not even thought of. Americans still call breast feeding 'nursing' – an example of archaic English surviving elsewhere.

The comic nurse in Shakespeare's *Romeo and Juliet* started her stay at the Capulets as the heroine's wet nurse. By the eighteenth century some wet nurses had metamorphosed into nurses, having stayed on after a child had been weaned – they were then aptly named 'dry nurses'. The first reference that Jonathan Gathorne-Hardy could find in his book *The Rise and Fall of The British Nanny*, published in 1972, was in a letter in 1711 from Lady Mary Wortley Montagu to her nurse calling her 'Dear Nanny'. By the next century the job of a nursery nurse was established. Every good home had one. By the early twentieth century the word 'nanny' had become common parlance, though nurse, 'nursie' and 'nana' remained current up to the Second World War. Nursery nurses were in demand during the war, running government nurseries so that mothers could contribute to the war effort.

Nanny is an odd word. We talk about nanny goats – the female of the billy goat, and there may be some link between the wet nurse as suckler and goats who were milked. 'Nan' and 'nanny' are diminutives for granny, apparently originally popular in

1

Wales and the Midlands, and 'nan' has survived among the working class even today. In the past nannies took on the surname of their employers sometimes, and thus became known as 'Nanny Caldecott' for example. Some research seeks to prove a connection between 'nanny' and the christian name Anne, as it was a nickname for Anne. It is just possible there is a link between granny and nanny and St Anne – she was the mother of the Virgin Mary and therefore a granny.

Why Do You Employ Other People to Care for Your Children?

It is not just the people who can afford it who want to employ someone to care for their children some of the time. Some feel that child care is a never-ending task which no one has found a way of mechanizing. Other women would love to have some help with their children, but feel it is a luxury they can't justify unless they have a job.

Today mothers admit more openly than they did in the past the desperation and claustrophobia they can feel after days and weeks of looking after their offspring single-handed. Once it was the norm up and down the land for mothers to grin and bear the relentless demands of whining voices and clutching hands. They would not have found a sympathetic ear for their grumbles. After all, caring for kids and keeping the home fires burning had been a woman's lot since the cavemen.

Mothers give the following reasons for employing carers for their offspring:

I need another pair of hands. I don't want all three dragged everywhere each time one of them is collected from somewhere.

To keep my independence and to stop me going potty.

I have to be able to work away from home at any time. I couldn't be with children 24 hours a day.

I like to have some energy left for my husband at the end of the day. This way I can work part time and enjoy my children.

Business entertaining is part of my life and so I have to have someone to dilute my other responsibilities.

I would be an appalling mother if I had to be with the kids all day.

I'm 41 and run my own business. I find babies exhausting and restricting.

To try to ensure that the kids have a cheerful person with them most of the time. She is also good back-up if I'm ill so that the children's routines can go on. This is very important to me.

Freedom to do other things rather than just be a mother.

The Nanny Explosion

It was natural for Jonathan Gathorne-Hardy in his book *The Rise and Fall of the British Nanny* to write about what he thought was the last gasps of a dying breed. Ironically, just as the ink had dried, the dinosaur, as in Jan Pienkowski's *Meg's Eggs*, began to uncurl.

The big reason behind the rising demand for nannies and every kind of child care is the fact that more women work than ever before. The latest figures, published in 1984, showed that women account for 10.9 million of the labour force (men at work total 15.5 million). This represents 41.4 per cent of the total workforce, compared with only 38.9 per cent in 1975. The increase has come mainly from women doing part-time work.

In 1983, 38 per cent of working women had dependent children and over two-thirds of these worked part time. Of women with children aged four or under, 25 per cent worked, and this is probably an underestimate because many women are part of the undocumented 'black economy'.

In 1983, 5 per cent of families with children aged four and under had both parents working full time. This tiny, pioneer group is still too small to make an impact on national statistics, but it is greatly significant in the nanny world. Double income families, particularly in cities and towns, contributed significantly to the jump in demand for nannies and mother's helps in the 1980s. Upwardly mobile urban professional couples (Yuppies) start out as Dinkies – double income, no kids. Then they turn into Tinkies – two incomes, nanny and kids.

People still tend to think that the upwardly mobile who hire help for the children are wealthy city slickers. Some of them are of course, but there is many a middle income couple, who live in the London suburbs and in southern England particularly, who can afford and find space for a resident young nanny or British or foreign mother's help, or an au pair in their three-bedroomed semi-detached. Today, people whose parents wouldn't have dreamt of, let alone have been able to afford, living-in help for their children, are doing just that, and they include factory workers, clerks, secretaries and nurses.

Feminism in the 1970s helped turn around women's, and the media's, attitude to their role in society. The introduction of statutory maternity leave, pay and allowance in the late 1970s made it easier for many women to return to work after their first baby. It is now the norm for women to work, married or not, and it isn't entirely acceptable any more for a woman to sign off when she starts a family. Being 'just a housewife and mother' is no longer fashionable; today a woman is defined by her work. Flexi-time mums say incredulously of the full-time mother with school-age children, 'What does she *do* all day?'

Women who do not need to work are choosing to do so in this generation. Their mothers actually gained social status by giving up work to have children. The arrangement was considered fine by both husband and wife. In fact it was only the wives of poor men who had to work. The poor still work and never feel a guilty pang – they don't have the option.

In 1989 a survey carried out by the Office of Population Censuses and Surveys (OPCS) found that 41 per cent of mothers with children aged under five worked, and 23 per cent of that number worked full time.

There is a trend for women of all kinds to start their families later and go back to work afterwards sooner. Over the period 1950–79 the median time of return to work after the latest birth had fallen from around seven and a half years to just over three and a half years, and all the signs suggest that the trend continues.

Geriatric mums are becoming commonplace: Ursula Andress was 43, Priscilla Presley was 42, and Felicity Kendal was 40. In 1987 Kathleen Campbell became Britain's oldest mum at 55. At 35 a woman used to be described as an 'elderly *primagravida*' (first-time mother) by the medics, but at Queen Charlotte's Hospital in London they report 'the expression is obsolete. We just don't call them anything any more. We see 40-plus mums almost every week.'

Medical advances in obstetrics, ultrasound and amniocentesis, as well as better nutrition, increase the chances of the survival of the foetust. So more women feel it is safe to postpone child-bearing till their middle and late 30s and even well into their 40s, and these women are even less likely to stop work than those in their 20s. A study carried out by S. Dex and S. Perry in 1984 found that the more work experience a woman has, the more likely she is to have work-committed attitudes.

As well as all the sociological changes that have occurred in the 1970s and 1980s, there has been a big emphasis on pregnancy, birth and children. The media, the manufacturers and the advertisers have joined the bandwagon. The post-war baby-boom generation – the young of the 1960s – are now parents in their 30s and 40s with money to spend on their children. At last there are changing rooms in motorway cafés and crèches at airports. There are American-style restaurants that provide high chairs and menus for the under-fives. There are Alton Towers, Thorpe Park and many other variations on the drawing board.

There has been the growth of the National Childbirth Trust (NCT), followed more recently by the Maternity Alliance and the Working Mothers' Association. Not to mention the proliferation of child care and birth gurus like Sheila Kitzinger, Le Boyer, Gordon Bourne, Hugh Jolly, Penelope Leach and Miriam Stoppard. The royals, headed by Princess Diana's progeny, have helped fuel the fashion.

A working woman today, married or single, now doesn't want to be saddled with children too soon. If at all possible she likes to get the mortgage payments underway and kit out a home. This is all made so much easier by a double income. If she lives with someone, she and her partner want to enjoy what two incomes bring them – sunny holidays, a bigger, nicer home, a better car, even two cars, at least for a while. Many enjoy two incomes so much that they don't want to suffer a drop in lifestyle when they do have children, and they return to work as soon it is feas-ible.

If they have a professional training – and more and more women have – they can pursue a career and have a family in comfort. They are fortunate in being able to earn a big enough salary to afford an NNEB nanny and go back to work straight away. Even if a mother isn't earning a great deal, a childminder will make returning to work economic sense.

More women are divorced and find themselves the major

breadwinner for the first time. More divorced men now get custody of the children and need child care. There are more single parents who have to work too. Some mothers work because they don't wish to rely on social security benefits. Others work and still have need of Family Income Supplement and rent rebates.

How Many Nannies, Mother's Helps and Au Pairs Are There Out There?

According to J. Martin and C. Roberts in their *Women and Employment*, 5 per cent of children up to the age of four of full-time working mothers are cared for by nannies and au pairs at home. Three per cent of babies aged less than nine months are cared for by this group. Relations, childminders and nurseries look after the vast majority of the children of working parents.

However small a percentage of the overall number of non-parent child carers nannies and au pairs account for, it is a percentage that has been rising steadily. There are scant statistics to illustrate this rise of the last 15 years, but judging by what agents, nannies and employers say, the industry is booming.

No one has much idea of the size of the in-home child care market. Based on the few figures that are available, a very minimum guestimate could be somewhere in excess of 100,000 of girls working for families in the UK.

There are 5,000 National Nursery Examination Board graduates each year, about half of whom take jobs with families. So, assuming that they stick to nannying for five years on average, then about 12,500 are in circulation in any one year. If we double up this figure to cover the other nanny qualifications, like B/Tec, NAMCW and City and Guilds, this brings up to 25,000 the number of trained nannies on the market.

There are absolutely no figures on British and foreign mother's helps; there may be 25,000. We do know that around 7,000 Western Europeans living outside the EEC enter the country under the au pair arrangement. If the number is multiplied by 10 to account for the undocumented number of EEC girls who come to Britain to work as au pairs, then the grand total for nannies, mother's helps and au pairs could be over 100,000.

Three Types of Mother with Dependent Children

Full-time working mothers
Most working couples would prefer some flexibility in their working hours to allow them to spend more time with their children. In practice, to compete in a conventional job you must keep conventional hours. If you do, you have to delegate the greater part of your child's upbringing to a hired hand. After aeons of the cavemen approach, it is not surprising that the modern career woman feels guilty about this abdication of her role as mother. It doesn't half hurt. The anomaly of this arrangement is that if she pays a lot for substitute attention and security, she feels less guilty.

Part-time working mothers
Another group of women challenge the dilemma by working part-time. This enables them to satisfy feelings of responsibility and duty to their children as well as achieving something for themselves. They lose the kudos of a career, but feel that this halfway house has much to recommend it.

Full-time mothers
A third group do not have the problem. They toil not, neither do they spin full or part time – at least not gainfully. Some of them, however, may not *necessarily* spend more time with their children than the other types, though it is fair to say that most do.

Full-time mothers are often excellent organizers. Some see themselves as 'be-ers' rather than 'do-ers' – they may enjoy exhibitions, squash, home-making, hunting, shopping, socializing, cooking, entertaining, charity work and fund raising, interior decoration and travelling. Usually they are married to men on comfortable incomes or they live on a generous divorce settlement. Some are the wives of busy men who need a consort. Husbands who are diplomats, MPs, businessmen who have to entertain clients, farmers or men in the Services tend to share their jobs with their wives.

Many members of all these groups of mothers have one common denominator – they employ nannies, mother's helps or au pairs. For a vast variety of reasons they want some time, space and/or peace, and they have decided to buy it.

It doesn't matter into which category you fit; it is a shock at some point to every new mother to find that a child is there to stay and cannot be left at all. You cannot go out alone to shop; you can't pop out to the letterbox without it becoming an expedition; you and your partner can't go out without arranging for someone to babysit. A Moses basket at supper with friends is feasible for a few months only. Any sort of peaceful, uninterrupted work is out of the window until you have found care for the baby.

The Working Parents' Problems

It is plausible to argue that the less time a mother spends with her child, the less time she wants to do so. Unless a working mother is determined to know her child well at all costs and squeezes in time in the morning and/or evening most of the working week, the symbiotic pleasures of parenthood may not be as strong. Some contend that if you are unpractised at something you get less pleasure from it, though it may be questionable to align raising a child with the obvious analogy of playing the piano.

Combining children and full-time work is not easy, and requires a great deal of discipline and stamina. A strategy used by those who want to achieve a guilt-free trip to work in the morning is to hand over the child to the chosen carer as soon as is decently possible after the birth. The agencies report that the shortest period is two weeks, though six weeks is a popular cut-off point. All the mothers say, 'I fed him myself.' Career women make a point of breast feeding to help bond – just like the books tell them.

If you escape your baby's charms – and Mother Nature arms the Cupid fearsomely – by the time he is two years old, you've done it. You are over the maternal hump and the chances are that your armour is impenetrable. Happily, in no time he is off to nursery school, so he wouldn't have had any need of you for half the day anyway, and full-time school is on the horizon.

Women are prepared to risk feeling guilty now and possibly regretting their behaviour much later when their children have grown up and moved away. They believe that it is possible to have it all – and it is. Many people manage to combine a career and children. They don't always do it without a hitch, but they do it well enough to make the envious world gasp.

More and more working mothers believe firmly that it is the

quality rather than the *quantity* of time spent with their children which is the most important thing for both them and the child.

Absentee Parenthood

For some employers the nanny is a commodity. She provides a service just like the car cleaner, the carpet-cleaning company, the home-delivery butcher and fishmonger, the interior decorator, the window box gardener, the visiting valet and the silk flower arranger.

Employers shell out for their window cleaners and house painters but many skimp on child care. Uncharacteristic bargain hunters proudly announce that they've found an inexperienced mother's help to look after their three children 'for a lot less than an NNEB', before dashing out to work or to do the bulk buy. It can be concluded that the quality of child care is not as visible (if at all) to other people. Young children are not regarded as objects of conspicuous spending by these parents. Thus their care doesn't receive the same attention and financial outlay as things that friends and neighbours will register, like the new kitchen floor or the better car.

The children of absentee parents are not processed in quite the same way as the house, the car and the garden, but their children's caretaker has as much control as she did in the Golden Age of the nanny. She has total responsibility for them for all or most of the week, and a few employers can't face the weekend without support.

Nannies are more likely to receive less enthusiastic and relevant comment and appreciation for their work with children from this type of employer. The more they do, they find, the more they are asked to do. 'It's give, give, give, with this lot. If you didn't love their children you wouldn't stay a minute,' says one nanny resignedly.

Nannies do like sole charge. But they don't generally approve of working women, unless the nanny becomes the mainstay of a lone parent. Most nannies' mothers didn't work and many say they won't when *they* have young children. More than that, they do not approve of families where young children are seen and not heard, and where the parents do not spend much time with their offspring.

Employers have to watch to see that their nannies cope well with being with children all the time. One nanny writes, 'I sometimes feel like a single mother. I feel trapped. I wish I had more money and more time to myself. It's a great job for a couple of years but no lifelong career.'

One nanny who is effectively a surrogate mother says: 'If the parents are away from home for long periods the children rely on me for love, security and comfort. Children always behave differently with their mothers, testing their love and pushing them to the limit. The parents don't seem to realize that the child needs *their* attention as well as mine. I find myself taking complete responsibility for the children's emotional welfare especially if the parents abandon their responsibilities.'

To wind up the contentious theme of absentee parenting, one Hampstead author says: 'Motherhood has had a bum rap of late. Women don't want to consider how much power they have handed over by not being around that much while their children grow up. Children are little vessels into which any amount of good or bad may be poured and stored. If you put in crap, that's what you'll get.'

'Why do mothers not realize that children are part of them? They will also become partly like those who take care of them. How can they fail to?' says Jeanne Magagna, child psychotherapist at the Tavistock Clinic.

The Hangover from the Old Guard and the Modern Nanny

There are two main misconceptions about nannies. The first is rooted in the real-life memories of a tiny minority whose families were cherished by devoted women sequestered on the top floor. Many of these memories have found their way into literature (Evelyn Waugh, Nancy Mitford, M. J. Farrell, A. A. Milne, etc.). Many people have heard about Winston Churchill's adored nanny, Mrs Everest.

The famous royal nannies were Clara Knight, the Queen Mum's and then her daughter's nanny, and Mabel 'Mambo' Anderson, nanny to the Queen's children, who was later re-enlisted to cope with Peter Phillips. Then the mould was broken by Nanny Barnes, nanny to the little princes at

Kensington Palace. Although, like other royal nannies in the past, she had no formal training, Barbara Barnes hit the headlines when she left the job before Prince William had reached the age of five. The media reckoned that she went because there were classic nanny employer/employee problems – those in the know went further and said that she was not strict enough and Wills was getting a bit wild.

The other fantasy version is to be found in stage, screen and literature. Julie Andrews reinforced the image twice – as a singing and dancing mother's help/governess in *The Sound of Music* and, of course, as Mary Poppins. In *Peter Pan* a Dulux dog was anthropomorphized into 'Nana' – a dog who cared for the children and was more aware of danger than crusty Mr Darling, their father.

Nanny was presented as a cosy omniscient, as familiar as a piece of nursery furniture, in the world of A. A. Milne's books about his son Christopher Robin. Wendy Craig, who played the nanny in the TV series *Nanny* whose career spanned the post-war period until about now, presented a more realistic picture of nannying. As did Rachel Billington, one of the many children of the Earl of Longford, writing in the *Daily Telegraph* about the family's notorious nanny who gave 'little whiffs of gas to quieten her over-energetic charges'. In a panic her mother appealed to her father about what they should do. He replied, 'We must watch and pray; you watch and I'll pray.'

The hangover from these images causes problems today for nanny employers and for nannies themselves. Employers in the main still cannot believe that the nanny will clock off at the end of her working day and lead a 'normal life'. She will not be so devoted that she is always to be found in her room darning a child's sock. Sex and a full social life were never an issue in the good old days.

Some parents find boyfriend trouble too threatening. A magistrate mother says: 'Our Norlander's boyfriend was over six foot and built like a barn door. He had tattoos in unexpected places and several convictions for GBH. As he muscled his way through the narrow passage of our Chelsea house, he snarled, "Where's yer toilet missus?" He and the nanny spent a lot of time in the bathroom together and intimidating and uninhibited noises would echo around the house. In the end she had to go, though the children loved her.'

Many parents avoid 'it' by employing older women. There are few on offer and even fewer are clones of the old school. As the divorce statistics rise, so there may be more mature nannies joining the market who have brought up their own children and need a new direction. This has been the pattern in America. In Saudi Arabia, nannies over 30 are considered the best bet.

Employers blank out of their mind that 'nursery duties' of yore were much more limited than today. An old-fashioned nanny did not clean, cook, shop, pay the milkman or answer the door. She did have specific skills, at which her successors rarely excel, like smocking, darning, knitting and sewing for her charges. She was completely reliable because she had nothing else but the children to occupy her. It was a vocation. Her employer gave her a secure home for ever. She experienced life through the comings and goings of her adopted family. Her fulfilment came from her great pleasure in her charges' development over the years and from the way everyone relied on her. She was the lynchpin, the only person who knew where the mothballs were kept and she provided the shoulder to cry on for every member of the family she served.

Nothing could be more of a contrast to the modern nanny. She is probably the life support system to working parents. She may have most evenings free and may live elsewhere. She may spend her weekends as she chooses and may well not accompany the family on holiday. She is unlikely to stay longer than two years at the most. Today, nannies want a change and move on. One mother, brainwashed by fond memories of the old guard, says bitterly, 'She just treats your child as a job and is as fickle as the office junior.' She may leave after six weeks if her employers don't know how to treat her.

Historically nannies and parents were on the same side. Today too often nannies and parents are at loggerheads. The profession is full of prejudice and there is little balance between two extreme views. Employment agencies, training colleges, unions, employers and employees pick sides and stick to them. One faction holds that nannies do too much for too little without enough appreciation from snooty, divorcing, demanding, mean employers. The other bunch insist that nannies don't know the meaning of work nowadays and they are sex-crazed and over-paid, and employers bend over backwards in vain to please these unreliable little minxes.

This polarization is unhelpful and unprogressive. The Them and Us syndrome is always good for a grumble on both sides whether it involves age, social class, educational background, north and south, town and country, money, privilege, holidays, sex as usual, appearance, tastes, opinions, phobias, role of parents, or myriad other minor clashes. Any or all of them can have the effect of chalk grating across a blackboard. Part of the point of this book is to enable employers to spot looming difficulties and deal with them amicably.

The current heyday of nannies is likened by some agencies to the golden days of the secretary in the mid 1960s to the early 1970s – the good ones were in short supply and everyone wanted them so they were paid a packet. There are plenty of nannies available, but now there is a chronic shortage of *good* ones; too many fussy employers are chasing too few effective nannies (particularly the case in London). The result is that nannies' wages are beginning to look quite competitive with 'ordinary' jobs for the first time. Many argue that the calibre of nannies has dropped as salaries have risen. Employers complain: 'When I put an ad in *The Lady*, I am lucky if I come up with a single, remotely worthwhile applicant.'

Unemployment has helped bridge the gap between supply and demand for mother's helps at least. Girls from the north particularly are encouraged by their parents to travel south and seek work as mother's helps. Many agencies make monthly recruiting visits to Leeds, Manchester, Solihull, Walsall, Nottingham, Rotherham and points north. Girls of 16 and 17, most with little or no specific training in childcare, work for a whole range of employers, many on small and medium incomes, once again concentrated in London and the Home Counties. Many of the jobs are not well paid and involve much responsibility and long hours while parents are away at work.

The green baize door has gone, but parents still have to maintain the relationship of employer and employee with their nanny, mother's help or au pair and it is intrinsically uncomfortable. Lack of space and mutual claustrophobia are peripheral to a central dilemma – that of master and servant.

A servant is defined in the Oxford Dictionary as 'a person who has undertaken, usually in return for stipulated pay, to carry out the orders of an individual . . . especially one who lives in house of master or mistress receiving board and lodging and wages and performing domestic duties'.

At the heart of the matter is the fact that a nanny's status remains low compared with what her peers do. This stems from her willingness to live, in effect, at the beck and call of others. She has given up part of her freedom and has joined one of the few jobs left that is closest to unwaged labour. Nannying, like housekeeping or being a butler, is an anachronism. But it is a popular choice for many today because there *are* major compensations, particularly when other work can be hard to come by for an 18-year-old.

The British are as embarrassed by employing domestic help as they are about death. In the late twentieth century it is not socially acceptable to describe a nanny as a servant. A nanny 'helps out', she is 'part of a team', and sometimes a 'real friend'. This is the very most a nanny is prepared to be – her training, her mother and her peers tell her, and rightly, that she's not there to serve a family, and that she should beware of being treated like a servant. Nannies were never described as being 'in service' in the past, but they knew their place. Luckily the whole master/servant relationship was easier then because the nanny had her own separate accommodation on the nursery floor. This was her domain, shared with the children; parents and other staff visited.

Today's almost extinct substitute for the harmonious set-up of bygone days is the daffy, socialite mum who is delighted to see the children in their dressing gowns briefly before she goes out again. She may employ an excellent trained nanny who runs her nursery floor impeccably. They don't meet much and they coexist happily and separately.

The reality of most people's domestic arrangements is comparatively chaotic. There is not room to swing a cat, the parents are devoted to their kids and want them there most of the time. The nanny copes well, but far from infallibly in a maelstrom of unsynchronized plans. The smallness of most homes means that all personal details are everybody's business.

There are still vestiges of an old-style approach to a nanny being a loved and trusted servant in the house and this may verge on straightforward snobbishness. One nanny says that she was upset to be asked to eat in the kitchen rather than joining the adults for dinner when they were spending the weekend away.

'It's very hard when you are a member of the family at home.' This can be described as a kind of imagined snobbery, but it does illustrate how quick to take offence some people may be.

Colonial types, like the Canadians, are aghast at the inherent snobbery which abounds in everyday life in the UK. They are detached and amused by their employers' embarrassing views. One New Zealander says: 'I can talk to my employers easily, but there is a basic distinction about what we think is important in life. Bluntly, I am not such a snob as they are. But I suppose I accept the differences here and my status in their house.' An Australian says: 'A lot of my employers' friends give the impression that they cannot be bothered to talk to you or even say the pleasantries to you, let alone treat you on equal terms.'

Some employers appear to be inverted snobs. They are embarrassed that they have a nanny: 'Believe it or not, we have a nanny' or, even more uneasily low profile, they talk about 'someone to help out with the kids a bit' when they have a full-time trained nanny. Quite rightly, nannies themselves dislike being explained away, so if an employer is sensitive to the stigma of not doing all the child rearing single-handed and being able to afford proper help with it, she should not belittle her role to acquaintances in front of her. Trained nannies don't like being described as 'help' and mother's helps badly want the appellation 'nanny'.

There are nanny pecking orders which are as confusing to the uninitiated as a knees-up in a masons' lodge, but vary considerably depending on the location. Roughly, it goes something like this: nannies trained in residential colleges mostly have friends trained similarly and tend to come from more middle-class backgrounds. Other trained nannies stick together quite a bit, a few experienced mother's helps may join the clan as honorary members. The au pairs mostly spend time with other au pairs or foreign friends; unless they have good English they won't stand a chance with the NNEBs and even with the ordinary mother's helps. As usual, the Antipodeans and North Americans are different and, because they are not easily pigeon-holed by their peers, get on with all strata.

One nanny sums it up:

You have to learn to live with lots of people being a nanny and living in. You have to get used to their little habits, their personalities, fit into their lifestyles and be flexible. You have to learn to respect other people's homes and not abuse certain comforts, perks and privileges. They must learn to treat you as a nanny, as an equal, not a low servant. You have to learn to get on with each other and have a happy relationship.

A Nanny's Job Description

A nanny's or mother's help's job is to make sure that the children in her care are nourished emotionally, physically and intellectually. The crucial point is that she's required to do all this to someone else's specification. Her way is only as good if it is the same way as her employer's.

Nannies have to be flexible because there is no right and wrong in child care; there are hundreds of families that do things quite differently. This is one reason that employers say they like young nannies – either so they can boss them around without encountering too much resistance or/and because the girl has just left home and she will be more used to restrictions. One common misapprehension among nannies is that they will be their own boss as a nanny.

A sensible nanny realizes that her job is like many other jobs, albeit with a number of important differences. Long hours, babysitting and some weekend work, even when employers give ample warning of their own plans, will play havoc with a girl's 'normal' social life. It is also tough to live and work with people who are not family or contemporaries, and to have to adapt to their way of life – their diet, plumbing, budget, manners, habits, smells, affectations and worse intimacies. Most employers have not experienced live-in help before, so they probably will not have practised the little rituals of politeness and respect which decreases everyone's sense of trespass.

People agree that the following attributes are just a few of the pre-requisites for a successful nanny: enjoyment of children, kindness, discretion, willingness, patience, stamina, unflappability, stability, efficiency, flexibility.

There is a general trend for some qualified and unqualified nannies to underestimate how necessary it is to be organized to survive the day satisfactorily, from everyone's point of view. The employer's dream nanny is aware of the benefits of 'time and motion'. She plans for the next day, checks that things work and where they can be found. Employers complain again and again that their nanny cannot, or will not, adopt a reliable routine. The trouble is that the minutiae of the job are petty and it is troublesome to get every detail exactly as someone else likes, particularly if they are being petty too.

It takes all sorts to make a nanny and all sorts to hire them. One woman's nanny can be another woman's nightmare. Both sides need self-control, discipline and the will to make the affair long-lasting, which is what it is all about. Given the artificial nature of the relationship, it is vital that the employer *likes* the nanny she chooses.

Why do nannies want to look after children?

Most of the time children are fun to be with and life is never predictable.

It's what I enjoy doing and feel that I am good at.

I enjoy seeing a child develop and have pleasure in playing a part in his growing up.

I honestly just love children. I love their company. I also feel that it's the best experience that anyone can have who wants to bring up three children as I do eventually.

I prefer working in a home rather than in a day nursery because I'm not very outgoing and do the job best with a one to one relationship.

An experienced trained nanny comments:

I love working with them and find it a rewarding and fulfilling career. Nannies nowadays do an important job and most of them realize that it *is* a job, not an excuse to stay at home and be a slug and do nothing all day but watch TV. The general opinion of nannying is that it's a cushy option and that it's not really working at all. Just a great round of tea parties and socializing.

A good nanny treats nannying as a career if she does it for at least five years. Mrs Louise Davis, principal of the Norland College says, 'It's not a job with a career ladder. There is not much difference between two and ten years' experience in terms of pay and appreciation of the years dedicated to children.' There is slightly greater scope for promotion for NNEB graduates who decide to work in day nurseries and nursery schools rather than become nannies. NNEBs find it frustrating that they are not supposed to 'teach' the under-fives in nursery schools, that's the province of the teachers.

Most nannies and mother's helps genuinely want to work with children. A few want to leave home, go to a city, travel abroad, be part of a lifestyle that they will probably never be able to afford and get off the dole. The second-rate reason why too many girls go into nannying is that they can't think of anything else to do. Sadly, even some NNEBs do the training without feeling strongly about it either way and when they reach the job stage they can *still* take it or leave it.

The Elusive Professional

'It is a weird job for a young girl nowadays when you stop to think about it. Living in someone else's house and abiding by all their rules is so unlike the way of the world now,' muses one employer.

Theoretically, training and experience will have moulded a nanny into a professional. As a professional she will be able to handle the restrictions and acknowledge employers' rights if she is resident in their home. In practice, will she remember to be 'professional' when it does not suit her? It takes maturity, discipline and a sense of honour to do as you said you would when there is no one there to see. No one but the children that is, and they won't tell or know the difference. There are some nannies who can hold their heads high from the start to the finish of their nanny careers in ethical terms. Some nannies behave professionally, but many do not know what the word means.

Trained nannies may never have heard the word 'professional' in two years of college. Untrained nannies, mother's helps and au pairs may never have considered the concept. Professionals do not sit on their boyfriends' knee while on duty; they do not take the easy way out with their tasks – for example, giving the children excessive sweets, TV or soporific cough medicine – wilfully disobeying instructions. They do not spend hours having long-distance telephone conversations with parents and friends, and their boss has a right to know what they are doing and where every moment that he is paying her. Nannies mean well, but many of them don't do their job professionally, trained or not.

Throughout this book we encourage employers to behave like professionals towards their nannies. What do we mean by this? To inform ourselves and to produce a consensus about the best way to be a good employer of whoever cares for the children we have gathered advice from employers, employment agencies, nanny unions, nannies, mother's helps, au pairs, training college tutors and their principals. By the end of the book, faithful readers will know what is expected of the employer who is professional.

Another big problem that employers find difficulty in coming to terms with is that live-in child carers are not hired primarily for themselves but for the services they provide. However much an employer may feel that it is essential that she employ a nanny, she still may dread the whole business. Many employers resent sharing their private space with the hired help and they can find the commitment it takes fairly demanding.

One mother who had au pairs and mother's helps for her first family, treated herself to a nanny for the only child of her second marriage. Her nanny stayed nearly three years. 'When I recruited her replacement when my daughter was three, I realized that I just didn't have what it takes any more. The elder children were all at school, Elspeth was at nursery school. When the new nanny from Wakefield got homesick, I decided I'd rather manage without any so-called help ever again.' This is typical employer burn-out.

Another example of an employer cracking under the strain is when a mother felt she must leave her job and return to either full-time or part-time motherhood because she couldn't take her nanny's unreliability any more. This mother was too worried to work effectively. Nanny fatigue finally took its toll.

Oddly enough, it may take an emotional hiccough or drama – divorce, illness, redundancy, another baby, a death – to cause a mother to reconsider. If for whatever reason she feels vulnerable, it is probable that she will feel the need to be closer to her child than before.

One type of nanny that employers may become sick of swiftly is the one who starts to identify with them and their lifestyle overmuch. Tell-tale signs of this emerge when she asks questions like 'Where did you get your new dress?' and 'What did it cost?'. She tells you that she, too, would like to give a dinner party and will you be out next Tuesday? She starts going to charity dances and so needs time off to get her hair done and iron her dress and she makes you feel like Cinderella's stepmother if you demur. Nannies employed by Sloane Rangers may start wearing puffa jackets, Barbours and pearls. She can direct the builders as well as you can, and she knows exactly where to find them in your address book. A bit spooky.

It is a rare nanny who can maintain the balance so that you all stay friends over a long time. 'After three years she still calls me Mrs Braithwaite and never oversteps the line. When she leaves at Christmas, I shall miss her. I rely on her as I would a friend and even as a sister.'

High Turnover

Women worry, when they have a high turnover of nannies in a short time, that it reflects badly on them. They're right: it does. Consistency of care should be the prime objective of every employer – you don't need more than elementary psychology to know that children can display disturbed and even neurotic behaviour if they feel insecure. It has to be far from ideal if whoever is closest to them a lot, or most of, the time, changes frequently.

A high turnover can mean that the employer is deliberately, though unconsciously, selecting an inappropriate nanny because she does not want to relinquish the maternal reins. The hiring and falling out go on indefinitely. Other employers may not interview perceptively and form an inaccurate picture of the girl's character. They may pretend the job is something it isn't and are found out within days; they may have delusions about themselves and the sort of people they want to live with, or they may be impossibly exacting. It is unlikely that an employer is jinxed time and time again.

Some employers have no idea what a nanny ought to do. Their nannies continue to leave in droves when they've been ordered to clear up the dog mess and the employers still wonder why. It reflects well on the nannies that these employers are often dazzlingly rich and offer fat whacks and juicy perks, but they desert them notwithstanding.

A Final Word

Much of the angst generated by the employer and her nanny or mother's help is self-inflicted. Some people become a little unbalanced about the whole gamut of problems they feel the nanny is creating for their perfect family.

Both employers and child care employees have to hold tight to an optimistic and positive approach to their life together.

The Breese/Gomer line is that employers should: think and talk about it; set up good pay and conditions; work out their rules; interview exhaustively; grill referees; give the employee clear instructions; avoid asking for favours; and not stand for any nonsense.

Try to make your children's welfare come first and insist that the nanny does so too. If a nanny convinces you that she puts their needs before her own convenience and that she enjoys being with them, you will find yourself liking, respecting and trusting her.

Read on. This book tries to tell you how to achieve all this – and heaven too . . .

2

House Rules and the Big Four

House Rules

If guests and fish are supposed to stink after three days, how is a family to put up with living with someone who is staying indefinitely? The need for House Rules is clear to the experienced employer, the residential training colleges and the employment agencies. House Rules may vary greatly, but everyone agrees that the wise employer will have decided on their consistency before even interviewing a nanny. Rules can always be relaxed but it causes problems when they are made up as the occasion arises. Do discuss the broad principles with your husband and/or anyone else who may be affected.

To make your lives together work, it is essential that you think through as precisely as possible what your views are on the following: smoking, drinking and drunkenness, boyfriends and curfew, what you are called, how the nanny is to use the car if at all, where in the house the nanny may or may not go and what she may or may not use without asking, when and how often she may use the phone, who may or may not stay and for how long, how much time you intend to spend in her company, and the need for confidentiality on both sides.

House Rules do not cover 'Sackable Offences', though you need to be even clearer about these, and have thought about them properly before interviewing. Turn to page 45 for a discussion of Sackable Offences. Having said that, a House Rule, if ignored repeatedly and after warnings, can often turn into a 'Sackable Offence'.

Many new employers will wonder justifiably why it all has to be so complicated and regimented. In the 1990s a proportion of employing mums have a 1960s style liberalism towards other people's ideas and habits. Almost all employers start out that way; many have the sense to do a swift volte-face and metamorphose into House Rules devotees after the first few months of employment. Some exchange written contracts with their nanny. Information about these is detailed on pages 325–8.

What should she call you?

Most employers prefer to be called by their first names, as is the norm for a boss and his/her secretary and in most jobs. One mother says: 'It's impossible to live with someone so intimately and not think it absurd to be called anything but your first name.' Others make the distinction according to the employee's age; some like to change tack after a few months, and some say that it depends on the girl herself and her attitude. One mother argued for first names on the grounds that remarriage meant that her name kept changing, which made everyone giggle.

Some employers confuse formality (i.e. Mrs) with respect, believing that 'some barriers must remain up if you don't wish to breed contempt'. Finally, one experienced employer who has tried it both ways says: 'It doesn't matter really. The relationship either works or it doesn't.'

There is a small number who like 'Mrs X'. Actually, if she is called Mrs Higginbottom the nanny will probably come to the usual cosy compromise and call her Mrs H. Significantly, most of these employers have living-in nannies and they give a number of cogent reasons for their choice:

I'm too informal and it reminds us who is boss.

It creates an air of authority.

They're young enough to be my daughters, what do they call their parents' friends anyway?

I was taught by my first nanny who said she much preferred it, because when there are problems or disagreements it makes the situation clearer.

When in doubt nannies use 'you', as do au pairs. A few call their employer 'mummy' which takes a bit of getting used to; one titled employer claims she prefers it to all the other misnomers.

One old-style agency deplores the use of first names, while another states that the use of Mrs distances the employer from the nanny to the nanny's advantage – like a uniform, it protects the nanny from being put upon and from too much over-familiarity.

Whatever you feel about this one, one employer suggests that the nanny addresses her employers' friends and family formally until they invite her to call them by their first names.

Confidentiality

The Norland and Federation of Recruitment and Employment Services (FRES – see page 341) model contracts of employment state that 'it is a condition of employment that now and at all times in the future you keep secret the affairs and concerns of the household and its transactions and business'.

It's not just the royals, rock stars and Hollywood who care about their privacy. There are instances when the nanny's discretion can matter very much to you, particularly if you are nearing the divorce courts, are rich, political or important in public life. Your child could be an abduction target or the press could be riveted by titbits about your private life.

Anne Diamond, a TV presenter, won an injunction granted over the telephone from the judge's home to stop the presses and silence her former nanny. It was granted on the basis that the nanny as an employee owed the couple a duty not to reveal confidential information acquired during the course of her job.

Even if an employer is not obviously vulnerable, it is sensible to mention to your nanny that you do not like her to gossip about your family and friends to anyone. Of course, if she is human she is bound to chat about her job, but she should be made aware that it is unprofessional and potentially trouble-making. The onus is on the employer to be discreet; blackmail could be a temptation to a nanny scorned, or in the very rare circumstances when an employer hires a complete nutter.

The nanny's dress on duty

Fewer and fewer employers like their nanny to wear a uniform; many feel that it is too formal and ostentatious. There are a number of employers who keep a nanny and her uniform as a status symbol to some extent. This keeping up with the Jones's syndrome is prevalent but rarely so unsubtle. It is illustrated by

Mrs Townsend of Chiltern remarking that, 'One of my girls worked for a family who made her wear uniform when the children were visiting their paternal grandparents. They were a bit more upper crust than the other set.'

Not surprisingly, the three big residential training colleges – Chiltern, Norland and Princess Christian – are proud of the identity that their uniform gives them, and the girls are encouraged to wear it if that suits the employer. One Norlander reacts against the whole idea of wearing her uniform. She feels that it is uncomfortable, over-formal, and anyway she 'wouldn't want to work for anyone who was more interested in me as an obvious status symbol than in their children's happiness'.

A graduate of an NNEB college doesn't have an official uniform like the private colleges, but sometimes an NNEB creates her own version and prefers to wear it. The advantage of a uniform (and like the image-conscious NNEB mentioned above, it is easy to buy an adaptation) is that there is no risk of her wearing what an employer might consider to be unsuitable clothes. It is not chic to wear an apron, but many nannies wash their clothes constantly (which is expensive) as a result of wearing trendy numbers which the baby wrecks with sick and dribble. Smart clothes may inhibit the nanny from initiating any sort of mucky play like making mud pies or pretending to be snakes along the floor.

Another and less obvious plus about the uniform for the nanny is that when she is out of uniform, she is visibly not on duty. This reminds everyone that she has working and non-working hours which should not be so 'flexible' (a favourite word of employers) that she never has a moment to relax and be off duty.

Wearing a uniform does not guarantee a smart appearance of course. One mother says that one of her nannies looked so scruffy in uniform that she suggested that she wore her own clothes – the result was a great improvement. It would be politic to ask the nanny how she feels about her uniform, particularly if you are in two minds about imposing it. Remember that many girls enjoy putting together outfits and accessories and having to don a uniform every morning if she yearns to sport an emerald track suit, with big white earrings and white sneakers, might not be the best way of keeping morale high.

Don't forget that a uniform can be an added expense. It is reasonable that an employer pay for or contribute towards replacing a worn-out uniform as well as footing any dry cleaning bills that are necessary. Some employers give their nannies a uniform allowance. Some generous ones give them a clothing allowance.

Most nannies feel more comfortable in mufti, but that makes it the employer's job to comment on its practicality if necessary. Do so straight away. It will continue to annoy you but be harder to bring up later. One mother couldn't abide her nanny sitting down to lunch al fresco in her pink bikini and requested that she dress for meals, please.

Footwear is often a problem. Several mothers raise the vexed question of pink fluffy slippers with high heels. Not so much the slippers, but the fact that some nannies and mother's helps like to wear them all day around the house. High heels are ruinous to wood floors or lino and are dangerous up and down the stairs when carrying a baby or child. They also discourage the girl from running with or after the children. In an emergency a nanny moves quicker in flat shoes. There is a lot of bending and stretching when looking after children, so trousers or jeans are sensible.

Smoking

Ninety-nine per cent of employers prefer non-smokers. A growing proportion are militant about it and will sack a nanny who lies about her habit. Some are more lenient and ban it while the nanny is on duty and a few, some of whom may themselves be smokers, just don't mind. Some employers insist that smoking only occurs outside the house; others let the nanny smoke in her own bedroom. One realistic working mother says that she has to 'leave it to the nanny's discretion, but hoped that she didn't'. Several nannies told us that they were well aware that their employers disapproved but didn't want to bring up the subject.

Both Norland and Princess Christian Colleges are strictly non-smoking and the latter guarantees adherence to its rule because it has smoke detectors. This attitude provides an excellent example and good training for nannies who are highly likely to be unable to smoke at the home of their employers. Surprisingly, when you think about it, the students at the Chiltern College have no restrictions on their smoking.

All the agencies report that employers are becoming increasingly mindful of the health and fire hazards caused by smokers, so that almost no one wants to employ a nanny who smokes, any more than one who can't drive. Nannies are well aware of the current trends, but can't, as Mrs Davis of Norland College sagely comments, 'give it up the week before taking a job'. Never trust a self-confessed 'social smoker' not to be a pack-a-day girl on the quiet.

If you run a smoke-free household, don't forget to remind her that you won't like her friends smoking either. Any new mother has only to imagine her reaction to the sight of an eight-month-old baby reflectively chewing a fag end left around by his nanny, as one employer reports, to understand why this subject causes feelings to run high. Another thing to remember, if your nanny is allowed to smoke in the house (one employer allows her nanny to smoke only in the garden), is to ban her smoking when she is ironing. One mother was so cross when a large stack of freshly laundered clothes stank of tobacco that she insisted that it all be washed again.

It is not part of a caring professional nanny's image to smoke. It would be helpful if the NNEB and other courses spelled this out to trainees. Apart from the fire and health dangers, a committed smoker needs a cigarette as often as she can make time for one. This does not bode well for her charges and their schedules. Shortness of temper and of breath and dealing with the nicotine craving are far from ideal for a nanny.

Drinking and drunkenness

Like all good things, a bit of drinking is fine so long as it is not overdone. One employer sums it up succinctly with, 'I don't mind as long as they don't get pissed.' Most people agree that nannies should not drink while on duty and shouldn't drink their employer's liquor unless it is offered. Some employers go so far as to prime the nanny straight away that when she is offered a drink by anyone when she is on duty she should not accept more than one glass. Many employers, however, offer the nanny a drink at the end of a hard day and exchange news and views over it.

Drunk nannies are a rarity and there seem to be few instances of hangovers, falling up the stairs at night, or passing out on the bathroom floor at 4 am. These real reported examples are probably exceptions. Beware Australians and New Zealanders; they receive a dishonourable mention here.

It is not sensible to give your nanny or babysitter a bottle of wine before exiting in your glad rags. Having drunk half a bottle, could she get three children out of a burning house? One of the principals of the private colleges reminds us: 'Young girls in London for the first time, and not used to drinking, do get drunk.'

Tell your nanny if you allow her to use your car that she may not drink and drive whether on or off duty. Regardless of any moral view, it invalidates the insurance if she is involved in an accident.

Just as you would rather be oblivious to any effects of drink on your nanny or mother's help, similarly she shouldn't have to cope with drunk employers.

Where and what is out of bounds

Almost all employers' stated aim is to make their house the nanny's home. However, when they think about what this actually means in terms of loss of privacy and peace, their list of exceptions is lengthy. Here is a characteristic response: 'Absolutely their home, but they must ask to use the phone, there won't be any dinner party invitations, and our working lunches don't include her.'

Another conflict arises, frequently and justly pointed out by nannies, that although most employers are jolly glad to have a nanny on call at any time, many of them resent their physical presence when off duty and don't want to meet them around the house. Unless you are lucky enough to be able to offer her 'a separate flat in the nursery wing' (a stately home/green baize door option), it is unkind to make her unwelcome. Hope to heaven that her training college will have mentioned the employers' need for time alone in the evening, and that it won't be necessary to lecture her about the strains on a modern marriage.

Anyone who employs a trained nanny or even an English-speaking mother's help need feel no guilt about telling her to amuse herself after work. It is less easy to take this line with au pairs; part of the deal is that they need to practise their latest English word on you and they are meant to be part of the family (see chapter 8).

The majority of nannies eat at the same time as the children and therefore leave you and the kitchen free to entertain your spouse in the evening. A few nannies take a tray to their room, some are 'always out when we are in' or 'are anywhere but where we are'. One mother disingenuously comments 'she has always been part of the family, but she prefers meals on her own'.

Some employers are not particularly privacy conscious; others quite enjoy a bit of companionship. A third group are the sort who live up a long drive in the country and are extremely glad to have the nanny around a lot of the time. The nanny, of course, may have her own plans.

Most employers are agreed that their bedroom, their own bathroom if they have one, and the living/drawing/sitting room are out of bounds to the nanny especially in the evenings when most employers like to be alone together. It all depends how much space you have. Obviously it is unfair on the nanny to be confined after work entirely to an eight-foot-square bedroom and a galley kitchen. If you have lots of room(s) she won't feel deprived, and you needn't feel mean if she has a large comfortable one to herself (see chapter 5).

Other no-go rooms in some families include the study, the dining room, the husband's dressing room, the cellar and the attic. Most employers are quite relaxed about the nanny using a particular room for a bona fide purpose, like, for example, an au pair asking to use the piano in the sitting room.

Possessions can cause problems. Employers want to believe themselves to be sharing, caring and generous with their goods and chattels, but mostly they find it easier to be generous with their cash. It is sensible to tell your nanny not to borrow or use anything without asking. What is *anything*? Tell her exactly what you are sensitive about, be it your food processor, sewing machine or stereo equipment. You are entitled to be irritated if having pointed out the no-go areas of the house, the nanny uses any objects found in them. As one mother put it, 'I respect their belongings and would like them to respect mine.'

To summarize, the employer's home is not the nanny's home and however much you may want her to feel 'at home' for your own purposes, don't get confused and give the nanny inconsistent signals. Clear messages from the start about the way you want to live in your home should help reduce future friction. Both parties need to learn respect for each other's 'space' and to nurture a mutual, and entirely healthy, desire to be apart some of the time under the same roof.

The telephone

Even the most open-handed of employers grumble ferociously about their nannies' abuse of the telephone. What is most upsetting is that an employer has to recognize that she is virtually impotent. One working mother speaks for thousands when she says: 'The telephone is always a headache. I get very cross inside, but do nothing about it except complain to my husband, who says do something.'

To the question 'How much do you use your employers' phone?' the stock response from nannies is 'not a lot'. Very few choose not to use the phone often, but this is such a common understatement as to be a misapprehension by the nanny, rather than a conscious rip-off. Most have never seen, let alone paid, a telephone bill and their hurt innocence, when first confronted with the beast by an irate employer, is legendary.

This is one area in which the employer may feel quite free to act as if she were the nanny's parent. Do not feel inhibited to say 'Please Jenny, get off the phone' after twenty minutes long-distance off duty, or after three minutes mid-morning with two children round her feet who might rather be otherwise entertained. A neat way out of such crass confrontation is to say quietly 'I must ring my mother now, I'm afraid.'

The received wisdom on this issue is that employers request that nannies ask before making long-distance calls and are otherwise free to make local calls when and as they wish, although there is usually an embarrassed mumble about off-peak times. Remember to mention to any Canadian, Australian or New Zealand mother's help that she must not make overseas calls without the operator ringing back with the cost. Also remind her that local phone calls do cost money in this country (unlike in her own).

An employer expects her nanny to make arrangements to meet other nannies and children, to check times of engagements and to organize her own social life. These conversations should be short and to the point; most employers resent anyone gassing about the joys of the night before on the morning after. As one mother says, 'I always recommend off-peak times, but I am out most mornings and she starts phoning as soon as I've left. I sometimes can't get through for hours.'

What do you do about a phonaholic? Mercifully British

Telecom's itemized phone bills have taken much of the friction out of the issue. The nanny can be shown her long-distance, lengthy calls and their cost. Some employers will pay a percentage of her calls, others deduct from her wages each quarter. Even with itemized phone bills there are always the local calls which add up alarmingly with a phonaholic. At the first sign of uncontrolled chit-chat, show her the last phone bill and say that it is not expected to double in the next quarter. When it does, show her the new bill, jump up and down if it is your style, and threaten to make her pay the difference next time.

Phonaholics have friends with the same problem and they all do it all the time – even at midnight and at 6 pm, when little children are bound to be in the bath. When you answer a phone call from the mother's help's best mate at an inconvenient hour, say 'Can you ring back later please' or even, cheekily like one exasperated mother, 'She does work you know.' Apart from crises, tell your nanny you don't expect her friends to ring after, say, 10 pm.

One employer's wheeze is to give the nanny her own phone and pay the rental. Another's is to install a 'tell cost' machine which will make it clear how much she is spending. *In extremis* and Getty style, either have a pay phone or add a locking device. The latter seems over the top, not least because the nanny might need to dial 999.

Naturally enough, nannies need to be in touch with their families and this should be encouraged. One employer deals with this by inviting the nanny to ring home once a week from wherever she is (her job takes her abroad frequently), and she never fails to remind her. If you don't offer her a specific time to ring home each week, she may, as another mother reports, take the initiative and enjoy a lengthy talk every time her employers go out in the evening.

In fairness to nannies, it is silly to pretend they are unique as employees in ignoring the ethics of the whole thing. As anyone who has ever worked in an office knows, one of the accepted perks of the job is ringing long distance when in the mood. This awareness is summed up by a nanny, 'Yes, I use the phone a lot, but I'm not supposed to.' Employers, as so often, don't set the best example, by gossiping to girlfriends at peak times. Cordless and car phones are becoming more and more common and if the office pays the bill, employers do not seem in the least restrained.

Use of car

These days employers need nannies – mother's helps and often au pairs too – to drive and the agencies and training colleges do all they can to encourage a girl to acquire her driving licence. Some employers generously help finance driving lessons – this is genuinely altruistic because the chances are that she won't have become a competent enough driver during her stay with them to be able to help out on the school run and the like.

Use of a car has become an expected perk of nannying and it is not uncommon for employers to provide a car exclusively for her use. Most people now let the nanny use the car or the second car if there is one, when they don't need it. It is expected that she ask before driving away and always give her employer priority and reasonable notice.

She must be insured to drive the car, and it can be an added expense for the employer, and especially punishing if she is under 25 and with no 'no claims discount' (see page 329). Tell your nanny the terms of her cover (comprehensive, third party) and explain any excess clauses, i.e. that the insured, not the insurance company, has to pay the first £50 or £100 or whatever of any claim. Remind her that often it is best that a car owner doesn't claim on insurance for a minor bash, in order to protect his no claims discount, but the car still needs to be fixed and the bill paid.

Again, employers often don't give a good example by being much too casual about damage done to a company car. Keep quiet about the fact that the car is company owned if it is. The perks of your job are not her business. Cynically, in the knowledge that young nannies are accident prone, they are frequently allocated the company car to reduce the repair bills that come out of the employer's own pocket.

Some mothers have a blanket rule that their nanny never drives the children for safety reasons and peace of mind. Others make quite sure that the carer is a competent driver before letting her take the children out in the car. Any sensible parent lectures her on the absolute necessity of child safety belts, and of course her own. A nanny failing to put on a child's seat belt is negligent and is asking for the sack.

Petrol can be a perk, though most employers ask the nanny to refill the petrol tank after her private use. Employers don't usually expect her to contribute to any of the running costs but may restrict how far she may travel in the car. One employer, for example, doesn't mind her nanny using it in and around London, but objects to a long trek home to Cornwall every other weekend because of the wear and tear on the vehicle. Mention this early on, as undoubtedly the girl will soon figure out that using the car is much cheaper than even her Rail Card to get home.

Incidentally, another and less obvious reason for the nanny's preference for using your car for the trip home is that it is a tangible sign to her family and friends that she has a real job in which she is valued. For any young person a car is a symbol of status and independence, and it doesn't do the employer any harm that the nanny is bucked up by being allowed to use the car and show it off at home. In central London, where there is a nanny to every square yard, there is an overt one-upmanship about what make of car different nannies drive – the Mercedes, the Porsche and the convertible Golf GTI versus the Fiesta, the Renault and the Montego estate.

Accidents *do* happen and often to nannies. Many recently qualified nanny drivers have very little experience still of driving and particularly in big cities or abroad. Employers are amazingly long-suffering about 'nanny's little prangs'. They often excuse her, saying: 'It wasn't really her fault', though one says ruefully: 'Our experience hasn't been great so far; three dented cars and one write-off.'

If the school run dominates your life, au pairs are not ideal as they are used to driving on the other side of the road. The household bike is often on offer to take them to classes, though there is the safety angle to consider. Think of your explanation to her Barcelonan mama when she is strapped up in the local hospital.

Spell out to the au pair how often and how quickly bikes get stolen, particularly in a city. Tell her about the padlock, fixing to the railings, *never* leaving it unpadlocked in the street and even then not for long or overnight. If it isn't insured, warn her that if it is lost, damaged or stolen she will have to fork out for its replacement cost, if that is what you have decided. Given this litany she may well decide not to bother and that will cut out probable future irritation.

Some employers are keen that the nanny use the car at night as a protection against assault or mugging. Many recognize that employers are far from delighted to pay up for accidents incurred when off duty. One drawback of being 'good about the car' is that you may soon see it bulging with giggling nannies who can't quite remember where they live, all yelling instructions in your nanny's ear. You are the only one in the street to have provided a taxi service for other nannies and there could well be a crash round the corner.

When the inevitable happens, her fault or not, you have to deal with her shock, injury, possibly other people's. There is also the embarrassment of her having to tell you and you having to be decent about it, not to mention possible loss of the no claims discount or an unwanted repair bill. There seem to be few circumstances in which an employer can assume a combination of a nanny and wheels which will not be time- and cash-consuming.

May they stay?

If an enlightened employer is keen to have a long-stay happy nanny, allowing her to have friends to stay is a perk to offer which shouldn't cost much or cause trouble as long as you lay down a few guidelines. A nanny's parents may be glad to spend a weekend in the house if you are away, so that they can have a look at the way their daughter lives and spend some time with her. It is nice for her to feel she can play hostess to them and her friends too.

Most employers restrict a nanny's overnight visitors to 'great girlfriends whom we know' and 'members of her family'. Some girls prefer visitors to descend only when the family is away, no doubt realizing that it is a worry for employers to leave a nanny behind alone in a house at weekends with or without the children (especially if she is young and in a big city for the first time).

A few nannies think it best that visitors are only invited when the employers are in residence. Employers are unanimous in discouraging weekday overnight visitors; requiring proper notice of anyone's arrival; and making it clear that any stay should be limited to a night or two only. They also evince a definite preference for female visitors.

'It's all right in principle if it suits us'; 'if they ask me and it isn't a man', and 'as long as we don't become a doss-house for all sorts' are characteristic caveats. An experienced mother is precise: 'With permission, as long as we and they know them well i.e. that the friend won't be casing the joint, drink all the booze or be a nuisance to us in any way.' Another adds: 'No to the friends she might have met the week before.'

Letting the nanny have a friend or her mother to stay can suit everyone. Parents treating themselves to a weekend away from the children tend to feel more confident if the nanny has her mother with her.

The issue is different, as always, with au pairs and foreign mother's helps because they don't usually have any kith and kin in the country. But beware of being kind and letting her friends transform your home into the local YWCA. The travelling friends of Antipodeans are magnetic when it comes to spare beds.

Inviting people to sleep over, as the North Americans have it, is a fun thing to do, if you have the space and it's no trouble because you won't be there and you trust the nanny with the house in your absence. Score high by being the first to raise the topic. A convertible sofa in her bedroom is particularly appreciated. Try to emulate one mother who writes 'I know her friends, like them and welcome them. If the nanny sticks to our rules then they can all have a good time.'

Curfew

With a responsible nanny who has a professional attitude to her job, the need to give instruction about when she is expected to be home at night does not arise. It has been mentioned before that it is not a good idea to make up rules as you go along and it is especially hard when you are already cross and/or disappointed with a nanny's behaviour. Be realistic every time. It is much easier to relax the rule when you are entirely satisfied that the nanny has boundless energy and good humour in the early morning which is sustained throughout the fun-filled day. Many mothers are sure that their nanny or mother's help can cope after a night out and don't have a curfew.

In contrast, some employers are adamant about a strict curfew. They like to lock up; they have sensitive ears and don't want to hear her footsteps up the stairs when they are trying to go to sleep, or hear the sound of her ablutions in the bathroom. Above all, a few of them actually worry until they know their nanny is safely tucked up in bed. This feeling is more prevalent when she is still in her teens and is with a London family. The same concern is more common with young au pairs and mother's helps from abroad. One advantage of insisting that an au pair or nanny is back by midnight is that the employer doesn't have to lie awake debating whether it is time to start ringing police stations and hospitals at 3 am when there is still no sound of creeping footsteps.

Mrs Davis of Norland says that employers must not forget that their nannies are young with lots of energy. This is a timely reminder to those former Yuppies who assume bedtime after the News at Ten has become the norm.

One delightful curfew story tells of the couple who returned after a night out to see their Dutch au pair Saskia all dressed up for a night on the town. Often her night began when they returned home. She used to go to the West End and have a whale of a time. They were surprised by this strange social life, but as she was excellent at her job and never showed a sign of fatigue after returning at 6 am from her outings, they let her carry on.

An incidental bonus of a curfew is that it renders your nanny just about ineligible to babysit for other people and get exhausted that way. Employers who hire babysitters, especially if those babysitters are also other people's living-in nannies, might think about being conscientious and returning at the agreed time. Don't take advantage of the fact that the babysitter is never going to say to you: 'Please be back on time, I need to get up early.'

Imposing a curfew assumes that the nanny is working the next day. It could be sometime between 11 pm and 1 am. Most employers lift the curfew if she isn't on duty in the morning. Many allow, nay encourage, the nanny to stay out all night when she is off so long as they know in advance. Others are not so keen and allow the carer to stay out the night for a specific reason like a friend's all-night birthday party. Many employers insist that she telephones if she is going to be exceptionally late or, if there is a curfew and she is not going to be back in time, she ring and explain why.

The trouble with instituting a strict rule about when to be in at night, is that the employer must enforce it if it is ignored, if he is to retain credibility about the rule and about all the house rules. An employer who says 'Be sure to be back by midnight' is wasting everybody's time if a new nanny comes in even ten minutes late, and he or his wife does not mention this fact and ask her why? If he isn't strict about the curfew the nanny will quite understandably feel that it doesn't mean anything.

Mrs Townsend of the Chiltern training college says: 'A nanny must not put her needs and social life before children and family.' Every employer and good nanny will agree.

Boyfriends

To misquote Dorothy Parker, it could be said that if all the nannies in Kensington were laid end to end, no one would be the least surprised.

A mother and her three-year-old daughter were walking in an idyllic Dorset valley one weekend having just admired the farm animals. Reflectively the little girl remarked: 'Billy the bull, mum, what's he doing?' 'Making babies, darling.' They walked on. 'Is that what Kathy and Abdul were doing yesterday afternoon?' In this way one mother discovered how her child was entertained while she was at work. On Monday evening the mother tackled the nanny and her boyfriend together. Abdul saw the point and agreed not to cross the threshold unless the mother was there. He was soon bored with the nanny who then attempted suicide while left in sole charge.

This may sound an incredible story. It did happen. It points up only a few of the myriad problems associated with allowing the nanny's boyfriends into your home. It also brings home the fact that a sensible, trained nanny (which this one was) may turn into an unrecognizable, love-lorn wreck within weeks once smitten. There are countless examples of this sort of thing occurring.

Some employers may imagine that their youth was spent in gentle romantic pursuit of the opposite sex and, whatever else, it certainly took longer to score in those days. Today the pace can be quicker and plenty of pre-marital sex is the norm. AIDS may slow down the process somewhat, but don't be shocked if your young nanny or mother's help assumes the whole business of sex to be a matter of fact.

It is hard for an employer to deal with this area successfully. There is no other subject which exercises both employers' and nannies' tongues more energetically than what to do about boyfriends and sex. The truth is as one nanny puts it: 'If you are residential you really can't have an affair; men and nannying just don't mix.'

The most important piece of advice to a new employer from a mass of experienced ones is: 'Don't agonize over it. There is no solution that will suit everybody. But remind yourself, "He who pays the piper calls the tune."'

Experienced nannies are well aware that this subject is the bitterest pill of a live-in job. It's the main reason that they become daily nannies if they can. It's also the main reason why employers would prefer a daily nanny, if money and highly organized routines presented no problems.

It is hard for nannies not to feel that a ban on boyfriends in the house smacks of a hangover from Upstairs Downstairs when 'followers' were shown the door. Several comment that they don't understand why their employers are prepared to trust them with their children, but don't trust them not to choose a boyfriend who joins his girlfriend while babysitting, has a plate of baked beans, nicks the silver and heads for Rio.

There are a few nannies pro the boyfriend ban: 'It is difficult. Never have a boyfriend in the house, then there are no problems and employers don't have to worry that the kids are neglected as they would if the boyfriend stayed the night.'

A Norlander with years of residential experience says, 'I think it's a bit of give and take on both sides. Obviously discretion is the key note. No one has ever given me rules exactly, but employers are within their rights to lay down a few guidelines.' Another says, 'My boyfriend, now husband, was welcome at all times. It's the same as living at home, you don't have as much privacy as you would like. Yes they can make rules, it's their house, and they are concerned for your welfare.'

Employers relate a wealth of horror stories from their friends and relations and often from their own experience too. The most common rules are 'no men in the house at all'; 'no men in the house unless we are there and then out by midnight and never upstairs'; 'no men ever in the house while on duty' and variations on that theme. Obviously a sane employer will relax the rules for a steady boyfriend – but this is where we meet a problem of definition.

Many employers report that their nannies become affianced surprisingly often. One nanny divulged over the cornflakes that she 'got engaged last night and it didn't half hurt'. Just as 'engagements' are not always what they seem, so also the 'steadiness' of a boyfriend can be called into question. Out once with a guy and he's a boyfriend, twice and it's 'steady'. Some mothers reckon the boyfriend a feature of the household after a couple of months; others think this is an absurdly short time and don't acknowledge anything less than six months' courtship.

If an employer has to consider the vexed question at all, she would prefer a long-standing stable relationship which was in place when she hired the nanny. This assumes that the first passion is spent and that he lives nearby (vital), preferably with his own pad. It can be disastrous to hire a nanny who has a serious boyfriend living far away. The most caring employer will probably fail to settle the lovesick girl or the faithless man will drop her within weeks for a local lass and you will have to pick up the pieces.

A Wiltshire mother remembers, 'When one of our nannies discovered the opposite sex, it blew her mind. When out of love she was moody and when in love she could think of nothing else. The children were forever being taken to wherever her current beau was employed in the village.' To say that the reason for this restriction is that the nanny may not be paying your child adequate attention is superfluous; it can be dangerous too.

One working mother was told by a neighbour that she had passed her nanny embracing a man on a seat at the Round Pond in Kensington Gardens. Before her very eyes the little boy she was meant to be looking after fell into the water. The nanny hadn't mentioned it to the mother and had threatened the boy with a beating if he did.

There is no other job which permits an employee to sit on her boyfriend's knee half the afternoon and get paid for it (apart from the notorious casting director's suite and the same sort of boss's secretary). Don't stand any nonsense on this one. Boyfriends are not allowed to accompany nannies in or out of the house while she is on duty.

Back to babysitting. If you have a daily nanny or mother's help and you get her to do occasional overtime, which means babysitting, she may not want to come unless her boyfriend is in tow, which is why she 'lives out'. A babysitter may feel the same way. It is very common in North America for the devoted couple to arrive together. Many British parents buy this line and let the boyfriend come too, because they are between a rock and a hard place and know they have no option. The employer of a live-in nanny does not have this problem, but even so many are generous and feel that babysitting is not 'on duty' in the strict sense and, feeling guilty about being a curb on young love, invite the boyfriend to sit in too.

Nine times out of ten this is fine. The tenth time is graphically described by many employers. 'Imagine my fury when I discovered Sandra with her policeman boyfriend snogging on our drawing room sofa while the kids went unpotted.' There are other things nannies are reluctant to do in front of their admirers especially being covered in sick by a teething baby, feeding a bawling infant who refuses to burp quickly. Just like the Billy the Bull story, no one wants their nosey eight-year-old snooping round the door and witnessing a torrid scene.

Such behaviour is unprofessional in the extreme. One employ-ment agent says, 'If she leaves the door open so she can hear the children, it's fine if her boyfriend is there while she's babysitting.' This is irresponsible advice to a new mother. When you know your nanny very well and her boyfriend is someone you like and trust then maybe it's OK, but only then can you decide.

The fear that boyfriends may burgle is not a fantasy that employers dream up to spoil nannies' fun. Any nanny talking to a strange man about a weekend away with her employers or their plans to take her on holiday puts the household at risk. Copying a key takes seconds. And you haven't yet invited them past the front door. Tell your carer that careless talk costs money. Some readers may think that this sort of detail is a bit paranoid, but in cities the crime rate is rising and who wants to be part of the statistics?

It isn't the case that most employers mistrust their nannies, but they cannot be expected automatically to like and trust her friends until they know them. One agent with 25 years ex-perience, who describes herself as a dinosaur on matters moral, says:

If the boyfriend is allowed in the house then he must only be entertained in the sitting room or nursery and must leave at a proper time. The nanny may not do as she wishes in someone else's house. I may be very old hat, but that girl should not be in a residential job. Employers are cowardly and don't want to deal directly and correctly with their nannies, because they don't want to have to sack them with all the ensuing fuss and bother. They ought to be clear and say 'the human race must go on but not in my house'.

How can you avoid the boyfriend problem? Some nannies are cosy, homely and not particularly keen on going out or acquiring a boyfriend. They may also be less than lovely and may often be overweight. It is cynical and rather unkind to bank on your nanny limiting her life to your children – a prisoner of her spotty face and lack of discipline with the doughnuts – or to hire her with this ulterior motive. Many employers choose nannies and mother's helps whom, they hope, will not attract boyfriends, and, even better from their perspective, won't have any social life.

Some employers rejoice in the fact that their nanny's idea of a good day off is to be huddled in bed with a box of Milk Tray and the fourth Mills and Boon of the week.

Sex and nannies

Oddly enough, the subject of lesbians hardly emerged in all our research, although a few mothers had had vague indications of this proclivity, having observed a few rather unbalanced same sex relationships. One funny story starts off with a family and some friends having a drink in the garden one summer evening and hearing titters from the au pair's bedroom. Lo and behold, a pair of frilly knickers floated down into the delphiniums nearby. Suspicions were confirmed, the employer had noted no boyfriend and a butch girlfriend. Nothing was mentioned and the au pair's leanings presented no problem.

There have been many cases of nannies' and mother's helps' pregnancy and abortion reported to us by employers. Sometimes the nanny is too scared to tell her parents and the employer feels herself responsible for arranging the abortion (sometimes paying for it too), and dealing with guilt and possible other side effects. The way to avoid all these hassles is to talk about it and point your nanny in the direction of the nearest family planning clinic.

Working parents were astonished recently when their nanny confronted them with the words, 'I've liked your baby so much, I

41

want one for myself, so now I'm five months pregnant, will it be OK if I go on working for you?' They weren't convinced that she would have the stamina or time to do her job properly and so had to tell her to leave.

A few employers do keep their nannies and even au pairs on throughout the pregnancy. Sometimes they marry their boyfriends, or eventually go home to mum. Rarely, they remain nannies in the household and look after theirs and yours together. At this point an employer has not only adopted a parental, but also a grandparental, role and one can only wish them luck: no job description can be this flexible.

Sex and employers

The classic story of the husband getting off with the Scandinavian au pair sounds rather dated, possibly because real life is rarely that straightforward. For example, a nanny and her employer were having an affair and the employer's wife announced that she was expecting another baby. The nanny gave in her notice at once, outraged that her lover had been two-timing her so flagrantly. The agency to which the nanny returned for tea and sympathy was furious with her, quite rightly, for her lack of professionalism.

Male employers with a dim recollection of Tom Jones and Fanny Hill who entertain the fantasy of a modern nanny wilting with desire while he exercises his *droit de seigneur* are out of time and out of luck. Wives are beadier than ever, and some recognizing their dear husband's little ways, tell the agencies not to send pretty nannies. Jamie Turner of the eponymous agency says of his Australians and New Zealanders, 'Occasionally girls are too good-looking which poses a threat to the exhausted mum of three who is not feeling her best. She can't cope with some sensational bit of crumpet driving the old man crazy.'

Unless employers and their friends are being super discreet, the instances of male employers jumping into bed with the nanny are too few to focus on for long. However there are many instances of territorial and macho display; nannies have some priceless recollections about this peacock behaviour.

Apparently, husbands walk into nanny's bathrooms, bedrooms and lavatories much too often to be so amnesiac. They walk around the home intimidating all viewers with their dazzling boxer shorts and hairy pot bellies. 'Short towelling dressing gowns open to the navel are off putting at breakfast', and 'he gets undressed anywhere except his own bedroom' wail two nannies. This can become in some cases almost harassment, although it does seem almost unconscious and nannies are very forgiving: 'I just laugh', they say.

Infatuation may strike the nanny too. One father went upstairs to get a suitcase and was amazed to find in a cupboard a shrine to himself. His photograph was mounted and surrounded with lipstick kisses and buttercups, Indian beads and burnt joss sticks. He beat a hasty retreat and guess what happened? As usual nothing.

Nannies sometimes date employers' friends and relations. This can be tricky. Tread warily, she may end up as your sister-in-law. Discourage weekend guests from corridor-creeping, the un-fairest part of this is that the lustful guest departs and most employers feel they have to sack the nanny for lack of discretion on Monday morning. If there are signs of vital business clients or your husband's boss murmuring to the nanny, take urgent action and explain why her intimate relationship with either would be considered a Bad Thing.

Robert Chantry-Price, director of the NNEB, mentions employers' double standards. He says, 'Why shouldn't a nanny have a boyfriend in the house when her employer may be having an affair?'

It is a fact of nannying that an employer can say 'do what I say and not what I do' and mean it. Living in makes a nanny privy to secrets that no one else is in a position to comment on. It is not logical for a nanny to think she can do what you do. You pay her and your private behaviour is not intended as a model for hers. Having established this as a point of principle for any residential staff, it is obviously far from ideal for a nanny to be forced to observe her employers behaving like alley cats. Don't expect respect. Do-as-you-would-be-done-by is the good rule in all personal dealings and a nanny may leave if your standards are too different from those you insist she live by.

Nannies can be bricks – and even mortar – in a crumbling marriage when it is essential that she doesn't let on that she knows anything about what is going on, turns a deaf ear to all rows and shields the children from the fall-out. 'Practising for a play again, dears' is the line when the parents are shouting at each other. One nanny tells us that she is staying on in the job after five years there already and by giving evidence in court she hopes to ensure that the mother isn't granted custody of her charges. It is unfair of employers to put pressure on a nanny to stay for the sake of the children in these sad circumstances, and most nannies and mother's helps are well advised not to become involved.

Honesty

Apart from any moral view, it is not practical to keep someone in the house who tells lies or steals money or valuables. Some employers are apparently so desperate to keep a 'good' nanny, that they turn a blind eye to the disappearance of the odd fiver, and ignore a bit of glossing over the exact facts of the case whenever she is discovered to be in the wrong.

Experienced employers will know the thin end of the wedge. Honestly has to be a House Rule for the protection of your children. If a nanny can lie, fib, prevaricate, cheat or fudge about little things, even by omission, you do not know exactly what is going on. This is your right as an employer.

Once a nanny has forfeited your trust you have to be on the look-out until some time has passed and you're sure it was uncharacteristic and is unlikely to recur. Some parents can't cope with the insidious erosion of trust or the stress of the anticipation of the next time, and consider it a *sackable offence*. One mum says, 'It can be the most dangerous thing there is if you don't know exactly how and why a toddler hurt himself. How is a doctor to produce a diagnosis?'

Some people think it anachronistic and even pious to insist on the whole truth. Qualities such as integrity, honesty, honour, courage (much needed for owning up) and loyalty are essential for all jobs like nannying that involve much discretion and responsibility with other people's possessions, including the most important, their children. They are never out of date and employers should prize them above any other consideration. They are just as vital as professional competence. A nanny should say what she does and do what she says.

Sackable offences

Employers and their partners will have to be clear before they hire a nanny precisely what 'beyond the pale' means in their household. In other words, what a nanny could get up to for which you would sack her at once. It is only fair that she should be quite clear that certain behaviour, in or out of your house while in your employ, will mean summary dismissal. Also, it makes things easier for you.

One clear example of summary dismissal is provided by one employer who, having refused permission for any boyfriend to go into the house, returned after an evening out to find her nanny and a man in the employer's bed. She was told to pack her bags and she left that night.

It is difficult to pontificate on what constitutes a Sackable Offence Situation (SOS) for different families. Employers sack nannies for many reasons. A specimen statement of employment produced by FRES (page 341) mentions 'theft and drunkenness as examples of reasons which might give rise to summary dismissal'. It also lists 'reasons which might give rise for the need for disciplinary measures:

a   causing a disruptive influence in the household
b   job incompetence
c   unsatisfactory standards of dress or appearance
d   conduct during or outside working hours prejudicial to the interest or reputation of the employer
e   unreliability in time keeping or attendance
f   failure to comply with instructions and procedure'

Employers report that the following Sackable Offence Situations have provided grounds for dismissal if, having been warned, a nanny does nothing to correct them: dirtiness, unkindness to children, theft, dishonesty, smelliness, smacking, general bad temper, moodiness, rudeness, neglect of children, swearing, sulking, boyfriends overnight, men in beds or anywhere in *flagrante*, getting off with the husband, drunkenness, insincerity, favouritism, irresponsibility, loose behaviour, arrogance, being a know-all, insolence, pregnancy, sluttishness, slovenliness, overfamiliarity, hypochondria, unpunctuality, idleness, selfishness and shopping for herself on duty.

If you need to take disciplinary action they suggest procedure might be: 'first – oral warning; second – written warning; third – dismissal.'

Pick your own and be reassured that if you see any signs of the above, you are not alone. One father summed up many employers' SOSs as 'theft and fornication on the premises'.

The Big Four: Pay, Time Off, Holidays and Perks

The price of nannies doubled plus a bit in the 1980s. As there are too few trained and experienced nannies for too many jobs, so they are earning the most they ever have in real terms.

Each proven rung up the nanny career ladder will add to the cost. So, you get what you pay for – the well-worn cliché that if you pay peanuts you get monkeys is indubitably the case in the nanny market. An untrained 18-year-old mother's help will expect not less than £60 in the early 1990s in London, a bit less than that in the country.

The new NNEB nanny will cost more – £90 plus all found is the bottom line for London, a bit less elsewhere. Experienced (i.e. around two years in a job or two) NNEBs may earn between £100 and £150, occasionally more in London. Nannies with less well known qualifications (see pages 165–70) are a little cheaper.

If you are taking a girl from one of the residential fee-paying colleges (see chapter 7) – expect to pay more. Even a Norland probationer commands a basic £100 a week, but when fully fledged after her nine-month probationary period with your family, it goes up. An experienced nanny from any of the above colleges (and experience means more than two years) earns in the range of £120 to £200 all found. The upper end of the scale is most often afforded by working parents, though these nannies can earn double this figure in North America or the Middle East.

Daily nannies are expensive and you will have to spend extra on babysitters or pay the daily nanny more to babysit occasionally, if you can persuade her to do so. A daily nanny will cost you £30 to £40 per day for about 10 hours every weekday. Daily nannies are usually trained and experienced, but there seems to be less variation in earnings. In a city a babysitter will cost you about £2 to £3.50 an hour and a lift or a taxi home.

Obvious and hidden costs of live-in help

- Employer's National Insurance contributions; pay rises; bonuses; overtime pay
- Extra help when she is away
- Employer's presents and treats for the nanny
- Time spent recruiting and cost of advertising and/or agency fees and organizing her tax and National Insurance payments or paying an accountant to do it
- Lighting and heating her bedroom
- Hot water for washing, bathing and laundry
- Electricity – elsewhere for her use. TV, radio/cassette, sewing machine, the hairdryer, etc.
- All her food and drink
- The telephone
- Use of vehicle(s) – wear and tear, possible extra insurance, cost of accidents, possible cost of losing employer's no claims bonus
- General wear and tear on the employer's home and probable need for redecoration in the nanny's bedroom and bathroom – carpets, chairs, tables (effects of cigarette burns, nail varnish and coffee spills), sheets, towels, etc.

There is a premium for hiring a temporary nanny, reflected in the fee to the agency for finding her and the transient nature of her stay with you.

Part-time nannies are usually also mature and their rates are to be compared with those of the daily nanny.

The whole aim in sharing a nanny is to reduce the cost. The family with whom she lives and boards usually contribute less to her wages than the family whose child she also cares for. For example, an experienced NNEB might expect £100 to £120 for looking after two children from separate families. The host family might expect to pay £40 to £45 of this figure.

There are three sorts of mother's helps; the untrained English girl, the Australian or New Zealander and other girls from overseas whose mother tongue is not English. Mother's helps are employed to do the housework as well as to look after the children, although the Australians and New Zealanders do mostly go to households where a cleaner is also employed. The minimum wage for full-time foreign and English girls is £60 per week in London, the younger English girl (about 16 to 18) will make just about exactly this, but the older and more experienced girl may make as much as a new NNEB, at which point she graduates from the kitchen floor and is called a nanny.

Australians and New Zealanders don't care much what they do, but must be paid a good whack. In the early 1990s this means a starting salary of £100 a week.

Foreign au pairs are the most exploited of this group of child carers. They can be paid as little as £20 per week for well over the Home Office guideline of 30 hours a week. In London, the going rate is around £30 a week; the au pair plus arrangement means that she works longer hours and is paid more.

Childminders are paid between £40 to £50 a week, and more in London. The hours are similar to those worked by a daily nanny, to fit in with office hours.

One employer comments, 'You start by paying as low as you dare and you raise it by a few pounds every four to six months'. A second says, 'A decent wage pays dividends in terms of results: quality of child care, loyalty, and length of stay.' Another has a strict 'invest in the best' policy which she reckons is particularly vital morally to the working mother. 'The difference between a fairly ordinary nanny/mother's help and a really reliable nanny who can safely be left on her own and let me live a trouble-free life is the price of a good meal each week.' Yet another says smugly, 'She is expensive and worth every penny.'

Be honest from the start about the nature of your own finances and only hire a nanny whom you can afford comfortably. This is sensible because otherwise you will resent the drain on the family purse and this will become obvious to the nanny, whose perks won't measure up against those of her friends and she will leave you sooner rather than later.

It is short-sighted to pay below the going rate. This is less easy to do, of course, with a trained nanny or in London where there are plenty of comparisons nearby. Having discovered the extent of the discrepancy between her meagre pittance and her contemporaries' fat pay packets, she will either ask you for a rise, or just leave.

It is easier to get away with paying a mother's help and particularly a foreign mother's help less than what is currently accepted in the area. The scope for paying au pairs way below what is acceptable even for so-called 'pocket money' is even greater. It is disgraceful how many people take advantage of a girl who isn't staying long in this country, and has no means of knowing what is reasonable. Even if she does realize she is being genuinely exploited, she is probably returning to the fatherland shortly and won't confront her employer.

Salary rises

There are lots of reasons for raising your nanny's salary, none better than another, but the good rule is to do it as often and as generously as you can afford. Some people say raise it every six months. In the early 1990s this meant around £10 a week rise a year. The important thing is to have a 'carrot ahead always' says one mum, so that a wonderful nanny will stay that little bit longer. Also keep a weather eye on other local nannies' pay and rises, and try to be sure you are slightly ahead of the street.

Employers link their nanny's pay to the inflation rate, another gives them a rise for 'extra experience' as often as she remembers. One working mother gave her nanny a pay rise when she received one herself. By contrast another says flatly, 'I give a rise when I'm asked for one.'

Any nanny will anticipate a salary rise linked to the arrival of a new baby and her increased responsibilities and probably increased hours too.

Bonuses are a way of giving your nanny a pat on the back. Christmas and Easter are good opportunities and a bit of extra cash for her holiday in Switzerland or wherever is a nice thought. Some employers go so far as to discuss a bonus scheme in the interview; others prefer it to be a spontaneous gesture of appreciation for a job well done.

Time on and time off

A nanny's hours on duty are very long compared with those of an ordinary job. In effect, many nannies spend most of their week on 24-hour duty. Robert Chantry-Price, Director of the NNEB, points to the fireman analogy, meaning that a nanny may be asleep but at any minute is required to leap into her boots and sort out a night-time crisis, just like a member of the fire brigade.

Of course, he, like many others who defend the rights of nannies to prevent their possible exploitation, forgets that a nanny who is expected to be on 24-hour call five days a week is likely not to be *en poste* for the next. Why should she stay with such treatment? In all our research, it is clear that the aim of most parents is to keep the nanny happy, well rested and content with the job, so that she will stay for as long as possible. In fact, 90 per cent of employers reckon it is their job to deal with their children at night (see also page 134).

Asking nannies to do more hours than were discussed and agreed at the interview is, nevertheless, a common transgression by employers and one which causes a lot of resentment. You must be clear exactly what you want your nanny to do from the beginning. If you are a working mother who may occasionally be caught in a 6.00 pm conference, don't say that you will always be home by 6.30. It raises expectations and is disappointing. Warn her by phone the moment you know it is going to happen, avoid doing it often and grovel if you have messed up her evening rendezvous. It is a form of blackmail to behave unreliably with a nanny's time off, because obviously she cannot leave the baby alone in the house. In an office job, she would be able to clock off on time.

If you are a busy working mother who cannot guarantee to be back when scheduled all the time, spell it out to her at the beginning that it will be that sort of job, and you will be wise to pay her over the odds for inconveniencing her. This is the way people think in London where there are lots of well-paid jobs and too few nannies. Exploitation will occur more where nannies are isolated and jobs are scarce. Relocation presents a great problem to many nannies, which is a pity for them.

One employer's neat ploy is to tell the nanny that 'she is to keep the children's hours', but in reality this is from 7 am to 7 pm in most households. Obviously au pairs are different (see chapter

8). Babysitting comes with the job. It may be a 12-hour a day job but most nannies tell us that they have quite a lot of time off during the day when their charges are asleep or at school. Some employers suggest a quiet time for all after lunch so that the nanny can have a break.

There are many different formulae for giving nannies time off. A nanny graduates to all weekends off after several years, or sooner if she can swing it. Nannies who are in sole charge during the week expect every weekend off and mostly get them. Increasingly the trend is towards the nanny's job becoming a 5-day-week affair. This trend is supported by the rising numbers of working mothers who want to look after their children themselves at weekends.

Here are some examples of time off arrangements: one weekend a month and one day off a week in the week after the nanny has worked the weekend, i.e. five days off a month (this is the least we encountered); two weekends a month and two extra days; one weekend working a month and a day a week off; half a day a week off and every weekend; one and a half days off a week and a whole weekend off once a month; every weekend off.

If you have a chance, be generous with extra time off. Do not impinge on the nanny's free time at all. If she is in the house on her day off, it is not good enough to say, 'Can you keep an eye on the baby who's asleep upstairs while I pop to the shops?' Remind everyone in the house when it is the nanny's day off and, if she is sleeping in, to be quiet.

It depends a lot on the atmosphere of the relationship, but, unless you are quite relaxed when your nanny is around, it is not unreasonable to expect her either to stay in her room or to leave the house on days off. You cannot be expected to have to hoover around her and you won't enjoy her watching how ineptly you deal with the chores. Long weekends, i.e. starting on Friday lunchtime right through to late Sunday or crack of dawn on Monday, are a treat for everyone on occasion. Splitting a day off mid-week into two is, incidentally, a bonus for the employer and sometimes agreeable to nannies too. Be flexible with reasonable notice about her granny's 50th wedding anniversary, and swap days off if requested.

Holidays

Holidays should be paid. The range is from two (mean) to four (generous) weeks. Bank Holidays often are not honoured but should be or made up in some way. Some employers save on the expense of holidays by offering, say, three weeks paid and one or two weeks unpaid.

Often foreign mother's helps and au pairs don't seem to merit holidays paid or unpaid. This is partly because they are usually here for a finite stay, ranging from six to nine months on the whole (see chapter 8). The English have a tendency to insist that being abroad makes every day a holiday, and because the foreign girls, unlike the outspoken Australians and New Zealanders, don't demand it, they miss out. If the latter work for six months they get two weeks' paid leave.

Perks

Bonuses are a perk. Experienced nannies say that in their first job or maybe two, they focused on salary to the exclusion of other factors like perks and the employer's personality, but that the quality of their lives became increasingly important to them. In other words, the nicer the accommodation – spacious, gracious, warm, comfortable – the nicer the food – varied, exotic and generously available – the nicer the holidays – hot sun, well staffed hotels, general luxury and impressive postcards to send home – the better. And that is just the beginning.

A rich employer who is happy with her nanny may be an endless source of bounty. It is not just the Middle Eastern employer who can lavish presents and treats on an employee. All our researches have shown that English employers can be extremely generous and inventively so, though a few have no conscience. One London agency says, 'They promise a girl perks in lieu of better pay and then the perks never materialize.'

Some examples of a worthwhile perk are totally self-contained and well-decorated accommodation with a separate entrance and telephone line; a smart car for the nanny's exclusive use and petrol, service, insurance all paid, of course; the employer may make available her hairdresser, dressmaker, masseuse, exercise class, manicurist free of charge to her nanny.

There are also recreational facilities like the tennis court, the indoor and/or outdoor swimming pools, horses, jacuzzis, saunas, helicopters, yachts, and even complete gymnasiums.

Holidays and travelling generally can provide well-known inducements to a nanny to stay that extra summer or year. In fact, some employers are amusingly cynical about the way in which they oh-so-casually mention that the toddlers are going on safari in the autumn, though they engineer the conversation to coincide with the first signs of discontent during the previous winter.

Sensible tactics also comprise the inclusion of the nanny where practicable in any treats and luxuries. Simultaneously, the employer must remain aware of how an expensive lifestyle may transform the nanny from a simple, appreciative, willing young girl into a spoiled, idle creature who complains of the service on the Air Canada flight.

Less exotic and more affordable nanny entertainment can be provided by tickets to pop concerts, musicals and the ballet. Fund them to take the children skating, up the river, and to the local Disney offering. Extra time off is always popular.

Most employers report themselves embarrassed by their nanny's largesse towards them and their children on birthdays, at Christmas and on such unlikely festivals as Father's Day. One way of repaying their kindness is to give them carefully chosen special presents at Christmas and on their birthday. Remind whoever is travelling abroad to include a token for the nanny in their baggage when they return.

3
Pick Your Own

The Ideal Nanny

It might seem patronizing to try to generalize about the character of the nanny. Nannies were simply women and as various as that: there were witty Nannies, devious Nannies, murderess Nannies, and lesbian Nannies (rare), drunk Nannies and scholar Nannies . . . all occupations that demand particular qualities or impose special conditions inevitably tend to make those that practise them resemble each other in certain respects or attract people with the qualities required by the conditions. This is particularly true of vocations – that is, occupations to which people feel called because of some special skill or need, occupations which frequently demand sacrifices they are willing to make to fulfil that need or use that skill.

Jonathan Gathorne-Hardy, *The Rise and Fall of the British Nanny*

The question of whether an ideal nanny exists is confidently answered by many employers who can't speak highly enough of a present incumbent. In fact, it may be observed that celebrities, from Mick Jagger to Esther Rantzen, given the chance to talk about their private lives, all take the opportunity to give their nannies a puff – a good insurance policy for a warm greeting on returning from work.

It is surprising, given how much time this book spends discussing the problems of the nanny/employer relationship and its pitfalls, how often both parties like each other and get on famously. Everybody's human, and regrettably nannies are no exception. Even an ace has her weak points. It all depends how much you trust, depend on and genuinely like your nanny as to whether you focus on her minor faults and they drive you mad or whether you choose to ignore them almost entirely because she's so great in virtually every other way.

Employers rather feebly cite Mary Poppins as the ideal role model, though one wag was a shade closer to reality with her desire to recruit the Princess of Wales for her household. She is, at least, clued up about the difficulties, though hiring and firing is more her style than sterilizing the bottles.

Another powerful namesake, Diana Forney (NNEB, NN, RSH, consultant to the nanny profession in America) commented aptly on this subject in the National Nanny Newsletter:

A good nanny has a stable and happy disposition coupled with a good sense of humour. She is not subjected to intense and obvious mood swings or bouts of unpredictable behaviour. For this reason most successful nannies have already passed through the teenage years. She has a good sense of herself, likes herself and knows how to take care of her own needs without requiring guidance or constant direction from the outside, since nanny work is frequently isolated and can be quite lonely. She needs to be trained and alert enough to recognize the value of good nutrition and exercise to maintain good health.

She needs to be independent enough to be able to make friends and find entertainment outside the household in which she is working. To this end she needs hobbies and interests outside of child care work. She has resolved her relationships with her own family in such a way that she can work professionally in another family without involving her past experiences and relationships in ways that may not be healthy. That is to say that she knows what the role of nanny is and should be, and she is not seesawing back and forth between playing the role of another child in the family or competing with the mother for her position.

The successful nanny is also the realistic nanny. She is the one who is working in this profession because she likes the work not because she craves the money or power of association with wealth. She knows that the work is difficult and at times tedious in whatever circumstances . . . those nanny applicants who perceive their work as a casual job are certain to be disappointed (as are their families).

It needs to be noted that the successful nanny is a person who has a strong sense of ethics and responsibility coupled with integrity and honesty. She is kind but firm with the children in her charge and is honest and respectful of the privacy of the household in which she is working. . . .

Finally the nanny must be wise enough to negotiate the business aspects of her professional work, i.e. understand the contracts and deductions and wage issues and be assertive enough to discuss and resolve disputes as they arise in the job. Absolutely every job has some elements of personality conflict which will emerge. It cannot be helped when one is working so closely in a household. The successful nanny is the one who can discuss conflict without ruffling feathers unnecessarily. She can assert her own needs while respecting the other point of view. She operates as a professional from her knowledge and intellect, not from emotion or instinct.

It might be helpful to read the following comments before discussing what type of nanny you want to live with. A top ten of qualities employers most prize in their nannies is listed below in the order in which they were most frequently mentioned:

> cheerful
> clean and neat
> sense of humour
> flexible
> punctual
> polite
> reliable
> fun
> child-loving
> honest

They also like them to be: enthusiastic, affable, wholesome, attractive, creative, friendly, hygienic, sympathetic, generous, loyal, dedicated, immaculate, reliable, kind, strict, affectionate, observant, trustworthy, conscientious, caring, warm-hearted, even-tempered, unflappable, tidy, stable, tough but tender, resilient, imaginative, calm, easy, firm, organized, professional, unmoody, hard-working, intelligent, quick off the mark, efficient, nimble, considerate, funny, tolerant, pleasant, patient, healthy, unselfish, out-going, serene, robust, good-natured, educated (both well and highly), well-groomed, middle class, smiley, gentle, unobtrusive, tender, sensitive, consistent, charming, inventive, practical, keen to learn, cuddly, safety-conscious, engaging, adaptable, perceptive, jolly, resourceful, down-to-earth, enterprising, easy-going, imaginative, persevering, unflurried, direct, straightforward, demonstrative, ingenious, aware and instinctive, loving, sensible, mature, presentable, lively, industrious, energetic, competent and happy.

They don't want much do they?

One sage old mum puts her finger on some of the best nanny attributes with this definition:

A good nanny knows she has to win the child's affection and respect before she can tell him to stop picking his nose. Our best nanny said she hated putting the children to bed because she wanted to go on playing with them. Once that level is reached there is never any problem with discipline.

Another comments that the 'ideal' type of nanny you want and/or find changes as the children grow older. The loving, warm person who cuddled the baby may not be the best companion to kick a football with five years later.

Perhaps the most telling commentary on a nanny's role was provided by the employers' remarks about their own needs:

Attractive in an unchallenging way and friendly and polite
Kept me in good order so I never took her for granted
Always has a sweet smile specially at breakfast
Sensitive to our set-up
Has a quiet voice
Likes music and sings to the children while they bath
Cooks easily and efficiently
Organizes toys and clothes well
Plenty of ideas for amusing kids
Seemingly effortlessly keeps the place in order
Always learning
Quick to learn a good routine and not thrown by the odd exception or
    diversion
Never cuts corners
Nothing too much trouble
She mucks in with anything
A ray of sunshine
Doesn't do the job by the book

All this sounds more like applying for a new wife by mail order, than an employer paying someone to be capable and pleasant. It is essentially an entirely personal choice.

Nannies were less voluble about their ideal employers, but because they all said the same thing, their top ten created itself:

> easy-going
> down-to-earth
> kind
> friendly
> appreciative
> sense of humour

> fun
> fair
> reasonable
> ordinary

The amusing aspect is that the only two adjectives in common on the two lists are 'fun' and 'sense of humour', so if employers think they can't grin and bear it they had better start trying. Nannies pray that you will laugh like a drain when they have flooded the bathroom. 'Laughing it off' and 'luckily she saw the funny side' are common pronouncements, which will make any experienced employer grind her teeth.

Readers will quickly get the picture from the following comments that how employers behave towards a nanny matters crucially. There is only one, a mother's help, who says, 'They must be courteous and reasonable but I need not like them.' All the others say:

Extremely important that I like my employer
Looks at me as an equal
A bad relationship causes a bad atmosphere and is sensed by the kids
My employers are great people and I respect them
Somebody friendly, which matters a lot if you live in
A relationship with an employer is like one with a friend or a guardian and is bound to go up and down. Your overall feeling must be liking them.
I like a boss who doesn't become too friendly and nosey
You'd better like her. Your employer is your charge's most treasured possession.

Different Options

Your choice is limited straight away by what is available, where you are, whether you are at home or out at work – full time or part time, how much money you have, how big your home is and whether you can stand the idea of sharing it with a stranger. Just as important are the matters of whether you feel you *want* help with your children and can reconcile it with your image of yourself – will it embarrass you to be an employer?

On offer throughout the country, although the choice may be limited if you live somewhere remote, there are the following options for child care: a living-in full-time nanny, a living-in part-time nanny, a living-in full-time mother's help, a living-in part-time mother's help (probably shared), an au pair, a part-time daily nanny, a full-time daily nanny, a temporary nanny, a maternity nurse, a private or state day nursery, nursery schools, crèches at work, childminders and babysitters.

First it is necessary to decide whether you want your child looked after in your home or elsewhere. If the former, you then have to decide whether you want the carer to live with you or to come to the house every day – a live-in or daily nanny?

Many employers feel that it is unquestionably best that a child is looked after in his own home surrounded by his possessions, that he nap in his own bed, play in his own garden and have his own friends to tea. They also reckon they have more control of what their child gets up to during the day if the carer comes to the house.

Others feel less strongly about it and say that they like their child being with other children while they are out at work and provided the children have plenty of space and light and food, taking the child out of his own environment is fine. The alternatives to your own home are childminders and nurseries.

Childminders and day nurseries

This book is almost exclusively about in-home care and its stresses and pleasures for the employer, but this option is restricted to a tiny percentage. Almost all children of working parents are looked after by members of the family (at home) and by childminders (elsewhere). For details of childminding, see page 307. A smaller minority still attend state day nurseries. In practice, this is not an option. Due to the decline in the number of council-run nurseries over the last 20 years it is difficult for a family without major problems, like poor housing or very little money, to secure a place for their child. In most areas pressure on local-authority day-nursery places is now so great that being on the At Risk register is almost a *condition* of getting a place for your child.

Private day nurseries are another matter. Good for big city life, they are usually of a high standard and staffed by trained nannies. See page 322 for details.

Workplace crèches are mostly cheaper (because they are often subsidized) and the facilities are also good. Everyone wants more of these, there are far too few at present.

Live-in or live-out?

Now we come to the advantages and disadvantages of daily and residential in-home care, i.e. daily and living-in nannies and mother's helps. Let's start with all the cons of living-in help.

Live-in nannies need more food, light, heat, and hot water, and use of the telephone and car than daily nannies. In addition they use washing and drying machines, dishwashers, heated rollers and hair driers, their own TV and a whole host of other appliances on occasion. They take up space which would possibly otherwise be let or used for something else. In other words, residential nannies are the most obviously expensive options on offer, though it may seem that a daily one costs as much when it's time to pay her. Their salaries take a sizeable chunk out of an employer's post-tax salary.

Deprivation of privacy makes some employers decide they prefer daily help. Some mothers don't react well to the close relationship that a nanny may develop with their child or do not want to make the effort that it takes to live alongside someone else. Most employers do feel responsible for their live-in nanny, but it weighs on them. Some others dislike the usurpation of their role in the home: 'It doesn't feel as though we live there when we get back after a day's work. Depending on the nanny it either looks like a dentist's waiting room or a tip.' There is a major problem when either live-in or live-out nannies or mother's helps fall ill, go on holiday or leave without notice, i.e. there is no built-in back-up system, as in a day nursery with several staff.

Other possible disadvantages of the live-in help include her personal habits, her manners, her friends and, above all, her boyfriends. All these things will impinge on you and your family and can be ignored if the nanny leaves at 6 pm. A live-in nanny needs more appreciation, not just for the job she does, but also for herself as a person. The turnover of live-in nannies can be for all these reasons higher than with daily nannies; it is a bigger strain for everyone.

Neither live-in nor live-out nannies do any housework apart from the children's rooms, clothes, washing, ironing, tidying toys and preparing and clearing up meals. A live-in nanny will also clean her own room and her's and the children's bathroom (see page 113).

The pros of live-in help include flexibility, 'You don't get that rushed feeling in the morning or the frantic after-work dash', paid-up babysitting and tailor-made attention for your children. Many parents are grateful for the fact that their children come to trust and love another adult who is a constant in their lives. The hassles of snow, rain, transport strikes, traffic hold-ups and just being unpunctual (and using most of the latter as excuses) are blissfully irrelevant.

Two major pluses of a live-in nanny are that the employer can get herself up and organized for the day without having to wake, dress and feed the children breakfast as well. At the other end of the day she and her husband can go out without having struggled through mass bath time, safe in the knowledge that if a child wakes up, he will be tended to by his nanny who will have the advantage of knowing what sort of day the child had, and why he might be upset.

All the expense and fuss of organizing babysitters (see chapter 8, page 202) argues for the live-in nanny. Using a daily nanny will certainly ration your nights out and she will charge extra anyway.

Daily nannies

Daily nannies receive the biggest pay cheques of the entire group. If a nanny counts up all the perks of a residential post, she is quids in; but, and it is a big but, as the nanny gets older she values her freedom above cash in hand and perks. It is a normal progression in the nanny world after a few years to choose daily work. It follows that daily nannies are also more mature in every sense. They are mostly trained *and* experienced, and are wiser and more careful. They know what they are doing and what they want to do with any luck, though a few get unhappier with every year that they don't have a husband and their own babies.

What is wonderful about daily nannies is that they are not homesick and their relationship with their employer is less close in ways which cause friction. Some mothers report that they feel much more grateful and affectionate towards a daily nanny – familiarity sometimes breeds a certain wariness. It is also good that children are less able to play mother and nanny off against one another and 'know where they are' with whoever is around.

Some people will pay the earth not to have living-in help. Whether the mother works or not, some families mind less about the hassles of babysitting arrangements than keeping their home their castle. Their dislike of the living-in nanny and all the repercussions is so great that they would rather have a lodger in the spare room who babysits at night and have a daily nanny. 'We found this the best solution and we've tried every permutation. Our expectations of a nanny who has to live with us had become so low that we abandoned them,' as one mother relates.

For many people who don't go away for weekends elsewhere often, the strain of a nanny's constant presence off-duty can be a severe strain. 'It isn't that we make love on the shagpile in the living room or wash up Friday night's supper on Sunday night – but if we ever wanted to we could, without fussing about what a nanny will think. The moral is have a daily nanny.'

The biggest gripe about a daily nanny is that she may not be able to arrive punctually every morning unless she lives very close to the job. Transport hold-ups and deep snow, even if they delay her as little as five times a year, can be too many times to live through if the mother is a doctor on call or a barrister due in court in thirty minutes. The daily nanny must have a telephone. If she is ill, she must inform her employer as soon as possible – a temperature at 9 pm should mean a call at 9.05 pm to give you a chance to replace her and/or reorganize the schedule.

Not hearing much about her personal life and problems can turn into a problem. Few employers know when a daily nanny goes to bed at night, if she is experimenting with cocaine or whether her boyfriend beats her. Her lifestyle, unbeknown to you, may have an impact on your children. Try to talk to her about herself and her life when opportunities present themselves.

The other obvious difficulty is the babysitting. One of the main reasons that she is a daily nanny is that she wants her evenings to herself. Even if she agrees to a couple of nights a week babysitting in her contract, don't expect her to like it. Many employers say it makes waves to insist and they resort to babysitters.

Employers comment:

It's impossible to have a daily nanny in the country.

An advantage of a daily is that they are not hanging about in the evening; this can be a bit of a problem with a live-in. Ironically, one who definitely doesn't hang about in the evening is also a problem.

Dailies are useless when I need them most: before breakfast, bath time and babysitting.

Your house is your own to row in, to undress in, to swear in, to scratch in, to drink in, that's why I don't live in a commune. Having a nanny from 8 to 6 is bad enough: no nannies after dusk, they turn into werewolves.

It is much easier to choose a daily nanny than the live-in kind. I have had wonderful daily nannies that I could never have lived with.

Nanny sharing

One way of making daily and living-in nannies cheaper is to set up a share arrangement, ideally with a friend or neighbour. This is an increasingly popular solution for part- and full-time working mothers and there are several ways of doing it. You can halve the week between two families, or halve the days, or the nanny can live with one family and care for both families' children at the other home. Both families share the expenses and, although the nanny herself (whether live-in or daily) is paid a bit more for the extra responsibilities and work, it is a lot cheaper per capita.

A few very capable nannies say that they earn most by giving five different families a day a week or variations on this theme, partly for the money and partly for the interest. An enterprising nanny may advertise on local newsagents' notice boards and organize this gruelling regime herself; alternatively mothers can get together and work it out. A few agencies are happy to cooperate.

Nanny sharing is a happy option for families who wish to keep a long-staying nanny; they can arrange that she is kept busy out of the house looking after other people's children a couple of days a week in their home and defray the costs of her salary, as well as caring for the host family's children after school. It can also be a boon if two families have only one child each. Some think it a plus if they are much the same age; others think that a gap avoids the problems of looking after 'twins'.

There are built-in problems to the nanny share. It is essential to like and respect the people with whom you share a nanny and, some swear, they have to know them very well. However hard two families try to be fair, someone always thinks they are losing out and that their children are getting a rawer deal. If something straightforward, like a car pool, or something intimate but short-term, like a shared family holiday, can cause stress, the scope for trouble with a nanny share is great.

Discipline, theories about diet, potty training and manners are examples of child-rearing issues which some employers feel strongly about and others don't – the twain should never meet in a nanny share. One mother who wasn't that twitched about healthy food says: 'I was a little impatient of the endless supplies of dried apricots and sugar-free low-fat this and that I was expected to provide for their child – it pushed up my grocery bill something chronic.'

One of the families sharing the nanny may upset the applecart within months: they don't get on with the nanny/can't stand you/think your child an unruly vandal/move house/Dad is made redundant/have quads/or the other mum decides to become a full-time mum, so the nanny share has to be redesigned. Time and time again with childminders, day nurseries and shared nannies, mothers finally get fed up with the complications and hire someone for their exclusive use.

Temporary nannies
Some nannies make temporary nannying their life. They like the high rate of pay, comparative lack of friction with employers and the detachment from their charges that nomadic life ensures. They look on temp work as a busy efficient job. The good ones tend to have had lots of experience, they may be 25 or 26 at least. Many of them share flats where they return between jobs. They are used to sole charge and well qualified to have it. They are the crack troops, the Flying Squad, who expect to sweep in and take over with the minimum of explanation and hand-holding. See Agencies, pages 283–97, for those which specialize in temp work; this is an area when a steady relationship with an agency pays dividends. For an old and valued client a good agency will find a good match within hours.

People employ temps when their usual childcare arrangements break down. They need a temp when they take holidays, because mum is sick of mumming and wants a holiday, but with the children, or when her usual nanny is taking her holiday elsewhere simultaneously, or when there is a family holiday and mum wants help. Temps are also sought when the nanny is ill or something pressing has happened back home.

It is an expensive way to buy your way out of a crisis. It can also present a new set of problems rather than provide solutions.

Coping with a stranger at short notice may prove an organizational and emotional strain. Do not skimp on references just because you are in a hurry. Rely on word of mouth or a reputable agency. One agency says her temps 'are stunners, the best of the lot. They are adaptable, flexible, have few hang-ups and don't bore for Britain about their boyfriend problems.' One temp with years of experience says, 'It's much harder work but it suits me. I love it. If there are problems with the family, I can say to myself in two weeks I'll be gone.'

Mother's helps

Mother's helps are a cheaper version of nannies. They are not trained, they do housework, and some of them graduate to being called a nanny after several years' experience. Then they stop doing housework and get paid the same as a trained nanny. People increasingly like age and experience better than training and no or little experience. It is a common misapprehension of new mothers that new NNEB-trained nannies are ready for sole charge posts. Many employers want cheap help, and don't want someone who knows her rights. As one mother puts it: 'An untrained nanny doesn't carry a red book.' There is much less opportunity to exploit a trained nanny and a good thing too.

Many mothers feel that aptitude has nothing to do with training and they value common sense and integrity alongside age and experience. As Robin Rice says in *The American Nanny*, 'Intelligent, sincere, child loving candidates are rare enough without demanding training.' Another reason why employers like mother's helps is because there are lots of them about and they are easy to replace. One mother who could well afford a Norlander much prefers to train her own 18-year-olds and pay them generously if they listen hard and do the job well – her way. One of the things that experienced employers can't stand is being dictated to by a nanny who thinks she knows it all when she has just qualified.

For further discussion of mother's helps, including Australians and New Zealanders, see chapter 8, page 196.

Au pairs

Au pairs are another form of part-time nanny, shared with their language courses. They are very good value, young, inexperienced with children, want to spend time *en famille*, often have poor English and don't stay much longer than about six months on average. See chapter 8.

Having reviewed all the choices, work out with your spouse exactly what you think will suit you best and plumb the depths of your pocket. Afford as much as you can; try and treat hiring a nanny like buying a car – people always spend a bit more on that special trim or extra feature – but don't overdo it or you'll end up resenting the weekly drain on the family coffers more than appreciating the smoother ride. The cliché that 'You get what you pay for,' is so relevant to the nanny world.

You Know What You Like

Once you've decided what sort of child care you need, and for how many hours a day, and how much time you expect to spend with the nanny or mother's help, then it is time to examine and analyse your own preferences and prejudices. Be dead honest and insist your husband is too; consider your children's apparent likes and dislikes. Consciously dredge up your unspoken biases: you don't have to reveal them to anyone; just be aware that they inform your thinking more than you usually want to admit.

The ways in which people confess to prejudging the issue tell us a lot about employers. Employers do not want: militants (we think this means left wing), fanatics of any kind particularly in the time-honoured battlegrounds of health, religion and politics (in fact anyone who bangs on about anything often), gossips or 'thickies'. One is exhaustive in her dislikes: 'I won't have starchy, snobbish, uniformed racists.'

Employers can't tolerate nannies who are: chippy (this makes them most uncomfortable), bossy (too much competition), over-confident, self-conscious and shy, apathetic, humourless, trendy and punky, dreary, phony or fantasizing. Many of them complain of unattractive accents and vocal pitch, summarized by: 'I couldn't employ a cockney/Northern/Irish/South African/Anti-podean/refained taipe, however marvellous they were with the babies.'

Geography

One mother says that she 'can't stand sulky, stuffy, southern, stuck-up types whom you know will not be loyal to one'. She likes girls from the north, particularly from Yorkshire. It must be said at once that if an employer has had a successful nanny from one place, she will tend to imagine that everybody from there will make ideal nannies for their family. In fairness to them, such silliness does often seem to unearth a string of good girls who are compatible. Perhaps if the employer is prejudiced in favour of a girl from a particular geographic area, expectations are self-fulfilled, rather as your stars come true.

Many others say that the Australians and New Zealanders are terrific – 'hard working, fun, adaptable, enjoy the outdoors; they generally muck in and don't faint at the sight of a scrubbing brush.' One might suggest that for some people familiarity breeds contempt and they prefer anyone with a different outlook – a Close Encounter in fact. Maybe this is what many an effete Londoner imagines he discovers in the hardy, down-to-earth, no-nonsense girl from the borders. Others claim to find them incomprehensible and untameable and, worst of all, they find they get homesick. Often they don't stay long with the Sassenachs.

Every would-be green welly, easily recognized by the brace of black labradors crammed in the back of the school run Range Rover in Clapham, insists that his nanny is born and bred in the country. They have a rose-spectacled view of apple-cheeked wholesomeness in these girls. It usually escapes their notice that nannies can become bright-lights-big-city as fast and as completely as though born within the sound of Bow bells. Their ideal is to net a girl who will be as much at home at the muddy point-to-point near the renovated weekend cottage just outside beautiful downtown Newbury, as she will in the Smallbone swagged, dragged and gagged interiors of Wandsworth. 'You don't want a townie,' they all chorus.

The real thing want 'someone who will treat the farm as an adventure playground rather than a prison from the razzle dazzle'. Several mothers complain that 'English country girls are spoiled by their mums and are lazier and chippier than any foreigner' and 'within days they can't stand staying with granny away from the discos'.

Background

'Background' consists of another set of prejudices about the nanny's or mother's help's family which is supposed to provide you with further comforting indicators. 'A happy background is vital' – so many mothers say this that it's hard to imagine any nanny being foolish enough to reveal the mildest dislike of a sibling or letting on that she has lived away from home since she was 17. Unfortunately most employers are right to suspect that a nanny will treat children as she was treated herself as a child, but you would have to be psychic to know the details in advance.

No employer wants to be bothered with 'anything complicated' for choice, and the preference is unanimous for a nicely brought up girl with nothing less than perfect manners. When people ask nannies 'What do your parents do?' they hope to find that mum is a housewife and devoted to her brood and with high hopes for them. Ideally, dad is a policeman or something vocational, or anything self-starting, a volunteer at the local youth club and a pillar of the community. Employers hope to ascertain that the nanny's background is 'legal, decent, honest and truthful' and also confident, motivated, and well ordered.

As for the nanny's own achievements to date, employers are delighted to hear about the Guides, the Duke of Edinburgh's Award, the Church choir, the school swimming team, and anything that sounds healthy, active and therefore laudable (all very Edwardian – a combination of cold baths and the team spirit).

Physical appearance

Prejudices about how and whether a nanny or mother's help looks the part professionally are personal in the extreme, to the point of offensiveness. Employers are outspoken in their dislike of bad skin, spots and greasy unkempt hair (especially teased peroxide spikes or coxcombs). Untidy, torn or dirty clothes in emerald and orange are too eye-catching for safety. Tights or stockings should be neat and unexceptionable and shoes should gleam dully. No diamanté bows, chains or studs anywhere about her person. Finger nails bitten to the quick or talons like Cruella de Vil are not popular. Anything else unhygienic is frowned upon too – bad teeth and breath are taboo. Slouching and slack posture receive minus points. Employers feel nervy about anyone larded in make-up.

Fat is a feminist issue but not in the world of nannies. The archetypes of Posy Simmonds and her ilk, for all their stated enlightenment, don't want a fat, ugly nanny in the house any more than anyone else does. The Sloane types are more likely to be sympathetic and associate bulk with comfort, succour and affection.

'Hugely fat and therefore hugely lazy', as one mother said dismissively is an unjust generalization, though even fat nanny employers admit that the long haul up the London staircase and the daily dash to the ducks looks like a big effort and resembles a Babar illustration too much for complacency. No one minds an unlovely face much, as long as it is creased with smiles and comes with a loving personality.

Colour
There are a few black nannies working in England now and a few Asians as well. The agencies report that sadly there is still resistance to employing a black nanny, and, where the chance comes up more often, a mother's help of a different colour from the employer. As has already been discussed, most employers want to hire nannies who look and behave as much like themselves as possible; it makes sense (unattractive though it is) that they should feel the need to be as consistent in this area as in the others.

It is hard to put much faith in some employers' assurances that they would naturally *like* to hire a black nanny, if they have never done so. The unavoidable claustrophobia of a residential job may make someone of a different colour that much harder to relate to. 'There are enough imponderables', said one mother hopelessly, 'without a multi-racial challenge.'

A black nanny who works in Fulham tells us that she has always insisted that she wears a uniform when she goes out with her white charges. Other blacks are insulting if they assume the babies are hers.

It is telling that the Race Relations Act Section 4 allows discrimination within a private household where a private employer can discriminate on grounds of race.

One family employed a member of the Xhosa tribe for ten years in the depths of the English countryside. She weighed more than 20 stone, could balance a tray on anything and carried the entire family's laundry on her head. Foreign diplomats import every nationality as child carers; it seems that everyone likes what they know best.

Health

Most employers do not ponder the vital areas of health and a positive attitude to illness. Thanks to the AIDS spectre this subject is more to the forefront now than before. Most employers would not altruistically take on a nanny who is disabled, or has a history of mental instability, is epileptic or suffers from diabetes or dismenorrhoea (painful periods). If you are to be spared, you must be prepared to ask these questions.

Male nannies

An increasing number of employers would consider hiring a male nanny; and particularly as a daily nanny. Australian and New Zealand males are the popular pioneers here. Correspondents who thought they might hire a man tended to have sons and plenty of space.

He could kick a football with our lads.
Specially useful during the holidays and cricket season.
Daily would be best. I don't want to meet a man in my dressing gown late at night while both of us compete for the teething baby.

In the US the expression 'mannies' has been coined or – by one family who always had them for summer holidays – 'nanny men'.

There are a few male NNEBs, most of whom go into state nursery jobs. One who qualified from Brixton College says he enjoys being a novelty factor and 'children often show a preference for me rather than other members of staff, which can be a bit embarrassing'. He is adamant that he would not want to be a private nanny which he considers 'the least stimulating experience'.

There are no rules yet created about male nannies and pretty few thoughts. One thing is sure, as usual – if employers want what they know, they won't choose this route to hassle-free child care. A husband's reaction may be negative in dealing with another male in the house to whom he is not related. The Naked Ape is notoriously territorial. Most women are still too modest to be relaxed with a male employee, especially when it comes to underwear mix-ups and communal washing facilities.

AIDS is mentioned straight away by employers when quizzed on the male nanny option. This is too devastating a question to bring up during an interview with a male nanny for most parents, but it is clearly not one to be avoided. Any employer will want to know why the man wishes to be a nanny and be entirely satisfied that his needs from the job are normal. Employers may also be concerned that they expose their little children to homosexuality: this may be stupid, but it exists as a fine example of knee-jerk prejudice.

One employer says, 'It would be fine as long as he was comfortable in this position.' Some mothers feel that 'the need for a female lap' is important and so will not employ a man. Another echoes, 'Girls are better with little girls.' The last word goes to 4-year-old Harry: 'Good idea, we could hit each other.' His sister said she'd be too shy and her mother sides with her.

Age

As one sensible mother comments, 'Maturity varies tremendously' and another agrees, 'If older meant more mature then I like them older. But it's not usually the case.'

The current career pattern for a professional nanny may be outlined as follows. Unless she attends residential college she is qualified at 18. She may spend two years working alongside a mother in the country (probably near her home). Then she may move to London and work with two children and a baby (a more demanding job) with a part-time working mother. Her third job may be residential still, but plenty of sole charge is considered to be promotion and she may stay for two years. After this she could well take a post abroad for a while and then return to live in a flat with friends and be a daily or temporary nanny.

Most stop being nannies at about 25 when either they help run a nursery school or day nursery or take other child-related jobs, or they get married. There is, as Angela Hovey of Occasional and Permanent Nannies agency points out, a difference between a 'career' and a 'life nanny'. The latter are the traditional sort who find the constant care and cherishing of other people's children sufficiently fulfilling to continue as a nanny indefinitely. They should have a conservation order on them because they are so rare, but not quite extinct.

The favourite age range is 18 to 23. Many prefer 24-year-olds but 'I always end up with the green 18-year-olds. They should pay me for what I teach them after years of indoctrinating new nannies', is a common gripe from experienced employers. For this reason many will consider anyone up to 45 'and possibly older if she had been living in a family for years'. Another section positively avoid the older nanny: 'In the winter they sit at the Albert Memorial gossiping and they move like transhumant goats to the bandstand in the summer. Awful old black crows.' Another observes uncharitably and accurately that 'they are a dying breed'.

The super-responsible and highly paid jobs, involving weeks of sole charge and/or extensive travel and a life shared with security guards and kidnap risks, go to more mature nannies of 35-plus with a proven and impeccable track record. Most ordinary families have no need for such a paragon.

Age can have its drawbacks. A mature nanny is more likely to be 'right', i.e. to know how to handle a tricky child after years of experience and may insist that things are done her way. She may also be that irritating type that knows that there is a 'right' way to do things and makes sure that everyone knows when 'standards' slip. She may also reminisce *ad nauseam* about the well-ordered lives of her erstwhile employers in comparison with the chaos around her now. No one likes a nanny lording it over them. In fact most mothers know that they want to be boss. As one mother put it, 'She needs to be younger than I am.'

It may also occur to the sensitive mama that nannies of a certain age may much regret not having had their own babies. Menopausal problems can be just as hard and more embarrassing to deal with than the teenage kind.

As a generalization, it is true that 18-year-olds are more likely to cause difficulties than 23-year-olds. They are mostly away from home for the first time, they are likely to be man-mad, they may resent any sign that you are protective towards them, and they may not have enough confidence or experience yet to take criticism gracefully. They have a great deal to learn still and leaving them in sole charge ('even of your cat', as one agent says nastily) is asking for trouble. If it passes you by, it will be due to sheer good luck, not good judgement (see page 123 on Sole Charge).

Where To Find Her

But if it were me . . . well, I should get somebody to put in the *Morning Paper* the news that Jane and Michael and John and Barbara Banks (to say nothing of their Mother) require the best possible Nannie at the lowest possible wage and at once. Then I should wait and watch for the Nannies to queue up outside the front gate . . .

Mary Poppins, P. L. Travers

That was in 1934 and a lot has changed. The art of selling your family as attractive bait and hooking a good one who doesn't have to be thrown back instantly, either to grow up a bit more or because she was an odd fish, is damned hard work. The ones that got away may sound fun in the telling, but are very wearing for all concerned at the time.

People will do anything to get a good nanny. The reckless will risk losing old friends by trying to poach a desirable one. More likely, the present employer won't know the predator at all and her nanny will be approached at the One O'Clock Club or clinic. Even then she'll be lucky to learn about it at all and only if the nanny decides to reject the overture . . . this time.

'Word of mouth' is an oft-quoted source. Its great advantage is that it doesn't cost a bean and reduces the time taken up by interviews. Don't let the fact that the 'mouth' belongs to a great friend inhibit you from ploughing through your usual question-and-answer session with the available nanny. Tell everyone you meet that you are looking for a nanny or any other type of carer and ask them how they found theirs.

Hiring daughters of friends or friends of friends can be risky. One mother remembers taking on a Sloane mother's help, the daughter of friends of her parents back home in Northumbria. She found the arrangement a little awkward. 'We found ourselves eating with her every evening and I became embarrassed about giving instructions.'

It is far from ideal for the nanny whose parents are friends of her employers. One such got so fed up of the covert pincer movement to exploit her and clip her wings that she left the job and the country simultaneously when the joint pressure became too great. 'Whenever I did something wrong my Mum and Dad were told by my employers at once and they gave me a rocket too. I never got a pay rise and my parents were unsympathetic. It was a bad idea from the start.'

73

If you fancy the top brass, apply direct to the Norland and Princess Christian college registries. The Chiltern nannies put their names on the agency lists. Several recommend telephoning or writing to their local NNEB college, or to any that they have heard are particularly good. For details see chapter 7.

Agencies cost money. They may save time, however, and be conscientious enough to save you hours of interviewing by phone and in person. Their experience may guide your decision. How do you choose an agency and how do you know if it is any good? See Agencies, page 283.

Advertising
Employers' favourite organ in which to place an ad for a nanny, mother's help, au pair or any kind of help for their children whether full time, part-time, shared, live-in, or live-out, is *The Lady*.

It is a fuddy-duddy, rag-bag of articles on anything from the Aland Islands (between Finland and Sweden, we note with interest) to 'Score with Scones' (how do you do that?). The magazine has a faded, missionary/Simla/Miss Marples nostalgic feel. It is hard to pigeon-hole its market, so it is the more surprising that its fame has travelled from Calgary to Canberra with stop-offs at Lisbon, Stuttgart and Malmö. It sells 69,000 copies each week but claims a readership of 300,000. Every would-be nanny and trembling employer from Truro to Uist via The Wirral buys it from their local newsagent.

Its copy is wedged between two wadges of 'hotels, guest houses and board accommodation', 'activity and interest holidays', and 'houses and flats to be let'. The vital part is billed as 'Domestic Situations Vacant in the British Isles' (Cooks, House-keepers, Mother's helps, Nannies), followed by a brief 'Situations Wanted'. The last is always worth checking out and do this well ahead of time, as the advertisers are often living abroad and often give addresses and box numbers rather than telephone numbers.

The Lady's publication day is officially Thursday, but it's available by lunchtime on Wednesday in the London area. 'Prepaid classified advertisements' instructions appear near its end. It is good value at well under £20 for a short ad. It won't take instructions on the telephone. The most vital bit of the small print is to send your ad *to arrive no later than the first post on the Wednesday of the week before you wish the ad to appear.* Don't forget that Bank Holidays cause chaos and mean that your ad must arrive even sooner; check exactly when if you need to cut it fine and always allow for the vagaries of the post.

One mother cursed when she chose to use a box number because she was in a hurry to get someone and giving her phone number would have speeded the process. Most employers reckon that box numbers, like being ex-directory, are more of a nuisance than an advantage, and having one costs more. A few employers with time on their hands like box numbers because they prefer communicating by letter rather than by phone.

A few use *Nursery World* because this is the magazine of the trained, career nanny; it is quite pointless to advertise for any other type in it.

A growing number cling to *The Times* in the rather quirky belief that their sort of nanny will see it there. The funny thing is that sometimes they do. London dwellers may chance their arm with the London *Evening Standard*. It's impossible to predict what sort of response you will get, if any. It is not a net for trained nannies but it can be worthwhile for au pairs and mother's helps. The trawl will probably produce some highly unsuitable applicants. Its greatest advantage is that it is cheap and quick, and you know fast – within 24 hours of placing the ad – whether it is going to produce anyone remotely possible. The downside is that it is here today and gone tomorrow unlike a periodical like *The Lady*, which has a shelf life of about three weeks and also gets passed around the nanny network.

One mother always scans the CGA magazine (the Country Gentleman's Association) where nice gels' 'member's daughter' adverts appear as they fill their time between school and university looking after kids, dogs etc.

If you specifically want Australians and New Zealanders, advertise in the London give-away magazines LAM and TNT and put a card in New Zealand and Australia Houses. Also consider putting cards in shops or anywhere else with a high concentration of them, such as the ski shops in Kensington High Street or the travel agencies in Earl's Court. For further information on how and where to find them see Agencies, page 283 and chapter 8.

Advertising in local newspapers either in London or in the

country, may produce a good NNEB candidate, or a mother's help, whose parents live near you and this may be a big plus. If you are a Roman Catholic or think that they have indubitably more moral strictures placed on them by being so and you want to cash in on it, go for the Catholic press. Employers report success with cards in newsagents, laundromats, clinics, surgeries, church newsletters, grocery shops, chemists, sports and leisure centres, second-hand children's clothes shops and schools. For advice on au pair hunting, see chapter 8.

Writing an advertisement
Employers are as opinionated as ever about the compilation of an arresting and effective ad. In summary, they belong to two groups: those who rabbit on fulsomely about their darlings and comfy houses, and those who despise the gush and keep it short and plain. The latter is cheaper. It is not necessarily better; it must depend on the personality of the nanny reading it and on how she feels that day as to whether she wants to wallow in the details or likes the brisk, no-nonsense approach. One mother's help tells us that she always goes for the warm-sounding advertisements, which give the names of the children. She also likes big ads on the simple grounds that the family is more likely to be well-off and pay generously; there must be many nannies and mother's helps who think the same way.

Some mothers swear by the upfront approach. They are happy to spend the extra, even splashing out on the semi-display kind because they think it's advantageous that the nanny conjures up a partial picture of the type of family she may join straight away. At one end of the scale this revelation may meet your eyes:

Lady Paddington needs a
very kind, reliable,
trained or experienced
NANNY
(21 years +) from May

To be lovingly responsible for Harry (7), Charlotte (2), and to take charge of a new baby expected in the summer when our maternity nurse leaves in October.

Louise (11) is at boarding school and Emily (10) will be separately organized.

Large, very comfortable, London home. Some weekends and holidays in lovely country house in Suffolk. Above average salary for the right applicant. Time off excellent. Other help in the house in every respect. Non-smoker, animal-lover preferred. Car driver and good references essential. Applicants must be looking for a permanent position (one year minimum) as continuity of loving care especially for little Charlotte is a priority.

> Please apply with references and
> telephone number to:
> The Countess of Paddington,
> 29 Arundel Gardens,
> London W8

Presumptuously, we can learn a lot from this slightly altered real-life example of an unusually up-market ad. Only Princess Michael can rival this style in *The Lady*.

It is amusing to note that even Lady Paddington doesn't have high expectations of the duration of her nanny's stay. It depends on your view, but what else could she offer? It seems a short time for any job, let alone one in which the applicant is probably a top-rank career nanny.

One experienced au pair procurer always spends her pittance on the lowest possible deal in *The Lady* thus:

AU PAIR: non-smoking, good English, for two tinies. 071 937 3276

She says that this weeds out the foreign girls who speak no English and is designed to gather potential interviewees who will learn more by telephone. She does admit that a detailed ad should lessen the amount of time needed to sift the applicants on the phone. Employers of au pairs write much shorter ads anyway, because the job is part-time, short-lived and training or experience is not expected, though they are usually longer than the above.

Employers recommend that if you have a difficult or unusual family set-up, like a one-parent family, or a disturbed/handi-capped/or fostered child, you are advised to be open about it in the ad. It is better to attract a nanny who quite likes the idea than one who is put off on arrival for interview.

If you like lists of qualities in your advertisement, take your pick from the Ideal Nanny definitions listed on page 56. Otherwise it is pragmatic to mention any perks that will catch the jaded job hunter's glance, like foreign travel and holidays, weekend houses, own car and separate accommodation. It is stupid to be flashy in ads as elsewhere, so don't try to impress.

It is noticeable that people don't stipulate the salary, or mention the Big Four (see page 46) except with carefully considered adjectival vagueness. For example: 'good' as in 'good salary to the right person'; 'flexible but generous time off'; 'ample holidays'. Understandably, employers prefer to spell out the terms and conditions of the job once they have had a look at the applicant. This lack of specifics has a purpose. It enables the employer to be flexible, particularly about pay if she chooses, at the interview. If a smashing NNEB walks in whom you know is a bit above your price range because of her experience and references, then it is still possible to offer her £10 per week more than you originally intended to pay to secure her.

The best months to advertise for nannies are December (employees like to make a move in the New Year) and June (to catch the new NNEBs or school leavers for the early Autumn). Au pairs are best recruited in the summer for September; this is the most likely time to achieve a year-long stay; January is the other time to do it. For Australian migratory habits see chapter 8. In general, avoid March, April, November and December for an immediate start.

The depressing story from many employers is that however widely their net is cast, even with money no object, sometimes they are just plain unlucky and they don't even interview a single good candidate. One mother says that after a semi-display effort in *The Lady* she received 'fifty replies on the phone and ended up with only five hopefuls, two of whom didn't appear and one of whom turned out to be the best ever. A damned close-run thing.'

Suppose your ad has flopped. What next? The interview processes and the 10-day time lag in *The Lady*'s schedule have rendered you desperate. Some experienced employers anticipate this and book the ad to appear in two consecutive weeks. You must cancel fast for a refund, but if you hope not to be knocking on the agencies' doors, which is going to cost a great deal more, a consecutive ad is a sensible precaution.

If this whole procedure fills you with gloom and nausea, particularly if you have spoken to sixty nannies and mother's helps and seen six, all of whom were mediocre, reconsider the agency option.

Insist to yourself that you *will* find the right person for your family. It is so easy to feel demoralized, but that won't find a nanny. Brace yourself, drop your shoulders and start again.

4

Interviewing

By Telephone

Telephone interviewing is time-consuming, hard work and can be confusing, particularly if your desire for an au pair outstrips your knowledge of her language or if a nanny's broad Yorkshire might as well be Swahili to your cleaning lady who answers the phone for you if you are out.

An advertisement in a magazine or newspaper elicits a great deal of telephone interviewing. The only way to avoid this is to give a Box Number inviting candidates to write with their details first. One mother asks them to write the moment they put the receiver down. If there is plenty of time before the job starts, a written application can work well, but there is then the big risk that many nannies, mother's helps and au pairs rightly reckon that they are worse on paper than in person and can get a job with someone else much more easily and quickly – by telephone.

Some mothers are impressed by a clear and neatly written letter and feel that the fact that the girl *has* been bothered to put biro to paper is a mark in her favour. Often the girl who turns up does reflect the orderliness of her letter, but not always. One employer reflects drily that, 'It was one of my major misconceptions at the beginning that anyone could write a decent letter. Six years as an employer has taught me that my best nannies have all been "awful spellers" or appallingly illiterate by my standards. Now I couldn't give a fig how they spell banana on a shopping list. I'm just pathetically grateful that they are buying them.' Nevertheless, asking for a written CV is one way of cutting down on applicants, if you have a huge response, and it may also provide clues to personality.

You will also have to interview on the telephone if you decide to use an agency. The employer is usually given the name, phone number and details of a suitable girl or vice versa, but in either case, the telephone provides your first contact. Some agencies will ask you to fill in a questionnaire and will have given the applicant a similar one which you will have read; this will cut out some of the questions. A quick chat with the agency about CVs and other details that you may receive should weed out some obvious duds.

It is a sensible idea to cancel outings in the evenings and plans to go away for weekends during the interview period, unless you mention your intended absence in the advert.

Before the phone starts ringing, remember to consult your spouse about whether he intends to appear at the interviews and find out if he will be available during the allotted time span. Don't stray from the phone for long for at least three days after the publication which carries your ad hits the streets.

If you go out, try to arrange that the present nanny takes down the relevant details and give her the basic telephone interview equipment (see below). If she is capable, get her to arrange the interview schedule. Incumbent nannies can be excellent telephone interviewers and, if they sound positive about the job, will also give your lovely family the thumbs-up.

Decide what you want to do about paying or contributing to the applicants' travel expenses – trains, tubes and maybe a taxi. Make it clear whether you are or are not prepared to reimburse them. Agencies press their clients to pay them. Some mothers think it the done thing; others think the applicants can perfectly well arrange other interviews on the same day and shell out themselves, as indeed they would have to do for most other jobs.

Telephone interviews should be kept fairly short – especially if you have invited applicants to reverse the charges in the advert. Write down a list of major questions (see page 82) and keep it by the phone. Also have ready your Filofax or a large sheet of thick paper or card (it doesn't slip so easily while writing with one hand) for names and details and find two biros that work. Leave them by the phone. The whole business is fraught enough as you juggle a baby, a phone and a burning saucepan not to want to worsen the experience by failing to find something with which to write.

Attempting to memorize some half-heard mumbles about Hull

About the applicant

- What is her full name?
- What is her telephone number? (Get this down immediately; it's surprisingly easy to forget about it entirely.)
- Does she smoke?
- How old is she?
- Where is she living now?
- When can she start? (This often does cut down applicants. It's amazing how many insist on starting tomorrow or not for at least a couple of months.)
- How much experience has she had with children? How old were the children and how long did she work in each job?
- Has she any qualifications? NNEB or equivalent, CSEs, GCSEs, Os and As?
- Can she drive?
- Has she organized references for herself? Could she please bring them with her to the interview? (No references, no interview.) It depends on her experience, but she should have at least 3 (1 personal and 2 professional as a minimum) if she is experienced.

Tech, while the 'beep, beep, beep' goes is no fun. A frazzled mother can't think when a nanny rings her from a call box. Take down her number at once and ring her back straight away.

If you have more than one telephone, ideally try to keep this equipment safely by one *all the time* and use only that phone in that room for all incoming calls for the duration.

Many employers hire mother's helps and au pairs over the phone without a personal interview, because they have no choice; the girl lives too far away, i.e. abroad. Many agency au pairs or mother's helps have to be taken 'blind'. This does increase the risk of landing a no-hoper but it is often successful. It is always best to set aside the time to see anyone who is going to look after your children and/or live in/work by day in your home. Even if you hire a temporary nanny for the weekend, and in whatever crisis, don't rely totally on an agency's assessment of personality.

Many employers reveal the Big Four (see chapter 2) over the phone. Others feel strongly that applicants should turn up for an

About your family

- Tell her about the size of your family, the ages and sexes of the children; mention twins or children with special needs if you have them.
- Describe the type of accommodation you live in and will provide for her.
- Be honest about communications – buses and trains – particularly if you live in the country. Tell her if a car is provided for her use.
- Give her a brief job description making it extremely clear what type of help you want. (Employers/employees are too often vague about what exactly an au pair or mother's help is expected to do.)
- Tell her if you have a cleaner (a big plus).
- Tell her where you live and how to get there. Offer her travel expenses if you have decided to pay them.
- Mention pay (see below), holidays etc, particularly if attractive.

interview and find out about the family before enquiring what they are to be paid. The other considerations that make up the package – the perks like holidays abroad, her own wheels or flat, a swimming pool, or a charming, amusing and entirely delightful family (harder to sell this one) – should count for something. They may make an average salary bearable.

Obviously, from the girl's point of view, she doesn't want to travel miles and go through the whole interview only to be told that she will be offered less or the same as she is paid at present. Incidentally, several nannies told us that they went to interviews having been attracted by a big salary advertised in *The Lady*, only to find that the employer never had any intention of paying that amount and had just used it as a ploy.

It is best to ascertain what the nanny is earning currently over the telephone, then she has to hope that you won't be a goof and offer her half that sum.

It is comforting that Mrs Townsend of Chiltern advises her

students to: 'Go for the job you think you'll be happiest in. Money is important, but use of car, if you think you'll be well fed, your own bathroom and TV and travelling are all to be borne in mind. You must be happy or there's no point in any of it.'

Some parents spend some time on the telephone interviews and then say to the girl that they *may* ring back in a matter of hours to invite her to come for an interview. This gives the employer a chance to put the phone down and write detailed comments of her impressions of the applicant. Was she articulate? Friendly and easy to talk to? Did she sound doubtful about anything? Was she enthusiastic? Did her description of her previous experience make it sound ideal/OK/barely adequate/grisly? Do you care if you never speak to her again?

This may sound like mind-reading being passed off as intuition to someone who is not used to using the telephone as a means of screening people professionally. Many agencies place great store by these skills and some are extraordinarily perceptive after years of experience. Don't mistrust a funny feeling; if something niggles nastily, take note and mull it over during the day.

Another little-used technique is to encourage the nanny to ponder what you have told her about the family and job and to call again if she would like to come for an interview. Unlucky for some, this seems extremely cocky to many employers whose instinct is to haul in all comers. If she does ring back, it means she is keen and it also avoids wasting time arranging interviews with nannies who may not bother to show up (quite common).

A nanny may not come because she has already found another job and doesn't make the effort to inform you, but, as often as not, she has not liked the sound of the job. It may well be that she only took down your address and laborious directions because she couldn't think of a way of telling you that it all sounded hellish and was unable to bring the conversation to a close.

Another tip to avoid wasting time is to ask the nannies nicely to ring you if they find another job or if anything crops up to prevent them from coming. Explain humbly that you have a few things that you could be getting on with instead of waiting for her non-appearance. Often they will respond to your plea.

Never pursue someone who doesn't ring back and never hanker after those who don't turn up. Apart from the bracing spilt milk cliché, you may console yourself with the thought that they have a lot to learn and mercifully will not have a chance of doing so now at your expense.

When setting a time and day for the interview, be explicit about directions and give her the approximate time the journey should take. Punctuality gains marks, so help her achieve it.

Eyeball to Eyeball

The principal points which the parent must investigate for herself . . . have reference to the *moral qualifications* of the applicant: and if there is found to be any defect here, however healthy or otherwise desirable, her services ought to be declined. Temperance, cleanliness, a character for good conduct, fondness for children and aptness for their management are among the most important requisites. An amiable disposition and cheerful temper are also very desirable. It is unnecessary to allude to other qualities which a woman who is sought as a nurse should possess; they will naturally suggest themselves to any thoughtful mind.

Bull's *Hints to Mothers*, 1851

The employer hopes to discover much in a short time during an interview, but she must concentrate on organizing the data so that she is able to answer two crucial questions by the end of it. Do I think this nanny/mother's help/au pair will be good at this job? And do I like her enough to have her come and live (or be around the house a great deal – as in the case of a daily nanny) with us?

Many employers confess to being 'more nervous than the nanny' when they dealt with their first batch of interviewees, even though some had been quite relaxed about hiring and firing in offices for years. Comfortingly, most think that they learnt the ropes fast and that the experience of having talked to many applicants gives them the confidence to know what they want, judge it expertly and not settle for anyone who doesn't match up to their criteria. A few are still far from satisfied with their interview technique and dread it.

Everyone agrees that it is unlike an ordinary interview. It is just as well to treat it that way because your decision will make an impact on every important aspect of your life.

Some people say that their husbands like to interview nannies with them. If so, organize the double act so that you don't confuse the nanny by constant disagreement, hysterical giggles, quizzical looks or other distracting behaviour. Incidentally, some nannies say that two people make an interview more intimidating. Decide if you prefer to interview together, one after the other or let him second-guess your choice of brilliant finalists.

Choose somewhere comfortable to sit where you and the interviewee can both see each other clearly. Silence the phone, try to organize things so that the children are occupied elsewhere and you will not be interrupted. Now concentrate on the substance of the interview, relax, and be prepared to give the candidate your undivided attention.

An employer might think it safe to assume that all the obvious duds and kooks have been eliminated by careful telephone interviewing and that she is now going to view a parade of suitable candidates. You may be in for a shock. A 'good telephone manner' is a most deceptive tool.

If you don't like the look of the girl, can't understand a word she says or can see only dimly what looks like a nightclub hostess slumped on your sofa wreathed in Turkish cigarette smoke . . . *cut the interview short*. You will save both her and yourself time, trouble and further embarrassment if you firmly and politely show her the door.

Some mothers and nannies claim to hate a 'formal' interview and 'despise a bombardment of questions'. Although techniques of interviewing differ widely and you will need to vary the questions to suit individual applicants, the fact remains that you will kick yourself later if you don't cover essential ground. Your job is metaphorically to spin an impenetrable web in which bad nannies may entrap themselves across your front door, thus effectively denying a bad carer access to your children. It is best to be able to assure yourself that you have performed this task conscientiously. Since this is your only chance to grill an applicant (preferably subtly performed – she should not be aware of the heat), and to exchange a great deal of information, many questions and answers are inevitable.

Say to the nanny that you will tell her exactly what the job entails – warts and all. This is a better line than giving a misleading, or false, picture as too many employers do. Say that the interview will be direct and personal because both of you have to discover crucial details about the other and make judgements and decisions quickly.

Ask her

Training Is she trained (cooking, home economics diplomas), to do the job? Ask to see a photocopy of her certificate(s). What other exams has she taken? Where did she train and what did she think of her training? (See chapter 7)

Experience How many jobs has she had? With how many children? What were their ages and sexes? How much sole charge has she had? Why is she a nanny? How long did each job last? Where were the jobs and why did she leave them?

References (she should have brought them with her). Were there any jobs from which she was not given a reference? If so, why? Has she shown you what her tutor said about her if she did the NNEB or other training? Will she mind if you talk to her mother? (Obviously this would seem a most peculiar request if you are interviewing someone mature, but with a young girl many employers mention how very frank mothers can be about their daughters. Others go further and insist that a good mother equals a good nanny, especially they say, if she has only just left home.)

Her home and background Where does she live? What exams has she taken? What are her parents' jobs? How do they feel about her coming to live where you live? How does she get on with them? (Big red flashing lights if she says she hasn't seen her mum since she was 16; it is important that she has a home to return to in various circumstances, not least illness.) Will she be homesick if she lives a long way from you? Has she got brothers and sisters? What are their jobs? Are they a close family?

All this aims to give you a reassuring picture of a happy, disciplined and stable background: if divorce, remarriage or recent deaths emerge, it is a good idea to ask searching questions and satisfy yourself that the nanny has come to terms with the event. Most employers insist that their nannies come from a stable home environment.

Boyfriends Does she have a boyfriend or fiancé? How will he fit into her life in your home? When will she expect to see him? Does he welcome the idea of her taking the job?

About herself Does she smoke? Does she drive? When did she pass her test? Has she driven in other jobs? Does she have a clean licence? Has she got her own bike/car/moped?

Does she practise a religion? What are her hobbies? How does she spend her free time?

Does she know the area where you live? If going to a city, i.e. London, for the first time, does she have friends or relations there? If she doesn't, how will she make friends? Does she like the countryside? Is she knowledgeable about it? Does she enjoy walking or playing on a beach (or whatever you need her to enjoy while on duty)?

Would she say she was quick, patient, resourceful, efficient or any other qualities which you consider essential for the job? (Many interviewees say yes to everything but it can be instructive to see how she handles the query.)

Her health Is she generally fit and healthy? Has she had any recurring illnesses? Dismenorrhoea (painful periods)? Any major operations? Has she suffered from depression or any other mental illness? What about diabetes? Migraines? Epilepsy? (All these questions are vital if she will have sole charge and/or the employer works full time away from home.)

Think about asking whether she has ever had an AIDS test. No nanny or mother's help who thinks she may have AIDS should work with other people's children.

Many employers will be just too embarrassed to ask such a thing at an interview. But bear in mind that girls in their late teens and 20s, particularly if they were brought up in a city (Glasgow? Liverpool?), who may have had several boyfriends and/or are at all promiscuous are capable, in theory, of contracting AIDS. Obviously if any member of *your* immediate family has AIDS you must tell her about it. (It is possible that in the future AIDS Test Cards may have to be carried by everyone to prove to people that they were cleared at their last test.)

Hobbies Does she like taking exercise? Does she need a lot of sleep? Does she enjoy swimming, skating, cycling, or whatever your children most enjoy?

The children Does she know how to entertain children? Playdough, endless reading, colouring, painting? Puzzles and creative and educational toys? Can she sing or play a musical instrument?

Sole charge Does she insist on 'sole charge'? (no good if you are around during the day). Does she like the responsibility it entails? Is she alert to potential dangers to children in the home and elsewhere? Try a couple of quick questions about how she would deal with a common emergency, e.g. a child choking or a fat fire in the kitchen. These should be answered swiftly and confidently.

Her future What are her ambitions? What does she see herself doing in five years' time?

The next part of the interview is the best opportunity you will ever have to be opinionated – so make the most of it. At this point you have to decide whether or not you can cope with self-revelation. You should outline *all* your House Rules (having checked through the list in chapter 2) and reveal all or some of the eccentricities of your better half, adored offspring and cherished home.

Tell her

Her routine Tell her everything you can about a typical day's chores and responsibilities. Working mothers must discuss the 'sole charge' issue and watch out for nannies and mother's helps who seem too keen to be left alone with the children. One in 1,000 may be a nut; a greater proportion may be lazy and prefer not to look after the children as you would wish in your absence.

Mention the need for a generally helpful attitude, and that she will be expected to muck in with busy family life to which everyone has to contribute as the occasion arises. If she is trained, discover whether she will ever wash your tea cups or post a letter for you. Explain that you have no intention of exploiting her and you understand her job description, but you will take it to heart if she is stand-offish and waits for the butler – that's you – to do things that aren't strictly her job. Many nannies are rigid about their duties and if you want adaptability, better say so now.

Your children What are her views on discipline? Explain if you don't want the children to be smacked or shouted at. Do you mind how much TV they watch? Tell her everything you can about your children – their personalities, school routines, hobbies, friendships, likes and dislikes, any illnesses or other problems (grommets? speech therapy?) and what you want her to do with and for them. Try a couple of 'what if?' questions about how she would envisage occupying them and ten visiting children on the third rainy day on holiday in Gairloch.

Animals If you have animals, however big or small, and you will want the nanny to feed or care for them at all, tell her precisely the extent of her involvement. Is it mucking out a pony after breakfast or shoving the budgie a cuttlefish once a month? Don't be too astonished if she raises her eyebrows and claims she is allergic to all furry creatures. Seriously, better check.

House Rules There are many petty preferences and rules, i.e. use of phone, washing etc that are best left to the first week of employment (see chapter 5), but now you have to deal with those abrasive and revealing areas we call the House Rules (back to chapter 2). Be explicit and explain why you think they are necessary.

The applicant must understand that you feel *very* strongly about a few items. It is fatal to be wishy-washy – decide what you like and dislike and lay it on the line. Remember the hundreds of nannies who complain they were never told any of the rules at the interview and would never have taken the job if they had been. Better now than in a month or so.

Just to remind you briefly of the subjects that you should cover, here is the list: boyfriends, late nights, smoking, eating habits, friends to stay, dress on duty, confidentiality, out of bounds.

You and your husband's life If your family follows a religion, tell her. Mention any religious rituals observed by the family. Describe your own close relatives, particularly if they live with you or come and stay for protracted periods. Talk about your husband's job and travel schedules if relevant, and your own. How much time do you spend with the children and in the house? Mention any plans for the future or changes in your lives which you can foresee and which will affect her job. Moving house? New schools for the children? New baby planned? Getting divorced?

Your neighbourhood Outline the transport facilities, amenities, parks, swimming pools, shops, classes and anything else which might be appealing. Tell her about the existence of other nannies in the area and how you will make arrangements for her to meet them.

The Big Four (see chapter 2) – the nuts and bolts of the job that she certainly will want to hear all about: pay, time off, holidays and perks.

Ask her how much she is expecting to earn or has been earning – she may think of a number and double it, but you are stuck with her base line – and then tell her by how much you will increase it. However good you reckon your package to be, there's not much chance that most nannies will take a penny less than they got last week. So when she announces it was £100, there's not much mileage in saying 'Come, take fifty,' like the Mayor of Hamelin and reminding her of a chance to see the Matterhorn.

Explain your tax and National Insurance and sick pay arrangements (see pages 332–41) and any special bonuses.

Tell her how many days off she will have a week. How many nights, on average, she will be expected to babysit. What her working hours are. Explain any overtime terms – cash and/or time off in lieu. Do you expect her to get up at night for the children? How much paid and unpaid holiday will she have and when may she take it?

Mention the car and foreign travel. Think up anything else that your nanny-hiring neighbour doesn't offer or hasn't got – a jacuzzi, you will pay for her to learn to drive or learn to play the piano, you are a Cordon Bleu, your brother has a power boat, your father-in-law is good for Wimbledon, opera and theatre tickets, the holiday shack in the Bahamas/Hayling Island/Lake District or anything else you can flash in front of her eyes as long as she will genuinely benefit from it.

Some mothers think it is daft to chat intimately at an interview about exactly what you want in a nanny; they prefer to let the nanny pick up their preferences and dislikes once installed. Actually most nannies say that they are pleased to get as much information from a future employer as they can. The more open you are about yourself, the better she will be able to judge whether her behaviour and attitudes will blend with your own. Be as direct as you like.

First tell her of anything you can't stand, i.e. stealing, swearing, lying (in every form from fudging to bare-faced). Integrity and saying what you mean, and vice versa, is crucial in a nanny, being unkind to the children, racist views, untidiness, unpunctuality or anything that has driven you mad or you have come across in previous nannies may be mentioned. Of course she is not about to reveal herself as a kleptomaniac, but she'll either emphasize with you for bringing up such concepts, may look as if she does, demur or not react at all. Watch like a hawk.

Then you could talk about what you hope she is and will be: affectionate, observant, adventurous, patient, communicative, fun, sensitive to you and your husband's privacy, appreciative of the children, imaginative about entertaining them and aware of safety hazards. She should be able to cope calmly in crises, be reliable and responsible with other people's children when they visit, and able to fit in easily with your family and friends.

Speak of your need for consideration and honesty on both sides as problems arise and assure her of your concern and interest in her happiness in the job and well-being generally. She must feel that she can bring up difficulties with you, and that you will make time to listen and discuss things. 'The more you give, the more you will get' is the cliché that fits the bill. Don't be embarrassed to use it if you can guarantee that you are a good employer.

Either you have chatted your way through and round some of these suggestions and she has interrupted you constantly or intermittently in her queries or you should invite her to ask you any questions. A good, professional nanny will have prepared several.

Remember, all the time another process has been going on: the nanny or mother's help has been assessing you. She wants to be sure that you have enough money to pay her promptly and cheerfully and the intention and capability of raising her salary.

She also needs to check out the family and its attitude to having a nanny. One way she can do this is by talking to the present incumbent. This should be encouraged because it is advantageous to you too, unless you have fallen out with her. The departing nanny can be a great help in judging a contemporary and a potential successor. The cleaning lady, your mother, a neighbour or any old friend might be persuaded to appear to give her the once-over and/or provide another point of reference.

The applicant has a right to ask your nanny any questions about the personalities of members of the family, how everyone treats the children, whether she has been paid reliably, and if she has experienced any serious problems during her stay. A residential nanny must assure herself as best she may that the people she is going to be living with will be reasonable and considerate. There can't be a better endorsement of your family and lifestyle than from the current nanny. One nanny writes: 'Their previous nanny had stayed three and a half years and recommended the job; it counted for a lot.'

Show her

You will score points if you can show her written notes from previous nannies giving *you* a good reference as an employer – at least give her the phone numbers of old trusties, so that she can hear about you for herself. Incidentally, if you have had any or many failures, tell her now before she discovers the skeletons in your cupboard for herself.

Either you or the present nanny can now take her on a tour of the house or flat and point out the best features of the bedroom and bathroom she will use.

It's time to introduce her to the children, if they haven't already found you. One agent never interviews girls in an office. She doesn't feel that there is much point since she can't see how they react to children. She suggests that it is a good idea to try to leave the visiting nanny with one or more of your offspring alone. Make an excuse to go, and take this opportunity to scrutinize her references. Leave the door ajar and come back quietly, so you can get a glimpse of how she is getting on. If she is on her knees playing dominoes and helping the youngest cheat to win, that's good news. If she has made up her face again and is staring blankly out of the window while the children are jumping on the chairs, she has just lost the job.

Ask her again if she has any questions. If she seems to be a winner, don't risk losing her to the next interviewer; be definite and enthusiastic and tell her that, subject to having checked out her references, you will ring her at a certain time (preferably within 24 hours or you may lose her) and offer her the job. Unless you feel very positive about her and want to capture her without fail, don't raise her hopes. Say you have 'three or four others to see', but that you will ring her as soon as you can.

Time to Reflect

When she has left, it is good to remind yourself on paper about her responses and reactions. You may ponder some of the following:

Was she confident? What was her chief facial expression during the interview? Was she fun for the children to meet? Was she well turned out? Did she seem 'together'? Was she punctual? Did she whinge about the journey? What questions did she ask first (pity if she dwelt on money and time off)? Was she easy to chat to? What was she enthusiastic about? Did you like her voice and laugh? If you have steep stairs, did she bound up them effortlessly or sound like she was on the verge of collapse? Did she talk too much and have a lot of strongly held opinions? Do you feel worn out by an hour in her company? Would her appearance (height/size/spots/breath/moustache/choice of clothes) depress you day after day?

Recapture your reactions to her. Several mothers warn that ignoring hunches, gut reactions or their intuition may result in self-recrimination later as just the problems they had sensed at that first meeting materialized. Don't worry about being irrational or seemingly absurd; if anything bothered you about her, don't push it aside.

The vital thing is for the interviewer to be sure that her abiding impression is of having just met someone whom she likes, can respect, trust and talk to easily – in short, a nanny with whom she can live and who will put the children's needs before her own. You need to think that she will be capable of loving them and liking you back.

Chase Those Refs

Checking a nanny's and a mother's help's references are vital. Doing the checking thoroughly is a nuisance and time-con-

suming, particularly if the referee doesn't answer the telephone
and/or is not particularly helpful when you do get through to her.

References are not easy to write. Nor are they easy to read. First
impressions can often mislead and confirm the employer's rose-
tinted view of her chosen girl. However heart-warming a nanny's
references are, there should be at least three of them. Preferably
all of them should show that she has finished each job and been
given a reference – check at least two of them.

One employer was delighted with a nanny's references which
one Kensington agency said they had checked out thoroughly
when they read them to her over the phone. Several weeks later
the employer and nanny were at loggerheads and the employer
burst out in exasperation, 'Heaven alone knows why you had
such brilliant references from your last job.' 'They weren't,'
muttered the nanny, 'the agency said it was best to leave out the
last sentence.' After close questioning, the nanny revealed that
the last sentence had read, 'She can be short-tempered and
aggressive and is sometimes unable to cope.' The moral is
obvious – *always* check yourself.

Checking References

- Insist on at least two or three references and ensure that you
  see the originals.
- Ask to see a training certificate if the nanny is qualified. Ask
  for her tutor's name and telephone number.
- Require details of every gap in her CV.
- Remember that a reference from hotel work is not such a good
  guarantee of honesty as one from work in a private home
- You should be offered a reference for each job she has had.
  If not, investigate.
- Character references for first-time employees are much
  better than nothing.
- Don't automatically assume that if she was sacked in a
  previous job that it was her fault.

Checking references of nannies whether trained or experienced or both is essential and fairly straightforward. What
does take an effort is getting a young British mother's help to
organize references, even if she can't produce something related

to child care. It is even harder to get references for a foreign mother's help, let alone an au pair. Try to insist on references whenever you can, even if you are only hiring a short-stay au pair or temporary nanny.

It is an indication of how few employers value references, let alone care about checking them, that so many EEC nationals or Australians who have worked on and off as mother's helps for several families have just one or even no references to show for their experience. Many foreign mother's helps or au pairs who have worked for a British family often haven't known that they ought to ask for a reference before leaving. Their employers have not volunteered one.

The trouble is that the prospective employer doesn't know if the referenceless girl is just foolish and/or inexperienced or whether the girl deliberately didn't ask for a reference because it would not have been a good one. Any employer will wonder if the girl is pretending that she doesn't know about the importance of references.

Whatever she says, call her bluff and insist on procuring former employers' telephone numbers. If an agency is supplying the foreign girl then it should have taken up references responsibly. Some agents are extremely lazy about making a girl provide references and they rarely check them, particularly if the referees live in the girl's own country. A young, traditional type of au pair who comes straight over from her motherland to stay with a family should be able to send references or at worst, bring them with her.

The trouble with written references is that they can be faked. Sometimes this is obvious, like when, as one mother describes, 'Her one reference was in an uneducated hand; an unlikely looking piece of paper which had something unconvincing scrawled on it.' Just occasionally a checked reference is also a fake. A few nannies will go so far as to get their girlfriends to do a little act for them pretending to be Mrs Bloggs her last employer. The sinister part is that if a nanny will go this far, she may have done it often and the whole sting may be thoroughly convincing. Like a Hitchcock film, the nutter doesn't look nutty, in fact the kleptomaniac, child abuser or thief takes pains to look extra 'normal' and appealing.

Some employers tend to dismiss the likelihood of them landing a fruitcake, and say that 'hiring a nanny is all about trust anyway and it's silly to be paranoid.' Some go so far as not to put much store by written references or indeed verbal ones, because of the possibility of forgery. Others mistrust them because of notorious fudging on the part of former bosses who are too chicken to say that the nanny was just average. As one mother says, 'I tend to go on a gut feeling that the one I choose will work, and so far that has stood me in good stead.'

Like burglars, the tiny fraction of criminals who are masquerading as nannies (and they do exist), are probably amazed about how easily they con their victims and think what a gullible lot they are. Many employers can't believe that the psychopath nanny can breathe the air of their friendly suburb.

When this book first went to press an eye-catching case was current among employment agencies. A girl, let's call her Melody Scott, looking like a mouse and 'plain and accommodating' in a brown overcoat was wooed by every agent that interviewed her. She had wonderful references for the last four years which agents checked, but there were none for the previous four years when her boss had died, she said.

It emerged that she had been in Holloway prison and the judge had acquitted her of stealing jewels once. He wouldn't convict because of her plausible story and appearance. He felt that she was being set up by her employers. In Melody's next job she was caught stealing and was sent to prison. One leading agency placed her with an American family.

Another agency found out that Melody was working again and tipped off the agency which had placed her. The second agency, after some disgraceful deliberation and delay, rang the American employer. She said they were delighted with the nanny but had just sacked the cleaner of five years' standing for stealing designer jumpers and money. The employer refused to believe the agents' information, but agreed eventually to take Melody's spectacles off and check to see whether there was a scar across the bridge of her nose, which the convicted criminal had. Sure enough, there was the scar. She was sacked and blacklisted by the agencies, but is thought to have got another nanny job through *The Lady* recently. She and others like her are at large.

The case of one untrained mother's help who had one reasonable reference, but not a great deal of experience, was even more serious. She seemed pleasant and capable. Her employer became suspicious when after a few weeks she kept noticing bruises on the inside of her seven month old son's thighs. The mother's help owned up and admitted that she had done it. She had been pinching and bruising him hard and regularly when he grizzled. She got the sack of course.

She may never get another child care job again; even if she does she may never abuse a child again, but she very well might. She may be mentally ill and in need of psychiatric help. Unfortunately the employer did not tell the police nor did she get in touch with, or go and see, the girl's parents. Will her next employer have the sense to check whatever reference she offers? She may lie and say that she hasn't worked before as a mother's help; if so will the interviewer ask for a reference from her doctor, priest or teacher? These may not reveal that she abuses children but it might give some clue.

One more time . . . the moral is *always* check references. At the very least if your nanny does something appalling, at least you can console yourself that you made every effort to check that she was bona fide.

Making the phone call to the referee
Try to get through to the relevant person direct. Do not leave a message saying who you are and why you called. The idea is to winkle out of the referee an unpremeditated comment on the nanny in question.

If you get a cold response, or a sighed 'I've just written her the reference', be charming and apologize for taking up her time. Introduce the conversation with something like, 'Just ringing to check that you didn't have a gun to your head', or 'It's so important that I get the right girl, can you answer a few questions?'

Reassure her that what she says to you will be in complete confidence and that the nanny concerned need never know which referees you contacted. If the referee isn't voluble and forthcoming try to enlist her sympathy. Say that it is vital that you don't make a mistake and if she has any doubts about the trustworthiness or integrity of the girl, could she please be completely open? On occasion you may get a complete unbuttoning beginning with, 'I always loathed her, I'm so glad you rang . . .'

It is important to have an idea of the needs and lifestyle of the woman to whom you are talking. Her expectations of her nanny or mother's help may be different from yours. For example, she may want a high level of hygiene in her home but she may not be interested in whether the nanny enjoys playing with the children. You may live in a scruffy house, but can't bear the sight of a nanny not messing about with paint and board games with your children.

The first thing you want to do is to check to see if the interviewee's story and reference match what her former employer actually says. Remember the written reference may be a fake. Ask her how long the nanny worked for her and how much she was paid. Ask about her duties. What did the family like best about her? What was her biggest drawback? Ask the employer what qualities the nanny has which make her a good nanny. Could she become a better nanny? Ask whether the girl was sensitive, discreet, quiet or noisy. Ask about her friends, particularly boyfriends, and whether the employer had a curfew and did that work? Ask whether she was the gregarious type and always out of the house when off duty or did she like to curl up on her bed to read or watch telly? A crucial question *never* to forget to ask is 'Would you hire her again? And if not, why not?'

Ask how many days was she off sick? Was she healthy on the whole? Did she have any health problems that might affect her work? Did she ask for more than a reasonable time off to visit the dentist and doctor? Was she a good time keeper?

All health and punctuality questions are vitally important for the daily nanny or mother's help. If a nanny lives with a family it is a lot harder for her to reckon that a cold can keep her in bed. A daily nanny just has to get her boyfriend to ring up and say sorry, she is unwell this morning. She may be ill, she may be under the weather but capable of going to work, or she may just feel like a day off.

Make it clear that you want to hear about the applicant's good and bad points as perceived by her former boss. This will give you a clearer idea of the girl's personality. What irked her previous boss may not be the thing that would get on your nerves, but it may and whatever it is, it is all useful information. A referee may say, 'Well, don't expect her to do any of the washing up that isn't the children's!' or 'She is a sweet girl but you do have to spoonfeed a bit, memory like a sieve.' Weigh and measure these types of comment and decide if you are that bothered about small things, as long as she is competent, honest and nice to have around.

Listen intently to your interlocutress's voice and its tone. This can give so much more away than anything she might write in a reference. Many employers will not willingly volunteer disparaging comments about their former nannies. A change in tone, anxiety and hesitation on the line can all be clues that she is holding something back. Ruthless employers say baldly, 'I sense you hesitate – was there anything about Sheila's behaviour that makes you do this?'

Another common characteristic is for the former employer, anxious not to let the girl down, to harp on her good points. For example, a former employer might say, 'She was good with our two boys; very sweet with them . . . they liked her a lot.' At this point you must ask, 'Did you and your husband like her?'

A mother living in Harrow, used to interviewing professionally, drew up an impressive list of statements which she sends to former employers to react to before hiring mother's helps for her child. Referees are asked to mark their responses according to an ingenious scale split into four. Here are a selection of her statements put in question form:

Did she have strong views on many general issues which she expressed in forthright tones?/ Was she emotionally stable?/ Was she very untidy and disorganized?/ Was she imaginative with the children and did she show lots of initiative?/ Was she passive with a tendency to sit and do nothing unless told otherwise?/ Did she know about nutritious food and was she able to cook it?/ Did she adore the children, love them spontaneously or was being a nanny just a job for her?/ Did she play with the children or were they often bored because she didn't?/ Did she have an excellent idea of good educative play and spend a lot of time doing this?/ Did she ever let you down?/ Did she have no sense of discipline and let the children do as they wanted or was she a strict disciplinarian?

Put your best effort into reference checking. Rely on your judgement as you may, remember that it's the nanny's last hurdle – but your last line of defence.

Decision Time

Once you have checked her references, and talked to her mother, your nanny, your spouse or any other relevant person, ring the nanny as fast as you can to say yes or no and hear her decision. If you have decided against her, do the decent thing and don't leave her up in the air – ring and say no. Feeble excuses include 'I have taken someone with more experience/someone less experienced and therefore cheaper' or just say that you were spoilt for choice and it had been a hard one and that's that. Wish her luck and try to reassure her that she was a strong candidate, if she was. Don't squirm any longer, hang up.

If she cuts in with 'Sorry, I have just accepted another job', control yourself while on the line. Don't bite the flex and shriek four-letter insults. Once you have put the phone down, have a primal scream. It is surprising, given your brief acquaintance, how disappointing it can be when your ideal, or even best-of-the bunch, nanny tells you this. In a strange way it is difficult not to take her rejection personally. However, thrust aside these useless thoughts and console yourself that it may be for the best –she wasn't *perfect* after all.

If the next best was good enough, telephone her. Otherwise you may have your second classified advertisement in *The Lady* to fall back on, or you may have to re-advertise. This will take time to organize and produce results, so at this point it might be prudent to start ringing the agencies (see page 283). You may be lucky and nannies may ring up as much as two to three weeks after the advertisement appeared, but don't rely on this. Get weaving. Ring friends or friends of friends for any 'leftover' applicants to their ads.

At this point panic may set in, especially for working mothers due back in harness in two weeks' time. As mentioned earlier, try to leave months rather than weeks for the nanny search, so if the first ad fails to draw anyone good or the first choice fails there is time to find another girl.

If the nanny accepts the job, it is a good idea to write to her stating the exact date when she is due to start work and a convenient estimated time of arrival. Confirm the terms of the employment – pay, holidays, the contract if there is to be one, sick pay and notice – and explain any trial or overlapping period with the existing nanny.

Some mothers think that it is a good idea to have a new nanny come and work for a day, a weekend, a week or even two to see if they like each other. One mother says, 'It is good psychologically for the carer. She feels you are giving her a chance to assess the family properly. One did back out after a day. At least she did it then.'

If the employer wants to see more of a nanny in advance of a firm commitment, the weekend option may be worth considering. It may be expensive, but in the country particularly it can be helpful. Other employers say to the nanny, mother's help or au pair that she will be 'on trial' for two weeks, a month, even three months.

Suggest arrangements for how her luggage is to arrive at your home if she won't be bringing it all with her, and say you will meet her at the rail or coach station if that is the plan. Say an extra prayer that night, there's many a slip . . .

5

The First Week

From the moment your first nanny or mother's help arrives you cannot hope to live as before, unless you live in a huge house or are blessed with a separate nanny wing or flat. Even then having a living-in nanny touches on every part of life. This is not surprising, but it is less of a shock if you think a bit about how both of you will live together before she arrives.

The trouble is that initially, and possibly indefinitely, you may feel that you don't want a stranger living with you and the family, but you have decided you need her. This is the crux of all difficulties between nannies and employers. Some nannies are not suited to residential posts and some employers find the whole business of having a live-in nanny more stressful than others.

It also helps if you and your partner are good at leading a communal life and can curb emotions of most kinds in public. A nanny does not expect to be belted into a front seat at the amateur dramatics that are your private life. There is no need to meta-morphose overnight into a nagging prude, and the idea of living *pour encourager les autres* is dated, off-putting and smacks of Upstairs Downstairs. However, experienced employers report unanimously that a bit of dignity, distance and discretion is the only way to achieve long-term employer/nanny mutual respect. Experienced nannies concur. They don't like witnessing drunken scenes, or listening to tearful stories and personal revelations. You'll regret them as well.

It won't be a surprise to hear that setting such a marvellous example is a helluva strain. Even royal employers long to have scrambled eggs in front of the telly in their dressing gowns, so the rest of us, who aren't used to the endless discipline of hot and cold running servants around us, look forward to the nanny's holidays when you can jump in the bath with the children.

Employers claim they talk easily to their nanny, as do nannies. Topics of conversation most often include: anything to do with the children, the house, the nanny's family, the employer's family, friends, neighbours, what's in the news, on TV, on at the local, and the like. Employers say they do not talk about family finances, personal relationships and family tensions, nor do they gossip about friends, husband's or wife's job or colleagues. Employers do not want to turn into an Auntie Marje in constant discussions of the nanny's boyfriends and social life. The best sort of nanny does not want to work for employers who live vicariously or are 'too nosey and too matey'.

Mrs Davis of Norland recommends to her students and to employers that they 'should remember that neither of you are your normal selves during the initial period'. Be in no doubt that it is not going to be easy, prepare yourself and your partner for a different way of living at best and, at worst, a rough ride.

It will have a great effect on your child or children too, naturally enough, and the only person who can shoehorn this stranger into their lives successfully is you. If you are going back to work for the first time and leaving an older child, take him to your office and show him what you will be up to each day. With younger children give the nanny every aid and advantage in the first week. Send her off on favourite expeditions and give the children plenty of time with both of you around so that they can see that you are relaxed and confident in the new nanny's company.

Nannies, mother's helps and au pairs do not just arrive with their baggage; they also bring their opinions, habits, manners and little ways which can change you from the cool rational executive you hope you are into a paranoid, scratchy fish-wife. The nanny also has to cope with all your prejudices, foibles and petty rules. She is likely to be a lot younger than you, perhaps living away from home for the first time, and may find your home as alien as a crash-landing on Mars.

Be aware of the possible differences in your upbringing and experience. Focus on the variations of background, family life and education. For example, she might not yet have prepared an avocado, she may never have been abroad, she may not have heard of Beatrix Potter and you will have to show her how to open a bank account in the morning.

All this can be hard to deal with and many employers and nannies find these differences embarrassing. You may find that you are much more entrenched in the way you do things than you thought. The way you speak, the way you eat, the way you dress and how you expect the nanny to do those things with and for your children may be important to you. Spell out your preferences precisely and in detail; she cannot be expected to be psychic.

Experienced employers all mention the initial strain of dealing with these personal items but they get better at speaking plainly about 'areas of friction', as we call them. Start off with realistic expectations of the nanny, considering her age and experience. Assume she knows little about the art of living in someone else's house.

Recognize resentment and envy; your nanny may feel both. It is crude to leave estate agents' blurb about six-figure houses which you covet on the breakfast table and simultaneously ask her to try not to drink too much of the fresh orange juice. This is a serious point. You may take your microwave, video, expensive holidays and jewellery as a matter of course, but to her it may be testing to live alongside this wealth and luxury, which can be flaunted objectionably. Her mum isn't so lucky and works just as hard or harder, with much less tangible result.

Even if your new nanny has lived with a family, it may have had a quite different lifestyle from your own. Some people think that having a nanny who is 'experienced' will shortcut the process of 'house-training' her. To some extent this is true, but one man's meat is another woman's poison – and we don't recognize this simple fact often enough. There is not a *right* way of doing almost anything, just millions of personal preferences.

An aspect that must be tackled, and is related to class-ridden mores, is the subject of manners. The Pre-Select Staff Agency nanny information sheet sums it up: 'Manners maketh Man and young ladies into well-respected employees.' You may insist that you are a liberal, easy-going employer, but how well would you react to having breakfast with a tousle-haired, evil-smelling nanny reaching across your husband for the Weetabix with a grimy, scarlet-painted hand? Just one of those unlovely traits can make a brave employer quake at the prospect of an inevitable 'talk'.

Some nannies don't realize that unchecked BO is for some employers not only unappealing, but inappropriate to her role and girls have been sacked for not responding to tactful hints. One mother tried to tell her nanny what her best friend obviously had not dared. The girl took it like a lamb, so the employer crowed to her husband of her successful diplomacy. Within hours the nanny had left, and the employer found a note in the waste paper basket saying 'The bitch said I stank.' Perhaps this is a good enough illustration of just how upsetting the manners issue can be for both sides.

If you believe, like the classic old nanny, that 'manners are caught not taught', then watch to see that your nanny is aware of her manners in front of the children. Pray heaven you got this part right at the interview stage and it won't be necessary to deal with this now: you will know within hours. Things she needs to watch out for in your children's behaviour, if you care, include: farting, coughing, sneezing, sniffing, yawning, burping, elbows on the table, saying 'excuse me' at the appropriate times, and of course constant reminders to say 'please' and 'thank you'.

'Verbal class distinction by now should be antique'? Apparently not, though it isn't a subject many people enjoy tackling, though it may bother, nay obsess, them.

Jilly Cooper in her book *Class* has some apt comments on this touchy area.

The nanny/employer relationship is interesting because it is one of the few occasions when the classes meet head on, not just during the day, as people do in offices, but at all times, and the nanny has to adjust to a completely different lifestyle . . . Samantha Upward's au pair comes in very red in the face, saying 'Zacharias refused to say "Pardon".' Whereupon Samantha goes even redder and stands on one leg saying 'Well actually we always say "What", don't know why.'

One mother resorts to saying to her nannies that in the south it is more usual to say 'loo' than 'toilet'. Another explains that it helps the child to hear just the one word – hers – when he is being potty trained. Perhaps, if you care about these things, it is best to say 'I prefer x to y' with no further explanation. One confusion which can need clearing up is when the nanny refers to Granny as 'nanny' or 'nan'. Other words that grate include such old chestnuts as: lunch/dinner, pudding/sweet/afters, tummy/belly, bottom/bum.

There are also a whole range of grammatical grouses and other misuse of words like boring, dirty and ignorant. There are a few nice malapropisms like, 'It's six of one and a dozen of the other if you ask me,' and a few nannies drive their employers barmy by their oft-repeated aphorisms, for example, 'Once funny, twice silly and three times naughty.'

Some nannies have very strong regional accents and the children and employers may genuinely have difficulty understanding her. 'It was agonizing,' says one mother, 'she said please may I have a *something*? She said it eight times before I twigged – by which time we were both puce and she was close to tears and I was desperately trying to make her see the funny side – but I challenge any southerner to interpret the word "cup" as it sounds in broad Yorkshire without some practice.'

Another miscellaneous point to raise is that of babysitting for other people, or indeed her acceptance of any kind of extra work while you are paying her wage. Many nannies babysit for other families and supplement their salary. What is wrong with that? Most employers of live-in nannies find that it is impractical and exasperating in practice. Their friends and neighbours keep the nanny babysitting until 2 or 3 am and she is worn out and bad-tempered the next day. Say no and avoid having to backtrack later. You have no reason to feel guilty about this if you are paying her generously.

It is kind to think hard in advance, or from previous experience if you've done it before, about the things that irritate you. For example: loud music, dregs of petrol left in a shared car, your husband's mayonnaise disappearing in the midnight binge, her underwear left in the bathroom. Tell her about these things straight away. It will be tougher to mention them three weeks after she has arrived, and you'll kick yourself for your silence.

When she has discovered you are irrational and impossible to please, sweeten the pill by suggesting that once a week you sit down together (at a set time and on a definite day, so that it is not skipped) to have a News and Views session. This may not be your style, but, an American import, it is recommended by Mrs Davis of Norland as a safety valve for both parties. Communication is the most common word that both nannies and employers use to capture the essence of a successful partnership. All lines of communication should always be kept open. Neither should sulk, the children hate it, and as one mother says: 'There is nothing more awful than a frost in the house.' Nannies mustn't think that the News and Views session means that they can't make complaints or ask questions between sessions.

Tell the nanny what you hold dear – be it the cashmere sweater or the dinner service, the mangled silver spoon given by a doting godfather and gobbled by the waste disposal or the coffee rings on the oak dining table. These disasters happened simply because employers have failed to instruct properly and/or been too silly or lazy enough to allow the nanny to handle their precious possessions, most of which are outside her domain. It is all too easy to allocate blame and turn the nanny into a scapegoat for numerous little details for which employers should take responsibility themselves.

Do beg her to ask you about anything that she does not understand fully. It may be about child safety, emergency drill, folding the nappies, using the iron, about the food processor, sewing machine etc. And tell her what exactly is out of bounds to her, so that neither of you have unpleasant surprises and respect each other's privacy – another plank of the good partnership.

Our correspondents list the following items that their nannies may not use: their clothes and personal belongings, make-up, scent, jewellery. Some nannies do take and use these things without permission. Coincidentally, these are all good presents for nannies. First-time employers may be surprised to learn that the vast majority of employers report little or no dishonesty on the part of their nannies (this is confirmed by the agencies) – it is quite rare and almost all the instances we have unearthed have been cases of kleptomania. Casual thieving is far from the norm.

Jobs for the Employer

If you have a written contract with your nanny (see pages 325–8) your first duty is to ensure that you both sign it and keep your separate copies safely.

If you have not employed a nanny before, try to make her room as hospitable, practical, spacious and pretty as possible. A basin is an advantage. Lots of cupboard, drawer and storage space will help her to keep it tidy. There should be enough good light, at least one comfortable armchair, a table and desk to write at, a bed you would be happy to sleep in, a washable bedspread, a TV (preferably colour), and as large a pinboard as you can fix to the wall. The idea is to make it as much like a bed-sitting room as possible, so it is also a good plan to provide a few mugs, an electric kettle and perhaps a toaster too.

Employers should never forget that the nanny's bedroom is a symbol of her independence, privacy and her own and possibly only little world in your house. Ideally, you should allow her to do what she wants with it. It is significant and encouraging when the nanny makes the room reflect her own personality, draping it with scarves and posters from floor to ceiling. This is a sign that she is settling in. Don't ruin this good feeling by being possessive about the colour co-ordinated Laura Ashley.

Always knock on her bedroom door (and hope she follows your example) before entering, ask her permission if you need to go into her room for any reason. Try to treat it as a foreign embassy in your country — inconvenient on occasion, but sacrosanct and not subject to local law.

Remember to tell your children that they may not wander in and out of the nanny's room; entrance is by invitation only. The door must be capable of being properly shut, even locked. This is also to protect children from her pills, potions and make-up. Remind her to be conscious of how inquisitive and foolish toddlers can be.

Miss McRae erstwhile principal of Princess Christian comments, 'I expect to be able to knock and walk in, as I would for a daughter.' Slovenliness, squalor, including unwashed dishes, coffee cups, left-over food, unmade bed, airlessness and smelliness need not be tolerated. 'Don't forget she is not in a flat doing her own thing,' says an experienced agent. It is not reasonable that someone in your employ should rejoice in a pig-sty – and it's not most people's image of the ideal child carer.

If you are a seasoned employer, you should dust the highest shelves, muck out the cupboards and remove all traces of the former occupant, redecorating as necessary. If the result is gloomy and barracks-like, you did it wrong. Start again and think as for a daughter. The nanny has to spend a lot of time there and you want her to be happy in it and proud to show it to her friends and family. It is advantageous to you in the long run to ensure that her room is demonstrably nicer than those of her contemporaries who are daily nannies living in flats, otherwise she'll wonder what she's missing. Understandably.

It is a nice gesture to equip her with a pair of bright trainers and wellington boots, if she has none. Make sure that she has a watch which works and also an alarm clock. She may have to be lent or given effective waterproof clothing; this is specially your responsibility if you hire her for a city job which involves visits to the country. Fill up and organize the sewing basket and show her the nail scissors, sellotape for mending books, glue for fixing toys and shoe polish.

Even an experienced residential nanny may feel homesick, if only in some cases for the familiarity of the last job. Tell her about the Under 24 Rail Card. Persuade her to be in touch with any friends in your area and suggest she rings home in off-peak hours at least twice a week in the first month. If you live in London, explain the underground and bus weekly pass schemes, buy her a bus guide and an A–Z. Extra efforts should be made for nannies and mother's helps in the deep country when public transport is minimal and nanny networks non-existent.

Don't leave your nanny too much by herself at first; invite her to accompany you occasionally, even when off duty, until she has made her own friends. Be overtly kind, friendly and appreciative. Introduce her to other nannies and show her the local clubs, exercise classes, sports centres, library, museums, theatres, cinemas and places of interest.

If you have recently moved house or if you are having your first baby you may not be plugged in to the nanny network in your area. Give your nanny the address of Nannies Need Nannies (see Useful Addresses) – a voluntary organization sponsored by *Nursery World* – and they will try to find congenial company in your area.

If your new nanny or mother's help has not lived in a big city before, it is important to talk to her about the dangers of urban life. In most areas it is not advisable to walk alone at night and public transport is no defence. Part of the reason that many employers impose a curfew on their young nannies is because they feel responsible to the nanny's parents and, if their daughter had not returned by 2 am, the employers think that they should call the police and hospital departments. In other words, they treat their nanny as they would their own teenage children when they behave unexpectedly.

Impress upon her that people are mugged even in 'smart' areas. Handbags are snatched or slit open. In discos they are stolen if put down on a table when dancing. Remind her never to put down the car and/or the house keys while she is out or, worse still, leave your address written down alongside them. She should not leave anything of value in the back of the car and ought to lock the passenger seat door as well as her own when she is driving around late at night. Nanny employers say that they have to have the locks changed or keys replaced because their nannies are ignorant or careless. One emphasizes: 'I had never come into contact with the police before I had nannies. They are always losing things in public places.'

Your nanny or mother's help may not have a bank or building society account. Encourage her to open both and be prepared to act as her guarantor for the first year of her employment, because most banks will not otherwise issue her with a cheque card, without which a chequebook is virtually useless. Spell out the necessity of keeping chequebooks and cheque cards separately.

It is advisable to register her with both a doctor and a dentist as soon as she arrives which will save time if she needs them in a hurry. Several employers pour themselves another gin and murmur the address of the local family planning clinic also. Some of the employment agencies run detailed medical checks on any nanny they send abroad. These, along with private security checks, may become the norm in the future, as they have in the USA.

Emergency Drill

A safety-conscious household will have, as a minimum precaution, two fire extinguishers, a first aid box, telephones and good neighbours. Introduce her to all of them. You should explain precisely what you want her to do in case of crisis in your absence.

If one of the children has a bad accident, she should not be afraid to call 999 immediately and ask for an ambulance. While waiting, she should consult the Red Cross book kept to hand and try to arrange for any other children to be looked after by a neighbour. It is better to call for an ambulance than to jump in the car with a sick or hurt child and get stuck in a traffic block while the child screams. If a fire breaks out which is more than a brief blaze, tell your nanny to leave the house with the children *at once*.

From the first day you relinquish direct responsibility for your children to anyone else (nannies, mother's helps, au pairs, babysitters, the cleaning lady, members of your family or friends), a list of emergency telephone numbers should be written out clearly by the phone. It should include both parents' work numbers, back-up local help (friends, neighbours, shop-keepers) other members of the family, doctor, schools and the address of the local hospital. Don't forget the plumber and electrician and someone who can service essential machines.

It is a good idea if the au pair writes down her parents' full address and telephone number, international code and all. Stick it up on the pinboard, rather than stuffing it in a drawer and searching for it frantically when fate does strike. This address is always useful after she has left anyway, so that her mail can be redirected.

If the girl encounters a burglar or intruder, she should not attempt to provoke or tackle him alone, but to do what he says if the children are around, then leave the premises as quickly as possible. She should be wary of approaches in the parks or streets, especially if the stranger seems unduly interested in her charges.

For a fuller discussion of safety in the house and with children generally see page 132. Several agencies and mothers comment, 'Too many nannies don't seem to realize that looking after children is literally a matter of life and death.' They feel that many NNEB colleges do not underline this or teach the necessity of safety measures.

Frequently your nanny will be responsible for locking up the house. Remind her to shut windows, doors, window locks, security locks as well as traditional locks and particularly garden doors. Most burglars try to break in during the day – when the nanny has taken the children out. Do not hide the door keys in super-obvious places. Explain the alarm system and if you have a number code for your door lock, make sure she takes a note of it and carries it everywhere. When she is inside the house, especially in cities, ask her to use the spy-hole if there is one, or leave the door on the chain and speak through the gap if she is in any doubt about the identity of the caller. If she is to be the last person in bed at night, or if she is looking after your children when you are away, make sure she knows about double-locking doors and putting the chain on too.

It is worth talking to her about the kinds of people who may call – Jehovah's witnesses, market researchers, freelance roof repairers, double-glazing salesmen, political canvassers, charity soap and duster sellers, hawkers and con men of all types – and that's before you start on the list of people who might be expected. The general rule may as well be – stop them in their tracks on the doorstep. On no account let them in. Don't give them a chance to practise their smooth patter; just instruct the nanny to say, 'My employer is out. I am afraid I am very busy.' Don't give a name or phone number. Forewarned is forearmed.

First Week Indoctrination

By the first week, you will have organized insurance to cover the nanny to drive the car and you should drive in it with her not only to familiarize her with its idiosyncrasies, but also to assure yourself that she is a competent driver. If she is coming to London or another city for the first time, do not let her drive the children until she knows the routes and basic skills of driving in heavy and competitive traffic. Safety belts for the children must be fitted on every trip however short. Don't allow her to drive other people's children without their express permission. One of the nastiest employers' stories concerned a nanny who took three children for a drive in the country in Wales. None of them was wearing a seat belt; they missed a hairpin bend, and went off the road and down a hill. The children were killed. The nanny survived. She was wearing a seat belt.

One way of alleviating the chore of having to show the carer the ropes and your every quirk in detail is to delegate it to the outgoing nanny. There is good and bad in this. The advantages include consistency for the children; they can get used to the new nanny gradually if the nannies overlap for a week, rather than being left with a stranger. Working mothers don't have much option and probably have to leave the children with the new nanny, so it is a good idea for them to arrange an overlap. If you have a cleaning lady, get her also to tell the nanny what standards you expect her to live by in her room, the children's areas and the bathroom.

It is generous and sensible to give a party for the nanny who is leaving so that the new nanny can meet the local nannies and mother's helps. It also helps to combat homesickness; someone else has done the job, survived and even apparently enjoyed it. The disadvantage of overlap is that it will cost you two salaries for a week. The nannies may not like each other. The outgoing nanny may not brief the new one effectively and leave out some vital aspect about the emergency drill or locking up the house. She may infect her with her own bad habits or get jealous of the children's dawning affection for the new incumbent.

If you decide against the overlap procedure, then you, the employer, must be around constantly for the first week to explain how you want your children to be cared for and how the house is run. Some mothers also hand over a written routine either for the week or by the day, or both. Others have covered these details in a written contract (see page 325). Still others deal with everything verbally. You will have a crash course in getting acquainted while you show her everything and that's a good reason for doing a lot of the indoctrination yourself. It will also give you ample opportunity to observe.

Overlapping is not exclusive practice for trained nannies. It can be useful for British mother's helps and, if their English is good enough, why not foreign mother's helps and au pairs?

Housework and Chores

Trained nannies expect to clean and keep tidy their own, the children's rooms, bathroom(s), the playroom, and to clear up the kitchen thoroughly after use. Some nannies do not have to hoover or dust or do basic cleaning, as there is a cleaner. Our researches show that this is unusual; most employers who have both a nanny and a cleaning lady reckon that the latter is there for communal areas and for the employer's private rooms, *not* to nanny the nanny. An employer is not entitled to expect a trained nanny to do anything else in the way of housework. There may be leeway for negotiation for any other domestic chores which don't concern the children, but they are a matter for discussion.

Housework causes friction. Some au pairs rather enjoy housework e.g. hoovering and dusting and cleaning the kitchen thoroughly. Some much prefer it to looking after children. A number of au pairs have never done any housework. This is because they are upper class girls and their mothers employ cleaners and maids. It is fair to say that the vast majority are not keen. The result is that they don't do it well.

As with mother's helps of whatever nationality, an employer will get a better result from an au pair if she shares the chores. An au pair with more than one child can't be expected to do that much housework properly anyway, and it isn't good for the child to be trailing round after the dustpan all morning.

One mother solves the problem by allocating an hour on a Monday for the au pair to tidy, dust and hoover the children's room, her own and their communal bathroom. On Thursday she asks her to vacuum the stairs and the hallway which takes about 20 minutes.

I don't think even with two small children to look after this is asking too much. I make a point of asking her to do nothing else, unless for some reason she is childless occasionally.

I do the rest of the house including the children's playroom. She can see me sweating over a hot hoover some days just as I pass her on the stairs on her vacuuming day. I will ask my children when they are teenagers to do the same, and most of my au pairs do that much adequately. Even then it is not a particularly thorough job, but they aren't experienced housemaids.

Remember during the first week to tell the girl *exactly* how to work all the machines. Many au pairs, for example, have not used a dishwasher, a washing machine or a British-style upright or cylinder cleaner before. Keep reminding yourself that her English is not good and speak clearly and simply. Be prepared to demonstrate and explain the workings of a machine several times. When in doubt au pairs tend to say 'yes' rather than 'Could you repeat that please?' Ask them specifically to say the latter as often as it occurs to them.

Every mother will tell a story about how the vacuum was broken by the au pair. Au pairs have a tendency not to empty the dust bag until the machine is so full it ceases to function properly. They let the brushes get so clogged with string and hair that they won't go round. They will run a hoover quite blithely over glass, large pebbles, hair grips, playdough, plasticine. When you show them the hoover's broken black rubber band they look mildly surprised. They are insensitive to any machine's condition, so

114

keep an eye on it. Unless it comes to a complete halt and, in the case of a hoover, the room is full of the smell of burning rubber, they will use it for weeks so stuffed up with bits that it picks up nothing.

All forms of help are potentially lethal with dirty washing. Au pairs, particularly from the poorer parts of Europe, may not have used a washing or drying machine before and if they have, probably not one as sophisticated. Every au pair and mother's help is likely to turn an entire wash either grey or pink at least once, just as their employer has done in the past.

Show her how the washing machine works and remind her that it is expensive to repair, and that she must be gentle with its knobs and knockers. Spell out the importance of sorting clothes into different fabric types, and the importance of separating *pale* from *dark* colours.

Wool is a major problem. She *may* be able to cope with a washable wool wash. Experiment with children's jumpers rather than your mohair creation strewn with rainbow-coloured blobs. Many mothers just don't risk it and do all wool themselves. The question to ask yourself is: 'Will I be utterly miserable if she shrinks my Aran sweater?' If so, then don't risk it, she may get it right twice, but sure as wool shrinks she'll get it wrong the third time.

Some girls are good at ironing but have an annoying habit of doing their own things first. Others take ages to get around to it, and seem to manage to leave the one shirt you would have liked to wear on the morrow unironed at the bottom of the basket *again*. It can be weeks before clothes reach the end of the washing/drying/ironing process. Some employers insist that the ironing basket is emptied daily.

Many girls are frightful at ironing. If she is the sort who, far from dashing away with the smoothing iron, manages to create creases as opposed to ironing them out, you will find yourself at 10 o'clock at night doing it all again. Added to this, she may be careless and scorch viyella, silk and wool. If you have doubts about her skill, don't risk anything precious like a child's party frock or a white silk blouse.

Many nannies will make sure that you are not going to exploit them before offering to do extra jobs. If you make feeding the cat at 4 pm feel like the thin end of the wedge, they have no reason to oblige you. Build a relationship first, don't take advantage of the nanny and gradually, if it is not enforced, a happy *modus vivendi* will emerge.

The Daily Routine

Other nanny chores include hairwashing, nail cutting, dusting, wiping paint surfaces (skirting boards and bookshelves), cleaning the bath and lavatory, keeping the children's books, toys and clothes in good repair, changing sheets and towels, packing

---

A Nanny's day

Imagine a family with three children and working parents. James is six, Emily is three and the baby is 9 months.

07.30 On duty. Get children up, washed, help them get dressed. Draw curtains, pull back beds, open windows.

07.45 Breakfast. After breakfast, while children go to loo, clean teeth, brush hair, collect school things, clear up breakfast table and kitchen (wipe up bits from floor and high chair). Put on washing machine.

08.35 All in car to take James to school. Collect extra child for carpool. Drop James at school 08.55. Everyone back in the car again. Drop Emily at playgroup and return home.

09.30 Make beds, tidy and hoover rooms. Put baby to bed for her rest. Transfer washing to drier.

10.00 Ironing and prepare lunch.

11.30 Baby up, play and read.

12.15 Collect Emily from playgroup.

12.30 Lunch for baby, Emily and nanny.

13.30 Baby to rest. Read and play with Emily.

15.15 Pick up James. Take all three out to play.

16.30 Prepare tea.

17.00 Tea. Clear up tea. Children play and James does homework. Clear up toys and playroom.

18.00 Bath, clean teeth and then read until mother or father returns. Put out clothes for the morning. Set breakfast table. Sort out washing and put away.

19.00 Bed. Off duty.

---

suitcases when going away, shopping, cooking and organizing meals, washing and sterilizing baby's kit, whizzing baby's mush, organizing nappies, making sure that the children's clothes fit, mending, especially name tapes, letting in electricians, paying the milkman and taking accurate telephone messages.

Imagine you have to add to that James's gym classes, Emily's dancing class and the baby's monthly clinic visit. All three like to attend the duckling class at the local swimming pool and to visit the library. One may get ill and the other two may catch it. All three have birthdays which need celebrating and so do those of their friends. These same friends and others frequently come to play and for extra meals, as do grandparents – up from the country to shop. Halloween, Valentine's Day, Mother's Day, Easter and Christmas are all energetically celebrated by children. Some mothers need their nannies to buy clothes and fit shoes for their charges. They will also shop for playdough, stationery supplies and the odd toy. After all, James is learning his tables, Emily is trying to read and the baby wants to walk and talk. It is a hectic schedule.

If you are a working mother, your nanny cannot possibly do all this alone. If you are working part-time or not at all, you can make her life a lot simpler and gentler by being a chauffeur and a bulk shopper, and by taking the children independently to the relevant activity, so that James is not attending the baby's clinic and the baby isn't forced to enjoy watching the gym class.

Given this list, it's amazing that so many nannies think they prefer 'sole charge' (see page 123). A nanny's duties are less onerous if there is only one or even two children to manage. Most employers tell us that they prefer to deal themselves with the children's educational and medical problems and contact with the school and hospital staff (homework and hearing tests). They prefer in the main to be responsible and responsive to their children's needs at night and make a big effort to be around after bath time to read, kiss, hug, sing or amuse.

It will take time for you to trust her but you should try to take that leap in the dark as fast as you can manage it and give her clear indications that you are doing so. Opinion is divided as to what is best done about petty cash. Some employers insist that their nannies account for every penny, 'not least because it makes

them *think* about the value of my money and not be too cavalier
with it or think I am', and others say, 'Be sure to give her a big
enough float to cover emergencies and don't insult her with
accounting for it – surely if you trust her with your child you trust
her with your money?' 'Er, sort of,' say a third group who start
strictly and ease up when they get to know their nanny better.

Time Keeping and Remembering

Time keeping, like a poor memory, particularly if you are a
stickler for either or both, can make employers twitch. Unless
mentioned, the nanny may be quite oblivious to the agonies she
is causing. The employer is tense, worried and after a bit, pretty
cross as she waits for her entire family to arrive home three-
quarters of an hour after she had asked them to be back to go to
the dentist. Try to avoid an outburst, but make it clear at the
soonest quiet opportunity that it is not to happen again and
explain your obsession. If routine rules your household, instruct
the nanny to be ready ten minutes *before* a deadline rather than
two minutes afterwards.

First check she has a watch and that it works as well as an alarm
clock. Buy both for her if necessary. Knots in handkerchiefs may
not be enough. One employer of a scatty au pair, in desperation
scrawled '12.30' in felt tip on the back of her hand. The girl was
quite amazed but it worked a treat.

Planning Ahead

Most busy families have a large communal diary by the telephone
in the kitchen where the nanny and the mother, and occasionally
the father, write down appointments, lunches, teas and all
comings and goings. Whoever logs their plans first gets priority,
more or less. Just because you have a live-in nanny or mother's
help who expects to babysit at your convenience, it is not fair to
insist that she be infinitely flexible. She should not often have to
change her plans to suit yours when you make them at the last
minute. Many nannies complain, understandably, that they
don't feel properly independent and can't make a solid plan with
their boyfriend to meet because 'you never know when they are
going to need you for babysitting'.

It is also important to be aware that Friday and Saturday nights are *the* night for nannies' socializing, so don't always insist on them yourself. Some nannies will only babysit two nights a week and will insist that this is written into their contract. If it is, you will either go out less, have to find an alternative babysitter or discover this limitation suits you fine.

Employers of trained live-in nannies need not feel inhibited about requesting babysitting, as required, within reason. With forward planning which is adhered to, it shouldn't be a great sacrifice for a nanny *sometimes* to have to babysit three or four times in one week. She can always invite her girlfriends or members of the family to visit when you are out (see the House Rules, page 22).

Don't let the nanny become bored. 'The devil finds work for idle hands' will become evident if you do. Be generous with your praise, thanks, and just as important, apologies for any inconsiderate behaviour on your part.

Ensure that her life is interesting and varied. Try to include her in the odd treat or special weekend. Encourage her to learn a new skill – to take driving lessons, evening classes, swimming or exercise classes. Always enquire if she is looking down or peaky and show concern and interest in her well-being generally.

Off Duty Activities

Many employers know surprisingly little about what their nannies do when off duty: out of house, out of mind. It is sensible to acquaint yourself with the whole nanny, not just the bit that works for you. Her hobbies and interests tell you about her health and current state of mind. If a nanny frequents the Hammersmith Palais nightly or is a born-again Buddhist in Battersea Park three nights a week, there is not a lot you can do about it, but it gives you a chance to prepare for problems. How the nanny spends her free time may have no connection with your family life, but it pays dividends to show interest. There is a bit of genuine altruism here, a desire to want her to have an enjoyable time, but there is self-protection too.

What do nannies, mother's helps and au pairs do when they are not on duty? Some like cooking, knitting, sewing, patchwork, embroidery, tapestry, practising music, reading, listening to tapes, resting, drawing, colouring, painting, dressmaking, writing letters, watching TV, having friends round to supper, giving a dinner party, and having a nice quiet night in.

Outside they like: walking, jogging, badminton, squash, exercise classes (aerobics, weight-lifting, dance), swimming, sightseeing, architecture, antiques, wine, photography, learning a new language, night clubs, eating out, night classes, the cinema, concerts, pubs, sunbathing, theatre, nightclubs (London nannies go to the Hippodrome and Stringfellows), running local Brownies and Guides groups, going to young people's clubs and societies, gardening, skiing, shopping, and joining a friend who is babysitting in the evening.

On weekends off nannies may go to their parents' home, 'which I still regard as mine as opposed to my work home', says one. Some stay with local friends or go and visit friends in other parts of the country and a few go and stay wherever their boyfriend happens to be. They also have their friends or relatives to stay in their employers' house when they are away.

There may be a complication here if an employer has not previously ascertained that the nanny has a family in this country with whom she is on speaking terms. One employer warns:

I didn't think it was suitable to leave an 18 year-old alone in a very large London house over an entire weekend. She hadn't made any local friends because she had only just arrived and I thought it could be lonely and frightening for her. We couldn't take her with us to stay with friends. So I said, 'Why don't you go home?' She looked at me fiercely and said 'They don't want me there; this is my home now.' 'Fine,' I said out loud. 'Heck,' I said to myself, 'what happens if she's seriously ill? Is everything about her to be my responsibility from now on?'

A happy nanny has friends. She meets them at the park, at her exercise class, at playgroups, ballet classes, One-O'Clock Clubs and in local shops, churches and clinics – anywhere where there is a crowd or a queue or where people have time to talk.

Encouraging a nanny to be busy is part of a good employer's job. It is a relief to see a nanny organizing her time off purposefully and looking after her social, emotional and physical needs. Employers always feel cheered when nannies take some exercise rather than hearing the perennial moan about 'running up and down stairs all day is enough exercise for me'.

Modern employers no longer expect much in the way of

domestic skills. Gone are the days of the nanny who spent her free time knitting, sewing and making clothes for her charges and their dollies. Few employers get more than minimal mending: sewing on buttons and name tapes and repairing a hem is about the limit: even a zip can cause trouble.

If an employer finds that she has hired a quiet and/or anti-social nanny, she may feel guilty if the nanny doesn't go out much and seems incapable of making plans and initiating outings with friends. No employer wants her nanny to describe life with the family as 'lonely' as so many nannies do. Equally, an employer cannot be expected to do more than encourage the nanny to make friends and have fun and enjoy herself when not nannying.

6

The Roles of a Nanny

This chapter concerns the subject of continuity of care. It is not helpful for a baby or young child to receive conflicting or contradictory messages. Mother and nanny need to discuss and decide on what their responses will be to given situations in advance.

Synchronizing reactions is not easy. Some obvious areas of difficulty can be illustrated in the following ideas: 'Eat up what you're given'; 'Because I said so'; 'It's better for the child to walk than to be carried'; 'It's rude to walk about with nothing on' and 'Crying exercises their lungs.' These areas, if dealt with inconsistently, can cause a child to be perplexed and frustrated.

Keep in the forefront of your mind that what matters is that nanny and mum should work as a team for the children's good. It is only when the team is working well together that a mother will relax, and trust can grow and interference will not be necessary. Try to talk these things through and, if you find that the nanny is firmly but immutably disagreeing, then there is trouble ahead.

When is a Nanny not a Mother?

Employers have strong views on this subject. Many say that when they are around, the nanny is not a mother. A few expect their nanny to be mother-like when the mother isn't there. Some give more detailed comment:

When she doesn't remember details and can't plan ahead . . . at bed time except very rarely . . . also when the children are ill, or when they need congratulating when something good has happened . . . you need a mother rather than a nanny to scold and lecture seriously when a child is dishonest, cruel or manipulative . . . in most ways she isn't a mother: she can't deal with schools, teachers and reports, hospital and other tests and she can't be expected to cope with some crises alone.

At the age when the children themselves consider they have grown out of the nanny.

A nanny is never a mother. The relationship is quite distinct; children are always quite clear about the difference. The nanny is an additional relationship for the child, not instead of.

Although nannies are very involved with your children, the ultimate responsibility is never theirs. They go off duty.

At evening prayers.

What nannies say:

A mother doesn't have to be working not to see much of her children. I can't understand why they don't find a three-year-old good company some of the time. She prefers to go to the hairdressers, shop and have lunch with friends.

I can't understand why they had children when they can't be bothered with them.

I treat Jacob very much as if he was my son. I wouldn't treat my own children any different.

I'm going to leave this job so I cannot and should not become too emotionally involved.

You can never take the parents' place. You can't help loving them and getting close to them, maybe too close, but then you are the one bringing them up, almost.

I tell the children that I am not their mother and that I'm not one of the family. That's very important.

Nanny as Sole Charger

Sole charge is nanny jargon and most new mothers have no clue what it entails. Nannies cannot know in advance whether they are fitted for such responsibility, but ideally the wise employer will not give a sole charge post to any nanny who has not had at least two years' experience. The reliable employment agencies feel this strongly and refuse to let untried nannies take sole charge posts. If an employer is paying for an NNEB anyway, it is silly not to pay a bit extra for experience and avoid a new nanny's mistakes – she'll get her chance at sole charge when she has learned a bit in a supervised job.

'NNEBs too often have an inflated view of their own ability. They want a job without the mother around and insist on sole charge,' says a long-established nanny agent. 'I tell them that they are only 18 with no practical experience and that I would prefer them to work where there is a mother to alleviate the responsibility.' There is no doubt that part of the attraction of working alone is simply to do with a novice's wish to practise – and make mistakes – in private. Another agent reports that a father started working from home while writing a book and the nanny rang up to complain, 'He watches everything that goes on.' The agent responded, 'Is there anything he can't watch?'

This last point may well give working mothers cause for concern. Many confess to telephoning the nanny constantly to see how things are. They worry a great deal about what goes on in their absence, and have to fight back the fantasy (they hope) that their beloveds are sitting in a row in front of the telly Test Card munching liquorice allsorts.

The temptation for working mothers to trust the nanny to get on with the job responsibly and unsupervised is strong. This is how executive working mothers are treated by their superiors at work. Their bosses have complete trust in how they do their job and give them autonomy in their offices. So it suits them to treat the nanny with as much respect. Wonderful, but what if she abuses the mother's trust and how on earth is the working mum to know what's going on in her absence? The boss at work is at the most a floor or a lunch away; the absent mother has no opportunity of checking on her employee's ability to get on with the work in hand.

Many employers are wrong in thinking that they needn't worry about what the nanny or childminder does in their absence so long as their child can talk and tell them what happened that day.

Some children aged two or three are capable of saying, 'Joyce hurt me today on my leg' or 'Joyce was cross today', which provides a little information to go on. Other children may not even give this much away. It is probable that if a child has been pinched, slapped, shut in a cupboard or generally roughly treated that he won't mention it. They may not tell about less extreme but nonetheless undesirable events, for example: 'We watched telly all day. Joyce had a little sleep.' 'When we cry Joyce says shut up 'cos she's on the phone for ages.' 'We met Joyce's boyfriend in the park and we had three lollipops each.'

Hoping that you will hear about any oddity from the children's lips is vain. One member of The Working Mothers' Association from Harrow tells of the time that she came home early on a hot day and the house was like an oven. There wasn't a single door or window open. The children and nanny were sweating in the playroom.

It emerged that her nanny's fear of creepy crawlies was so strong that she hadn't let the children go out into their large pleasant garden for the nine months she had been in sole charge of them. They had been denied the paddling pool, sandpit and swing week after week throughout the summer. The nanny had always opened the windows and doors ten minutes before her employer's estimated time of arrival.

A working mother must rely entirely on the nanny to report humdrum happenings like whether the children painted, made paper hats, read the new library book, fell over in dancing or decided they liked spinach. She has to be trusted not to take the easy option with their nutrition, play, manners, nappies and in running the home.

How can a working mother prove to herself that her nanny is to be trusted? Shirley Conran in *Superwoman* writes:

Check on your minder. There is no reason to trust her until she is proven trustworthy. If you can't hop home unexpectedly yourself, get someone else to do so. This sounds nasty but they're *your* children and you can't take risks. Also check carefully with other parents about your child-minder, playgroup or nursery school. *Never stop checking*.

One full-time working mother turned overnight into the part-time-from-home kind:

I arrived back at lunchtime to pick up a file to find our new NNEB and another nanny with their feet up watching the TV in my sitting room with three under-twos on the floor behind the sofa. My daughter, aged 11 months, had a biro top in her mouth. There were no toys in the room, swilling potties graced a bookshelf and the room was full of cigarette smoke. I kept telling myself that I did not need to feel guilty, but *something* made me choose that day to walk in on that scene. And I am damn glad I did and I'm now around enough to ensure that all that will never happen again.

Working mothers have various tools at their disposal if they want to monitor the home front. They can ask the nanny to keep a log, diary or scrapbook of events. This can serve several purposes. It helps a mother and nanny communicate, allows working parents to keep in touch with the day's events and makes them feel more involved in their child's upbringing. It also provides details of developmental changes which the nanny observes in the children, i.e. little Johnny didn't hear the doorbell; Henrietta spoke her first sentence. This is not much to ask; a trained nanny will have done her 'observations' on her course and will probably enjoy doing them again.

Who can an employer co-opt for the job of checking up, if she is stuck in the office herself? A cleaning lady is an obvious answer, if you have one. Appoint her official spy and make time to hear her full report, maybe an evening call once a month. Don't ask her to mention just major problems; you want to hear *anything* of note. If she's not that sort of cleaning lady, what about a mother, a mother-in-law, a sister, neighbours, other local mums, the WMA or NCT network (see Useful Addresses)? Arrange a secret rota, ideally at least one person to look in on different days and different times to give an independent report.

The temptation is to ease up after a month or so, but err on the side of caution. Keep going for longer than that and rely on your greatest friend to be a brick and go on calling. Nannies can change overnight with a new devastating experience – good or bad. Watch out for the new love. Vigilant mothers ask nursery school teachers to get in touch immediately if they feel at all concerned about the nanny's attitude to the child, her road safety drill or anything else. Local shopkeepers can also be a help in keeping an eye on comings and goings.

Make sure that the house diary is full of friends and trades-men's calls – the more your children are seen by third parties, the more you can relax, so arrange a couple of lunches and teas a week with other nannies and their charges, and/or with a friend who is at home. Local activities like swimming or gym are all to be encouraged. It is important to organize these yourself if your nanny is clearly not taking the initiative. It is a ghastly prospect at the end of a long day at a desk, but an outing a day keeps the guilt at bay.

If your nanny is the gregarious type, you can't relax either. You want to know exactly where she is taking the children; check it is not too an ambitious a project – too far or for too long a time. Be sure to have met your nanny's best nanny friends, the ones with whom she is most likely to arrange outings. Prick up your ears if you gather that the children seem to spend the whole day out of the house, or for that matter in it with a permanent *ad hoc* crèche going on in the playroom and kitchen. Too much socializing with other nannies in the park isn't ideal. Many working mothers complain of too much nanny natter and not enough nanny and child playing/reading/painting.

Don't feel inhibited about banning other people's nannies whom you don't like or approve of when you are not in the house. Your nanny must accept your veto about where she goes and whom she sees while on duty. If she doesn't then she shouldn't be working for you.

The working mother/nanny relationship is less stressful all round if the nanny doesn't live in. The simple fact that their paths barely cross makes friction minimal. But other problems are legion. One of them is when to talk; the baton is handed over from one bleary-eyed minder to the other at dawn and swapped again at dusk when both are even more weary. Who has the strength to care about the potty-training progress reports or what they had for tea today? Once a week both nanny and employer should get the log, sit down quietly and have a News and Views session.

Working mothers get frustrated by being unable to prevent nannies doing things their way, even when they know that their employer would disapprove. One working mother sums it up: 'I have always felt that my little prejudices – food, creative play and the like are treated very seriously when I am around, and are out the window when I am through the door. I fear that if you hand over your home to what is in effect a housewife, she feels entirely justified in doing things her way in her domain.'

Nannies like sole charge because it is more peaceful not to have another adult in the house. She can do the routine exactly how and when she likes. If a mother is not around to object, it is not surprising that she leaves the bits under the high chair til! the end of the day rather than after each meal. No one interferes with her methods or second guesses her decisions. The children have no opportunity to ricochet from one adult to another – nanny is big boss.

Some mothers say that they would rather die than admit to their colleagues that having children entails responsibilities which may occasionally interfere with their job. At the moment many mothers simply lie about taking the day off saying they are ill, when in fact their nanny or childminder is under the weather and can't look after the children. This puts off the day when employers, whether a small company or a multi-national, accept that once in a while an employee who is also a father may have to be off from work to look after his child.

In Sweden someone who has to stay at home from work to tend a sick child under twelve years of age receives an allowance for 60 days a year. Days are also allocated for short-term child care and to visit schools. Think Swedish; persuade your husband to take a day off; come home early to deal with an accident or chat up teachers – do it 50-50. Why should he always be indispensable? Until child care is genuinely shared between working parents, employers will look askance when, as usual, it is only their women staff that go home in a hurry.

Don't overload the nanny or expect too much in your absence. All standards will slip; she will become exhausted and be ratty with the children. An experienced nanny will say firmly that there is too much on the agenda and Maisie just won't be able to do dancing that day. An inexperienced nanny won't have the nerve to say 'no'. She will try to meet all the deadlines and she or one of the children may well end up having a mishap. If this happens it is mostly the employer's fault.

Each additional child is a complication to the sole charge nanny. Three children can easily feel like twice two. A few parents who insist on a Rolls-Royce childhood for their offspring, and intend to continue to work full-time themselves, hire another pair of hands (a mother's help, an au pair, a daily or part-time nanny), to back up the nanny and work under her direction.

When a mother is at home when the nanny is on duty, especially if she is not usually there, she can feel curiously displaced. One mother says that she found herself asking her nanny if she could join her for a walk with the baby? Other mothers say that they wouldn't dare upset a nanny's routine.

While it is a fault on the right side that employers should listen to their nannies' wishes and advice, it is mildly idiotic to defer to them on all subjects. Betty Parsons, much loved and now regrettably retired guru and ante-natal-instruction-expert, advises inimitably: 'Rule your own roost. Find someone who will adapt to your particular household. No child should be left *entirely* in a nanny's care. Bonding with parents is vital. The nanny must realize that the baby does not belong to her. Remember *you* must get her to do things *your* way for *your* child.'

It is important that a mother tries to resolve her attitudes and thoughts about why she is working and not choosing to look after her children herself at home. This is the subject of at least one other book, but suffice it to say that guilt is a pain in the neck for nannies to deal with and to have to make allowances for as well.

When working mothers hire a sole charge nanny, both employer and nanny should be aware that it is an *extremely* responsible job. As one agent put it, 'I screen out nannies who think they can whizz on a coffee round and stick junior in a bouncy chair.' The nanny programmes a child's development – introduces the child to solids, encourages him to look at books and crawl – major areas which should be taken seriously and monitored carefully by the mother.

Ignore the mothers who claim they have 'complete confidence' in their nanny. It is healthier to respect and like a nanny *but* remember she is human and fallible. Be vigilant and energetic and *humble* enough not to be complacent about your choice of nanny and the way the house is being run at the moment. It cannot be ideal.

Nanny as Shrink

A committed nanny will give a child her undivided attention some of the time. From this will grow that wordless communication which is instinctive between mother and child. Some mothers cannot cope with the intensity of this closeness; some revel in it. Some nannies do not want it; others think it is that getting inside children's skin which provides the intense challenge of the job. But it is this loving understanding, which gives the child the security that someone minds specially about him, that prepares him for complicated events like the dentist, first day at school and being nice to Grandpa who's a bit gaga these days.

One old nanny says, 'The motherly instinct is lacking in modern nannies. You have to work on the kids for a long time before you establish a real rapport. I make sure that I do as Mum would do in every way I can. So I have a lot of observing and listening to do in a new job.'

Jeanne Magagna, child psychotherapist at the Tavistock Clinic, says: 'I always ask the question – is the meeting between caretaker and child generating love or promulgating hate, promoting hope or sowing despair, containing pain or eliciting persecutory anxiety, fostering creative activity or creating confusion?'

If you watch a child with a good nanny, you will see how she feels things *with* him. A mother can't help doing so. If a child is secure in the knowledge that people notice and care and act on his behalf, he rates himself highly.

A nanny may have favourites or even a chemical reaction against one of the children. If the latter occurs the employer probably knew from the beginning that there was a mutual antipathy and hoped things would improve. They may not. Maybe the nanny picks on one child much too often and you are uneasy that she quite enjoys her power over him. It is just as unfair when she thinks one of them is more cuddly and says so. Coincidentally, the one she is likely to want to cuddle most is the baby and his siblings may like him less. This is unprofessional behaviour and potentially damaging. Either the pattern is changed or the nanny must go.

One nanny played favourites. I had to talk to her and tell her to try and play fair as she bullied the less favourite and he knew it.

Another nanny liked the child she had been with since he was a baby and she didn't have much sympathy for the older one.

We had one nanny who was very fond of my eldest son and found it difficult to love the baby. I fired her in the end.

Nanny as Safety Net

On average, four children a day are killed in an accident in the UK. Accidents are the most common cause of death among toddlers and older children; the under-fours are especially at risk.

Each year one child in six visits a hospital casualty department where one in every three patients is a child. One in every six children in hospital is there because of an accident. According to Department of Trade and Industry statistics the home is as dangerous as the road.

Many nannies find it dreary that an employer wants a long discussion with them about safety. Mother's helps and au pairs may never have thought about any aspect of child safety; it's the employer's job to educate them. Even if they are trained, they may have had very little practical experience of living with children. Apart from the lack of practice in spotting possible hazards for a one-year-old or a three-year-old, nannies cannot be expected to have the supposed maternal sixth sense. They have to learn it and preferably not by their mistakes with your children. Do not play down the subject; defer to the training enough to say briskly, 'I'm sure you know all this already, but I will feel better if you hear it from me too.'

Do not rely on the carer's instinct to know when a child is about to have an accident. Prepare his environment properly in both home and garden to avoid dangers. When he is at the park, in the street, in other people's houses, and on public transport she will have to be extra vigilant and become the child's ears and eyes. Many parents only become safety-conscious after a frightening accident involving a visit to the hospital's outpatients department.

Accidents *can* be cut down if whoever is looking after a child is paying him full attention. Better safe than sorry. No parent should remain relaxed about a nanny who says, 'I hope you realize your son's accident-prone?' after the sixth visit to casualty when she and the boy are becoming a bit of a joke to the doctors. One baby's leg was broken when he fell from the changing table while his nanny was out of the room – the doctors did not call that baby 'accident-prone'.

Apart from trying to protect the children, every employer wants to save the whole family *and* the nanny from the awful repercussions of a serious accident. If it clearly could have been avoided had the nanny been paying attention, the loaded word 'negligence' rears its ugly head. (For a discussion about professional negligence, insurance and the law, see page 329).

131

Safety

> You know, at least you ought to know,
> For I have often told you so,
> That children never are allowed
> To leave their Nurses in a crowd . . .
> And Always keep a-hold of Nurse
> For fear of finding something worse.
> From 'Jim', Hilaire Belloc

One mother had the experience of driving down the High Street of her local shopping area to see her nanny posting a letter on one side of the road and her daughter beginning to climb out of her buggy on the other. Another mother threatened her nanny with the sack if she left the baby outside the shops again after two babies had been snatched in the same area in a month – she forgot again and was told to leave. Another had to go when a mother was told by a neighbour that her two-year-old twins had let each other out of their car seats, climbed out of the front door of the car, held hands, looked left and right and crossed the road to rejoin their nanny in the bank.

Tell your nanny or mother's help that there are *no* circumstances in which your children are to be left alone in public places. Explain why. A few examples to start you off – escalators to fall down, supermarket shelves stacked with heavy tins ready to tumble if the bottom one is shifted, strangers who may offer sweets or pretty puppies ('like this one in the car') and even dog mess in the park from which a child can contract a rare blood disorder called *toxicara canis* and become gradually blind. Do also ask your nanny specifically not to allow your children to pet strange animals, they may have fleas, bite or scratch.

A safe road crossing drill is vital. Nannies must always hold a child's hand. If the child is unreliable and impulsive and little, perhaps he should wear reins, but if this idea does not appeal it is essential that a nanny hold each child by the hand firmly. She should also teach them good habits of safety drill by setting them an example and be sure to use designated crossings and not jaywalk or push the buggy into the road from behind parked cars. Children shouldn't be allowed to hurtle along and then teeter on the edge of the pavement. Nannies should be aware of all this, but if they are young or have no experience of heavy traffic and city life, spell it out – and take them for a practice so that they can witness your responsible road drill and learn how serious you are about the whole routine.

The dangers in the country are often as great as in the town, though they can be different. For example, a weekending child can clamber on to a combine harvester, or wander down the middle of a lane thinking that just because he is in the country there probably won't be any cars and may be allowed to wobble about on the main road learning to ride a bike as the only tractor to pass that week swerves round the corner. He can be tempted by poisonous berries – e.g. yew and laburnum – or paddle in ponds, streams or bogs without being aware of the dangers. The *First Aid Manual*, issued by the Red Cross, should be read, marked and learned by anyone responsible for children's lives. It is essential to know *exactly* what to do in cases of choking, suffocations, burns and scalds, poisoning, cuts and falls.

It is not possible here to cover all aspects of safety with children in the home. The most important point about talking to your nanny or mother's help about the whole subject is to ensure that she understands that prevention is best. Remind her to beware of, among other things, children:

- suffocating on plastic bags
- choking on peanuts
- grabbing at boiling saucepans
- playing with matches
- unlatching safety gates
- climbing on banisters
- exploring power sockets and frayed wires
- drowning, unattended, in two inches of water.

She should be aware that the nature of the danger constantly changes with growing children. With each stage of maturity one clutch of hazards recedes and another batch looms – the baby who was immobile yesterday can roll off a changing mat tomorrow and the crawling child can suddenly clamber up to things that were previously out of reach.

Nanny as Nurse

The nanny or mother's help should always tell you if she notices any symptoms of illness, particularly high temperatures or a child's behaviour which is out of the ordinary. If she cannot get in touch with you, she should ring the doctor or the local clinic for advice.

Princess Christian, patroness of the training college, inveighed against the 'mischief of soothing powders and syrups'. The use of the latter can be controversial, given that Phenergan and Benylin expectorant are sold without prescription. Some mothers prefer the dispensing of medicines to be their exclusive province. Occasionally there can be a mix-up and the child gets a double dose or none at all, so whatever you decide, be consistent and consult closely. Incidentally, remind your nanny about the contents of children's medicines; there are sugar-free options.

If you are around, take it in turns to nurse and entertain a sick child both by day and by night. The same rule applies for teething, colic and feeding babies in the middle of the night. Trained nannies certainly expect to do this as part of their routine, but if you aren't working long hours yourself, it is important that you relieve her, so that she can catch up on her sleep to do her daily job as well. Mrs Davis of Norland recommends that 'three nights in a row are enough for any nanny without support'. Mrs Townsend of Chiltern warns that 'many employers don't realize that nannies need to recharge their batteries'.

Most parents sleep within earshot of their children and usually cope with a wakeful child. This is one reason for the parent to bother to go personally to hear if anything is specifically wrong or has upset the child during the day.

One employer says: 'Good nannies sleep like logs. If they are unmoved by the racket during the day, it is no wonder that they are unmovable at night. I used to think it was deliberate, but they are just like my older children – they sleep like babies but my baby doesn't.' Another says, 'He who hears first, deals.' Some reckon that 'night duty is for parents'. This is definitely the case with au pairs.

Nanny as Cook

It will be a bonus if your nanny or mother's help cooks well and has heard of modern nutrition and diet. Trained nannies are meant to have learned about food values, a balanced diet, and vitamins. The chances of meeting a nanny who is fond of brown rice, pulses, beansprouts, wholemeal bread and spaghetti, low fat milk, polyunsaturates, steamed veg, fresh fruit and grilling rather than frying are slim – and the nannies aren't.

Before you flounce in and throw a fit about the nanny's cooking and choice of tins, frozen food and instant whips for the children, remember that this is a very touchy area. You are criticizing her mum's cooking, which may be pre-war in outlook and includes a new-to-you recipe for cooking cabbage. Start with cold water, boil for twenty minutes and serve straight from the hob in a slotted spoon when it has sat in the water for another half an hour before lunch. One raw carrot would be more nutritious. Raw is good for you, and this is a positive plus for lazy nannies.

Keep a sense of proportion; it is not vital that every meal is served and prepared as you would choose, but don't ignore its content. A large majority of employers have the same criticisms to make: more fresh food, inventiveness and use of recipes, less fat, sugar, salt, cakes, biscuits, orange squash, chips, fish fingers, sausages and tomato ketchup.

Employers often say that they greatly dislike their nannies giving their children sweets as treats – not least because they feel that this is the province of the parents. The nanny may not be using sweets as a bribe (very naughty) but, even if she is just being generous, it's a good idea to persuade her that raisins or a big juicy red apple can have the same effect. It helps if they lead the way.

Don't forget to remind nannies that children and especially babies do not need added salt in their food. One mother tells us that her baby was fed an Oxo cube a day by her NNEB-trained nanny and had to spend several weeks in hospital after severe dehydration.

Certain 'E' numbers and other additives have been definitely linked to certain allergies and problems such as hyperactivity, eczema and asthma. This is the worst aspect of having a nanny who is idle or unaware of healthy eating. One family is so against such additives as tartrazine (E 102), sunset yellow (E110) and benzoic acid (E210) that they instruct their nanny to read every label on everything she buys. She has learnt to enjoy being a tartrazine-spotter, but she was always keen on the subject thanks to a good NNEB course.

Mothers often put aside enough food for the children's lunch from their cooking the night before because they know how hard it is to break habits of a lifetime. Almost all the mothers we consulted put themselves in charge of the weekly bulk shop so that they could monitor the intake. It is quite a good idea to decide together on weekly or daily menus, then an employer does not have to nag at every meal. If your nanny has never encountered this entire subject before, do not get cross if she thinks you are a bit barmy – recapture your own reactions to the first health food freak you met years ago. Many people prefer butter to marge and always will.

You will need to agree about how much and what your children are to eat. Some people feel they would rather their children ate anything, rather than everyone having to suffer rows over muesli, greens and fruit. Some nannies are rigid about children finishing what is on their plates and can take punishment too far for wayward eaters. It is necessary to know the nanny's approach before leaving the children's meals to her. As Katharine Whitehorn writes in *How to Survive Children*, 'A food is not necessarily essential just because your child hates it.'

If you have a nanny who is too bullying about your children's eating habits, remind her that she is at least twenty years older than the miscreant and that it surely cannot be true that confrontation is the only way to get what you want from the under-fives? Suggest that she gives smaller helpings, cajoles, persuades and avoids too many rules.

Nanny as Disciplinarian

If babies could speak they'd tell
    mother or nurse,
That slapping was pointless and why;
For if you're not crying it prompts you
    to cry,
And if you are – then you cry worse.
'Bringing up Baby', Roy Fuller

It is a truism that people vote as their parents vote and bring up their children as they were brought up. In other words if *they* once experienced violence, shouting and swearing, they are not inhibited about treating their own child or children in their care in the same way. One of the main reasons for discussing the subject of discipline during the interview (see chapter 4) is that attitudes are diverse and people hold strong views. It will now be obvious why a stable and happy family background is very important.

Norland nannies are taught that it should never be necessary to smack a child and they will refuse to do so regardless of the parents' wishes. Whatever you think is right, you must agree on a plan of action for dealing with a naughty child *with* the nanny. Work on the principle of reward for co-operation: for example, 'Please tidy your rooms quickly then there will be more time for a story/play/Blue Peter.' Encourage the nanny not to stand for any rudeness to her and to make 'sorry' after a misdemeanour the absolute norm. Don't both bellow at the children in unison if you can avoid it.

Having decided between you on the course of action to take on discipline, there should be no public disagreement about an issue. Ask the nanny to stick firmly to an agreed policy. Don't let the children play one off against the other, but present a united front and talk about it later.

Nannies hate having their authority undermined, justifiably, as in the classic case of when the nanny says 'no' to another sweet and mummy comes in and consoles the doleful child with one. It is particularly irking when toddler manipulation wins out. Never succumb to the temptation to let the nanny know who is boss when it is not appropriate. Do not score points. You will repent in the leisureless weeks after she has left.

In an office, if a colleague is boring, irritating or behaving unreasonably, the bloke who sits in the next desk knows that he cannot attack him physically, however exasperating he may be. Yet in many families adults do hit their kids for those very reasons. Max Patterson, a past President of the PPA (Pre-school Playgroups Association) says that 'Much child abuse comes from parents' failure to perceive themselves as adults. They feel their child is being vindictive, so hit back in revenge, just as a child might react to another child.'

Even trained nannies with little practical experience may punish a child who is behaving in a way which is entirely appropriate for his age and stage, out of sheer ignorance. Correcting aggression with more aggression can only lead to confusion in the toddler. And he's more likely to be aggressive to his brothers and sisters so it can be counter-productive.

Many parents regard smacking as violence, and in a society where we agree that children should not be beaten at school the Norland approach seems reasonable. Those same parents admit to the occasional smack or wallop when at the end of their tether. It is for them a cathartic gesture, but a nanny should not need such an emotional outlet. For some parents, smacking is indeed a Sackable Offence (see pages 45–6).

If you give your nanny a lot of sole charge and anyone, be it neighbour, friend or distant acquaintance, mentions however obliquely and whistling the while, that she has seen your nanny behave in a way that she feels you may not have approved of, try not to dismiss her as an interfering old bag. It is not a subject people raise lightly. They don't have to be sensitive to know that you would far rather not hear bad news of your nanny, nor feel guilty about your own lack of judgement in having employed her. Investigate the criticism thoroughly and, if proved fair, be grateful and sack the nanny without delay.

Suggested disciplinary alternatives for your nanny to practise include: scolding, banishing from the room, sending up to the bedroom, standing the child in a corner, a quiet firm verbal reprimand eyeball-to-eyeball at the child's level, taking them aside and having a little chat, withdrawals of privileges and carrying through *any* threat.

Be aware that non-residential NNEB courses scarcely tackle the subject of children's discipline. The broad line is that nannies should take the lead from the children's parents. So give them one.

A long-established agent says that, 'The employer should assume that the children won't tell them how a nanny disciplines them. They are too frightened of what she might do to them next time the employer leaves the house.' A Scots employer warns: 'The awful truth is that nannies are more subtle and devious than we like to know. Discipline should be discussed, agreed on and stuck to.' She goes on to mention a nanny who was with her family for 18 months and when she left both the children were quite clear they didn't mind if they never saw her again. She never quite knew why, but always felt guilty that she had not been around enough to protect them from whatever the nanny had done to frighten them.

Parental child abuse is the one instance when the nanny is incontrovertibly within her rights to go against the rule of confidentiality between employer and employee, especially in a residential job. She would be likely to be sacked instantly but should be reassured that she is morally and legally in the right and that the law of 'unfair dismissal' was drafted to cover such an occurrence. She may take her case to an industrial tribunal. PANN, the nanny's trade union, (see page 343), would take up her cause.

It can arise that an employer feels uneasy about a nanny's relationship with a child. Do not suppress this reaction as being beyond the pale. There are cases when young teenagers are initiated into the joys of sex by a younger sibling's nanny. A live-in 'Mrs Robinson' is far from most people's idea of the perfect nanny. It's inevitably a Sackable Offence Situation.

It is entirely natural that a toddler grabs or fondles his nanny's breasts, but even then she should gently reprove and remove his hand. A seven-year-old clearly should know not to do so. A nanny who permits or encourages such behaviour is guilty of abuse. A disturbed child may use the sexual contact of climbing into bed with a nanny often as a way of making himself feel safe and good. The carer should make physical boundaries for a child at a certain age – there are grounds for some minor confusion in the relationship, unlike that between parents and children who have the incest barrier to illuminate what is 'right' and what is 'wrong'. A tiny number of nannies who are not receiving physical or emotional gratification from an appropriate source may come to rely on children's affectionate gestures and insist on them.

One of the most common and heartfelt complaints from parents concerns the volume of the nanny's voice. They find this never more objectionable than when a nanny is chastising their offspring. Several mothers mention that they tell their nanny at the outset not to shout or insult the children; parents have no need to pay someone to do that for them. Verbal abuse is the first cousin of physical abuse, and can hurt some individuals a lot more. A nanny who continually yells at a child must go. It is not a pretty sight to witness a girl showing off her power over yours or another's child in front of other nannies and children. Object strongly and deal with it firmly – and quietly.

Nanny as Scaredy Cat

Irrational fears are part of everyone's upbringing but the last thing you need as an employer is a nanny who makes no attempt to hide hers in front of your children. A child is deeply affected by seeing an adult, and particularly one in whom he places his trust, obviously frightened or reduced to a jelly. It is not surprising that whatever has given the nanny hysterics is likely to give the child problems in the future. Spiders, flies, snakes, creepy crawlies, bats and mice are common bugbears. Water presents a threat to some.

Some people also dislike: black men, homosexuals, tattoos, seaweed, walking under ladders, flying, boats, cows, geese, horses, the dark, the heat, the cold, the wind, the rain, thunder, lightning, heights – and some of these people are nannies.

You asked her specifically in the interview if she had any particular fears or prejudices. Do not be too sympathetic if she now reveals herself to be an agoraphobe. She really should have told you before. You can't be expected to re-write the job description, as you would need to if you always go away at weekends and she is constantly car sick.

It is a good idea to talk about any fears or prejudices she has, but the important thing is for her to understand that she may not shriek in front of the children when she sees a spider.

Nanny as Potty Trainer

Usual thing: talk about it beforehand, have a party line and both stick rigidly to it. The subject and people's attitude to it is clearly related to discipline. Try to persuade your nanny to treat the training process as though dealing with the child's eating habits and not to get emotional, or bullying, and to avoid confrontation at all costs.

Try to instil into the girl the need for her to become the child's bladder or body alarm clock. In other words she must think about when and whether the child should/need/want to 'go'. Remember to standardize your vocabulary and check out the words the playgroup use. In the 1990s 'pee' and 'poo', 'willy' and 'bottom' seem to be fashionable and employed so universally that both employer and nanny can use them uninhibitedly.

Make sure that the nanny plays fair with your child and protects him from his own 'accidents' by always going out with a potty secreted about her person, as well as trainer pants and perhaps a disposable.

Don't let your nanny be relaxed about her own or anyone else's carpets – the stains are the worst. She must not blame the child nor use the popular but totally inept words 'dirty' and/or 'naughty'. Any trained nanny should understand why not, and if she skipped the relevant lectures at college, refer her to Penelope Leach, Dr Spock and, indeed, Freud.

Incidentally, if your nanny has not yet encountered the 'dirty protest' – when the child smears crap all over the cot and walls and eats what's left – if you are around, deal with it yourself. It is uniquely disgusting, particularly if you are not the child's mother. Don't stretch the vocational instinct to its limits.

Nanny as Educator

If your nanny or mother's help isn't naturally voluble, do try to get her to talk, talk, talk to a small child. It doesn't matter how trivial it is; like learning any language, practice makes perfect. If you think she is self-conscious and will feel silly having a dotty conversation about pink dragons-baggons and fiery blanc-mangey-mangey, talk to her about it and set a good example by making sure she hears you sounding silly too.

Get her to discourage stereotype roles. If she hears the four-year-old lad say to his two-year-old sister 'Girls can't be cowboys, only boys can', remind him that there are cow girls who are quite as capable of riding a bronco. Tell her not to ignore silly, impolite comments about other races even if they are meant innocently. She should make it clear that what has been said is unacceptable and should explain why unemotionally.

Books are the biggest boon to child entertainers. Most children adore being read to. It is a good thing to read to them after a period of activity. It can calm them down before a meal, or before going out, and, of course, before bed. No playroom can have enough books. Research affirms what common sense knows already: the more a child is read to, the better it is for his intellectual development, not to mention his reading skills, before, during and *after* he has learnt to read. Nannies of working

141

mothers should be schooled particularly about the importance of lots of reading all the day through and if the parents can't be there at bedtime, the therapeutic effect of a quiet read of at least 10 minutes (the more the better, so long as the child is absorbed).

Encourage your nanny to tell stories as well as read them. Children can then add their embellishments. They love to hear about themselves; in written stories they identify with the heros and heroines. It is easy to weave a story around them and their circumstances.

The nanny should encourage her charges who cannot read yet to 'read' books with her, to enjoy the pictures and tell the story with her and to her, to enjoy books on their own. Enjoying books helps a child concentrate, learn about people and situations and use the story and pictures as a spring-board for his own ideas and stories. All the time he is becoming familiar with letters, words and numbers. He is also developing his language and thought processes.

It may give your nanny satisfaction to see herself as much as a teacher as a carer. She will gain a sense of achievement, as will her charge, when she helps him learn the alphabet and how to count. Of course, she must be sensible and sensitive about it and not become hectoring, or insist that the child guesses letters when he doesn't want to.

Keep an eye on the children's tape cassette collection: does your nanny put on the same tapes (possibly her favourites rather than the child's)?; does she use them enough?; do you find a tell-tale cassette of her favourite rock group in the machine at the end of the day? Ask her about it. Encourage her to sit and read the book that goes with the tape with the child, rather than always leaving him to get on with it.

Nanny as Square Eyes

The use of TV and the video is a flashpoint for many parents and nannies. A few parents feel strongly that they want their children to sit in front of a TV for as short a time as possible, particularly when they have a nanny to amuse them.

Many parents are not happy about the amount of TV their children do watch, but find it a godsend. What a boon to plonk the little dears in front of a video of the *Wizard of Oz* on a wet

Wednesday afternoon while you get on and prepare supper for eight, encourage them to watch Breakfast Time so the parents can have an extra hour in bed on a Saturday morning, or switch on Play School so that mother can whizz round with the hoover. Some children come back pretty drained after a day at school and immediately slump in front of the telly for an hour and more – it's called 'vegging out' in America.

Other parents try hard to plough a middle course. They believe rationed telly is a Good Thing. They feel it widens a child's understanding of the world and how it works and familiarizes him with visual techniques like cartoons, hand and string puppets and animated models like Thomas the Tank Engine. They relish their children watching the wild life programmes, anything related to what they are doing at school and generally approve of all the mass of colour, enthusiasm, imagination, skill and information that goes into good children's programmes.

Many parents find irksome the passivity of a child (always 'in a heap'), who watches the box for 40 minutes. This is increased when the nanny is sitting beside the child filing her nails, talking to another nanny or reading a magazine. The parent may well break up the quiet scene if the sun is shining and the window is closed as well.

You may have touched on TV during the interview. Talk to the nanny again and remind her of your views if she shows signs of wilfully ignoring what you asked her to do. Employers have every right to be tough about the telly if they want to be. It doesn't have to be used as a surrogate minder – not turning it off is a parallel to giving children daily doses of Phenergan so that they don't wake at night.

Agree that TV can be a life enhancer *if* she is responsible and selective about the programmes and channels she lets the child watch, if she watches *with* the child and if he is given the chance of talking about it with her afterwards. All this has to be spelled out most emphatically with a nanny who is in sole charge for long periods, particularly if the mother doesn't feel that the girl shares her opinion.

Nanny as Entertainer

Too many employers express discontent with their nanny's,

mother's help's or even au pair's attitude to children's play. If a trained nanny doesn't show sufficient interest in, and enjoyment of, her charges' play, then she is a lot more culpable than an untrained mother's help.

Play helps a child develop practical skills, makes him think, calculate, ponder and use his imagination. It gives him greater understanding of the workings of the world and people. Play gives his limbs, lungs and muscles plenty of exercise; his senses – sight, sound, taste and touch – are continually stimulated through play. Last but not least, the trained nanny will have learnt how a child's play with other children and with adults contribute to the child's socialization, making him into an acceptable member of society who shares his toys willingly and with politeness, a child who doesn't kick, yell, snatch and scratch. Play enables him also to experiment with certain kinds of behaviour, reactions and emotions.

Good child carers *enjoy* playing with their charges, adapting to a child's ideas and wishes. She must be able to take a secondary role in a child's game while also being able to direct him to do something specific, like a puzzle or drawing a picture, at other times. Employers become annoyed when they are paying a trained girl £100 a week and she doesn't show initiative and imagination when with the children.

A nanny should think of herself as entertainments manageress and have something planned, either in her head or on paper, for most days. She also needs the flexibility to give up her fun-filled programme when the child is clearly too tired or just plain unwilling to do it her way. Play should never be forcibly directed.

If you are unlucky and have a nanny who isn't much good at entertaining the kids in a purposeful, energetic way, and it worries you, there is only so much you can do about it short of hiring someone else. Some girls will respond to suggestions and guidance, but if they haven't a great deal of imagination and minimal *interest* in their charges' high jinks, it will be an uphill struggle. If she has more than one child to look after it will be a test of her skills anyway to make time for creative play. That is why it is always a bonus to hire a girl who has bags of energy. You want to avoid a nanny who feels like a wet rag having given the children breakfast, dressed and changed baby, cleared up breakfast, made beds and tidied toys and it is only 10 am.

However limited you may feel a particular nanny is when it comes to amusing the children, it is worth writing down a detailed list of suggested activities. Don't leave it entirely to her to decide when to do painting/water play/playdough. It may happen once every four weeks, when it could happen once a week at least with a bit of guidance and nudging from you.

She may improve noticeably once she becomes used to thinking about ways of amusing her charges, and they will also draw the fun out of her and insist she does zany things with any luck. Parents can help a good deal by setting a precedent and doing things with the children which might not have struck her.

Remind her that play should be fun, varied and enjoyable. She needs to direct and stimulate the child while allowing him to express himself fully and do his own thing a lot of the time. If a child doesn't want to do potato prints today and he isn't just being contrary at the moment the nanny suggests it, leave it for another day. Tell her that play is for its own sake. Play is often about a child taking the initiative, or taking it with another child or an adult. It is also all about choice, and the player likes to be in control.

Like all employees, nannies and mother's helps prefer to use nice, new equipment. Imaginative entertainers can get by with remarkably little formal equipment to amuse a child. Some parents argue that too many primary coloured toys and games can inhibit a child's imagination.

However, it is best to be on the safe side when it comes to carers and, finances permitting, provide plenty of the following: shapes, sorters, nesting and hammering bits, bricks, puzzles, games, packs of cards, things to thread and make, things to construct and push together like Duplo, Brio Mec and Stickle-bricks; toys to pretend with like toy soldiers, knights, forts, castles, zoos, a Noah's ark, train sets and tracks, telephones, cash registers, cooking utensils, brushes and a dustpan, dolls prams, push chairs and houses, farm and wild animals, tractors and farm machinery and on and on.

Make sure the nanny encourages plenty of constructive and creative play: cutting, sticking, printing, colouring, making scrapbooks, collages, mobiles; don't forget the ubiquitous egg box which has a thousand different uses, as have empty loo rolls, kitchen rolls and squeezy bottles. For imaginative play she could

145

organize a Dressing-up Box, transform a clothes horse or playpen into a tent or purloin the kitchen scales and a collection of empty jars and boxes for the grocery shop.

Don't let the nanny deprive your child of his ration of messy play, be it digging in the sandpit, 'cooking' with flour and water in the kitchen, emptying buckets outside or from making mud pies in a discreet corner of the garden. Remind her that children also welcome quieter times with finger and toe games like 'Here's the Church' and 'This Little Pig', 'I Spy', opposites and action and nursery rhymes. Whatever the activity, explain that children love attention and their play is enhanced if they have someone who is prepared to share it with them.

Nanny as Hostess

Tea, lunch, outings to the park, expeditions to museums or the zoo are more fun for both nannies and children if they are shared with their contemporaries. As an employer you encourage it within reason because it keeps everyone happy and busy. However socializing can be overdone, and is meant to be, after all, for the benefit of the children when it takes place with the nanny. Inappropriate ages and stages of children, some of whom may be unknown to you, are signs that the nanny is putting her social life before the children's.

However, bear in mind that many experienced nannies consider socializing on duty a perk. It is one of the few aspects that make nannying preferable to a 9-to-5 job. They enjoy the necessary organization, catering and the alleviation of drear routine and loneliness. Indeed, some socializing is to be recommended for nannies looking after babies and toddlers as they can become bored and out of touch with local life.

No mother likes to see a ring of gossiping coffee swilling nannies while the children go unheeded. Working mothers won't experience this exasperation, but it may well happen. One mother who works upstairs says she interferes boldly on this occasion but no other, and with a loud voice says, 'How about something that everyone can play? And less jumping on the furniture please.'

Too much emphasis on sociabilities is peculiar to large concentrations of nannies and children, i.e. in London. When children are old enough, about three years plus on average, they have reached the point when they can come and play on their own. Remind your nanny to invite the child alone.

If you have an inexperienced nanny, don't feel inhibited about vetting surreptitiously any friends she brings to your house and steer her away from the rough trade in the nanny world. You don't want her to pick up bad habits and a world-weary expression.

7

Training

The ability to stick at a course for one to two years and survive the experience of being tested at the end of it speaks of a certain dedication in a nanny. This stamina is less likely to be found in the kind of girl who may leave to serve in the local department store sale within six weeks of arrival. Some employers don't like trained nannies for many reasons, but all agree that attending a course bestows some maturity and more than a passing interest in the subject.

One employer who has never had enough money to afford a trained nanny says, 'In my inexperienced days I pooh-poohed the need for a trained girl. Nowadays I think that someone trained is more likely to stay longer, be more professional and know more about ways to entertain young children. Another plus is that a trained nanny would not need the sort of intensive child care course that someone untrained has to go through for at least a month alongside me.'

Another mother who has always employed Princess Christian nannies says: 'I think training is vital. Not so much for the knowledge they gain but for their attitude to the whole job. If they bother to take a training course I think they have a genuine interest in children and in being professional.'

Other employers have mixed reactions:

Standards seem low, but it's a mercy that there are any.

Training takes time and shows initiative. All our trained nannies have been extremely efficient and organized.

How to do 65 different things with an egg box is not necessarily all you need, though of course splendid at times.

The nannies themselves are equally wide-ranging in their comments:

148

Lots of girls were doing the training because they couldn't think what else to do and they thought the jobs would be easy and well paid.

The courses were designed for the social services and didn't give me much idea about nannying.

I feel more confident as a nanny knowing I'm trained.

However, there is not much chance of nannies being treated as professionals unless a high proportion of them are trained. The untrained after years of experience acquire eventually a sort of honorary trained status, like Prince William's former nanny Barbara Barnes.

The prevalent attitude that 'anyone can look after children' will not go away unless training and its standards are recognized, understood and seen to be excellent in practice as well as theory. The editor of *Nursery World* writes:

Training is often described as 'concentrated experience' and is a short cut to good practice which avoids many mistakes which may otherwise only be corrected by bitter experience. Formal training, when it is thorough, is a shorter route to excellence. It is not necessarily better than experience, however.

Trained nannies will at least have been exposed to many different theories about child care and should emerge with clear ideas about what is best for the child, rather than what suits his carer. They will have been taught about the emotional, physical, intellectual and social growth and well-being of an infant and, with any luck, may have picked up a number of professional tricks of the trade.

The biggest objection to training is that a little knowledge can be a dangerous thing, especially if only partially understood and not put to the test with practical experience. Many employers and employment agencies complain that the trouble is that girls are given exaggerated ideas of their competence by training courses. Both groups agree that training course standards vary too much to make effective generalizations about the graduates.

The NNEB Course

The National Nursery Examination Board (NNEB) exams are taken by students at local authority colleges, like further education colleges and technical colleges, and at residential fee-paying colleges as well.

The first NNEB Certificate was awarded in 1946: a direct result of the war. Nursery nurses were needed to look after the children of young mothers who joined the War Effort. The NNEB board is now an educational trust whose members include the Associations of County Councils, the Federation of Recruitment and Employment Services (known as FRES, the employment agencies trade association), the National Association of Nursery Nurse Tutors, NUPE (National Union of Public Employees), the Royal College of Nursing and the National Association of Health Authorities in England and Wales.

The NNEB is still the only training of which most private employers of nannies have ever heard. It is no longer the highest ranking qualification for a trained nanny. The B/Tec diploma (see page 169) is of higher status, and the mushrooming of other qualifications in recent years and the plans by the National Council of Vocational Qualifications (NCQV) to restructure completely child care qualifications could make the NNEB course look very different before long.

The course is open to men and women; it lasts for six terms and takes two years to complete. Students are mostly 16 years old at the start and each place is funded by local authorities. Over 5,000 students graduate each year. There are a few male graduates – about half a dozen a year. A high proportion, around half, of graduates become nannies in private homes.

Those who don't become nannies work mostly in the public sector as nursery nurses; a number continue in further education. The courses are immensely over-subscribed. Robert Chantry-Price, Director of the NNEB, says that on average one in five applicants are accepted on the course though competition can be much stiffer in some particularly popular courses or in populous areas. For example, the college in Lincoln has eight applications for each place – it is the only college in the county and the second largest county in the country.

Officially an applicant need have no qualifications of any sort because the course is reckoned to be a 'vocational education'. If it is over-subscribed, colleges look at GCSEs as a way of weeding out applicants. For example, the College at Birmingham's minimum requirement is English GCSE for a school-leaver. At one technical college the demand for places is so high that at least three GCSEs at grade three or above, of which one should be English Language, are needed.

Older applicants (even a 40-year-old can make it) are treated differently and their experience respected. Some courses make a special effort to include those whose natural bent for children is palpable, but who aren't good on paper. Academic achievements, school reports and personal references are considered before candidates are invited for interview. One course tutor who interviews says: 'I choose those that are out-going, mix easily and who know a little bit about what they are letting themselves in for.'

Many NNEB students receive some sort of grant from the local authorities. Their course is free, but depending on their parents' income and assets, students may apply for extra money for textbooks, travelling to 'placements' (see page 152) and college, and for a living allowance.

At the end of their first year students take a written exam – those who fail are not thrown out, but given a pep talk. Students are given an hour and a half to do a Multiple Choice Question (MCQ) exam in their fifth term and a three-hour essay paper in the sixth term. Their college work and placements reports during the six terms contribute to the final assessment.

The exams are marked by the course tutor and by external examiners who visit the college. A moderator reads border line papers and makes her decision whether to pass or fail. Previously, if a student failed one of the three sections, she failed the whole exam. Now it is possible to pass by 'compensation'. If a candidate fails the MCQ by one or two marks then, provided she does well in the written paper, she will scrape through the entire exam. The NNEB has introduced this compensation system in order to be fairer to border line cases.

Eighty-five per cent of students who take the NNEB pass; recently students have been permitted to receive distinction if they excel in their written paper assessment. This is a good thing for tutors who are happy to distinguish their star pupils from the lazybones who larked about in the back row: it is also an excellent recommendation to an employer.

The child care theory taught for three days a week includes: health and nursing a sick child; safety; nutrition; a child's psychological, physical and social development; language progress, and learning through play. Students also do the 'complementary studies' mentioned above. The detail of the course can include useful items like cooking for children's parties, stocking a fishtank with tadpoles, setting up a child's bedroom, creating glove puppets and jam making.

There are more academic themes to do with current theories of infant problems, e.g. genetics and hereditary diseases, dyslexia, the only child, Down's Syndrome and other disabilities. Premenstrual tension, pregnancy, alcoholism, role play and imaginary situations, form filling and job hunting may also be tackled among other subjects.

Two days a week are spent gaining practical experience called 'placements' in child care. Students are sent out to hospitals, day nurseries, family centres, nursery schools, private homes, childminders, and to centres and homes for handicapped children. They work under supervision and are expected to record their experiences in written 'observations'. As well as this, some colleges encourage students to 'adopt' a neighbour's child, visit him regularly and note his development over the two years as a project. One NNEB says, 'We were also encouraged to find a job with kids in the holidays.'

'Training' placements differ from 'experience' placements. Colleges resort to the latter when they cannot find enough of the former. The idea is that students spend some time in a family working in a 'mother and baby placement'. To count as a training placement which goes towards the student's final assessment, the mother must be either an SRN, NNEB or the equivalent. If she is just an ordinary mother, the student's time with her is put down to 'experience' only.

The NNEB allots two days a week to placements. In practice the same amount of time is split up differently so that the course tutor can juggle classes and placements successfully. For example, rather than a girl spending three days at college learning child care theory and two days on a placement, she may do a block of about two to three weeks on a placement at, for example, a hospital and then do a block in college. Alternatively, she may do four days in a placement on the trot, followed by six days in college in sequence.

Gripes about NNEB training as preparation for nannying
(gathered from employment agencies, employers, nannies,
college principals and union officials)

- Too little properly supervised practical experience.
- Inexperienced girls given exaggerated ideas of their
  competence.
- Course standards vary too greatly to rely on the product.
- Not enough emphasis on work as a nanny in all its aspects.
- Health and nutrition not always adequately taught.
- Domestic skills not emphasized sufficiently, i.e. laundry,
  mending, etc.
- Sixteen is too young for most students to be committed to
  the course (sometimes as few as 15 per cent of the entry are
  still working in child care within two years of qualifying).
- Entry qualifications should be higher. Many girls without
  any academic qualification have great difficulty coping
  with the course.
- Very little teaching of employer/employee relations.
- There is no proper nanny-employer representation on the
  NNEB Board (many suggest that the appointment of a
  couple of experienced employment agents would remedy
  this).
- Apart from a newsletter, the system currently provides no
  support, aftercare or advice.

The NNEB has been much quicker to react to change than in the
past. Its greatest innovation has been the setting up of a graduate
register which enables employers to check a nanny's credentials
quickly, allows graduates to keep in touch with each other and,
all important, ensures that any NNEB with a criminal record or
who has been proven guilty of professional misconduct can be
struck off.

The NNEB Director, Mr Chantry-Price, is proud of the Board's
now overt policy of equal opportunities and the 'NNEB's role in a
multi-ethnic society', as well as the course's emphasis on child
abuse and AIDS. He thinks that nursery nursing is more
demanding than it used to be, particularly in the public sector,
because of today's social problems. He is also pleased that there

are more mature students and more men taking the course. Students now receive a better preparation for the demanding task of coping with 'at risk' children and parents; more of a social worker's job than a childminding role in many inner cities.

Mrs Townsend of Chiltern Nursery Training College, who teaches the NNEB course to her students, comments: 'The course is by no means perfect and there are quite a lot of loose ends to be tied up and weak areas which are being updated and widened. At the moment we are all waiting with interest to see what happens to the course structure in the light of all the big changes which are in the pipeline.'

Employers of nannies in the home may feel that a few more basic standards need upgrading as well, and that the questions of minimum qualifications and a higher age limit should be addressed too.

The NNEB used to be like a very large crude carrier in that it took five years (as opposed to five miles) to change direction. But fortunately the NNEB has turned into something more like a container ship, becoming quicker off the mark, now that the NCVQ is preparing to make child care courses much more flexible. The plan is that students can collect credits and hop about between different teaching bodies. This should create some healthy competition between City and Guilds, NAMCW, NNEB and B/Tec (see pages 168–9).

Residential Fee-Paying Nursery Nurse Training Colleges

Fifty years ago there were over thirty private nursery nurse residential colleges, but with the proliferation of free NNEB courses in technical colleges funded by local authorities, this number has dwindled to three – the Norland Nursery Training College, the Princess Christian College, and the Chiltern Nursery Training College.

All colleges do the NNEB curriculum of six terms. Tuition and board at all three colleges costs between £600 to £7,000 for the whole course. It is rare but not unheard of for students to win local authority grants. The established colleges are all non-profit-making charitable trusts. Choosing to pay, as is always the way, makes students and their parents take the course seriously. Also, because the graduates are so much in demand by employers, parents know that the investment will pay off. Apart from college pressure to do well, no parent is likely to allow their child to do it in a half-hearted way.

The three colleges all have educational requirements – they demand three GCSEs of grade C or above. English Language must be one of these for Norland, whereas Princess Christian and Chiltern will accept the softer option of English Literature. All students who have their English Language or Literature GCSE are eligible to sit the Royal Society of Health Diploma in nursery nursing.

All students start at 18, though they can apply at 16, be accepted and go away and do something else for a couple of years. The students live closely with each other 24 hours a day, away from their homes and parents. They are supervised day and night, live in a structured world and have to obey the college rules – not unlike an employer's House Rules. Boyfriends are not allowed to stay overnight, smoking is banned in two of the colleges, and manners, appearance and general behaviour are corrected. The net result is the nearest thing to working in a private home.

Another major advantage that the residential colleges have over the public sector equivalent is that they all boast on-campus nurseries for the under-fives for their students to gain hands-on experience.

The emphasis on domestic science and home economics is evident in all three colleges. Every student will learn about additives, allergies and sugar-free recipes. There are also fancy aspects to the cooking courses with the use of woks and food processors. The same goes for needlework and crafts.

Reunions, membership and newsletters flourish and the college in-house employment registries continue to place nannies for much of their careers. They wear uniforms and may receive badges. Any graduate guilty of conduct unbecoming that is reported to the college, investigated and condemned is struck off the register, with no hope of redemption.

For those who pass out with flying colours, the confidence given them by the college propels them into the outside world and continues to give them a sense of belonging and of being answerable to their college and its expectations of them. The old college mafia provides a world-wide network of contacts, friends and jobs the student may slip into like a pair of old slippers (for ease) or on to a magic carpet (for experience).

Chiltern Nursery Training College

The Chiltern College is in Caversham, Reading, and is situated on a residential road in a big, red brick, gabled house with modern additions. It was founded in 1931 and today accepts about 50 students each year. Most live in and there are 100 students at the college at any one time. Its prospectus tells us that 'the Chiltern now has the most modern facilities of any nursery training college in Europe'. They include a new day care department and nursery school for children aged between two and five who come daily. There are 24 babies and 30 toddlers.

Mrs Pamela Townsend has been Principal of Chiltern since 1981. She was trained as a nursery nurse as well as a primary school teacher and is a keen grandmother. She is a homely, warm and friendly person who is fond of the girls in her college and obviously enjoys her job. She says that employers often misunderstand the training that nannies receive and many of them are so confused that they apply to her when they want to hire a Norland nanny!

Her thoughts on nannies at Chiltern run thus:

Their family backgrounds are widely varied. High standards of speech, appearance, morals and personal hygiene are of paramount importance. Nannies must set an example and educate children along similar lines. I like my students to be proud of their uniform, but I feel that it should be worn only when it is appropriate, i.e. when handling small babies or as a traditional sign on special occasions. Some people prefer their nannies not to wear uniform in this day and age.

The trained nanny should have a set of standards to work from, and a great deal of knowledge and understanding. This has been added to her innate love of children and desire to care for them. She should have professional common sense at her finger tips, a sense of humour and the ability to give support and cope with all eventualities. She must also be adaptable.

Mrs Townsend says that in the past the college used to foster children who were in local council care. They don't do so any more, but she would like to have mothers and babies needing support to come and stay in the college together. 'Our students need experience of 24-hour care. They have to understand how tiring it is getting up in the middle of the night.'

Mrs Townsend insists that the applicants' GPs fill in an exhaustive medical report. It is headed by the bleak comment that 'applicants with a history of the following conditions are rarely accepted: blackouts or epilepsy, significant uncorrected defects of hearing or vision, mental illness requiring psychiatric super-vision, anorexia nervosa, drug overdose, drug addiction, diabetics needing insulin, major forms of physical illness.'

Her students are allowed to bring their boyfriends into the college and there is no curfew. They are also allowed to smoke in the college when they are off duty. She encourages her students to do local babysitting and temporary nanny jobs at weekends. The uniform is coloured navy and madonna blue – skirts, tabards, trousers, capes, aprons and plain black lace-up moccasins.

In the evenings and at weekends students manage their own common room and its affairs and organize a dance each year. They have numerous video evenings and join local clubs, classes and churches in Reading.

Once qualified, Chiltern nannies find their own jobs; there is no college register. Mrs Townsend feels that at 20 they are well capable of finding employment for themselves, but she is available to give advice and guidance before they accept their first post.

Chiltern College reflected Mrs Townsend's cheery personality. The students greeted visitors confidently. The buildings were modern and pleasant, but not exactly spacious and neither was the garden. There was a relaxed and happy atmosphere. It was entirely unoppressive and refreshingly uninstitutional. Students joked with teachers, there was a hubbub at lunch in the nursery, and it looked as though a jolly time was being had by all.

One Chiltern graduate comments: 'I really enjoyed my time there. Reading is a dump, but Chiltern's a lot closer to London than Norland which I could have gone to. We had an excellent training with good tutors who ran the place.'

A few employment agencies and past employers comment:

Chiltern's standards are not as strict as the other two.

It is more human than either of the other two, and the girls are always friendly and willing.

It's more like hiring an Australian than a Norlander. They are good at mucking in.

Norland Nursery Training College

Norland is synonymous with the trained nanny. It was the world's first nursery nurse training college, founded in 1892. It is to be found at Denford Park near Hungerford, a gracious and imposing Georgian house set in its own 150-acre park. There are tennis courts, a chapel, an outdoor swimming pool and beautiful views of the Downs. It is the only residential college of which most people have ever heard.

Norland has the largest number of graduates – 65 to 70 each year. There are toddler and baby care units for 30 children between three months and three years.

A unique feature is that the students receive 24-hour experience of residential child care. Members of the public who are going away on holiday can pay to leave their children up to the age of seven at the college. The children who come to stay have their own small rooms. Each child is cared for constantly by one student nursery nurse; the aim is to give him a secure one-to-one relationship for the duration of his stay. She has a bed in his room. The visiting children also have a big playroom, a quiet sitting room and a dining room. They play in the gardens, sandpits and climbing frames. It is designed to be as much like home life as possible and seems to succeed.

For those who may wish to consider this means of obtaining temporary child care, sending a child to Norland for a week *all in* costs about the same as a temporary nanny. Bonded mothers may throw a fit at the whole idea of abandoning their offspring thus, but those parents who do it are pleased with the service.

Another feature of Norland is the Maiden Scheme. This was created in 1904 to help young women unable to afford the training. It is organized so that two to three girls are able to contribute to their fees by doing light housework for a year. If they show signs of promise they then join the formal course and pay reduced fees.

It is striking that Norland seems to head the field in its thinking and teaching on the subject of nannying in the private sector.

Students are taught about child psychology and employer/ employee relationships in depth, in fact, everything to do with the art of living in someone else's house. Their craft and needlework standards are high too – a smocked garment, a rag doll and clothes, a wall-hanging and competence in knitting are all compulsory.

Impressions of the students were favourable. They seemed friendly and busy and fun – not in the least the type to be described as starchy or stuck-up – just nice, normal, girls going about their well-ordered routines. There is a residue of sour grapes about criticisms – often from agencies whose offices they do not frequent or from employers who cannot afford their salaries.

Towards the end of the second year students sit the Norland Final Exam and they also take the NNEB Certificate and the Royal Society of Health Diploma of Nursery Nursing.

All students spend three months in a hospital working in the paediatric, maternity or special care baby units. They aren't paid but stay at the hospital free of charge and they receive a meal allowance. Only when they have completed this term successfully do they qualify to receive the Norland Preliminary Certificate.

On graduating, students become probationers having passed all their exams including the final Norland Assessment. The Norland diploma and badge is only awarded to students who have completed 'nine months of satisfactory work as a Probationer Nurse in a private residential post approved by the Principal'. They can stay for longer than that with the family, though employers must raise her pay when she is fully qualified. The college suggests a minimum starting salary and it holds a copy of the contract of employment. There is no pussy-footing with Norlanders on tax and National Insurance (see page 332). They know just what the employer should be doing – so don't try it on and look foolish.

The probationer period is Norland's special invention and highlights its commitment to turning out nannies who are ready for and capable of the task – but only after they have had experience of working and living in a family for nearly a year. The most basic tenet for the Norland philosophy is that a trainee does not become a nanny just by passing her NNEB exam, which is only one of several hurdles. This is an entirely different attitude from the local authority courses. The probationary period is a clever way of avoiding employers' grumbles about newly qualified nannies.

The vast majority of Norland probationers go into private homes. The Principal, Mrs Louise Davis, says: 'The training was the first ever co-ordinated particularly for private homes and there will always be an emphasis on this. The self-contained nature of Norland College is such that each child care section is finely structured and disciplined. We control our own standards of practice in every area.' It is a big plus that any Norlander having been put through the mill 'will not normally expect to meet such demanding tasks in such a variety of settings again'.

Students are distinguished by brown bonnets, black for winter. The rest of the uniform is brown and beige. There is a college magazine called the *Norland Quarterly*. The Norland registry is over-subscribed and many employers get irate as they are apparently never eligible for a Norland nanny – and they are never told why either. Put yourself on the register months before you begin to need a Norland nanny and do not be at all surprised if you still fail to be offered one.

Mrs Davis has several children and employs Norland nannies so she is in the excellent situation of sampling whether her nannies practise what they are preached. Currently, she is the only principal who employs nannies. She is a dynamic, efficient person, who leaves a lasting impression of dedication to the college and its fine traditions. She has a clear vision of excellence and is an ideal representative of the college when she lectures elsewhere and abroad. As a true professional herself, with both feet firmly on the ground, she sees her job as instilling the virtues of application and common sense into her trainees.

A few employers and agencies comment:

They use the register for their first jobs. Agencies often do not see them until they are about 23. We find them excellent.

Norlanders think they are the bees' knees.

Not all Norlanders make fantastic nannies, though better educated and more mature than most. They have a stiffer upper lip.

I have never had a bad Norlander.

Princess Christian Training College for Nursery Nurses

The Princess Christian College was opened in Manchester in 1901 under the direct patronage of HRH the Princess Christian. She was born Helena and was Queen Victoria's fifth child. She married Prince Christian of Schleswig-Holstein. Princess Christian was much involved in many forms of charitable work. She was a founder member of the Red Cross in 1870 and set up Princess Christian's District Nurses in 1894. The Princess was keenly interested in the training college from the start through her involvement with The Gentlewomen's Employment Association.

Mrs Elsie Rigby took over as Principal from the redoubtable Miss McRae in 1990. Her previous career has been in managing services for children, particularly in the care of the under-fives. Mrs Rigby sees herself as building on the impressive reputation of the College and emphasizes excellence in the training of her students.

She says:

I want this College to meet the needs of the nineties when so many exciting things are happening in child care. Despite recession, many women are going back to work and there is a great demand for good quality nannies. I think the profession is beginning to be taken more seriously with the current shake up in training, and the new emphasis on post qualifying studies offer interesting opportunities for NNEBs.

Mrs Rigby is a confident judge of character and knows what she wants to see in her new students. 'Eye contact and body language I always watch because nannies must be able to communicate easily and, even by the age of eighteen, should display some sense of poise.'

There is a general feeling about the College that students are being treated as adults and adult behaviour is expected of them. Rules and restrictions are kept to a minimum and only imposed when strictly necessary. Mrs Rigby does not see herself as a pseudo mother or guardian but as a trainer. She comments: 'My first responsibility is to make sure that each individual gets the most out of a very high-quality course. Then I hope I am also a caring adult who is happy to give sound advice either personally or professionally.'

She has distinct views about the NNEB course, which her girls study: 'I feel that nursery nurses provide an almost unreplaceable service in this country. The standard of the NNEB course is improving and I think it is both demanding and testing of my students. Academically it should be better recognized.'

The College is, quite properly, reticent about the number of nannies who take jobs in royal households worldwide, but over the years there has been a good number. As with the two other residential colleges, there are ten posts available for every girl.

The building in Wilbraham Road, Fallowfield (a surburb of Manchester), is a Victorian monstrosity, but this is mitigated by the fact that it backs on to a pretty park with a lake, lawns and a pets' corner, ideal for the nursery children. Inside it is a charmless warren of corridors, lino and fire doors. Everything is spotlessly clean but not exactly cosy. The most striking feature of the building is the extensive security arrangements outside which are necessary in the area. The students in evidence gave the visitor a positive impression of being nice and neat and tidy.

The College takes 56 students a year. Students have the day nurseries for various age groups organized into three nursery units – a baby unit for nine babies aged six weeks to two years plus, and two others for the two to five age group. The uniform is brown, beige and cream. Like Chiltern, it consists of tabards, trousers, dresses and capes.

At least 95 per cent of the students become nannies. It is informative to listen to Mrs Rigby musing on their role:

The job of a nanny should not be underestimated. There are a wide variety of types of lives for nannies nowadays. My emphasis is on sharing the care of the child with the parent. There are enormous opportunities for travel and examining different cultures. While caring for a child, a nanny can get involved in a mass of community activities. They lead varied and useful lives and they have the great advantage of being able to improve their child care skills as they work.

The College has its own employment register and students are encouraged to use it. Agencies are regretful. Graduates are issued with a beautiful brown Testimonial Book franked with the College imprimatur. There are blank pages so that future employers' references can be stuck in. 'They should be regarded as the passport to your career and should be kept safely. They cannot, under any circumstances, be replaced', the girls are warned. Employers are required to fill in an official testimonial form. It is then stamped by the college, which keeps a copy and the nanny is sent the original. Truly a reference worth its salt.

The five-year badge is awarded to nannies who have totalled five years nannying, though they may have been qualified, say, eight years.

Employment agencies and employers say of Princess Christian nannies:

We can't get enough of them. They are down to earth, cosy and informal.

Fabulous.

The London Montessori Centre

The London Montessori Centre is quite unlike any of the residential colleges, but almost as unlike a local authority college NNEB course. It is a fee-paying daily NNEB college situated in the heart of London, just off Oxford Street. Its unique feature is that students not only achieve the NNEB certificate but also take the Montessori Childcare and Teaching Diploma, for which they study simultaneously. Normally it would be a one-year course.

It is an expensive option, costing more than the residential colleges and there are no board and lodging thrown in. Maybe it costs more because it is not a charitable trust like the others, but a profit-making concern. 'You get a very good course', says a Montessori teacher there. 'It is special to us.' Not only an excellent course, but two qualifications for the price of one.

Dr Maria Montessori (1870–1952) had both a medical and academic background and was the inventor of the Montessori teaching method. When Maria Montessori taught, children sat in rows and learned by rote. She felt that they would respond better with more imaginative and indirect methods. She introduced a planned environment where a child could grow and learn by using her own patented devices, for example, counting beads in blocks of tens, hundreds and even a thousand. Through touching and counting the golden beads the child is introduced to abstract arithmetic.

There are also unique Montessori teaching aids, like the famous Pink Tower with its fitting cubes, the Geometric Tray to help a child identify shapes, the graded cylinders, beautifully turned in wood, and sandpaper letters a child can handle. Music and dance and nature – all have their place in her syllabus. Her dictum was that the teacher should not abandon the child to total free play.

A Montessori teacher does not instruct in a straightforward sense, but rather directs children's natural activities so that they can learn spontaneously. With patience and the gentlest of guidance, she leads her children to explore and discover a carefully structured classroom, take from it what they need, and lets them develop stage by stage at their own pace. Today this kind of enlightened 'voyage of discovery' type of teaching is the norm; every nursery school, state and private, has plagiarized some aspects of Montessori teaching.

The NNEB course at the Montessori Centre was started in 1984. Mrs Lesley Britton, Principal of the Centre, was prompted to introduce the course by her experience of worldwide travel and watching how everywhere women want to work and are demanding better standards of child care and education. One of the main reasons for the course's particular success was the excellence of its placements. This currently remains a major strength.

The College has a good scholarly atmosphere; it vibrates with activity and is full of Montessori teachers and students. There is a Montessori Nursery School on the premises, so NNEB students, alongside students from other Montessori teaching courses, can visit the school to do their 'observations' and some of their training.

Students live in hostels or YWCAs, many of them come from outside London and some are from abroad. One or two per year get grants. There is no room to provide any sort of social life within the college. 'But because it is a small group in a small college all the students know they have access to us and they have lots of personal contact and involvement,' said one of the NNEB course tutors.

Correspondence courses are available world wide in the Montessori method. In one year workshops were held in Penang, Bahrain, London, three in the USA, three in Africa, Trinidad and Malaysia.

The Isle College, Wisbech

The Isle College, Wisbech, does not fall into any neat category. It is a residential course for some students; it does not do the NNEB; it only lasts a year and there are those who say that its graduates are 'as good as Norlanders'. It has an intake of 20 students, of whom more than half are usually in residence. The college recruits nationally and some students get local authority grants and some pay for themselves.

The Principal of the College is Mrs Sandra Ward, who has taught in nursery and primary schools and has employed nannies from the college in the past.

The course is designed to train students to be sole charge nannies in private homes. They study for the College's own certificate, which is externally assessed. They also do in a single year a range of other courses: NAMCW level two, City and Guilds Communication level one and St John's Ambulance First Aid and Care of the Sick.

Mrs Ward comments:

Apart from emphasizing the role of the nanny in the home, I have also introduced swimming, riding and languages to widen the course. We also encourage them to take driving lessons.

The students have local placements and a number of employers go back to this little known college again and again for dedicated nannies.

Other Qualifications

It is increasingly necessary for employers to acquaint themselves with a whole maze of acronyms other than NNEB. Many an applicant for a nanny job now has various letters and certificates to proffer the bewildered employer. There *is* no equivalent in this country to the NNEB, as many people fondly imagine in their ads in *The Lady* when they advertise for 'NNEB or equivalent'.

Employment agencies are just as bemused: 'There are new courses arriving every day.' But most of them say that it is a pity that many parents only know of the NNEB, especially the first time mums.

An editor of *Nursery World* says:

We find the maze of different qualifications for child care very confusing.

And if *we* find it hard to keep up with the latest offering, goodness knows how a school leaver can find out what to do. It would be really useful if some independent body were set up as a clearing house for information and guidance.

Let's start at the bottom.

Youth Training

The Training and Enterprise Council (known as the Tec) sponsors school leavers on its Youth Training. It provides them with two years' work experience in various businesses and trades which gives them a better chance of getting a job at the end. They receive a training allowance financed by the Tec (everyone is careful not to call it pay), roughly equivalent to what they would receive on social security.

Thousands of 16- and 17-year-olds join Youth Training to do 1,001 different sorts of jobs. Most of their time is spent in 'on the job training', learning different aspects of various trades such as building, catering, warehousing, hairdressing, retailing, clerical work etc. There is also 13 weeks' 'off the job' training in a year often taught by the local technical college. Some of the schemes enable trainees to work in 'the community' and that's where nannying comes in.

The Tec hands over the administration and organization of courses to 'managing agents' which may be a large multi-national or a company set up to do nothing else but organize YT students. All over the country managing agents organize courses on behalf of the Tec for which they receive a fee.

It is impossible to generalize about the contents of a community and/or health care course on which a YT student may have been. Her experience *may* have been relevant to nannying, but the employer should not expect much. Depending on the course, she may have spent time with a childminder, or in a public or private day nursery. She also might have learned something from her work with the elderly, the sick, and the physically and mentally handicapped.

There is a City and Guilds (see page 168) course called Practical Care, referred to as course number 356, which is aimed specifically at YT trainees. YT trainees elect to do the City and Guilds 356 course in community care and receive a C & G certificate at the end of it as well as their YT Certificate. From the employer of nannies' point of view, a girl who has learned to help bath an elderly man, organized a game of cards for a group of pensioners at a day centre, and has helped dress and feed someone who is mentally handicapped, should have more idea of the demands and practicalities of child care than the school leaver with no experience at all.

Students who have completed the two-year YT course receive an official YT Certificate which gives prospective employers some idea of how well the student has performed during the course. However, the Tec counsels managing agents that 'statements on the Certificate should only indicate what has been achieved and *not* failures to achieve'. Suspect any other certificate (unless it is bona fide like the City & Guilds Certificate) that a YT graduate may have been issued with at the end of the course. For example, one managing agent (a college) was reported to be offering applicants a nursery nursing training as part of YT and saying that on completing the course they could put NN (Dip) after their name. This sounds like an abuse of YT.

CCC and CPVE
The Child Care Course (CCC) is two years long and can be studied at school, alongside GCSEs. The first year gives some practical training.

The Certificate of Pre-Vocational Education can be studied at college or school and it can get a student on an NNEB course in lieu of GCSEs.

PRCC and PSCC
The Pre-Residential Child Care Course (PRCC) and the Pre-School Care Course (PSCC) are like NAMCW (see page 168) but they last only a year. As one agent says, 'A girl who has done these courses usually has the right sort of attitude for nannying. These courses give a good basic general grounding. If the girls have common sense and are good with children, after three years they may be as good as an NNEB.' In other words, according to some, the intensity of the theory taught on any of these courses all comes out in the wash.

With the PRCC and the PSCC a girl is sought after by those caring for mentally handicapped children and handicapped young adults. She can also be a good bet for a mother's help.

The Pre-School Playgroups Leadership Courses
The Pre-School Playgroups Leaders' Foundation is a one-year, evening class which teaches young people about children's play and recreation. Students' experience includes hospitals and playgrounds for the handicapped. It gives a diploma which is highly thought of by employment agencies, particularly for work with older children. The Pre-School Playgroups Leaders' Further Course is a three-term course for those who have done the foundation course.

NAMCW
The National Association of Maternal and Child Welfare is an increasingly popular two-year course among would-be nannies who may not have been accepted on, or applied too late for, an NNEB course. It is generally considered lower grade than the NNEB. Its rating *vis-à-vis* a City & Guilds qualification is debatable: some think it is superior; others think it less good. These conclusions are based on an individual's performance and it very much depends on the girl's personality as to whether she is a good or bad advert for whichever course.

Some students leave after one year and are awarded the NAMCW Certificate but if they stay on the second year and take Parts II and III, they receive the NAMCW Diploma.

Someone who has an NAMCW Certificate is to be considered a 'young nanny' requiring supervision until she becomes experienced (similar to a sensible employer's approach to a newly qualified NNEB). She is one up from a mother's help. Those with the full diploma are taught 'more than they need to become a nanny', as one college tutor reports. Certainly, they may have attended a good basic course, but will have received very little relevant practical training.

It is often available at local council colleges, as is the NNEB. A girl will probably gain a place on the course with as little as a couple of GCSEs. 'They should be highish GCSEs, because otherwise they can't cope with the exams,' says a tutor. 'They have to be 16, they must demonstrate a "proven commitment to children", meaning babysitting, and they should be practical and sensible', comments another course tutor.

City and Guilds
The City and Guilds of London Institute devises courses which can be taught all over the country in Further Education colleges and the

like. It has been providing education in practical skills like catering, painting, decorating and upholstery for years. Trainees must be at least 16 and courses usually last for two years. At the end of it, the successful trainees receive a City and Guilds Certificate. These are valued in both the private and public sectors.

A potential nanny might have done the City and Guilds Family and Community Care Course, number 331, which combines college study and work experience. The numbers attending this and related Courses (3521 – Community Care; 3241 – Caring for Children; 356 – Practical Care) are rising annually and have doubled in the last few years to between 10,500 and 17,500 people (exact figures are hard to assess). The advantage of these courses is that they qualify holders for other caring jobs with the old and disabled as opposed to concentrating just on work with the under-fives, unlike the NNEB.

PCSC

The Preliminary Certificate in Social Care (PCSC), a two-year full-time course, is approved by the Central Council for Education and Training in Social Work and is available to 16- to 19-year-olds. The CCETSW says, 'These courses allow young people the opportunity to learn about work in the social services including work with children and to see what career opportunities there are.' A tutor describes it as a 'foundation course for people who want to work in residential care'.

B/Tec

The Business and Technician Education Council, known by everyone as B/Tec, has introduced its National Diploma in Caring Services (Nursery Nursing) and another one in Caring Services (Social Care). The courses have been going only since the late 1980s but are proving popular. Diplomas are awarded after a full time, two year course. There is also a Certificate in the same discipline which is awarded after a two-year *part-time* course, which has the same value as a Diploma but where the practical experience gained from the student's job makes up for the more theoretical course of the Diploma.

It has to be said that B/Tec's Diploma is already a 'first choice' for employers as against a candidate with the NNEB certificate. However, it won't take away the vast majority of NNEB prospective students even if it was able to, as it appeals to the more academic

16-year-old who wants to do practical training but is capable of 'A' levels. The Diploma is regarded as equivalent to two 'A' levels, unlike the NNEB exam, which does not count as anything, though this should change shortly (see below). Unlike the NNEB, where students do not have to show any academic qualifications in theory at least, four GCSEs are the minimum for acceptance on the Diploma, with English Language being obligatory. Some B/Tec course tutors say that they like Maths and/or Biology GCSE as well.

The best thing about B/Tec students, as members of the crack regiment of nursery nursing, is that their existence has made the NNEB more introspective and more aware of its shortcomings. The whole 'care' training industry, including nursery nursing, is in the melting pot because the National Council for Vocational Qualifications is in the process of introducing seismic changes which are unlikely to leave any examining body unchanged, including both B/Tec and the NNEB.

One tutor says, 'The great thing about the B/Tec is that it enables students to keep their options open. We find that about half go off to be nursery nurses or nannies and the rest go on to higher education for social work or nursing.'

Further Qualifications

Your nanny may want to leave you to take the one further training course tailor-made for the NNEB graduate with a minimum of two years' experience as a nursery nurse. This is the CPQS (the Certificate of Post Qualifying Studies). It is available at a few colleges and there is stiff competition for places. This sandwich course is made up of six 'modules', each consisting of 60 hours of class work and 60 hours of project and private study.

Those who have already completed it say that they enjoyed greater job satisfaction having studied some areas of child care in detail (e.g. autistic children, problem parents and children and their needs of a day nursery), and it also increased their chances of promotion and better pay.

Some nannies and nursery nurses want to do the Certificate of Qualification in Social Work (CQSW). This is the professional qualification for social workers. The minimum age for starting this four-year degree course is 20 and it is open to anyone. The Certificate in Social Service (CSS) is a two-to-three-year course of a lower calibre than the CQSW.

8

Au Pairs, Mother's Helps and All Sorts

Part 1: Au Pairs

This section deals primarily with au pairs, who work part time, but as there are many foreign girls who work full time, i.e. they are mother's helps, inevitably it covers both categories of child care. It is relevant to anyone wishing to employ a foreigner whose mother tongue isn't English.

'Au pair' is from the French meaning 'at par'. According to the Oxford Dictionary, it is 'applied to an arrangement between two parties by which mutual services are rendered without consideration of money payment'. In other words, the two services are equal or balanced. One of the earlier references in print to an au pair arrangement was in the 1920s where a German woman lived with a family and in return taught the children her language.

Today an 'au pair' girl receives pocket money as well as board, as it is reckoned that so many hours' work a day cannot equal a straight swap of bed and board.

The chief characteristic of an au pair girl is that she is not British. She works part time and she usually goes to 'English as a Foreign Language' (EFL) classes to learn English. Some employers talk about having an 'English au pair' but this is a confusing use of the term. What they mean is that they have an English *part-time* mother's help (see page 196). The confusion comes about because many foreigners are mother's helps. They tend to stay longer than an au pair (for nine months to a year), and don't go to classes, or go in the evenings if they are keen.

A great many au pairs are Roman Catholics, as they come from the Catholic countries of France, Italy, Spain and Portugal. Some Dutch, German, Swiss and Austrian girls are Catholic too. This may have no significance at all to the family that employs them.

Many girls are lapsed Catholics or have chucked entirely. Others still believe and are keen to go to Mass on Sunday. Some employers choose Catholic au pairs specifically because they hope that the chances of them being morally well-behaved will be higher. Sometimes they are right and sometimes they are wrong. Certainly a *practising* Catholic is the best bet for these employers.

Au pairs have been a popular form of home help and child care since the war. One guestimate is that over 60,000 of them a year come and stay with British families. We are lucky to have access to this cheap form of labour in such quantity (unlike other European countries). The reason is because everyone wants to learn English – the international language.

Au pair plus

This is a term that has been made up by employers and employment agents to explain why the au pair is working more than the Home Office recommended maximum of five hours a day, six days a week. Some agencies offer to place a girl on an 'au pair plus' arrangement. In such cases some girls may work 36 to 40 hours a week.

Asked to comment on 'au pair plus', the Home Office says, 'It is against the spirit of the law for an au pair to work more than 30 hours a week and we don't approve.' However, most employers don't feel guilty about going for an 'au pair plus' if it is sanctioned by the agency, the girl is happy and if she is fairly paid for the extra hours. Since most of the girls who are 'au pair' are also members of the EEC and can therefore work as many hours as they like, in most cases it is not an issue anyway.

Thousands of responsible employers, and irresponsible ones, choose this type of employment because it means they get help in the mornings – breakfast, lunch, and again for an hour or so in the evening around the children's bath and bed time.

For many employers who want to spend as little as possible on a home help who has nearly full-time duties, the au pair plus is the most cost-effective choice.

Demi-au pair

This phrase, meaning 'half au pair', has been made up, like 'au pair plus', to describe the au pair who receives board and lodging and a very little pocket money for a few hours' work. In a sense

172

this arrangement is closer to the spirit of the Home Office guidelines than the 'au pair plus', as the girl has plenty of time in theory to pursue her studies and her 'pocket money' is just that.

Some employers don't want five or even four hours of work a day from their au pair. They need someone to organize the children's breakfast and school rush, do an hour or so of housework a day and two nights' babysitting a week. Thus they like to pay a few pounds a week for about three hours' work a day, perhaps only for the weekdays. So long as the au pair is fully aware of what type of job she is taking on, and has some money of her own to supplement the paltry sum, then the demi-au pair arrangement is not exploitative as such.

Unfortunately, all too often, the girl doesn't know that she will not be able to see the sights and keep herself in toothpaste on her tiny wage and she may think that this is a standard au pair deal. The other problem is that unscrupulous employers describe the job as 'demi-au pair' in order to pay the minimum, when in fact it turns out to be a three-quarters au pair job.

Summer au pair

Agencies (see page 297) are happy to provide foreign girls for two to three months at a time, usually in the summer holidays. Many families with children find a bit of extra help useful during July and August. The au pair goes on holiday with them and has a much greater chance of being 'part of the family' than she does during term time. She also sees more of the British Isles, and/or even better, may experience a sunny spot in Spain, France, Greece or wherever for a couple of weeks.

Mothers complain that just when the girl has got the hang of the family and her duties, she returns home. Others persuade her to stay on into the autumn with them. Agencies get cross, understandably, when a family doesn't pay them anything extra for a summer au pair who ends up staying six months or a year.

Which foreigner may work here?
Non-EEC and non-Commonwealth nationals
Foreign girls who are not in the European Community or the Commonwealth who come to the UK to do any kind of work for remuneration must apply for a work permit and in most cases will find it hard to get one. Thus for example, Brazilian, American,

Mexican, Japanese or Chilean nationals, who do not have a work permit and are full- or part-time mother's helps, are 'illegals'; they are breaking the law under the 1971 Immigration Act. This does not stop them finding work with British families without difficulty.

Many non-EEC and non-Commonwealth nationals have little or no chance of obtaining a work permit, but thousands of them, particularly in the big cities, work in hotels, restaurants, shops and pubs as domestic servants and as full- and part-time mother's helps. Many of them enrol in 'English as a Foreign Language' classes or other educational pursuits which enable them to have their stay extended without much trouble by the Home Office.

Most employers of Brazilians, Chileans, Mexicans and Filipinas who cannot get work permits report that they don't have much trouble with the authorities. If their mother's help has signed on at a local college and can show the Home Office that she is registered for so many hours a week to study, there isn't usually much difficulty in getting her passport stamped for a further period. Some foreigners take a trip abroad when their 'leave to remain', as the Home Office calls it, is about to expire. They re-enter a few weeks later and often are allowed to enter for another six months.

The police require that non-British nationals allowed into the country (including EEC and Commonwealth citizens) must pay a fee to register after six months, whether they are working or not. They need to take their passport and two passport-sized photographs to their local police station.

European Community nationals
European Community nationals are admitted into Britain initially for six months and can do whatever work they like; they do not have to procure a work permit.

Many nationals of the EEC, even though they are free to work in this country without restriction, enter under the 'au pair arrangement'. The scheme is of special value for those who are *not* EEC nationals but live in Western Europe (like the Norwegians, Swedes, Icelanders, Maltese, Cypriots and Turks). Under the scheme these nationals are allowed to come to the UK and improve their English while staying with, and doing some part-time work for, an English-speaking family.

Spain and Portugal joined the EEC in the 1980s, but until they become full members in 1993 their nationals cannot get a work permit as a matter of course. Thus their young women rely currently on the 'au pair arrangement' to gain entry into the UK for any length of time.

The exact wording of the Immigration Act concerning au pairs runs thus:

'Au Pair' is an arrangement under which an unmarried girl age 17 to 27 inclusive, and without dependants, who is a national of any member state of the European Community, Andorra, Austria, Cyprus, the Faroes, Finland, Greenland, Iceland, Liechtenstein, Malta, Monaco, Norway, San Marino, Sweden, Switzerland, Turkey and Yugoslavia may come to the United Kingdom to learn the English language, and to live for a time as a member of an English speaking family . . . a girl admitted under an 'au pair' arrangement has no claim to stay in the United Kingdom in some other capacity.

When the immigration officer is satisfied that an 'au pair' arrangement has been made, he may admit the passenger for a period of up to 12 months with a prohibition of her taking employment. If a passenger has previously spent time in the United Kingdom as an 'au pair' girl, she may be admitted for a further period as an 'au pair' girl, but the total aggregate period should not exceed two years.

Note that the Immigration Act is sexist, young men cannot enter this country on the au pair arrangement. In fact, there are a number of foreign boy students to be found in London who look after children in return for board and lodging.

The Home Office guidelines supplementary to the Act on the au pair arrangement (which it will send you) say firmly that an au pair:

is not a domestic servant but may help in the house for *up to* [our italics] five hours a day for pocket money. Suitable tasks would be light housework and taking care of the children. She should have one day each week completely free and she should be free to attend language classes and religious services if she wishes . . .

The guidelines point out that the light household duties which the au pair does as part of the 'arrangement' are not regarded as employment.

Commonwealth country nationals
Nationals of a Commonwealth country receive special treatment.

They can work outside the work permit system under the 'Working Holidaymaker' scheme. A Commonwealth national like, for example, an Australian, a New Zealander or a Canadian, who is aged 17 to 27, can enter the country on the Holidaymaker scheme.

The scheme allows them to stay in the UK up to an aggregate period of two years on the condition they have sufficient funds to return home, do not intend to have recourse to public funds (i.e. will not claim social security) and wish to do some paid work. The scheme says that their employment is meant to be incidental to an extended holiday in this country. In other words, it sanctions Australians and New Zealand girls taking work as mother's helps for short periods as part of their Grand World Tour.

Exploitation
Many employers do not know about the Home Office guidelines on au pairs and do not want to find out.

Many employment agencies are vague or inaccurate about the number of hours recommended. In effect they encourage exploitation by their talk of 'about five hours' or 'six hours'. They shouldn't give employers leeway to push up the hours to six or six and a half. The net result is that the au pair can be, and often is, gravely exploited. Just asking her to do, for example, an extra hour a day, six days a week, pushes her weekly hours up to 36 hours and she is an au pair plus without any of the 'plus' money. And thousands of au pairs are grossly underpaid for the number of hours they work.

The trouble is that hundreds of au pairs arrive, usually in London, with no contacts or friends, and take the first job they are offered simply to get a roof over their heads. They go and stay in hostels like the YMCA or the German Centre but, because they have little money, they do not 'shop around' much. Even the cost of going to interviews in Greater London adds up. If a mother offers them a job, they usually take it. They may have liked the sound of another job but it is a risky business hanging on in hopes that the family will choose them rather than someone else.

Another problem is that too many employers make the job sound a lot more agreeable than it is. They say airily, 'Oh and then there is some housework, mostly hoovering really. I'll tell you about that if you come to us.'

Prospective employers use euphemisms and weasel words which merely sketch in the girl's duties without spelling them out. An employer would be less likely to indulge in this bad habit if she was interviewing an English girl, but because the foreigner misses subtle use of the language, she is unlikely to challenge the exact meaning of, for example, 'some housework, mostly hoovering really'. Having said this, many mothers do mean just that – hoovering and not much more. For many, however, this seemingly innocent phrase is another way of saying, 'Well, we have a 20-room house and while the children are at school I expect you to dust, hoover, wipe, tidy, straighten, spit, polish, plump up, fetch, wash, dry, iron, sweep, sew, not to mention chop, boil, steam, fry, grill, wash-up, dry-up – you name it, Cinderella.'

Parents forget to mention that they will expect her to walk the labrador twice a day on the Common. They don't say that the two step-children come and stay for a large part of the holidays and she'll be looking after them too. They play down the things they want her to do. They describe the job in such a way that it sounds quite leisured when in fact she is on the go non-stop. They don't say, understandably, that they are thinking of splitting up. So the poor girl is perplexed by the icy atmosphere and cryptic conversation whenever He is around.

Some talk about 'lots of free time' but this can just not happen or not often enough. Many au pairs take literally the phrase 'and of course you'll be one of the family', and are hurt and feel left out when it becomes clear that she is 'one of the family' on duty, and a lodger in the top room when she is not.

One phrase that employers take literally and most au pairs don't know about is the notorious 'mucking in'. It is a useful catch-all which employers use constantly. What many employers mean when they use it is that they expect the au pair to roll up her sleeves and do everything she is asked to do with a good grace.

Employers like to think they are pleasant, caring people, and particularly so when they are looking for live-in help. A great many are. A big proportion, once they have hooked the girl, forget, often, about all their good intentions to give her a reasonable time. These self-occupied types are in a hurry, have their own worries, and don't really want to know whether she enjoys their hearth and home.

If au pairs are asked to do long hours caring for many children for too little money, some of them leave. Others decide to stick out their six months with the devil they know. They put up with a lot more than other untrained carers, and console themselves by being able to visit a few tourist sights and enjoy themselves in their free time meeting friends and going to discos.

Employers of nannies and British mother's helps have to be a lot more careful and considerate, otherwise these girls will leave. An employer often gets away with cutting corners with a foreign girl.

Au pairs are the most exploited group of in-home child carers. They come from abroad, their grasp of the language is often minimal and it takes them a while to compare the arrangements that other au pairs have. They do not stay long anyway so it isn't worth their while to find a better job and hand in their notice to the old battle axe. Human nature being as selfish as it is, the result is that many, many employers expect their au pairs to work more hours and have much greater responsibility for children, housework and animals, than they should.

In an effort to reduce the numbers of exploitative employers, many agencies emphasize the necessity of the au pair to do *light housework* only, and the need for her to be treated as a daughter of

---

Au pair grumbles

According to *Das Au-Pair-Buch* (see Bibliography), au pair preoccupations include:

- Wanting a simple written work schedule
- Wanting to have a specific number of working hours
- Knowing exactly when 'time off' is
- Not being given plenty of notice when asked to babysit
- Being given too much responsibility when both parents work
- Having too much involvement with the children instead of doing the job *with* the mother
- Not being allowed to take enough part in family life
- Feeling isolated because the family lives somewhere remote with bad public transport

---

Employers' grumbles

Employers, while agreeing that au pairs are good value and not much trouble, voice the following complaints:

- Their difficulties speaking, reading and understanding the language
- The fact that conversation with them can be tiring and an uphill struggle
- The fact that many of them are not domesticated ('Does her mother do *everything*?' wails an employer)
- The way they break machines
- Their lack of initiative, their difficulty in adapting
- Their different cultural habits and mannerisms

the house, and, as the Home Office guidelines say, not as a servant. Agencies also remind prospective employers that the au pair may also need help finding English classes. Making these points enables the agencies to remonstrate more effectively with erring employers who do ask their 'slaves' to do too much.

Au pair considerations
Social status

Many employers are chastised by agencies and au pairs, quite rightly, for their off-hand approach to the girl in question. Because au pairs are young and usually new to this country and the family is, in effect, *in loco parentis*, they must be treated as social equals.

Nannies do not have quite the same status, though many families attempt to give it them and a fraction succeed. Thus an employer can say without guilt to a nanny or English or Australian mother's help, 'Could you give yourself supper in the evenings or eat with the children at 6 pm? And please, can you vacate the communal areas like the sitting room at night as me and my husband need a bit of peace and quiet together? – thanks.' With a professional nanny, an employer should not have to say any of this; the nanny will just melt at dusk.

There are countless instances of less professional nannies who should know better who manage to hang around in the evening.

Time and again polite employers grind their teeth but still find it difficult to be direct and say bluntly 'Please go elsewhere.' In contrast, with an au pair the much-used phrase 'one of the family' does have to mean that to a greater extent than when used somewhat euphemistically with a nanny.

Remember that the point of coming to the UK for the au pair is that she wishes to improve her English and wants to practise on you. Care of your home and children are a means to an end as far as she is concerned. She must have an opportunity to talk to you and the conventional place for this is around the supper table. Because she is on a par with a teenage daughter she expects to eat with the family and no self-respecting employer can deny her this.

Many employers try to avoid this duty by encouraging the au pair to be independent in the evenings. They let her catch up on her English conversation during the day when sorting the dirty washing with mum. Some girls are not particularly keen to have to make stilted conversation while masticating their hostess's idea of *boeuf bourgignon*. Others are tactful and know that hubby and wifey yearn to have a moan about the office, the size of the gas bill this quarter and what their darling Rosie got up to today at school, *alone*. These sensitive souls let them get on with it and take a tray upstairs.

Some employers, often new to the world of au pairs, are admirably conscientious about fulfilling their role as hostess with the mostest in a foreign land to the extent that the au pair is always in tow, even when they have friends to supper.

One couple was amused but slightly put off when their friends' Belgian au pair joined what they thought was going to be an intimate evening. 'First she had supper with us, so we all had to take turns in being polite and try to extract a sentence from her. Then she joined us in the sitting room afterwards and sat there like a lemon. By this time we had all given up trying and just ignored her, but it wasn't good.' Presumably after one or two more of such evenings the employer reviewed her generous 'one of us' policy.

Many employers are good about eating with the au pair if they are on their own, but say firmly if they are having friends that the au pair must eat in her room or early so that she is not queuing up for the fridge when her hostess is trying to stop the mayonnaise curdling. A good litmus test on this sort of issue is to ask yourself what would you tell your teenager to do? Many parents would ask them not to join the boring oldies for supper and say that they were to steer clear of the kitchen after 7 pm because Mum will be flapping over the flan.

The language problem

The big problem *all the time* with employing foreign girls is one of communication, which is why a few specify 'good English' in their advertisements. Some au pairs can understand barely a word of English, let alone speak it coherently.

The first-time employer of an au pair with poor English has to remember to speak slowly and to *show* her how to do things rather than just tell her about the ironing, the washing etc. The quickest way she can pick up her household duties is to watch how you do them. Always remember not to give too many instructions at one time. The chances are she will concentrate for the first bit and not have a clue about the second half, and of course she is likely to say yes, she has understood all you said.

One couple went to the theatre and rang home in the interval to find out if the Danish au pair was coping OK. 'The children all right?,' they asked, 'Ya,' she said. 'No problems?' 'Ya.' 'Is the house on fire?' 'Ya, ya' came the enthusiastic reply.

Explain to her the potential seriousness of her saying 'Ya', she has understood, when she hasn't. The instructions may involve something important about the child she is looking after, like the correct cleaning and mixing of bottles, or the temperature of his bath, or how to clean a dirty bottom properly. She may *say* she understands your run-down of what you suggest she does if the house does go up in flames. Make sure that she does. This doesn't mean she will perform as you instructed her in an emergency, but it may increase the odds. At least you can say to yourself after some ghastly happening that you had run through the drill with her properly, and feel better about it.

Some mothers are relaxed about the communication problem of au pairs. They hope that through signs and demonstration the language barrier will be surmounted, and it often is. By the end of the girl's stay, she should be able to understand most domestic vocabulary.

Others find all this too time-consuming and exhausting,

especially if they have more than one child. One mother called a halt to an interview almost immediately. A speechless Spanish girl had brought a friend to act as an interpreter. The mother told them both briskly that the interpreter wasn't going to live with them as well, so that the arrangement would never work.

The responsible employer who does not speak English as a first language should make this clear to the employment agency and any au pair she interviews. As quoted above the Home Office requires that au pairs stay in an English-speaking family, but in practice an au pair can find herself listening all the time to Chinese, Japanese, Hebrew and Arabic among other languages. One au pair told us that her first job in the UK was with a charming but completely incomprehensible Chinese family living in Windsor.

A foreign girl working for a non-English speaking family in London, for example, may encounter extraordinary difficulties with language, and diet and custom as well. Unusual dietary habits are rare but it can be something of a shock for an au pair used to smörgasbord to eat nothing but Kosher or Chinese food. She may also resent being asked to comply with eating and cleansing rituals if she has not been told about them before joining the family.

Classes

The au pair expects her employer to do a little homework on her behalf about her 'English as a Foreign Language' (EFL) classes. Go straight to the local yellow pages and look under Colleges.

The local Technical or Further Education college is a good bet for EFL courses, though the further away from a metropolis, the less likely it is that the college will run such a course. In London and towns like Brighton and Bournemouth, popular with foreign students, there are plenty of privately run language schools which charge commercial fees. Some have special cheap au pair courses. State colleges, particularly in London, are hugely popular because the fees are so inexpensive. In order to get a place it is often necessary to register the term before.

If your au pair or mother's help is able to get a place at a state college usually she can study for two hours a day either in the morning or the afternoon. If she is from the EEC she will pay very little per term. If she is non-EEC the fee will be much higher.

Money

The Home Office's latest guideline is £32 a week for an au pair's pocket money for 30 hours worked. This is set above the average so that it doesn't date too quickly. There is a huge discrepancy in what au pairs are paid. Some are genuine slave labour and receive under £20 a week.

London employers pay £28–£30 a week and more, depending on hours. Payment varies depending on the demands of the job. An au pair with one small child to look after could expect to receive less than an au pair with three children under six. An au pair who joins a family that has a cleaner may well find that she receives a bit less pocket money because she doesn't have to do much housework.

Pay drops noticeably the further from central London the au pair's family lives. Employers in the suburbs pay a bit less. Likewise, in the country, employers expect to pay an au pair less than the top rate, though often living there, unless she loves fields and views, is much less of an enticing proposition for her.

An au pair is not paid enough for her to have to pay National Insurance Contributions and tax, though she is free to make voluntary contributions, and this makes sense if her EEC country has a reciprocal agreement about social security payments with the UK. If she wishes to pay National Insurance, get in touch with the local Social Security Office about how she goes about this. Not surprisingly, 99.99 per cent of au pairs do not want to do such a thing.

Time off

By now readers must be clear that au pairs are meant to work a maximum of five hours a day. They must have one *full* day off a week. Many employers are naughty about giving the au pair a complete day off a week, and many shift about the full day off depending on their needs. This is all right within reason, but it isn't fair if an employer tells her on a Saturday that she can have next Wednesday off as the parents have organized a squash session for Sunday morning and she'll be needed to see to the children. As with a nanny, an au pair can expect to be asked to babysit two nights a week on average and it is courteous to give each other ample warning when either of you intend to go out (see chapter 5).

An employer who wants her au pair on duty on quite a few Sundays must make this clear at the interview, saying that she can have a day off in the week instead. The employer must also reassure the girl if she practises a religion that she may take time off on the Sunday to worship. This way the au pair can make up her mind beforehand whether she is prepared not to be free when her friends are, and she is less likely to flounce out when messed-up weekends affect her social life.

Holidays

One of the advantages of au pairs is that if they stay only six months then they can't expect to receive any paid holiday and they don't. The rationale behind no paid holidays is that the au pair experience is not a job as such and it is part time anyway. For all that, a case could be made for some paid holiday after a six months' stint and some generous employers do that with a successful au pair in the form of a cash bonus when she leaves.

There is moral pressure on employers who hire an au pair for nine months and more to give some paid holiday as well as about two weeks of unpaid holiday. Good employers of foreign mother's helps who stay nine months to a year give them two to three weeks' paid holiday. Many employers do give au pairs unpaid leave during their stay, often at Christmas.

Perks

One of the few perks of being an au pair is that, if she is with a responsible family, it will show her the sights or at least tell her how to get to them and be pleased to hear all about it afterwards.

'Being nice to the au pair' can be a chore, but it shouldn't be shirked, if you feel that she would appreciate it. Some are highly organized and independent and, mercifully, their one idea is to escape from the family in their time off. Kind employers take her out and about with them on their outings. They take her to other people's parties, lunches, drinks and even weddings. They take her to the Tower of London and Alton Towers and Madame Tussaud's. Less kind employers rather hope the girl will get on with it off her own bat.

In London all this is less of a problem as it is there on her doorstep, after all. Some employers make up for five months of touristic neglect by treating the au pair to Chatsworth or

Blenheim in the rain or something else they want to do that they feel sure that she will enjoy too.

In the country even the less kind employers feel they should help out a bit as travelling to tourist spots and even the local town can be expensive and complicated. No employer wants a moping au pair and as with the nanny, enlightened self-interest pays. Au pairs can feel lost and homesick, especially if they have just arrived in the country. They shouldn't be left to vegetate. A bit of introducing to other local au pairs and mother's helps so that they have someone with whom to go for a walk or to a pub, or whatever, can make a huge difference to their contentment.

The children
Somewhat curiously, au pairs are associated in people's minds with housework rather than children. Perhaps it is because this is where she differs greatly from the nanny. The latter only brushes up against housework when it is linked to the children. The au pair cannot escape. Also, many parents choose the vastly cheaper au pair option when their brood have reached school age and they feel that their full-time nanny or mother's help is not needed any more. It may be also because women who hire au pairs when they have young children are around much more than they might be if they had a nanny. These mothers concern themselves with the children while the au pair does the chores.

Sole charge
Apart from the part time nature of an au pair's work, she is also very much less capable of 'sole charge' than the experienced or trained nanny.

Au pairs can only be an option for working parents if all the children are of school age. Then her time can be split into a breakfast/get them to school shift and a collect them from school, tea, bath and bed shift. This gives her the day to go to classes.

More and more au pairs find that the mother has some part-time work which she does somewhere else in the house while the au pair is in semi-sole charge. The mother is around and can appear if she hears yells and screams, or if she wants to see how the au pair is managing. Generally, the modern mother – working or not – tends to spend a lot less time working with the au pair looking after the children and doing the chores than she did in the past. Modern gadgets, machines and carpets have reduced the grind.

Many agencies warn mothers that an au pair should not be expected to be in sole charge much, and certainly not for long periods. In practice many of them are, and often for most of the time they are on duty.

Mothers should be aware that the quality of child care can be a problem with untrained girls whose prime aim is to live in a foreign country for a while; many of them are not interested in enhancing a baby's or a child's play. An au pair, like a nanny or a mother's help, can leave a baby lying in his cot for longer than you would and listen to her music for an hour or two, alone in the play room, with a toddler left to entertain himself.

It is also important to feel pretty confident she has the nous and competence to cope alone (see page 110 on Emergency Drill and page 123 on Sole Charge). However wonderful you think she is, remember that she is foreign and if the child was streaming blood or the house was burgled, she would be under more strain than a British mother's help or nanny.

Parents often underestimate the skill it takes to keep small children tearless for long periods. They have developed their technique over several years. They know the child very well, his little ways and how to deal with them. The au pair is unlikely to have looked after two children on her own for any length of time before. She is probably unskilled in her timing of when to feed, play, encourage a child to go the lavatory, and when to put him down to rest. Remember that her knowledge about what to do with a whingeing baby or child may be minimal.

Another aspect which isn't important until the children are over a year, is the need for the au pair to get on with, and talk to, her charges. It is far from ideal for a child aged between ten months and five years not to be able to practise his own language learning with an au pair who has pidgin English.

Many mothers don't expect an au pair whose English is not good to be able to read books to the children, or have those delightful discussions with three year-olds upwards about the mysteries of the universe – what is thunder and why is it so hot at the top of the house on a summer's day? Many parents of two to five year-olds give up having au pairs and foreign mother's helps for this reason. They don't want to risk their children's language development.

Loads of experienced employers with small children solve the problem pretty much by taking only the Norwegians, Swedes, Danes, the Dutch and the Germans. These girls usually speak good English so that they can converse with a child and read to him comfortably too. Some girls of these nationalities are bilingual and, ironically, speak better grammatical English than many English.

Travelling

Some agencies say that their clients will pay a girl's fare to and from Britain, but no employer should be expected to provide this perk. The odd generous family does so. One mother went so far as to pay an unseen Brazilian girl to fly from Rio to be her mother's help. Unfortunately the girl was a complete disaster and only stayed with the family six weeks.

It is sensible to give an au pair from abroad plenty of help and instruction about how best to get to her destination. Families should try to meet her at the airport or station. Apart from the courtesy, she is sure to be burdened with luggage. In London she can be asked to jump in a taxi and the employer can pay on her arrival. It is mean in the extreme to let a 17-year-old au pair arrive at Heathrow to be met by a message telling her to get to Elstree, an outer London suburb. There was no crisis at the girl's employer's home to warrant this behaviour, just a lack of warmth and helpfulness for which British hostesses of au pairs have a reputation.

What type of au pair?

There are two types of au pair and foreign mother's help. There is the sort you are most likely to want and the agencies certainly prefer to place. She is usually 18 or 19, and is fresh in every sense – new to the country, new to the language, new to adulthood, new to men and she may be someone who is still under the influence of a no-nonsense mother who 'knows what is best' for her daughter. This type of girl tends to want genuinely to improve her English and enrol in classes. She may be taking a year off before going on to some sort of further education, or to train for something like nursing. She is likely to get on with her parents and siblings and come from a stable background.

This is the old-fashioned, traditional sort of au pair. This type was the norm throughout the 1950s and 1960s. Then Britain joined the EEC in 1971 and this opened the door to the second type, the EEC national who is free to work in this country indefinitely in any capacity she chooses. This group chooses to live abroad for years rather than months. It is almost exclusively a London phenomenon. These girls may do all sorts of different jobs, one of them being an au pair or a mother's help for a spell. They are usually older – 20 to 25; they may be as old as 28 or 30.

There is also the non-EEC national who can come within this second category. She is often from South America but could be from Japan or elsewhere in the Far East and is probably seeking work as a mother's help or an au pair illegally. She probably won't have a work permit but has registered at language classes in order to receive permission to stay in this country from the Home Office.

This type *can* make an excellent au pair and mother's help. Part of her attraction is that she knows about the British way of life, can speak the language quite well, has already experienced an English household and may know quite a bit about children. Because she is older than the fresh flower sort, she is more mature and may have graduated to a steady boyfriend which is a bonus. Many of this kind of 'mature' foreign girl take daily nannying jobs and return to their flat and their boyfriend in the evening.

There is a big 'but' with this category of au pair, however. Unlike her younger counterpart of the Alpine pastures or the farm in Holland, she is likely to be streetwise, and know all the pubs, clubs and discos of London from High Barnet to Morden. She is likely to have had several boyfriends while she has been working over here. Often she no longer goes to classes because her English is good. So her motives for wanting to live with a family to help with the children and the housework are very different from the traditional au pair's.

This sort of au pair is looking, primarily, for cheap board and lodging. If she is a good sort this approach won't necessarily interfere with the way she does her job, but the odds are higher that her latest steamy relationship may get in the way, as it can do with living-in British nannies and mother's helps.

If she is a bad sort she will be hell to live with and is to be avoided at all costs. She will regard your home as a place to wile away the daylight hours before the gaudy night begins.

One employer remembers landing just such one au pair member of the café society:

She was an Italian who lived way beyond her slender means, caught taxis everywhere, and spent hours in the bath steaming in Floris. We felt we had a would-be fledgling Bianca Jagger in our midst, but without the looks. She spent her pocket money on charity ball tickets which seemed to clash too often with our plans to go out and eat a humble pizza. She had to go.

What nationality?

Many employers are prejudiced either for or against particular nationalities. It may be the result of a bad experience with a girl of a particular nationality but often it is not. Age-old xenophobic comments about different nationalities come up time and again.

Germans and Austrians

They are highly popular and highly prized for their grasp of English. They are also described by a string of adjectives, not all complimentary, including: organized, intelligent, matter-of-fact, no-nonsense.

One of my German au pairs was a bit like the stereotype, the other wasn't at all, not matter-of-fact nor very organized, but rather sweet and gentle. They both had splendid English and were among my top five au pairs.

Swiss

Again, they are sought after because their English is good provided they come from the right bit of Switzerland. Not surprisingly, people talk about their precision and reliability, as well as their industry.

My Swiss au pair whose mother was a teacher taught me everything I know about domesticity.

We had an excellent, clean, well-ordered Swiss.

We had an Italian Swiss once who was hot-tempered and precious.

Dutch

This is one of the most popular nationalities, along with the Scandinavians and the Germans. Their English is very good.

189

They are full of life and enthusiasm and don't hang about and mope. I
hire nothing else now and have abandoned the British girl entirely.

French

Employers tend to be a bit wary of French au pairs, but they do
respect them for their ability to work hard and get on with
whatever needs doing. Some mothers say they have come across
several who are too detached, and too keen to look after Number
One to make ideal au pairs. Often mothers grumble about how
they do the job to the letter rather than the spirit. Superior, glum
and grumpy are some derogatory adjectives used about them.

One mother compared the French au pair to a cat, 'They walk
by themselves, thank you. At least they don't fawn for attention
like some others.'

Belgians

They tend to get tarred with the French brush, but nicer things
are said about them.

Scandinavians

Highly praised for their excellent English accents and grasp of
idiom. They are about the most popular group. Mothers seem to
be prejudiced pro the Swedes, Norwegians, Danes and Finns.
Somehow Scandinavians are associated in employers' minds
with attractive things like blonde hair, snow, enlightened attitudes to ecology and child care, and a healthy vigorousness.

Our Swede was the best. She spoke and wrote English well and read
endlessly to our son. She made friends, her parents visited. She went
to Uppsala University after she left us.

Our Norwegian was a delight, like having a permanent ray of sunshine
about the place.

I love the Scandinavians. They are unemotional, patient with the kids
and very independent.

Spanish, Portuguese, Brazilians, Argentinians, Chileans

People say the same thing about the Spanish and Portuguese –
that they are good sorts, warm and tremendously hard working.
Similar things are said about their Latin American cousins.

Many mothers say these girls are warm and good with the

children partly because many of them have at least three siblings. Some employers find the differences in culture and manners of some of the girls hard to take. A few say they can be moody, gloomy, stormy and sulky. They all grumble about the girls' poor English and accent.

Our best au pair was Brazilian. Grown-up, gentle, a natural child carer with bags of sensitivity and discretion and she never imposed on us.

Surprisingly our Portuguese girl had first-rate English. She did the job well and we both liked her a lot. We visit her every time we go to Faro on a package holiday.

Italians
Popular, considered gentle, charming and good with children. Often they have much better English than you might expect.

Ours was beautifully dressed and knew everything there was to know about Art. But I couldn't believe she didn't know how to make a bed or cook until she told me that her mother and staff did all the work at home.

The pros and cons of hiring a foreigner or going native
Whether to hire a foreign or an English mother's help – part- or-full-time – is a conundrum. Many employers experiment a bit to begin with before settling on one or the other.
Employers say:

I go for English until the children reach four or five then I go to a Catholic agency and choose either Dutch or Spanish.

I prefer the colonial types – more sophisticated and middle class than English girls.

Our au pair couldn't have been sweeter or more willing, but the language barrier was a problem with young children. So I went English.

Foreign help seems very adaptable and is prepared to work hard. Some lack initiative and like to be instructed about everything. Some tend to walk round things they don't think are their territory.

Prefer foreign girls as long as they speak good English. I like Aussies and New Zealanders because they are well qualified. They aren't resentful that you are better off than they are or because the work is, finally, menial. I think many English girls can resent this.

I prefer the English; no language problems and they can always go
  home.

Many parents are quite sure that they prefer their own
nationality without ever trying a foreign mother's help, largely
on the grounds that they can speak English. To a lesser extent,
they feel that there has to be more in common and that it is easier,
generally, to get on with someone from one's own country.

Others find foreigners socially and culturally more relaxing to
live with. Some members of the middle classes say that there is a
higher chance that an au pair from Europe will come from a
similar background.

A foreign girl is less likely to turn up her nose at her employers'
foreign food like chilli con carne, pork spiked with garlic and
lasagne. In fact, au pairs tend not to be fussy eaters and many
seem to exist on yoghurt and fruit. Many young English girls are
keen to try new foods and take an interest in menus which are not
all chips, peas and fried chicken, but the odds are that a foreign
girl will be happier to eat yesterday's murky stew re-heated.

There is more likelihood that a European may be cultured and
keen to visit museums, art galleries and historic monuments. She
may well go to see the same films, plays and concerts as her
employers and enjoy discussing their merits afterwards. It is not
important if the mother's help or au pair doesn't share any of her
family's interests and enthusiasms, and loads of them are not into
culture, but if it matters to you it is a definite bonus to have a
kindred spirit around.

Sometimes employers can experience culture shock with girls
from poor, unsophisticated families in parts of France, Italy,
Spain and Portugal. One Kensington mum recalls, 'I sacked one
and all my friends laughed. Her table manners were too awful to
live with. She would put her knife in the honey pot, lick it, and
put it back again. Ugh.'

Foreign girls are less aware of differences in income and class
than British girls. Many parents reckon that this makes living
with them more comfortable. It is less necessary to be aware of
what you say about politics, class and money when living with
someone who probably doesn't understand a good deal of what
you mean and whose frame of reference can be very different.

One mother who had employed foreign girls in the past

remembers her first, and probably last, 18-year-old English mother's help:

It dawned on me that, however nice Sheilagh was, she might have arrived from Outer Mongolia. She came from a Scunthorpe working class family with a lot less money than us.

It was her *attitude* to living with us that was different from a foreign girl's. She was perfectly polite, and good with the children, but I felt she thought our way of life was not hers and she didn't aspire to it either. After Sheilagh left we went back to the Ingas and Petras. Quite frankly they are less lumpen and didn't watch the box so much. Sadly, we have more in common with a girl from across the Channel than with one from north of the Humber.

Where to find an au pair or foreign mother's help
Au pairs can be found by word of mouth, by going to agencies, contacting various convents and organizations who run hostels as well as the churches of different countries, (see useful addresses), by putting ads in local shops and schools and by taking an ad in *The Lady* (see page 74). The advantage of an ad in *The Lady* is that, provided you live in and around London, you can interview applicants, rather than having to rely on a telephone conversation.

It is not necessary to be paranoid about the 'experienced' au pair who has already found her feet in the capital and avoid *The Lady* entirely. In fact, there are loads of 'nice' girls who do come straight from home to London. Often two friends make the trip across the Channel together, book in at a hostel or convent, or stay with friends or even a relation, and go and buy a copy of the magazine. Often a girl's home town convent may have contacts with one of the London convents, some of whom put girls up and will help find a job for a daughter of the Faith.

Outside London
Parents who don't live in London and its environs have much less choice. Many resort to provincial agencies, and failing those, London agencies. Some place an ad in *The Lady* and suggest that the girl makes a long trip, probably from London, for an interview and agree to pay her return fare. Some try to save money by deciding to take a chance and suggest that the applicant who sounds the most appealing on the phone comes

'blind', without a face-to-face interview, and both the family and the girl try each other out for a week.

For someone living in the country, away from transport and other young, the odds are long on finding an au pair who will stay six months. Thus those who are keen to achieve it could well benefit from the effort of putting an ad in *The Lady*, and interviewing girls personally at a friend's home or at an accessible spot such as the Commonwealth Institute in Kensington High Street or the Indian Tea Centre in Oxford Street.

Some employers succeed in finding, and keeping, au pairs in the country. Some are aided by the fact they they live in a country town rather than miles outside it. Others have the luck to secure a girl who genuinely likes views and quiet (rather than thinking it will do for a couple of weeks before finding something else), or have the sense to give the au pair the use of the car so that she can drive to see friends. Proper transport is essential. One Devon mother's Finnish au pair found the twice-weekly 20 mile trip by lift and bus to the city for her classes, and not being able to stay on and have fun in the evenings, frustrating. Very soon she flew from her unidyllic nest to the convenient pavements of Plymouth.

For deep country employers the straightforward but often unsuccessful technique is to deal with an au pair agency, which will probably be situated in the south east (see More Information: Agencies). More success in finding the right girl could be achieved by recruiting direct from her home town abroad (see below). Town and village twinning associations are often helpful. Also getting in touch with the local school's French, German and Spanish teachers may prove useful.

Recruiting direct

A few enterprising employers, often with friends in European capitals, and able to speak the language of the au pair they seek, put an advertisement in a foreign newspaper. This costs less than an agency (which advertises in the foreign press too), but it is labour intensive.

An ad for a foreign paper should give your name, address and telephone number and ask for a *detailed* CV written in English, plus a photo of the applicant. If you don't want someone who can't speak any English make this clear in the ad. Getting your girl can take repeated phone calls and can turn into an expensive and time-consuming process. Once through to her you have to conduct a long-distance telephone interview. Inevitably she will have left out vital bits of information in her letter which you have to find out – e.g. does she smoke and how long does she want to stay? – and all this on top of assessing her personality and grasp of English.

The would-be hirer is usually snowed under with applicants – sometimes as many as 30 but 10 is bad enough. She has to decipher each letter (discard any that don't include, as requested, a photo of the applicant), and if the employer is polite she replies to them all. She has to draw up a short list of, say, three girls and track them down.

You might think it would be possible to dial Spain or France and get through to the right person first try. *Hélas*, no. It is common to experience three almost incomprehensible conversations with people whom you think are her grandmother, her father and the woman next door who happened to be passing and picked up the phone, blast her. At best someone will tell you that your quarry is on holiday for two weeks/will be in tomorrow/has already found a job. With the first two reasons you have to decide whether to bother to ring again or put that one down to experience.

If you and the girl ever manage to communicate in each other's languages successfully, and you feel you have got a match, the next step is to suggest that she discuss the project with her parents and think it over for 48 hours. Another phone call should procure a yea or nay and then you can suggest a day and time for her to arrive at the relevant airport or harbour. The employer does not have to feel obliged to pay the girl's travel. Many agencies, incidentally, are happy for employers to feel that they should.

Then you wait on tenterhooks and hope that the girl doesn't get second thoughts and fail to turn up at the appointed hour. Once on your doorstep, there is still the chance that she is a no hoper. Then, instead of giving her two weeks' notice as you could with a girl you had hired in London, you have to help her search for a job and that means a warm reference as well. Then you curse your luck and crawl to the nearest agency for a replacement.

It doesn't have to be this bad, but it *can* be. The civilized thing to do is to ask a friend living in the au pair's country to ring the girls for you, do some sifting and even interview one or two herself over there. Anyone who has been independent and hired direct from abroad themselves begins to understand why agents' fees are so high.

Part 2: Mother's Helps, Australians, New Zealanders and Others

Mother's helps

A mother's help can be British or foreign. Most are British, a significant proportion are Australians or New Zealanders and a good many are from the European Community or beyond. There are lots of 'illegals' (see page 174).

The main advantage of a mother's help is that you do not pay for training. She is a lot cheaper than anyone trained and that includes NAMCW, City and Guilds and NNEB (see chapter 7). Many employers like the fact that a mother's help may be young and malleable and they feel more comfortable living with someone who in no sense challenges the way they live.

One mother says, 'Oh no, I couldn't cope with a smart, trained NNEB, quite apart from the cost, I'd have to redecorate the bathroom and get a cleaner.' One of the characteristics of a trained nanny is that if she is any good she is, by definition, going to hold views about how your child should behave and should develop. A few employers dislike anyone else having views about child rearing; they really want someone who does it like they do.

Employers also like housework to come within the child care package. Mother's helps hope to be asked to do 'light housework' only – they breathe a sigh of relief when there is a cleaner already for the heavy stuff. This means they won't have to mop the kitchen floor, scrub the loos, wash down the paintwork, spring clean, wash the front door steps, Hoover the stairs or polish silver and brass. If the family hasn't got a cleaner she can expect to do all these things. However, housework today isn't *that* heavy in most modern, centrally heated, carpeted homes.

The traditional idea of a mother's help is that the mother is broadly speaking, around to be helped. Although many mothers leave their children to be looked after by the mother's help, while they go out to work full or part time, reputable employment agencies frown on this practice, unless the girl has had considerable experience. After several years (three at the very least), experience may make any girl feel that she is on a par with her trained counterpart and with some justification. There are plenty of mother's helps with one or two years' experience who reckon they are as much a nanny as someone trained and they don't hesitate to describe themselves as such.

Most mother's helps are better supervised than left free range. A mother's help will do anything alongside a mother like making her employer's bed (so much easier with two), spring cleaning the sitting room together, the household's net curtains together –that sort of thing. She will even help clean the swimming pool or manoeuvre the puppy pooper scooper round the lawn. As long as it is together. A job shared is a job halved, as far as the mother's help is concerned – from the employer's point of view it is a job done properly.

If the employer acts like Lady Muck and reclines on the chaise longue reading magazines day after day, the housework will not be done well, if at all. A few mother's helps have a natural aptitude and enjoy housework; they are never happier than when sorting out the airing cupboard and reorganizing the marmites and marmalades. Some mothers have trained their daughters as excellent housemaids. The vast majority are just plain bad at it and bored by it and do it far too quickly and superficially for good results. They are either naturals or they aren't, so try not to get indignant about their myopia and lack of vim.

It helps to cheer up the whole housework experience if you give a mother's help all the modern cleaning gadgets you can afford, like a cylinder cleaner for the stairs and a sleeve board for the ironing. Make sure that old cloths get thrown away and don't be mean about the Ajax supplies and newish bog brushes.

Another bonus about a mother's help is that an employer can ask her to help with the cooking for the family and the washing up. Thousands of them can't boil a egg, but it is quite legitimate to encourage her to do it as best she may and, if she is foreign, try her national alternatives.

Katharine Whitehorn, in *How to Survive Children*, says,

Much easier are Mother's Helps who mop floors as well as tears. If you've hired them for qualities of cow-like tranquillity you absolutely don't have yourself, it's unfair to be furious if they take an hour and a half, reflectively stirring the water with one hoof, to do the washing up.

There is a species of daily mother's help – rather like a childminder on your turf. She is untrained, probably local and experienced with kids having brought up a few of her own. Some mothers who work full time prefer this sort of carer for their children. Americans refer to this type, confusingly, as a baby-sitter. Her children are grown up and she may be divorced or widowed. Unlike most mother's helps, she will probably work for you for several years – more like the job span of a cleaning lady than that of a nanny.

Whatever her age, the untrained mother's help should have the same qualities, ideally, that you look for in a trained nanny (see page 56). The essential stuff about liking children and being capable of spending most waking moments in their company all apply. Be sure that she is equable and sensible, responsible and that you *like* her. Do not compromise yourself or your children just because you aren't paying the earth.

One of the most important things to remember about an untrained, inexperienced girl is that she may have no idea about the importance of safety indoors and out. Buy her the Red Cross book and lecture her at length, regardless of her age or her experience with someone else's family (see page 132).

Another common problem with a younger mother's help, as with the new nanny, is homesickness (for remedies see chapter 4, page 109). You are employing someone young enough to be your daughter and she may have not have had any sort of training or relevant experience since leaving school. British mother's helps tend to to young – 17 or 18. For many girls, it is their first job. Employers should try to recall how crassly they handled their own. One experienced employer says, 'I always keep closely in touch with her parents if she is under 20. If I have problems with her, I will need their support.'

The big problem with the 17-year-old English girl is that often as not it is a toss-up between serving in the local chip shop, making beds in a hotel or nannying. Many an employer doesn't realize that her mother's help has not yet made any clear plans about the future. It is quite likely after several weeks in the job, when her employer is just beginning to relax, that the girl will smile sweetly and announce without a blush, 'My mum says there is a good job going at the local DIY shop. I think I'll give it a try.'

A few mothers have had the enlightened idea of encouraging their mother's helps to pursue some child-related training by correspondence and in night classes, with the intention of broadening their experience and expertise. Some examples include a pre-school playleaders course, a Montessori correspondence course and night courses at the local council college in storytelling, cookery, know your London, kids' clothes making, smocking, toy making and puppet workshops.

Australians and New Zealanders

Agencies and employers are unanimous in their enthusiastic support of this group. One agency says: 'If I could afford to ditch every British nanny and only deal with the Aussies and Kiwis I definitely would. They are trouble-free, happy, sensible and reliable – no wonder we all love them!'

Australians and New Zealanders present only two major drawbacks. They will probably not want to stay for longer than six months (the average seems to be about three or four) and they may not know how long that may feel and leave even sooner. The wish to travel is urgent and the Antipodean is definitely doing the job to finance worldwide travel for a year or two. However good she is with children, employers must psych themselves to accept the fact that she is a transient treat.

Aussies and Kiwis are good fun to employ and they are mostly gregarious. This is ideal for energetic large English families living in the country.

The most Antipodean-besotted employer admits that it is a bore at best to employ help for a mere six months. Parents tend to take a robust attitude to the numbers of Oz mother's helps needed in a year. 'Oh the kids get used to it.' This is OK as long as your children are over three and understand the rapid turnover. Even then, it is best if the mother is around to help children adjust to the new faces and habits so frequently.

It is also hard work and time-consuming for the mother to have to recruit several times a year; expensive too, as most people who choose Australians and New Zealanders like to stick with an agency with whom they build up a good relationship.

Australians and New Zealanders are particularly prized for their initiative and ability to 'muck in'. No one seems capable of an analysis of this essential commodity without mentioning housework. They are reckoned among the Seven Wonders because they will wield a scrubbing brush without throwing a fit. To enumerate the qualities of Australian and New Zealander mother's help is to list the shortcomings of the British nanny.

Another striking feature is that the Australians and New Zealanders are older – mostly in their early or mid-twenties – and often trained, not as nannies, but as nurses and teachers and in a whole host of other professions. Thus the employer more easily accords them respect. They have lived away from home and have crossed the world, so they have a better chance of being more amusing and sophisticated company than the average British mother's help or nanny. All of which means that communication is more direct. Antipodeans are legendary for their plain-speaking and their Pom employers are quite keen on it within reason because it can reduce friction. Polite/disorganized/timid/unforceful employers find it a relief to hear a sensible Kiwi announce that she will be doing, X, Y and Z this morning.

Typical attitudes not commonly manifested in English girls include an amazement that employers don't do the jobs they want to hire people to do themselves. Although Australians and New Zealanders are happy to be employed as mother's helps, housekeepers and 'couples', they don't think that those jobs are worth having, apart from the money. 'It's not like that at home' is a phrase commonly on their lips. 'Why can't she do the work herself?' As one agent says:

They ask me questions as often as not and I say because they have enough money to get you to do it. I have to explain that English employers are not much interested in discussing the ethics of who should be doing the job; they just want someone, preferably not them, to get on with it.

There are darn few Australian nannies in Australia, so most Australian mother's helps/nannies will never have done the job before. They may have no idea whether they will like nannying. They will probably do it anyway, and make the most of it for six months, whatever they think of it. As one mother says, 'It is an experiment for them. They have to live in to have a roof over their heads. They are over here to experience anything new and it certainly *is* different.'

Many Aussies and Kiwis think that British children are spoilt. They find the lack of discipline strange and the fact that children are not punished for misdemeanours is not in the least to their liking. If you are the mother of a tender flower, have a chat with the Antipodean mother's help about how you do and do not expect her to be treated. Most employers who deliberately choose Australian and New Zealand help tend to share their stoic, no-nonsense attitudes; that's why they get on so well.

Australians and New Zealanders are more expensive than an English mother's help – it would be cloud cuckooland to rate maturity highly and then not expect to pay for it. They earn at least £100 to £120 a week gross. The onus is on the employer to arrange tax and National Insurance, but most don't let this responsibility weigh too heavily – they'll be gone in six months and that's that. They mostly do not expect to do elbow-grease housework and tend to go to families that keep cleaning help. They prefer not to have their readiness to 'muck in' tested daily.

The whole class thing does not raise its ugly head. They sound different; they're foreigners; they do things differently, for the same reason. That's how employers see it. Many a public school employer misspent a year or more Down Under on sheep stations – even Prince Charles went to Geelong. They dreamed dreams, lost their virginity and got legless under the stars in the outback, so the vibrant tones of an Australian mother's help brings back happy memories.

The famous nursery nurse training college, Karatani in New Zealand, has now closed, but its students were and are much respected by English agencies. 'I reckoned it in the same league as the residential colleges here,' says one, 'it had world renown and produced excellent nannies. Now it has gone the only name we can rely on is the Tricillian hospital in Sydney. The nurses are brilliantly trained from there.'

There are several well-worn paths to agency doors. Look up Turner's, Lady Colwyn and Bligh, the specialist agencies who deal entirely with Australian and New Zealand help (on pages 283 – 97), and skim through the list for other agencies who are keen to attract Antipodeans. If you want to avoid agency fees, advertise in the free weeklies designed for Aussies and Kiwis living in London – LAM, TNT, *New Zealand News* and *New Australasian Express*.

The agencies are not about to ring Australia to check references unless you want to foot the bill for them to do so. They are not psychic and any employer runs a risk with taking an Australian off the street without a reference. There are bad apples, but there are very few stories about Aussies and Kiwis behaving badly to their employers, which is creditable given how footloose and fancy-free they are actually while working here.

Employers and agencies say:

They are bright and cheery and not evasive and depressing like so many English girls – even interviewing them is a positive pleasure.

They turn up and start work within hours of ringing the agency; that's what I like best.

I'm crazy about them. They just watch what you are doing and then do it better.

The moronic British mother's help is such a nightmare by comparison. We always have Australian graduates and they are such a help and so nice to have around.

Babysitters

> Ma's out, Pa's out,
> Let's have fun,
> Pee, po', belly, bum, drawers.

Anyone who has a real-life nasty story about a helper certainly has one about babysitters. The most popular and infamous tale concerns the parents arriving home early because they forgot their keys/got the wrong night/had a migraine, to find their babysitter with her boyfriend in the kitchen – both giggly and passing joints. The oven is on and the door is ajar. Then they see the tin foil stretched over the baking tin stir. Ripping it off, to their horror their six month baby is revealed in all his chubby nakedness, smeared with lard and with an apple in his mouth . . .

Dear, oh dear, most people's lives are not this bad, happily. The story has a lesson for many parents who do not make much effort to check out their babysitters thoroughly. Funnily enough, someone who is paying well over £100 a week for a swish daily nanny will often hire an agency babysitter they have never seen before in their lives. She is handed the children, the house, all the goods and chattels, and the employer assumes blithely that her burglar boyfriend will not arrive ten minutes after they go out for the whole evening.

There is no law to prevent anyone of any age babysitting in England and Wales, nor is there any law that says parents may not leave children alone in the house when they go out. In Scotland the legal minimum age for a babysitter is 16. At this age a child might reasonably be expected to behave sensibly in an emergency. It is a neglected area in England and legislation would be helpful.

An NSPCC representative comments, 'The law says that unless a person is over 16, he or she cannot be held responsible for the care of a child. The law on neglect is adequate, but babysitting should be specifically mentioned.'

The ad in the local shop looks fine. 'Responsible, experienced 14-year-old for babysitting'. Look at it again. How well would the average 14-year-old cope with a fire when there are only two minutes to extract the children from their beds? How would she cope with a frightening phone call, an odd caller or a burglary? And how would you feel afterwards about yourself, her and her parents should a tragedy occur? Is it worth risking this kind of anguish or guilt?

Choose a 16-plus local girl, whom you and the children know well, trust and like. Alternatively, find out about the local babysitting circle or start your own. The latter is a group of mothers, often as many as twenty, who babysit for each other free of charge. Some groups dish out tokens which may be cashed in when it suits.

Whoever it is, hand him or her an emergency drill written out clearly – the hospital name, surgery number and doctor's name, instructions for an ambulance driver, where you are for the evening and leave your phone number (*always*, even if you are going to a cinema, theatre or restaurant). Leave also the phone numbers of close friends or relations who live nearby.

Do make sure that your children know babysitters well enough so that if they wake up and are sad or thirsty, or have wet their bed or whatever, they can ask the babysitter without feeling too miserable that their parents are not around. Tell your sitter what pet names your children may have for their needs.

Decide beforehand what you feel about the babysitter's boyfriends or girlfriends coming to join her in your absence and state your view. The general rule is no to men, yes to girls. As for drink, if you like, fill a wine glass and make it clear that that's all that's on offer.

Agencies are expensive, not ideal nor in some magical way more reliable than a local arrangement. There are a few which earn their fee and a very few who guarantee a babysitter after an annual subscription to their service. Then their babysitters, who are trained nannies, will still charge £3 to £4 per hour on top, so this is not an option for many. 'A' level students, nursery school teachers, the greengrocer's daughter, the health clinic assistant, student nurses from the hospital, the teenage daughter of a neighbour or friend – all can be contacted via postcards in shops, clinics, hospitals and schools and if they live near you will charge half that price.

Other people's nannies are the first choice for people who are without them. Employers of nannies get very annoyed with approaches from comparative strangers and acquaintances on the school steps and in the park. As an employer, it is quite OK to say 'no' flatly. Most are kind and say yes, then they curse their stupidity, when the nanny is kept out till 3.30 am by neighbours and is not fit for work the next day.

Supper – ham and salad, no sweat – should be provided. A working TV is vital. If you know you will be later than midnight offer her somewhere to snooze, preferably close to the children, or suggest she brings her overnight bag and you will pay her until midnight. Otherwise, when you return, either you drive her home or pay for a taxi. Always err on the generous side; round up her pay to the nearest hour. If you treat her well consistently, it will pay off in the long run.

The granny substitute or proxy mother

Some employers don't have mothers who make perfect grannies and they do want to leave a nanny, mother's help or au pair in sole charge of their children while they go away with their husband for a holiday or on a business trip. So they sometimes want to employ a granny substitute to oversee the household.

There are agencies who deal in these super grans. The best known are Universal Aunts and Country Cousins (see Agencies for details). They are mostly about 50 to 60 years old, can drive, have had children of their own or are retired nannies and are entirely capable of running the nanny, the house and your children smoothly in your absence. Make sure that you check her references thoroughly and invite her to meet you and the family before your departure.

9
Friction

Stress and Conflict

Control yourself,
Contain yourself,
And if you can't,
Restrain yourself,
Then try to act
Agreeably on the whole.

Life is much too short
To spend it in a huff
Try to imitate
The guy who laughs
When things get tough.

Cleo Laine at Carnegie Hall

If you are bad at communal living, having a resident nanny or
mother's help may be a helluva strain. One full-time working
mother (who therefore sees comparatively little of her nanny)
speaks for many when she says:

The nanny/mother relationship appears to be full of conflict. You want
long-term commitment but few of us like the children feeling more
secure with the nanny than with the mum. You want them to be mature
but you reserve the right to treat them as teenagers. You don't want your
own position challenged but you expect them to behave as you would if
you were there.

Very few people can be said truly to *need* a nanny. Employers
hire one of their own free will and the mistake most of them make
is to think that money will somehow buy them immunity from
problems.

If you hire a super-experienced and highly trained girl to live in
and look after your children, you will cut out many of the obvious
stresses. But there will always be some friction, disagreement,
problems of adjustment and personality differences. And that is
just for starters.

Friction can cause fire, but the fuel which provides ignition is what any good employer, keen to keep a nanny or mother's help long term, needs to analyse thoroughly. Nannies and employment agencies report that if employers behaved more fairly they would have a much better chance of nannies staying longer. Employers say that if nannies were better prepared by their training colleges and/or agencies for the realities of living-in posts, they would cope with the strains better. It is pragmatic to learn to become a better employer. Examining the problems is far from being a self-indulgent wallow, or an excuse for a grumble.

Carelessness, thoughtlessnes and selfishness on either side are the root causes of stress. As Juliet Solomon puts it in her book *Holding the Reins*, 'Employers are permanent volunteers, nannies are temporary mercenaries.' Too often employers forget this and demand too much of the people who care for their children. Employers can also become dismissive and disdainful of the work the nanny is doing. Employers must respect the nanny's job. They have to take an interest in her and, while expecting her to be as professional as possible, they should not lose sight of the fact that she is human and fallible.

One parent says glumly, 'Normally most start off mediocre and stay that way or get worse. You straighten out the worst niggly aspects of their behaviour; the rest you ignore or get used to.' Another takes a more robust line, 'I don't like kids in dirty clothes, so I tell the nannies their standards aren't high enough and I put the clothes in the basket myself. Most of them tend to slacken off when they get to know the routine – I'm afraid familiarity does breed contempt very often. I have only had one nanny who maintained very high standards for two years.'

One can pinpoint periods during a nanny's employment when she is likely to be less than satisfied with the status quo and may well leave unless you take precipitate action. Mrs Davis of Norland says, 'It is human to slacken off after six to nine months and it is harder for the employer to reprove by then.' A London employment agency says that employers should watch out for the New Year which is a natural time for reassessment and itchy feet. One mother says, 'Two years seems to be the limit for everyone and they start to tail off well before then.'

Mrs Baxter who ran an employment agency for 25 years says, 'What nannies are told at interview often turns out to be untrue.'

The biggest cause of stress in nannies is when employers transgress their initial arrangements, particularly when it comes to the Big Four (see page 46). It amounts to a denial of a nanny's rights when an employer chooses to welsh on a contract, written or otherwise. It is also the ultimate sign of your lack of respect for her professional status.

The Nanny Connection agency in London says its 'biggest beef is with parents who take advantage of time off. It is the nanny's day off and the mum says, "Can I just run down to the shops while the baby is asleep?" The nanny doesn't want to refuse. Three minutes later the baby wakes, three hours later mum returns.' It is quite interesting how disingenuously employers may phrase such unfair demands – they are well aware that they are putting the nanny in an impossible position. They have set up the request in such a way that she cannot say no without feeling mean.

It takes quite a lot of gumption for a young girl to say in response to the question 'You haven't got anything special on tonight have you?' 'Well, not special, but I put it in the diary a week ago that I was going out . . .' The naughty employers still persist: 'Oh right . . . well do you mind awfully/just this once/my husband never usually gets back this early/we just want to go for a quick drink on the river . . .' At this point a nanny may agree to cancel *her* visit to the pub by the river, and it seems positively defiant for her to reply 'I'm sorry, but I need to take a break and get out of the house.'

This is just as bullying as bellowing at someone. Anyone would resent such trespass on their free time which makes them break arrangements and let friends down apart from being a dampener on the morale.

Even when the Big Four (see chapter 2) are conscientiously adhered to, nannies may still not be happy with the reality of the arrangement that you agreed mutually. For example, the Nannies of Kensington agency says that in living-in jobs nannies always want more evenings off. It doesn't matter that they know they are obliged to do three or four evenings a week babysitting. That doesn't stop them wanting to go out more than they can. One Norlander explains that many nannies, including herself, never relax when they are in the family's house. For her, unless she had shut the front door behind her and was tripping down the path, she always felt she was on duty.

A natural victim of a family that always needs help is a nanny who has the misfortune to land an employer who is desperate without many hands to tend her children elsewhere. Her waking nightmare is to find herself alone with a child. Open any door in her house and there will be another starched uniform performing some duty. The mother is a mass of white silk and Worth by night, a vision in a mink bed jacket and a tangle of telephones till noon. She is always frantically busy having her toes/portrait/jacuzzi painted. She just hasn't a moment for her children, though the shih-tzus are spoilt rotten and as neurotic as she is. No wonder many nannies insist on working for parents who are out of the house all day.

Nannies' comments are particularly tolerant of their employers' neuroses, hang-ups and egocentricity, though a few naturally enough have pithy criticism of their behaviour. Many of them think that they and their friends are exploited, often not a lot, but nevertheless put upon.

I get annoyed by their guilt feelings [sole charge] and their need to spoil the children and the lack of discipline.

One family treated me like a piece of furniture and never considered my feelings at all.

My employer is very untidy, she leaves her clothes all over the house, it drives me mad having to pick up her blouse in the playroom.

My employers lack basic common sense, the father eats noisily and hates children, and the mother reads *The Hobbit* to her daughter aged four.

However nice and pleasant your employer is, being a live-in mother's help makes for awkward, tense times.

Symptoms of Friction

Employers' paranoia and the Lucan Solution
Employers do get neurotic. They fear that their nannies don't like them and are rude about them behind their backs. Sniggers stop as they enter, tearful phone calls to the parents abound, the air is filled with melancholy sighs and speaking silences, the Sit Vac

page of every magazine is propped up on the coffee pot, and rather posh voices on the phone ask for Miss X. Employers' paranoia sets in.

Either this is all your fault, or she's making it feel that way for her own purposes. Your husband doesn't see as much of her as you do, so get his point of view on the evidence and ask him to tell you if you are going off your head. The Lucan Solution (remember he sought to solve domestic strife with murder and killed his nanny in error) threatens and the nanny is unaware that you have taken in all these details, and have been reduced to a gibbering wreck. She's sending out distress signals; you are ignoring them outwardly by virtue of your stiff upper lip and attempted maturity but you're crying inside too.

Your husband agrees that you are mad, 'but not to worry about it and do let's get some sleep. If I hear about that blessed girl again . . . oh for the day we won't need them any more.' Sure, but what about *now*? In fact, husbands can be tremendously helpful if they want. They can deal with potential pot holes like pay, overtime or holidays. They can ask the nanny to be considerate/under-standing/more sensitive. It is often easier for her to take this sort of thing from the husband rather than from the old hag.

Ring the agency which supplied her for advice, and don't hesitate to call the college that trained her. The three residential colleges encourage employers to ring them with their problems. Local authority college tutors are not meant officially to arbitrate and you can but try.

Snooping

At this point, several mothers confess that they have become obsessed by the need to have their suspicions confirmed. After a sleepless night, as soon as the nanny has taken the children out, the mother sneaks furtively to the nanny's room. Looking out for the full nappy bucket on the top of the door, which is luckily ajar, she enters the nanny's room and carefully, so as to escape detection, reads private letters and a diary and searches for any other incriminating signs. The waste paper basket is a magnet.

Snooping may take different forms – from eavesdropping to rooting through her personal belongings. Why is it done? Again there are many reasons. You may indeed need certifying; you may actually have nurtured a viper in your bosom (and very uncomfortable too); she may be a bit underhand (but not seriously so) or she may be on the move and is trying to let you know, albeit ineptly.

One mother felt that the nanny was acting oddly, but 'I couldn't put my finger on it. The only interesting item I found was a lesbian mag in the drawers under her bed. I had to keep checking for my own peace of mind and I used to go up once a week.' Diaries provide good ammo for the mother who suspects her nanny is conducting an affair under her roof. One employer was horrified to discover that her nanny had been having regular sex with her boyfriend in the house while on duty. According to the diary (which also sported gold stars as a score system recording each time she and her boyfriend made love), the tireless couple had climaxed sensationally on the landing outside the bathroom door while the children were in the bath.

One of the problems is what to do with these ill-gotten gains of insight? The person who can't face talking to a nanny normally about mutual problems is not likely to be any more capable of confronting her with the evidence of her wild sex life and explaining how she came by the information. Most find excuses, however lame, to sack forthwith.

Nannies snoop too, but more from nosiness than paranoia. They probably just want to get to know the nature of the beast.

Snooping is outrageous, unprofessional and the temptation to do so should be resisted. It is symptomatic of a badly conducted relationship which is close to divorce. Once again it speaks of a total lack of moral courage. Employers will not like themselves any better for resorting to such low conduct and ought to deal with each warning flare as it goes up. If a nanny sobs or sighs – ask her what is wrong. If she is silent and uncomfortable – ask her if she is happy and what you can do to help her. Mrs Townsend of Chiltern says: 'Don't let mountains flow out of molehills, discuss it.' It may take an effort and a bit of grit, but employers must bite the bullet, deal with problems as they arise and not let them fester.

Sources of Friction

Unrealistic expectations and prejudices
Even after months, intractable employers and nannies may still

cling to the stereotypes they first dreamt up for each other. This is particularly common when either employer or nanny is new to the game. A newly qualified nanny may have been told by other nannies, her tutor or her mother that employers are exploitative. Regardless of how the employer behaves, she may remain wary and untrusting. An experienced nanny may have encountered genuine exploitation and be once bitten, twice shy.

If she still selects the children's crockery and cutlery from the draining board, and leaves your cup and saucer, she is making a point. Enter your well-practised 'Let's have a chat' mode: compose your words, smile, and catch her eye. More like confrontation this time, as long as your conscience is clear that you are a good and fair employer. Say, 'What is the point you are making?' If the reply comes back like a dalek: 'I – am – an – NNEB – I – do – not – wash up – for – my – employers,' you either accept this mean-spirited reaction and think the worse of her, or realize that this is what people mean when they talk about 'mucking in' in their advertisements, and resolve to include this elusive quality in *your* next ad. This by-the-book attitude does not make for a happy give-and-take. After a time of you giving and her taking, you'll feel like an exploited employer and will have had enough.

Having said all this, many nannies do feel that this sort of nit-picking behaviour has to be resorted to as a desperate measure to stop employers taking advantage of them. Some employers never get beyond treating the nanny, or mother's help, as a resident slave, and even with employers who think they are fair, the nanny will find herself doing more and more, unless she takes a stand. One Australian notes acerbically, 'The English are up themselves. They will get you to iron their silk knickers if they can get away with it.'

Some nannies may set up in competition with the mother in several different ways. One mother says, 'If I have ever felt jealous of the nanny's relationship with my children, it is because I was intended to feel jealous.' Another says: 'Some nannies try to score off mummies.' A third comments 'I've not felt jealous much, well, perhaps a teeny weeny twinge once or twice.'

It is pretty much the employer's responsibility to discourage any nanny from usurping her role as a mother, housekeeper and social secretary. It is difficult if you are working to show a nanny proper appreciation if you are also feeling resentful that she has run your home, from dealing with the gas man to taking messages from your girl friends. She may know more about your life at home than you do, and this makes some employers jumpy. Not just jumpy, but positively paranoid. This can stem from general feelings of guilt and wistfulness that some working mothers suffer from because they are not watching their child grow up in every tiny way.

The most unkind way that this guilt manifests itself is when a mother wants to deny the reality of leaving the house and the children in the care of someone else every day. She doesn't want to visualize or think about what goes on in her absence and therefore she ignores the nanny in an attempt to block out the importance of her contribution. Not surprisingly the nanny becomes desperate for attention and tries to encourage the mother to read about her children's day in the log that she keeps for that purpose, and generally take an interest in their daily lives. The mother feels that the nanny is deliberately rubbing in the details of all she has missed, and is curt and dismissive. It must be soul destroying for a committed nanny to have to deal with such unbalanced behaviour.

Regardless of how incompetent/uninteresting/unloving/chaotic the nanny may think, or even know, her employer to be with the children, her training should have prepared her to care for them as their mother directs. Mrs Townsend of Chiltern College instructs her girls to 'remember that parents' wishes should always be adhered to, even if you are horrified by the way a child is being brought up. Bide your time; gain their confidence; it is not possible to make an impact on a child's upbringing immediately.'

Both nannies and their employers agree that the nanny's contract (see page 325) cannot be prescient about the small details and coruscations which can make both sides unhappy. Either party may be irrational and nit-picking and the other will either have to live with it and kowtow to their foibles or tell them they can't stand whatever it is and they must change it. It is not the individual niggle that matters *per se*, but rather the cumulative effect, which when allowed to snowball can metamorphose into a Sackable Offence. One Norlander tells us that, 'It is not the big issues that curdle a relationship; they are contracted for and discussed. It's just the petty things.'

212

There are stories of employers who wash eggs before cracking them, always keep leftovers (from bacon rind to half a cupcake) and recycle everything, refreeze the fish pie, pelt marauding cats with oranges from the top storey and insist that the nanny do so too. They ask her to say they're out when they're in, take a Fort Knox approach to locking every door, boil bathmats and flannels, and, as a child's tenth cold of the term starts, huddle the family under a huge towel to inhale Wright's Vaporizer and press the nanny to join them.

The nanny's problems: physical

Nannies' and mother's helps' health, diet and general ability to look after themselves effectively can cause considerable trouble to her employers. At the interview (see chapter 4) you may have screened the nannies for anorexia, bulimia, epilepsy and any psychiatric problem. Amenorrhoea and dismenorrhoea mean not getting periods and getting them painfully respectively. Menorroghia is when a girl gets them very heavily. If your nanny suffers from any of these afflictions, take them seriously and insist that she sees a doctor. The sad thing is that, although she may be helped with treatment, it is quite possible that she has a long-term problem which may disqualify her from nannying.

You obviously will not be overjoyed to find that your nanny is out of action for two or three days a month or, almost as bad, when she complains loudly and moans about her period. It is most difficult if she is accustomed to retiring with pots of tea and hot water bottles. PMT (pre-menstrual tension) is a buzz word and can provide a good excuse for bone idleness. Alternatively it may be for real and you should be sympathetic. Not easy, this one.

If, having talked to her, you feel she is making a fuss about the whole subject, tell her you think so and that you would be glad if she would take a couple of Panadol and get on with her life without involving everyone else. Mention that it helps communal living if some things are private.

Another important aspect of health is diet. What, how, when and where a nanny eats will tell you a lot about her. It will affect you if she eats too much, too little, too often or finishes packets, jars, the last tomato, crust, bit of pâté/dolcelatte/chocolate ear-

Nannies' and mother's helps' grumbles

- Not being paid on time
- Being given too short notice for babysitting
- Last minute change of plans
- Employers interfering with the nanny's handling of a child
- Employers cluttering up the kitchen/playroom, particularly while gassing with friends
- Employers not making up their minds
- Employers forgetting repeatedly to do something they said they would
- Employers getting drunk
- Employers shouting at and rowing with each other
- Employers saving up several grumbles and bringing them up unexpectedly
- Always running out of lavatory paper, cleaning aids
- Old, inefficient machines, e.g. vacuums
- Employers being mean with the heating in winter
- Having to leave everything tidy always

marked for you or your husband. If she is prone to this sort of thoughtlessness, suggest that she asks before swiping anything of which there's not much left.

If you try to lend a willing ear to the nanny's latest attempts to slim, it may pall when you watch her nightly flit to the chip shop with her mates. Try not to be irritated; remember that she is young and her good intentions will often fail, but you don't *have* to listen to them. Say once, 'I have heard it all before and I'll only want to hear again when you have lost three stone.' One mother bet her nanny '£20 a stone and she lost three in no time'. Recommend Weight Watchers and let them monitor the progress if you are plagued by a diet bore.

If you hired a fat nanny and she lacks energy and has a lazy outlook then that's too bad. If she gains weight noticeably while working for you, then it should concern you and it needs to be discussed. Say you are worried about her health and wonder whether her weight gain has been caused by too much children's

Employers' grumbles

- Not emptying the disposable nappy bin
- Pretending the nappy pail is infinitely expandable
- Not washing up immediately, entirely and thoroughly (employers are bad about this as well)
- Allowing thick dust and deep litter to gather in the children's rooms
- Allowing toys to get smashed or lost because they haven't been properly organized
- Not saying if the buggy/pram/high chair needs repairs
- Not dressing the children properly – grubby and/or unmended clothes, unpolished shoes, buttons hanging by a thread, inadequate clothing
- Children's unbrushed hair, dirty and uncut finger nails, tidemarks round the neck and behind the ears
- Unswilled, unrinsed, undisinfected and unscrubbed potties

tea or, heaven forbid, bingeing at midnight from loneliness/ unhappiness/homesickness?

It is sensible to steer clear where possible of subjects like diet and menstruation, because it can cause a confusion of roles; a professional nanny will not need a substitute mum or a new best friend, so however fond you are of each other, deliberately distance yourself. Period pains are the kind of thing she can talk to friends and family about. The insidious aspect of confidences is that they need to be exchanged and the employer, who may be naturally reticent about her personal affairs, can find herself making all kinds of revelations and, later, be cross with herself for having been too intimate.

Do not treat her as a teenage daughter, she may become one and you will both resent it in the long run. One agent is well aware of the converse problem: 'Some mothers depend on the company of the nanny. They don't realize how much they rely on it until their kids go away to school. Then it's just as sad for them not to have a nanny around any longer as it is to have the children away. They can get quite depressed.'

Several mothers have been alarmed to hear their nannies refer to them as 'mummy'. It starts off with the nanny making it clear to the children whom she is talking about, but can wind up with an employer wishing the ground would open and swallow her when the nanny calls her mummy in front of the milkman or granny. A few think the appellation is cosy.

A nanny who smells or has bad breath is a major horror for employers. The latter are deeply embarrassed and often don't know what to do about it. If they do not find the courage to talk to the girl about her problem, they stop spending much time with her, don't include her in family gatherings, and will shun her in many little ways. All this behaviour may be misinterpreted and cause extra stress all round.

Start the fresh air campaign with heavy hints. Open windows, stand well back, prime the children to mention it if they have already complained and you can rely on them not to cite you, give her soap, have a go at bringing the pomander back into fashion in SW18, and grab a clothes peg as she enters the room. Seriously though, you may already be searching for excuses to get rid of her on other grounds, because the stench has become unbearable and that for you has become a Sackable Offence.

Dread it as anyone does, compose your words and your smile, catch her eye, take a deep breath and say, 'I think I have noticed recently that you possibly aren't using enough deodorant? . .' (Pause to check the effect of this thunderbolt. Has she twigged instantly that you are talking about her BO which she is acutely aware of? If not, and that blank expression is set, take another deep breath and blunder on.)

'It really matters to me that my nanny should smell nice and fresh. I do hope you don't mind me mentioning it, but we *really* need to sort this out together . . .' (Has it suddenly penetrated? Is she scarlet and sobbing? If so stop, mop her up saying that it's all going to be all right *now*.)

The reaction may be swift and unpleasant: don't be surprised if your careful phrasing has insulted her deeply and/or she can no longer look you in the face, and she tells you she's off. Many employers don't attempt to solve this problem, because of the high odds that she will resign. It is an upsetting subject and no fun for anyone to have to deal with.

The nanny's problems: professional
Overload and underload
A nanny doesn't have to be physically ill to let the job get on top of her, and the prudent long-term employer will be well aware of periodic job dissatisfaction caused by overload and underload. When you hear your nanny's voice becoming more shrill and less patient with the children and she looks worn out, give the poor girl a break. When she returns from her longer than usual weekend, sit her down and talk to her about how to deal with the problems. If she says she feels too busy to do anything properly, either she needs a lecture on time and motion or she is overloaded, in which case you must decide jointly where to prune her schedule.

The other side of the coin is underload. This can happen to nannies who are looking after just one baby or whose charges are away at school for most of the day. She is lonely and bored (her best friend may have just left for Canada), and she may do her relatively few tasks either inefficiently and lackadaisically or efficiently and thoroughly as usual. Either way, you must take action. First, do a bit less yourself and think about ways to keep her occupied. Maybe her mornings could be spent with another family? Would she like to start a playgroup or song and dance group with a nanny friend to amuse your baby's local contemporaries? Or maybe you haven't realized yet that you don't need a nanny any more.

Both overload and underload can produce hypochondria. Headaches, making heavy weather of heavy colds, flu and endless upset tummies are all symptoms of the nanny needing a break or planning a complete change of scene where your lovely home and family do not feature.

Fitting in with the family
Fathers
One lurking drawback to the family – and far too many nannies discount his impact until too late – is the proud sire of her charges. Although countless fathers are supportive, appreciative, kind and helpful, many of them are the opposite and can be boring, obstructive, humiliating and arrogant, and also can undermine the sterling work their wives have put in to keep the

nanny with the family for that extra year. Some are genuinely distressing to a nanny.

Nannies are buoyant and sensibly dismissive of some types of dad. One's party piece for her friends is to take off her Hooray Henry employer preening himself in his Puffa jacket. He caught her at it once and 'his sense of humour could *just* take it'. One employer humiliated his nanny at a large lunch party by insisting that she sing 'that marvellous teddy song'. She refused but has never forgotten it.

One fat dad always came down to breakfast in his underpants. The nanny reports, 'I didn't know where to look in the mornings. I find it hard to talk to the man of any house, but it's worst when you see too much of them.' A mother's help remembers one horror who 'ate noisily and hated kids'.

During the nanny's first week fathers need to be reminded to be better about sharing the house. A score of nannies mention being burst in on by a dad wandering round the nanny's part of the house or flat. Some stopped being amused when he walked in on their ablutions too regularly with a stupid grin, and others were crosser still – with as much dignity as they could muster from the lavatory seat. If the poor wretched nanny can pluck up courage to mention his odd behaviour, a wife should not take umbrage but put locks on the door and insist that her spouse is more thoughtful in future.

One nanny had just got the children out of the bath and dressed, when she had to answer the phone. She returned to hang up the towels and let out the bath water to find a plump pink father waiting expectantly for her return. 'Will you scrub my back for me?' It's not so jokey if you are 18, it's your first job and you will need a good reference when you leave. On top of this his wife may well greet her tales of mass bathtime with cold scepticism.

Moving house
One employer complains bitterly that her nanny resigned rather than move house with the family. This seems unreasonable. If anyone's job relocates it is not taken for granted that the employees move without a murmur. Indeed, they can be offered redundancy.

Moving house is a terrific strain on everyone. Builders can cause unforeseen horrors. You may have to find an interim place to live. It might be a cramped flat, a damp cottage in the country, or the grandparents . . .

Grandparents
The relationship between the employer and the grandparents will set the tone of theirs with the nanny. Relaxed and loving grandparents enjoy their grandchildren and welcome the diversions and fun they provide and may often be a great source of support to mother and nanny in time of crisis. But, a prolonged stay, particularly if enforced by unfortunate circs, with the in-laws may cause too much tension. Employers mention the following problems with grandparents during any length of stay:

My mum is surprised that they have as much as two days off a week. In her day it was more like one a month and she often says so.

My mother-in-law cannot understand why I need help. She had four children without any.

They'll never get used to christian names and no uniform. I keep nannies and grandparents as far apart as possible.

I always hire an Australian temp to go with my children to their grandmother. Otherwise my nanny would leave me – no one could stand such barbed comments. I explain the difficulties, pay the earth and stay well away myself.

Most grandparents want to be involved with their grand-children, but this does not give them the right to make life more difficult by interfering with your *modus vivendi* with the nanny. When she is staying with them alone with the children, it is sensible to warn her of any old-fashioned views and foibles. It is probably also a good idea to prime your mother to curb her tongue and let the nanny do it her way unless she is floundering. In fact, if they are both told to live and let live, and that the other 'can be exasperating', then the chances are they will get on splendidly and even strike up a sort of friendship.

The best grannies have been trained to say: 'Young families today work harder and need all the help they can get' and they will not wish to rock the boat, but be supportive.

Change

Any psychiatrist will comment that change is stressful. Nannies and employers don't find it as good as a rest because it involves changes of job description, new thinking, instructions and discussions – in short, complication.

Family additions

Even something apparently simple, like a new baby that everyone is expecting, can cause a lot of change. The employer may be post-natally depressed, unexpectedly possessive and a bit dotty. Her husband may be moody or uncommunicative. The existing children will certainly react to the new arrival, who may present his own problems. The nanny is expected to show more initiative and do more. She may also have to cope with a maternity nurse, and possibly, if the mother is usually out of the house, the nanny has the added strain of getting to know her better and differently, for the first time.

Even though her extra duties were outlined in advance of the baby's arrival, the nanny may find the added workload exhausting and more than she expected. Many agencies mention the fact that some NNEBs are loath to look after babies – they know it takes a lot of time and effort and they do not like the restrictions of late feeds and the general mess. One tutor on the Birmingham NNEB course says that she 'would like to see more training in the 24-hour care of young babies on the course'. Norlanders have an advantage in having had experience of this, but then even they are under supervision.

Unless your NNEB has done this work before, don't rely on her training and leave her in sole charge of a new baby. Employers are frequently outraged to discover that their trained nanny doesn't know what she should be doing with a new-born.

Your visitors and friends

Grandparents, step- and half-brothers and sisters, visiting cousins and friends and ex-wives or husbands may all come to stay – some for a long time and, on occasion, for ever. Inevitably, this will mean more work for the nanny. Do recognize the impact this has on her job description, and talk about it before she approaches you. Encourage friends who leave hordes of children at your home to tip her generously. If a step-child who is an irregular feature of your life comes to stay for the holidays increase the carer's salary for the duration, unless you genuinely intend to take on the extra work yourself.

If you take the nanny on holiday, or to stay with friends, you'll be lucky if she can handle the change professionally and allow you to enjoy it too. Staying in other people's houses means that temporarily the nanny is living by someone else's House Rules as well as carrying yours around in her luggage, and gains another boss to boot. This can lead to trouble. One nanny says, 'We went away to stay with friends of my employers. The lady sent me out to the kitchen and treated me like a little nobody worth nothing. She told me I could probably find "something in the fridge" if I was hungry. She went on treating me bad all that weekend.' Whether the hostess was being off-hand or was just flustered by the numbers she had to feed, this is a good example of unhappy weekending.

By the by, weekend and holiday exposure to your friends and the ways that they treat their nannies are familiar trouble spots. Do not have post-mortem chats with your nanny unless they are entirely complimentary. To pre-empt the possibility of your good nanny picking up bad habits from a friend's sloppy one, drop a little hint that you *did* notice Mandy forcing lettuce down a child's throat with a fork, so you mentioned it to her employer, your friend. End of conversation.

Divorce and remarriage
Divorce, separation and remarriage affects nannies greatly and that's an understatement. If they don't like it, they won't lump it and off they'll go. Some will stay because they take to the new partner or lack of one, and others stay just long enough to tide you over the initial upheavals. This is extremely obliging, particularly if they aren't mad about the new regime and probable extra responsibility. The least you can do is to pay them more.

It is reasonable to expect a nanny to adapt readily to temporary changes. But how long is temporary? If you want to keep her, make her feel part of your plans, give her extra time off and don't be arrogant enough to assume that she will go along with all you do uncomplainingly. It's fundamental to any job that you check out employers before working for them. If the nanny's boss leaves her partner or swaps one for another, the nanny may wish to reassess her position. If her parents get divorced or remarry, similarly expect her to be affected and try to make it possible for her to spend more time at home for a while.

Death

Death is difficult to deal with. For everyone concerned. Obviously an employee must be given time off to attend any relative's funeral and she would be required to drop her plans and help you in similar circumstances. If an employer has a wasting disease, or develops a disability, the nanny will be in the extraordinarily awkward position of deciding whether to abandon the family, or stay on and risk martyrdom. Try and make it easy for her. Tell her your hopes and fears without any pressure on her to do what would suit you best. Spell it out that she is not to feel she must stay and also, that life will be very different from now on.

The death of a child – or even a terminal illness or grave injury – may be more than your nanny can cope with. In these circumstances, many nannies do leave and they can't be blamed in any way for wanting to get away. Like falling off a horse, a nanny might come to terms with her sadness and shock (and misplaced guilt on many occasions), if she lived through the grief with the sad family, but that's her decision. A cot death is uniquely traumatic.

It is embarrassing at one level for a nanny to find herself unable to work happily with a recently bereaved employer, who may be unapproachable and withdrawn in his or her grief. More complicatedly still, if the wife dies, the nanny has suddenly to deal with, in effect, a new employer in the widower. He'll be a novice at the job and may not have much idea about anything domestic.

If you discover that your real need now is for a responsible housekeeper or more mature carer for your children, explain gently to the nanny that because the situation has changed so completely she should find another job. She will probably be relieved you brought it up first.

A new side

Both employers and employees may reveal a 'new side' of themselves after several months or years of employment. This 'new side' may result from historic problems which emerge or re-emerge in a new form, or are thrust upon either party by fate or an act of God. A 'new side' is almost always a darker side.

Employers' problems which may impose on the nanny include: alcoholism and attempting to stay on the wagon (imagine her having to listen to a drunk dad beating up his wife and wondering what to do if he starts on the children next); unemployment (so she may be stuck with a depressed hulk under her feet who is keen to help with the children now and again); nervous breakdowns and recuperating from illnesses can also keep employers at home unexpectedly and require attention and effort; very pregnant mothers who have given up work to have their baby and who interfere with the status quo – the awful spectre, as Robert Chantry-Price, director of the NNEB mentions, of 'mum doing her mumming' and disrupting the routine.

None of these events are likely either to have been predicted, or their possibility to have been revealed at interview. In other words, circumstances do change. And for nannies too.

You may discover too late that the nanny's reportedly happy family life is tragically the opposite. One mother mentions her nanny's revelation on the doorstep, having been sacked for losing her temper repeatedly with the children, that she had been abused by her father as a teenager and this had made her cruel, she thought.

The 'social smoker' of six months ago may turn into a smoke stack. The glass of wine in the evenings may become an empty vodka bottle in her waste paper basket and, you note with growing alarm, that there weren't any friends to share it with last night. The quiet, controlled admonition to the children has turned into a harridan's shriek and the neighbours are complaining. The shrinking violet of yesteryear is only reflected in her electric purple boob tube (and how *they've* grown, as your husbands remarks nonchalantly . . . daily), and you recognize with a sinking heart that men and the discos beckon.

A frightening 'new side' to the carer may be in drug use. One agency reports that when they rang to check that the nanny was getting on well with the family, the grandmother was irate. 'Getting on well? I should think not indeed! I sacked her myself within days of her arrival. I came in from shopping and found the new nanny rolling about on my daughter's bed with an Irish labourer who was meant to be wallpapering and there were hypodermics all over the place. I look after the children now so no one has to see those kind of disgusting things again.'

But there is a lighter side, and employers were interesting in their general consensus that nannies' and mother's helps' confidence grew in the job. But, as one mother reported, 'Of course, any 20-year-old changes a lot in a year in her new circumstances, so expect it and hope for the best.'

Remember the House Rules?

You have either forgotten about these by now (in which case turn back to chapter 2) and that is why you have friction problems, or the nanny has adhered to the whole bunch of House Rules up until now and things are beginning to slip. This may start to happen at three or six months or any time thereafter. She is probably not doing it to test your memory, the restrictions are just getting to her.

Decide with your mate whether you mind maintaining your carefully constructed edifice of strictures as continued self-defence. You may want to rethink certain aspects of them. For example, you may now feel secure that you have netted a real goodie – a responsible nanny with a ton of energy who is well capable of getting up at 7 am after arriving home at 1 am or later. So, don't let this rule slide, giving her good reason to think that all the rules were a hollow show of strength at the start. Tell her that you noticed that she came in later than you both agreed last night, but that you have thought about it and have decided to trust her judgement about her bedtime for the time being. Does she think this is a good idea and she won't abuse it, will she? This is good gamesmanship and it is fun to be seen to be generous and it didn't cost you a thing. Nice one, Cyrilla.

It is worth saying that the best nanny/employer relationships seem to be based on a good deal of give and take. Nannies are great ones for not sticking to what their agencies, colleges or bolshie friends insist are their rights – if they like you and you are clearly not out to exploit their kindness, they will want to do many little extras for you. In return, after praise and thanks, next time you can show her that you really appreciate her flexibility, and it will be your turn to be more easy-going as well, and if she has any sense she won't take advantage of you either.

If all the House Rules are being bent and broken all over the shop and you haven't had the energy to enforce them for a month, don't put off the day of reckoning any longer. Either she lives the way you want under your roof or she goes. Unless you have changed too and anything she wants has become the rule. This is popularly described as 'trusting her totally'.

Quite how an employer can misjudge a character totally after months of living with someone is illustrated by the mother who liked and trusted her nanny implicitly. She allowed her to have friends to stay; she could go anywhere in the house; she was left in sole charge of the children while the parents went on holiday. So imagine the mother's horror when her bank manager queried some strange-looking cheques. It emerged that this much prized nanny had been adding noughts to her salary cheque and had forged her boss's own cheques. In all she had embezzled £3,000. Her employer was flabbergasted. Although history doesn't relate, it might be argued that this nanny was not a natural law breaker. She was just tempted by the ease of access to her employer's cheque book and could resist anything except temptation.

The epitome of a disaster nanny is summarized briskly: 'Over several months she broke into the wine cellar, hid the empties in the various loo tanks, flooded the house, and fled with the best jewels, leaving the children unattended.'

Employers may be forgiven on occasion for thinking that they cannot win. It is just a matter of how badly they lose.

Finding Solutions

Mrs Davis of Norland advises her students to: 'Be sponge-like, absorbent. Recognize the kicking the cat syndrome. You've got to be fairly tough-skinned and ignore someone being curt at the end of a long day. It is not aimed at you.' For the average nanny this is pretty grown-up stuff. Many employers assume too much *savoir faire* on the part of their nannies. They forget that the young are often gauche, crass, shy, easily embarrassed and sensitive to humiliation.

Employers love to think that they 'shoot straight from the hip' and 'tell it like it is' with 'no holds barred' to 'clear the air' or 'have it out' – in other words, nothing short of a stand-up fight with their nanny or mother's help. This is bullying, self-indulgent and rude, though entirely human. The cathartic effect will be short-lived and if she answers back, you have real problems (see chapter 14).

Although your attack may have been caused by over-reaction to a misdemeanour which affected the children, you have no right to shout at someone. You may deeply upset a young nanny by such behaviour. Remember that this would be most unlikely to happen in an ordinary job. Also, once you have rushed in and blown your top, there is no room for manoeuvre or face-saving if mitigating circumstances later emerge. After all, your whimsical husband *may* have given the go-ahead to some daft scheme. A salutary reminder is provided by one nanny who says, 'Any employer who's rude to an employee risks losing them. Most employers treat you badly at some time; I've learned never to let them do it twice.'

Even if nannies mean to be polite, they sometimes get it wrong as far as the employer is concerned. Many an employer is genuinely hurt when having taken trouble and given the girl a beautiful birthday present, or announced a handsome pay rise, she hears (just) a mumbled 'thanks' in response. And that's all she does hear about it.

Another obvious example of unintentional rudeness is when a nanny brings her friends to your house and you meet them in the hall. They advance crab-like, talking to each other over their shoulders and ignoring you. Finally the employer plucks up courage to say a tentative 'hello'. They barely respond. In time she will see how you make a point of introducing your friends to her and with any luck get the message. If she doesn't and it bugs you, tell her.

Don't think of it as confrontation. Try not to churn half the night or victimize your husband. Deal with the problems the moment they emerge. Do not ruminate or bore the mothers on the school steps or your colleagues at lunch; just say what is bothering you to the person to whom it matters, and try and teach her to do the same.

Don't forget to *listen* to what your nanny or mother's help has to say. It can be effective to say as little as possible to start with, hear her out. This way you learn a lot quickly. It also gives you time to prepare your response. Try to see the problem from her point of view. Why is she so fed up/cross/irritated? Be alert to what she is *not* saying. Often the unsaid may provide the clue to solving the problem.

When in doubt about a moan or a request, buy time. Before thinking about the query at all say automatically, 'Ah, I'll have to think about that/ask my husband/check in the diary.' The carer should use the same ploy too when she is being asked a favour or being asked to change her plans. If you have said yes to some plan and you later regret it, don't hesitate to say, apologetically, that on further reflection you have changed your mind.

Social graces are at a premium between employer and employee, especially with a living-in nanny. Many employers fail to have them at times when annoyed by their nannies. In spite of your natural desire to remonstrate in indignant tones, it is actually more productive not to sound cross and overbearing. If you can do it with a smile so much the better. Like Scott and Oates in the Antarctic, the need for self-sacrificing tolerance and courtesy is great. When the going gets tough, the habit of good manners will rescue you from ranting and raving regrettably.

Employers often moan about their nannies and mother's helps not showing enough initiative. Try not to be put out if she has done something off her own bat for once, but it is not quite how you would have tackled the problem. Try to praise her as enthusiastically as you can. Once bitten she'll be shy of doing anything similar again.

The art of saying what's wrong

Whatever happens, try to issue instructions and admonitions pleasantly. It isn't always easy to smile when you are in a hurry, frothing with fury or just plain tired, but it makes so much difference. It's a vicious circle; the nanny does something important wrong again, the employer has said it with a smile several times before and she doesn't want to give her a ticking off but feels she must, so she becomes tense, her brow furrows and in a strangled voice she deals with the whole thing badly. Rather than risk an eruption which you will regret and anyway could have been better phrased, (and that can be just as tiresome after the event), go somewhere else, think quietly about it, let time pass and compose your features into some semblance of sanity before tackling the subject once more.

Mrs Davis tells her students to start their complaints or gripes with the words 'I feel' or 'I prefer' or 'It upsets me when' and this is a sophisticated defusing device. An employer can take a leaf out of her book. When a nanny says 'I thought you said' or 'I didn't think you'd mind if', take a deep breath and then put her straight, politely. Some mothers report their paralysis when it comes to asking their nannies not to do something in a particular way, as well as general instructions. Such phrases as 'I wonder if you would mind?', 'Do you think you could?', 'It would be so marvellous/terrific/helpful/kind/useful if', 'Would you be an angel/duck/dear/pal and . . .', 'I'd be so grateful for . . .', do help to oil the wheels. This gush helps a nanny feel that she's not being got at and/or merely the recipient of a string of orders.

Don't get too subtle by cloaking your every need/wish/command in this way. She may interpret such flannel as you not meaning what you say. If she thinks you said 'It would be nice if you did X, but I'm not bothered if you don't get round to it today', then you overdid it. One parent admits to 'gabbling nervously and burying the instruction in the middle of a stream of chat'. In this case, the girl may well miss the instruction.

Eye contact means just that. Don't save up all your criticisms for long journeys where you can look straight ahead for hours, and don't issue instructions with your head in a broom cupboard. Two mothers reveal that these are their favourite venues for a ticking off. Closet employers will find that this cowardice is impractical and self-defeating. Apart from shopping lists and written reminders, don't resort to memos. Blasts should be delivered personally. Just as you ought not to yell, so you mustn't write hate mail to the top floor. This verges on the loony, but lots of people do it. If you find it therapeutic and it orders your mind, write it down, have it around for a few hours, but throw it away eventually.

Employers who wish to remain calm and reasonably happy with their nanny *have* to be tolerant and remember that they can't change a personality and turn it into a robot that mind reads and doesn't answer back. They indulge in too much ascribing of blame. Employers, like nannies and everyone else, find it difficult to admit they are in the wrong.

Postscript
It may be helpful to remind employers that the five stages of any project are popularly held to be:

1 Enthusiasm
2 Disillusionment
3 Panic
4 Search for the guilty
5 Punishment of the innocent

Try to be the kind of employer who recognizes that we are all human. Second chances given your nanny's youth and probable immaturity should be considered, unless she has done something that is *totally unacceptable*. Find out exactly why and how things went wrong, talk about it, sleep on it, and see if it won't suit both of you best if you forgive her. Remember priorities. The children may love her and she may be conscientious and kind to them; you are made of sterner stuff than they are.

10

Maternity Nurses

Maternity or 'monthly' nurses are often an employer's first experience of having a nanny in the house. The traditional maternity nurses are the residue of the old-style nannies. Far from teaching anyone much about the business of employing a nanny generally, a maternity nurse has specific functions and is specifically treated.

Are they worth it?
What's the point of having one? Opinion is sharply divided about maternity nurses; people either think that they are an indispensable part of the first few weeks of a baby's life or they can't imagine anything more idiotic and intrusive than employing one because they want to do everything for the baby themselves. One SRN mother says: 'I'm far too bossy to want anyone else and I always breast feed for months, so why bother?' And another: 'I didn't realize I'd feel so possessive; I couldn't bear anyone but Chris [her husband] and me to touch her. Next time I'll just hire an extra pair of hands to do the chores.'

Mrs Baxter who used to run the eponymous agency in Peterborough felt just that way with her five babies and says that there is far too much pressure on young mums from their friends to have maternity nurses. She reckons that they interfere unacceptably and that people should ignore such a silly fashion and have faith in their maternal instincts. She preferred to provide 'confinement helps' as an alternative – they walked dogs and other children, cooked, and helped do any odd jobs which you dread, leaving the mother free to look after the baby herself.

Nevertheless, many employers are sold on the whole idea. New mothers, especially those who want to be fit and well and back at their desks swiftly, say they appreciate a crash course in

230

babycraft (or indeed a refresher course if there is a sizeable gap between the new arrival and its sibling). They also like the peace and rest that is made possible by the extra help.

One devotee claims maternity nurses are 'a treat that everyone should try and afford. She makes an enormous difference to the happy running of the house, and yours and the baby's peace of mind.' Another confesses, 'I feel at a low emotional ebb having had a baby and need the comfort of someone else in full control. Not everyone can give birth in the paddy fields or behind a bush and get up and go straight on as though nothing had happened. Some of us have caesars and they need a lot of recovering from.' A third says, 'I wanted each baby to have that special care and attention that I would not have the strength to give them having just returned from hospital.'

A few mothers say that they always return to their mums after their babies, or their mums come to them to help out. One maternity nurse appreciates this need and says 'to be any real use, we must be a lot like their mothers'. Some families' old nannies come out of retirement to deal with any new baby born to the family, its cousins and occasionally old friends.

You can claim on BUPA or PPP for the fees if your maternity nurse is an SRN or a registered midwife and if you have had a caesarean or other complications at birth.

What sort do you want?
Different types of maternity nurses fall roughly into two categories: old and experienced or young and inexperienced. With a first baby most mothers are reassured by someone extremely experienced, organized and disciplined to teach them all about the baby. Many maternity nurses admit to far preferring the simplicity of the first time around. 'The best thing in the world is working with a first baby. Both parents are starry-eyed, all the equipment is new. There's such magic with number one.'

With later babies, it is more important that the maternity nurse is friendly and relaxed with the other children, and, though she is unlikely to give you much help with them, she should be prepared to include them in walks and bath-times and teach any nanny already in residence the ropes, so that the takeover will be smooth.

Good heavens, whatever next? A maternity nurse when

you've already got a nanny? You must be mad/rich/spoilt your in-laws may say. Ignore them, they haven't got to deal with the nanny becoming too exhausted from night duty with the baby to be pleasant to the other children during the day. But you certainly need someone who will deal tactfully with your nanny and not put her nose out of joint. This is a common problem exacerbated by the maternity nurses' characteristic grouse that young nannies don't work hard enough nowadays and they may say so too often and too loudly. This sort of professional competitiveness is tiresome; don't let the maternity nurse stir up trouble.

Some old nannies say that present-day NNEBs are snobby about their lack of training and one comments: 'I make sure I never cross swords with them. I know how to conduct myself. I just think, I'll keep off the grass with you my dear, and I am pleasant but never intimate with them.'

Many people are wary of traditional 'old-style' maternity nurses. The employment agencies often concur. One warns: 'I'm not doing maternity any more because too many of the old ones are a bit mental and I could never persuade them to retire before they became a liability. It was so awkward and cruel to be saying constantly that I didn't have any jobs for them, but it was the only safe thing to do.' Another reports: 'They are very nanny-knows-best and try to pressurize mothers to bottle feed so that they have complete control.' The last states: 'The old dears are complete pains in the neck. All the mothers think they are ghastly and even if someone dies in the house, their attitude is as long as the baby's OK that's not their business.'

Christine Hill, an obstetric physio who runs excellent ante- and post-natal classes from her house on the river in Chiswick, says that her mums 'are frightened of them and the babies probably are too. The young ones may create an uncomfortable feeling of the blind leading the blind, but anything is preferable to living with a battle axe.'

There are too many horrifying stories of old maternity nurses who are over the hill and don't know it for employers' and agencies' reactions to be hot air. The point is that if you choose a mature and experienced maternity nurse you will be well-advised to make sure that she is fit in wind and limb and capable of doing her job professionally and looking after *you* which is part of it.

Both employers and agencies agree that the good maternity nurses are like gold dust and a bad one is such a nightmare that you are better off doing the job yourself.

How long before the birth should you find one?
Everyone is agreed that about nine months' warning of the baby's arrival will already be too little notice to net the best maternity nurses. They are snapped up the moment the little poached egg shows up on the pregnancy DIY kit and the wise mother will interrupt her 'gynae's' speech of congratulations to ask if she may use the phone to book her special treasure.

One mother whose baby arrived a month prematurely and thus neatly evaded the dates for which the maternity nurse had been booked, hired a replacement from her hospital bed. 'It was incredibly lucky. She was much better than the one I'd planned to have whom I'd had before.' Most people are not so fortunate.

Where do you get them?
The grapevine hums with news of gems: 'My dear, she refused to take a minute off for three weeks and even the dog got breakfast in bed.' One maternity nurse has been employed exclusively by word of mouth recommendation for twelve years and says: 'Employers can check up on me with their friends. But I can also check up on them. It works both ways.'

Don't automatically assume that because X and Y like someone that you necessarily will too. You may discover entirely different attitudes in dealing with the baby, your husband, your fridge, other children, granny and a host of other details which make her entirely unsuitable for your family. Someone else's old nanny, however much revered by 'her' family, may not prove in the least good news as far as you are concerned. Having employed her, which everyone insists is a huge favour to you whatever the price, you may fall out with old friends if you decide that she is a self-opinionated old bag who needs a constant audience.

The grapevine occasionally contains a bad apple who continues working for 'everyone' by a sort of Emperor's New Clothes con trick combined with years of Chinese whispers. Someone once said she was fantastic, so no one along the line explodes the myth. If you do, you'll find several people back along the chain of recommenders who gave her glowing refs but readily concur with your criticisms of her shortcomings. They didn't want to be the first to mar the dossier and probably thought something was wrong with *them* for not liking her.

Several of the employment agencies (see pages 283–97) have maternity nurses on their books and one, Pembroke Maternity Service, is run only for maternity nurses by an extremely experienced and well-qualified ex-maternity nurse. The agency is small with a nucleus of highly trained old-style nannies, but can also provide young trained nurses too. You can also advertise in *The Lady*.

What do they cost?
The range in the early 1990s seems to be from £120 to £300 a week. There are also daily maternity nurses who charge about £45 a day. They all pay their own insurance and National Insurance contributions because they are self-employed.

Maternity nurses to twins must be some of the most heroic women on earth. They command the highest salaries and may safeguard your sanity in the first few weeks of unrelenting bawling and feeding, burping and changing. Employers of these martyrs are pathetically grateful for their calm and confident support.

'We would never have lived through it without her' and 'She made us see that there would eventually be light at the end of the tunnel' and 'always a gentle smile for each little face at 3 am – what a saint!' Don't haggle if it means losing one of these. It is uniquely hard work and if you have just performed the miracle of multiple birth no one needs a good maternity nurse more than you do.

Payment is obviously negotiable, but if she does not start on the day on which she was booked, because the baby is late arriving or you are stuck in hospital with complications of whatever kind, you must be prepared to pay her at least half pay for the first week of waiting and, after that, full pay even if she has not started.

Many maternity nurses complain that employers are extremely mean about this. The 'waiting' period is a grey area as far as payment is concerned and employers must resist the temptation to take advantage of this and not pay the nurse properly while she waits for you and the baby to do what you said you would do, and she is unable to earn her living elsewhere in the meantime.

Many Australian and New Zealand nurses do maternity work and are attracted to the high wages which enable them to travel soon after they have saved enough cash. No one would argue that it is money for jam, given that the restrictions of keeping a baby's hours preclude any social life during a job.

How much time off?
When your maternity nurse has worked for you for a week she is entitled to 24 hours off each week. She is on duty 24 hours a day.

How long will you need one?
Four weeks is the ideal time . . . don't hand over so completely that you are scared to death of her leaving and haven't a clue what to do with the baby because she hasn't let you touch it since birth.

Six weeks. Both times.

She stayed on for two years because she fell in love with the baby and then the gardener whom she eventually married.

We sacked her after three days; she was a tiresome old woman who drove me up the wall and it was mutual.

Some maternity nurses understandably don't want to do such concentrated work stints for longer than a month, though others prefer the continuity of an extended stay. There is no ideal length of stay; it depends on each individual and how much you are the victim of hormonal upheavals and emotional exhaustion, demanding husband or jealous children. Some mothers feel they need protracted support at this time.

What exactly does she do?
The Pembroke Maternity Service issues some guidelines to an employer entitled 'The Duties of a Maternity Nurse'.

The maternity nurse is a professional whose responsibility is the welfare of the mother and baby. This is a 24-hour-a-day job. She is not a domestic servant for family cooking, cleaning, washing and ironing, nor is she responsible for the care of other children in the family.

She is responsible for guidance and help in all aspects of feeding together with teaching a convenient routine to you and the baby. She is responsible for the tidiness and cleanliness of her room, the baby's room, the nursery bathroom and the nursery kitchen. All the baby's washing and ironing and care of clothes is also her responsibility. She will undertake simple nursing care of the mother if necessary and will advise on a suitable diet for breast feeding mothers. She will ensure that you get as much rest as possible throughout her stay so that you are 'back on your feet' by the time she leaves. Meals are normally taken with the family and, when possible, she will offer to help.

Agents and mothers agree that you should never employ a maternity nurse without a proper interview at home before the birth. You should do this well in advance. If you are a first-time mother, ask her to give you a shopping list for the baby. She is bound to like particular brands and have preferences for special items of kit, so you may as well humour her. If you have done all the shopping for a previous baby, show her what you have done already and make sure she uses it and doesn't utter a word of disapproval. Some maternity nurses despise disposables. Old-fashioned nannies also don't like baby-gros. They love beautiful shawls and long nighties and hand-knitted cardigans which they handwash far into the night as obsessively as Lady Macbeth.

Show her where she is going to sleep and how much other space you can allot to her in the house. Many maternity nurses do sleep with the baby, but if they do, then it's specially important to give them somewhere else to sit in the evenings.

Ask the maternity nurse about her qualifications, where she trained and *always* check references. Does she smoke? Talk about whether you want to demand feed or 'get the baby into a good routine'. Does this mean that she recommends you leave the baby to yell all night/at all? A very few take the toughest possible line and just shut the door and let the baby cry at night without going near it: one mother says she had to sack one devotee of this Draconian discipline for a week-old baby – both she and her husband cracked on the first night and asked the nanny to leave immediately.

Will she support you if you hope to breast feed? Sometimes a maternity nurse will come and wake you with a sweet-smelling baby and you return it to her to be burped and settled, while you snuggle down next to your burrowing husband, or she wakes you and you go and join her. Will you have the baby between you in bed or on the floor beside you in a basket or elsewhere? All these details will inform her what sort of mother you will be to work for. Any information you can give her about what you do and don't like will help prevent stress after the baby's birth, when you may be feeling exhausted and intolerant.

How much do you think you will want to be looked after? Breakfast in bed? One agent says, 'No one wants to be running around with trays for every meal, but to provide coffee and tea to mothers is common courtesy.' Some nannies can be bossy. Decide if you can stand it. Some people positively welcome it, find it relaxing and consistent with their recent institutionalization in hospital and thrive under the nurse's strict regimes.

All the rules are for your own good; it's just a question of whether you will agree to being dictated to or have an uneasy feeling that you are old enough to make up your own mind and the nanny may be overly enjoying her ability to do that job for you. They may enforce rest in the afternoons, refuse visitors, deny your relations a peep at the baby which could unsettle its routine and even prevent you from driving for the first three weeks or so.

This last injunction concerns post-natal amnesia and general dottiness, which is quite as common as depression but much less talked about and is, of course, impossible to quantify in advance of the birth. Hormonal changes can cause debilitating worry to any woman at this stage; to be cherished by a good maternity nurse can provide a wonderful bridge with reality. One mother describes the process as a 'need to grow back a hard shell or a new skin if you will. I do feel entirely vulnerable for several weeks after having had a baby.'

Talk to the maternity nurse about what sort of care she intends to provide for you and set clear demarcation lines of duty between her and the existing nanny if there is one and likewise the cleaning lady. Who will wash and iron your nighties? You may be glad of clean ones daily when you arrive home.

A maternity nurse will usually expect to be treated as a member of the family. One says: 'If employers don't feel they can eat with me then they shouldn't have me.' A peculiarly intimate relationship may develop so that you may feel the need 'to pour your soul out' as another put it. But maybe you will be quite yourself after the birth and that self will be as resilient and organized as ever and the last thing you will feel like doing is having to talk to a maternity nurse.

If there are separate catering arrangements for your existing nanny, it can be difficult to make an exception to the House Rules for the maternity nurse. Use your judgement having met and sized-up both individuals, but don't on any account be bullied into something you won't be comfortable with. Remember the remote possibility of skinlessness and be resolute now.

Young maternity nurses may not be fully conversant with the proper means of sterilizing bottles, because they have always had made-up bottles to give babies in hospital during their training. One agent says this causes so many complaints that she recommends that the mother show the maternity nurse precisely how she wants it done.

Any professional maternity nurse will recognize the need for the new mother and father to be alone, both with the baby and without. One old hand says, 'Some fathers get embarrassed if I watch them kissing and cuddling the baby, specially if it's a boy, so I always melt away.'

The Pembroke Maternity Service insists that their maternity nurses wear some kind of uniform, even if just a tabard, partly so they are treated like professionals and partly to guard against the risk of infection.

Agree the terms, the time off, the pay, and the exact day you want to start hiring her. Most mothers say that they like the nurse to arrive at home before her return from hospital to set everything out and bully the husband into turning up the heating or generally making the house babyworthy. Some ask her to come to the hospital to collect the mother and thereby attempt to avoid a sibling's instant jealousy by letting the maternity nurse be the one who fusses over the new baby at the start and introduces it into the household, leaving the mother free to be warm and loving with the other child/children.

One maternity nurse was funny about the problems of jealousy in the first few weeks.

Lots of dads hardly come near me or the newborn. They find the baby's arrival very messy and traumatic and strange and don't know how to react at all. The odd thing is that dad is invariably ill during the first month, just a little toothache or feeling a bit off-colour, but it's always because he doesn't feel he really has a role to play and wants a bit of extra attention.

I don't encourage them to stay at home for these imagined ills. I pack 'em off back to the office and am a bit brisk to protect the mums. No more trouble from *you*, I say quietly and they look at me in surprise like naughty boys.

Some maternity nurses are queasy about circumcision and particularly request not to work in families where it is the norm. This is coupled with complaints from maternity nurses that many mothers are exploitative. This means, by their definition, being asked to walk dogs, do the household cleaning, washing and ironing, being expected to clean out grates, look after the toddler, and make family meals. Then, they say, this type of employer has the nerve to quibble about the agreed salary and time off. Don't earn a maternity nurse's disapproval unless you want them to leave you holding the baby, which they certainly will do, and with the full backing of their agency. Unless *they* offer to do anything other than the baby, you should not demand it as of right.

This is far from saying that many maternity nurses are not immensely obliging and helpful in a million uncalled-for ways, as many mothers report:

She reorganized my store cupboards and did everyone's mending which had piled up over five years.

She arranged flowers terrifically well and was sweet to my invalid aunt who lived next door.

She was a gem and a strong gem to boot. She pulled a box spring double bed through a first storey window and moved loads of furniture with my husband.

One maternity nurse who has worked with babies for thirty years says:

I like parents who love and enjoy their children. I am happiest when it is easiest to leave knowing that the baby will be happy and secure and its needs considered unselfishly . . . I like an interesting, relaxed atmosphere, reasonable space and light and a grandmother's house in a pretty part of the country.

Maternity nurses are understandably driven mad by 'flighty mums who insist on breast feeding but refuse to express and then go out shopping or for a lunch date. They arrive back so late that the baby is screaming and impossible to settle and I feel much the same way.' 'Some new mothers are so silly; in the end they force me to make rules, so it is better to start with a few,' says another.

239

One mother wonders why maternity nurses ever do the job: 'It is an odd life. One minute she is so much needed and wanted and so close to the family and the next off she goes somewhere else and is virtually forgotten within weeks.' One maternity nurse of many years' experience replies: 'At long last I have discovered the depth of my feelings for these little scraps and why. I love them desperately and they never push you away nor make you feel unwanted and neither hurt nor reject you by look or by touch. I'm very secure in my baby world with each baby individually looked after by me and I really feel loved in return.' Many others simply reply, 'I just love/adore/am crazy about babies.'

Finally, the seeds of the relationship between mother and maternity nurse may grow into a lifetime of reminiscences for the whole family. Several maternity nurses report that they have been invited to be godmothers and/or are always invited to the christening, usually back on duty for the day. There is a special toast to her at the celebration afterwards and the treasured photos live in serried ranks round the maternity nurse's sitting room at home. Most employers say that their children always receive first birthday cards from the maternity nurse, and they particularly look forward to her visits so that they can hear the old stories again about how they behaved at three weeks at three in the morning.

11
Special Needs

Sadly there are no agencies which specialize in finding nannies and other help to care for children who are physically and mentally handicapped. There are a number which deal principally with the care of the elderly and to some extent with children. The best are registered with the UK Home Care Association. An excellent example of this kind of agency is Care At Home in Guildford, which is much admired by competitors. It takes on its books one in four would-be carers and provides an intensive day's training and interviews (see Agencies, pages 283–97).

A London agency, the Nanny Service, which has close links with nurses through its Childminders business (see Agencies, pages 283–97), is experienced in finding suitable nannies for less handicapped children with, for example, Down's syndrome and cystic fibrosis.

Mothers say that they also get nannies for children with special needs by contacting the heads of the residential training colleges (see chapter 7) and their local NNEB colleges. In both cases they ask if there are any students on that year's course who particularly want to work with children with special needs and whether the course tutor recommends them personally.

Some handicaps can only be dealt with by qualified nurses who may be contacted through the relevant agencies, by advertising in the *Nursing Times* and via hospital notice boards. Some mothers use *The Lady* and recommend that anyone with a handicapped child is upfront about it in the ad.

The range of different kinds of children with special needs is vast. Nannies are needed to help with slow learners and backward children, cerebral palsy, Down's syndrome, children with short life expectancies for a variety of different reasons, having a tracheostomy or colostomy, mentally and physically handicapped, blindness, deafness, tuberous sclerosis, low IQ, hyperactivity, car accident victims, multiple sclerosis, congenital heart and respiratory problems, cystic fibrosis, fits and epilepsy, behaviourally difficult, microcephalic, sickle cell disease, haemophilia, AIDS, paralysis, children on ventilators and on kidney machines, with pacemakers, tracheal oesophageal fistules, paraplegic, tetraplegic, quadraplegic – there are as many therapies and treatments.

Mothers and nannies should try to keep themselves aware of facilities which are specially aimed to help the handicapped. Play Matters/The National Toy Libraries Association runs a string of toy libraries, often mobile, for the disabled and the disadvantaged. It was the brain child of Jilly Norris, a Froebel teacher with two handicapped sons. Special toys for the handicapped are impossible to find and borrowing them from a toy library makes sense.

There are several magazines and newsletters dealing with subjects relating to the handicapped. The best known newsletter is *In Touch*, which links families with other families nationally and internationally who have types of handicap in common. A magazine was started called *Special Children* which deals with children with special educational needs. Contact-A-Family in London co-ordinates local groups nationwide so that they can get together for various activities and it also puts parents in touch with other parents to pool news and views on rare handicaps.

An adult usually has to accompany a handicapped child on specially organized holidays for the handicapped, and this is where a nanny could step in and give the child's parents a breather.

What Sort of Nanny?

Mothers of handicapped children all say that they want a jolly person and no martyrs in the house. No long-faced do-gooders, rather a positive, cheerful and matter-of-fact type. It is good if they have worked with ordinary kids before, then they have a yardstick and know what they want the child to aim for. A sense of humour is even more important than ever and the nanny needs to be caring to the child and sensitive to his parents. It can help if they have worked in special schools previously because this will have given them a little exposure to parents' feelings.

Employers also say that they look for:

Someone who understands my need for a break from my daughter and who is not as emotionally involved, though capable of being kind and reliable. Katie is autistic, quite tall and often violent. She terrifies me, but I love her. Can you imagine what it is like to love a child who may attack you with scissors from behind a door as you walk into a room? People don't understand.

Handicapped children need someone with a lot of patience who is prepared to repeat a task endlessly and to encourage self-help.

You definitely don't want someone who can't form normal relationships and thinks she is doing you a favour. It is not good to have a nanny who immerses herself entirely in your child without outside interests. No weirdos.

I'm always grateful to my young nannies for providing a hurly-burly sort of atmosphere. It is good when they are not too protective. A mother can never stop being so.

One nursery nurse speaks for many when she says:

I enjoy looking after the handicapped. It is a varied and rewarding job – the children are delightfully brave and loving. The frustrating thing about it is not being able to help the child communicate when they have no language ability. It is so sad not knowing what is wrong when one of them starts to cry.

To sum up what employers need of nannies for children with special needs one mother who used to run an agency for them has this to say:

They must be bright, have lots of self-confidence and be capable of making fast, accurate decisions. They must recognize when things have gone beyond their control and it is time to call in an expert at once. This can be a matter of life and death. I insist on the difference between trained and untrained – no bovine kind souls should be left in sole charge.

Sadly nobody now runs an agency exclusively for children with special needs.

Her duties

Duties of nannies and mother's helps are described respectively:

Nannies will be trained and/or very experienced with children, capable of sole charge of children and of every aspect of their care and upbringing. The duties and salary will vary, as will time off, from post to post, but a nanny may expect to take care of children's meals, entertainment, bathing, supervise homework, attend therapy sessions, stimulate intellectually and physically, take care of children's laundry, clean their rooms, her own nursery/playroom, some babysitting.

Mother's helps will not be expected to cope on their own for more than a few hours, will participate in all aspects of the running of the home and of the children's care, plus some housework, ironing, cooking etc. and some babysitting and to participate in the child's therapy sessions.

One example

Edwin is three and has congenital heart and respiratory problems and has a tracheostomy. He needs 24-hour care; his mother works part-time. She has to hire two trained SRNs and they need to have had specific experience; for example, some SRNs do not have tracheostomy care knowledge. So far he has had 21 operations. Below is reproduced the daily routine that she gives the nannies on arrival:

08.00 Edwin wakes. Has atrovent nebulizer (1 ml atrovent, 2 mls saline) and physiotherapy. Bath.

08.45 5 mls Septrin (take off syringe, squirt it into mouth), two drops of fluoride (orally).

Breakfast: four dessert spoons of Readibrek, one tin of fruit, daily dose of Wysoy. Warm for one minute in microwave. Fill beaker with Wysoy and encourage him to drink.

09.30 Second nebulizer – .5 mls of Bricanyl. Additional physio as necessary. On school days the above schedule needs to be earlier so to be ready for 9.15 – omit second nebulizer. [Nanny takes Edwin to the local Montessori nursery school and stays with him there.]

12.00 Atrovent nebulizer and physio. Change of tracheostomy or before tea i.e. whenever stomach is empty.

12.30 Lunch – a combination of mashed potato, baked beans, ravioli, mince, mashed carrots. (Saturdays my mother will have cooked him vegetables already, so no need to take food to her, only Wysoy.)

14.00 Bricanyl. Nebulizers to be given a minimum of one hour apart. Rest: put him in bed with tape recorder, and dummy and he'll have a good sleep.

16.00 Tea – baby rice, semolina, rusk, custard etc. (Dependent on bowels fruit can be omitted or added.) With tea – after it has been heated – add 5 mls of Ketovite liquid and 3 crushed Ketovite tablets.

17.00 Atrovent nebulizer and physio.

17.30 Bath or good wash, get Edwin ready for bed.

18.30 Supper – as for lunch – savoury or vegetables, followed by pudding if hungry. Again try and get him to drink.

19.15 Bricanyl nebulizer.

19.30 Bed – put Edwin to bed with a dummy, tape recorder and room humidifier. He should be connected up to Aquapack for at least five hours each night. Nappies at night.

Overnight – suction and physio as necessary.

The mother says that her nannies have many duties.

Apart from physio, suction, administering drugs via a compressor, a nebulizer and orally, they take care of all the equipment, cleaning, sterilizing, connecting it up, making sure it works, ordering replacements, spares and servicing: they also teach him to maximize his potential and do as much for himself as he can; use sign language and communicate, take care of clothes and all the usual nanny duties, emotional as well as physical.

Her pay

The state attendance allowances aren't too bad. Everyone applies for, and usually gets, the day attendance allowance and the higher rate, which covers 'night attendance'. Doctors are usually 'good' about this and press mothers to apply for the higher rate saying: 'I expect you *do* have trouble at night, don't you?' Always say yes.

Once the child has reached five, many are eligible for the mobility allowance provided they are 'unable, or virtually unable to walk'. Free milk is provided for children aged 5 to 16 who do not go to school and they receive a pint a day.

Obviously, the aggregate of the two will not pay for a trained nanny or nurse, but it will pay for a mother's help or au pair which may be fine if the mother is around. Whoever you employ, it is desirable to pay generously especially if you expect your helper to do more than average duties, which you probably will. Even with no sole charge, there is the extra responsibility which should be reflected in her salary. Try to give her as much free time as possible if the care is intense. The pressures are great and a nanny's burnout can be high in these jobs. Enlightened self-interest pays off. Think how hard everyone finds it to anchor a nanny normally; a mother of a handicapped child can do without the extra strain of frequent recruiting.

Her special needs

Remember that the carer of a handicapped child has a greater need to have a social life and to be able to 'get away from it all' than the average nanny or mother's help. A girl who looks after a child with special needs by day and who watches nothing but TV by night, needs your attention. In London more and more nanny groups have sprung up, and in Clapham, womb of so much child care consciousness, there is even a Special Care Nanny group.

While many mothers do not choose to socialize with other parents of handicapped children, many nannies do so, and they help their employers keep up with tips and advice like 'how Susie is persuading little Dominic to feed himself'.

Nannies may have to deal with unpredictable and complex reactions to their charge from the parents and other members of the family. Some siblings may treat the handicapped child like the runt of the litter. They may be embarrassed in public and cruel in private. Some are disgusted by their sibling's deformities and anti-social behaviour. They may resort to disturbed attention-seeking antics. It can be serious. Siblings may react by failing to progress properly, manifest psychosomatic disorders like asthma and migraine, truancy and anorexia. Nannies may be more able to cope with this than the child's parents, who are likely to be overprotective and overwrought by their other offspring's un-kindness to their vulnerable 'baby'.

The vulnerable baby syndrome presents problems itself. Some nannies listen to mothers talking glibly about the need to bring the child on and further his development, but watch with dismay as the mother insists that her 15-year-old handicapped son wears dungarees and a Mickey Mouse T-shirt more suitable to a toddler. One mum still baths her not very backward daughter who is now in her twenties. Very few mothers can bring themselves to be honest about the fact that they much prefer dealing with their handicapped children as babies and young children. Some mothers are happier for their child to mix socially with those younger than themselves as their handicap is less obvious. Often parents feel threatened by their handicapped child as he or she becomes older. The question of what plans to make for the young adult's middle age looms too close not to want to disguise the reality.

In so doing, mothers deny the nanny or mother's help her proper role. The nanny may recognize sooner than the mother that Simon is ready to use a knife and fork and can just about cope without a bib. This is not easy; the girl must brace herself in the interests of the child to have a gentle talk with his mother. Parents may fall back on the 'Does he take sugar?' behaviour with their handicapped children. A responsible nanny will set a good example by asking the child questions directly and waiting politely for an answer – from the child. Resist the urge to fill the silence – it may be cognitive for the child and gives him a chance to react aptly.

A family may resent their child's handicap so much that they deny diagnosis for a long time. Nannies find it extremely difficult to deal with this head-in-the-sand behaviour, which may do the child no good. Parents can be anxious to convince themselves and everyone else that 'There is nothing wrong with anyone on *our* side of the family.' Normal parents can become unrecognizably different to work for after a bad diagnosis of their child – it may be as late as two years after birth. The reactions to the news can range from anxiety, despair, depression, shame, inadequacy, isolation, embarrassment, to rejection and guilt.

If an employer has any worries about a nanny, in particular with her treatment of a handicapped child, don't hope that it will get better. As one experienced mother says, 'I have always regretted hanging on and praying she will improve. They have always had to go in the end if they haven't really got what it takes.'

Nannies of handicapped children may expect less leeway from their employers if they muck about with the House Rules. The parents are jumpy by definition. They are steeling themselves not to feel guilty about delegating the care of their much loved and often totally dependent burden, anyway. So any signs of an irresponsible attitude trips off all the alarms and nannies may expect their employer to blow a gasket.

Nannies should realize how great is the long-term anguish of the parent of a severely handicapped child, and how different the parent/child relationship can be from the ordinary. A special bond which can exist between the parent and her handicapped child is illustrated poignantly by one mother who says:

When the time comes and my end is near, I would like my child to leave this earth with me. I hope I shall find the strength to ensure that. I know many parents of handicapped children who have this feeling. I brought the child into the world, and I will see that I don't leave him behind, alone.

Mothers and fathers should be sensitive to the nanny's probable devotion to her charge. She will be as distressed as they after the child has had an operation or painful therapy. She may have given the child everything she's got, but it is in the nature of his handicap that he deteriorates and dies. The family does not have a monopoly on the emotions summoned by the sadness and helplessness of the child's plight. A family must try to share with the nanny the misery of knowing that while there is still life, there *is* no hope in some cases.

12
Why She Left

. . . Children I am very cross. Mary Poppins has left us . . . It's
outrageous. One minute here and gone the next. Not even an apology.
Simply said 'I'm going' and off she went. Anything more preposterous,
more thoughtless, more discourteous . . .

At the interview you discussed how long you wanted your nanny
or mother's help to stay. Indeed, if there was a contract you will
have written it down, perhaps nicely i.e. 'We hope that you will
stay at least one year.' Most employers make the big mistake of
thinking that nannies will stay for ever. Trained nannies may stay
as long as two years, a few stalwarts may manage a couple more,
but the average is a year to eighteen months.

One agent is extremely jaundiced about the swift turnover. She
says, 'They are a fickle lot; they get itchy feet. Like gypsies, they
amuse themselves better by keeping on the move.' Employers
should not be offended when after a happy co-existence the
nanny murmurs one day, 'It's time to be off.' The
nature of the job and its restrictions mean that it is only bearable
for many nannies if they keep moving, particularly for those who
have ambition. They feel they are going places, and they well
may with another family that goes abroad on holiday and
generally offers a more pleasant and exciting package. Often the
grass *is* greener when the next employer is richer.

Some employers do not want their nannies to stay with the
family for longer than a year, however good they are, because
they fear that their children will become too attached to them and
be very sad when they leave. The incidental advantage of this
policy is that employers get a good feeling of being more in
control of events as the chances are better that a nanny completes
a year. The disadvantage is that the mother suffers the recruitment process every ten months. It is partly for this reason that

when February comes round again and the nanny is still with them, employers rejoice.

Employers don't chat easily with their nanny about the possibility of there being another world outside and the like-lihood of the nanny wishing to rejoin it. Not talking about it is superstitious and ostrich-like. One mother, having clocked up a record two and a half years with her nanny, brings up the subject regularly, partly because she knows that all good things must come to an end and she wants to be the first to know when. It's also good psychologically, and much less stressful. If you can give the children a long lead-in to the whole idea, there is less upheaval.

Any employer gets cross when a nanny does not fulfil the agreed length of stay. Some employers are themselves the cause of the move and if they have transgressed the Big Four (see chapter 2), repeatedly or generally abused a nanny's willingness to 'muck in', she will leave before they planned and is quite right to do so. If a nanny leaves under these circumstances, some people get their own back unfairly by either not writing her a reference at all, or writing a bad or equivocal one, which is transparent in its luke-warm list of duties done. This is rough treatment to a young girl who has served the family well for over a year. The seriousness of this petty reaction to an inconvenience cannot be overstated. Her next employers will take a dim view of a gap in her CV, and she is defenceless against such evidence.

The employer can reasonably feel that she has been let down if the nanny resigns before her agreed time is up, because she feels merely tired of the job, or has been offered a more interesting one by someone else. It is too bad for the employer if the girl's mother is suddenly seriously ill and she wants to leave to nurse her. Other Acts of God which are exceptions are: employers moving house, bereavement, divorce – any major change in her job content or its atmosphere (see chapter 9).

Mrs Davis, Principal of Norland College, advises her students:

If you have decided you want to leave, don't be persuaded to take a fiver a week more. If you want a salary rise ask for one, if you want to leave, go. Employers shouldn't offer a little extra once a nanny has said she is off, it's too late by then. If she'd really rather have left then her nannying is not likely to be as good as it ought to be.

Employers are bound to have a shock when their carer gives no sign of wanting to leave and then out of the blue gives a month's notice. If lines of communication have been properly maintained both employers and employees will give each other much more notice of long term plans than a month. However, the accepted minimum is four weeks' notice.

Whatever the nanny thinks of her employers she should always try to give plenty of notice for the children's sake. Her first concern should be for her charges and she should try to minimize the disruption caused by her leaving.

One employer says: 'If you have kept your nanny a long time, you expect a lot of notice. Realistically, two months minimum is needed to find someone and achieve a smooth changeover.' Mother's helps should also give a month. Au pairs should give a fortnight, though many leave without notice.

In theory, both sides agree that lots of notice is a great idea all round but as another nanny put it: 'In my first job I was overworked and underpaid. I gave two months' notice as we'd agreed. I now think that was a mistake because my awful employer made those months feel like an eternity.' If relations have disintegrated so that you try not to meet in the passage, even four weeks will be miserable, and most of all for the children. Let her go, pay her off and, if you can afford it, call the agencies for a nice calm capable temp, while you start interviewing for a replacement.

Employers will be relieved to note that a nanny cannot take them to an industrial tribunal for 'unfair dismissal' until she has been with them for two years.

When employers want a nanny to leave without working out her notice, they vary enormously about how much they pay her in lieu. The honourable, who have spelt out these terms in a contract, pay the nanny her entire notice period, i.e. in many cases, four weeks' pay. Others don't behave so well, depending on how aggrieved they feel and pay just a week or two, or not at all.

Employers' stories about nannies leaving without notice make fantastic reading. Apparently trained nannies leave their charges unattended at midnight and scrawl inadequate notes left on the hall rug to say they have gone. Some don't even bother to do that. One nanny says she has never forgiven herself for doing just this in her first job. Even a babysitter, who hadn't any excuse for not liking her employers, so brief was their acquaintance, abandoned two children aged three and one in a big house in Richmond. The three-year old girl went out into the snow to tell a neighbour that her little brother was playing with the logs in the fire . . .

One employer of a North Country NNEB had gone out with her husband to the office dance. She and her husband returned at 3 am and kissed the children good-night. In the morning they found a note from the nanny in her bedroom saying that she'd left because she was homesick. Later they learned that a neighbour had heard a car drive up and away again, minutes after their own departure for the evening. Three little boys under five had been left alone for most of the night. Too late to sack her even if they could have; she was a candidate for the Lucan Solution.

Time to Go

The vast majority of nannies and mother's helps never dream of behaving irresponsibly and leave after giving notice for a wide variety of normal reasons, like these, say employers:

To get married.

To be a nurse.

Went back to Australia.

To become a daily nanny for more money.

Because we moved house.

The girls give additional reasons for leaving:

After a long stay with the grandparents, my employers started to take me for granted. They began to come home really late in the evening and generally put a lot more on me.

I left the job because I found it too hectic and it was hard to get holiday pay.

I left because there were four kids including twins and no routine. The final straw was that I was expected to clean up the dog mess all the time.

Many nannies remark that it is very sad to leave, especially the children. It's often more of a wrench than they think, though with experience they learn to distance themselves effectively.

Nannies and mother's helps who leave under normal circumstances should be reminded that any show of being upset,
however touching, will not help the children get over her
departure. The best precaution is to warn the nanny that you will
preoccupy the children while she makes a quiet exit. Floods of
tears, ululations and breast beating are not the ideal final memory
of a nanny for a child after two happy years. That's not how
grown-ups behave.

The last few weeks or days before a carer leaves are always a
touch fraught even when she has behaved impeccably hitherto.
Don't put up with a slide into anarchy; it won't help the new
incumbent to have to reinstate the routine and, again, it just isn't
professional. It is odd how often employers and nannies, the
light at the end of the tunnel approaching fast, fall out for the first
time over the silliest things.

Try to keep the parting sweet. It's not as simple as it sounds.
Most employers find it trying to listen to too much whoopee
about the nanny's new job and lovely plans, especially in front of
the children. Charts with the days crossed off are tactless. If she
hums 'Show me the way to go home', try to join in the refrain.

It is hard for a child to understand fully why the nanny is
leaving him and it is extremely important that he doesn't
interpret it as rejection. It can be a painful parting and parents
must not try to minimize the pain that a child may feel for their
own purposes.

Jeanne Magagna, child psychotherapist at the Tavistock, says:

A good nanny prepares the child for separation from herself when it is
time for her to leave. It is traumatic for a child when a nanny leaves – a
crisis to many children when the nanny has been there for 18 months or
more. . . . Children feel psychologically dropped at the carer's departure
which is very bad for their self-esteem and confidence. Parents should
acknowledge children's acute anxiety and share their sadness.

Don't wait till the morning of the departure to discover that her
room is a horrible mess. Suggest she occupies herself constructively in giving it a thorough spring clean. Get her to take down
her pictures, posters, scarves and mementoes – it may give her a
slight twinge that the place needs redecorating. If she is a brick,
give her a paintbrush. Ask her to change the sheets and towels for
the next nanny. Diana Forney, a Norlander who is an independ-

ent consultant to the nanny profession in America, recommends to nannies: 'If you are responsible for cleaning your own room and bath, do a thorough job. Small details speak well later for your recommendations.'

Remember that both of you want to part friends, draw a line under the whole experience and sign off neatly. Employer and nanny will then congratulate themselves on having won through, without a stumble when the winning post was in sight.

References

Don't be lazy about giving your nanny or mother's help a reference. Even if the nanny forgets/hasn't the sense/or simply doesn't know about its importance, be correct, write one without being prompted and give it to her before she leaves. Don't waste any lick on the envelope, she'll be dying to read it. It is sloppy to say that you will send it on because you haven't found time to write it. You may never get down to it and then what does she do?

Carve half an hour out of your life to compose an effective reference. Now you have to judge her character and how well she has done her job. Your composition will affect her future job prospects. Her livelihood may hang on your words. The business should be taken seriously and be given a bit of thought.

Agencies complain that nannies manufacture their own references all too often. For this reason a few employers take an extreme view and mistrust them completely. To avoid any possibility of identification or an edited copy being made, use headed paper if you have it, state your telephone number and post code and include any title or professional initials. The traditional way to address the unknown reader of the reference is 'To Whom It May Concern', with the nanny's name in full, underlined underneath.

Remember she will read the reference. If you have grave reservations about her and she hasn't been wonderful for any reason, you have three choices. One is to write a straightforward vitriolic blast which will almost certainly end up in your dustbin before she leaves. Another is to go to her and tell her frankly that any reference you could bring yourself to write would do her no good and that you have no intention of perjuring yourself on her

account. Third, admitting that you should h₂
months ago, you can chicken out and fudge s₂
her happy – and employed.

It is as hard to know how to write about the medioɬ
mother's help. It is easier to write a string of superlat₂
grudging line or two, than to compose a carefully wordeɬ
committal couple of paragraphs. After all, writing referencɬ ₂s
the art of omission. You pick out what they do right and leave out
what they do wrong.

You may choose to damn with faint praise, or to write with
such obscurity that the recipient has to read between the lines.
This is bad news for any future employer. The nuances are likely
to be misinterpreted and also be an impenetrable code to
someone with a different educational background or to a
foreigner.

A glowing reference

(an actual reference for an experienced mother's help from a
couple of working doctors in Hertfordshire)

Mary was employed as a nanny for two years and is leaving
to further her career. During this period of time she has
undertaken a number of other duties and has thus fulfilled a
wider role in support of our children and family. In all
respects I have been completely satisfied with Mary's work
while she herself can only be commented upon in terms of
the highest praise.

Mary's great asset is her outgoing, but not overbearing
personality. She gets on well with the young and old alike
and is sensitive and mature beyond her years. In particular,
our family is impressed with her adaptability, yet she is able
to interest and entertain children extremely constructively
whilst maintaining firm discipline. Her training in catering
has stood her in good stead and she is an excellent cook both
at the family level and also for entertaining.

I am also bound to speak of her selflessness and her
capacity to accept responsibility. My expectation of Mary
has been more than fulfilled and all our family are saddened
and sorry that Mary has to leave us.

It might be preferable to keep it short and get out of the problem by merely summarizing her job description and saying that she fulfilled it and that she was honest and hard working. The drawback with this is that she is likely to sense, and be disappointed by, your brevity and you will feel rotten. That's why people do the clever-clever thing and write to confuse. They have helped perpetuate the not-so-very-vicious circle of average nannies with average standards. But doing it doesn't boost the image of the profession or give it much respect.

If you write a prevarication of a reference, at least issue an open invitation that anyone who would like more details about the nanny should ring you forthwith. Make this a Belisha Beacon on the page.

Keeping in Touch

Once your nanny has left, all the inhibitions have gone and if you always felt that she was a kindred soul you may continue to be closely in touch with her for ever. One nanny was overcome when she learned of a small bequest in her favour in an old employer's will, who labelled it 'to my most faithful friend, our loving nanny'. It's more surprising that au pairs remain family friends and across great distances too. Most employers say that they maintain contact with the vast majority of their successful nannies for some time.

Where Are They Now?

> Other people's babies
> That's my life! Mother to dozens
> And nobody's wife.

Happily, nowadays most nannies want to get married, have children and do. More and more don't want them too soon, so that they can experience different things – travel, work in a nursery school, run their own nursery, set up an employment agency, become a daily nanny or a childminder.

One thing the majority of them say they *don't* want is to have a nanny to look after *their* children. The main reason for this is that they expect to enjoy bringing up their children themselves. One nanny is enchanting: 'I wouldn't have a nanny free of charge.

Why She Left

Children are so small, I couldn't miss out on the happy funny times bringing them up.'

Finally, one nanny seems to have marked, learned and inwardly digested much:

I hope that I will be married or, if not, travelling somewhere in five years' time. I think nannying has made me realize that having children too soon in married life is wrong. Enjoy marriage with your husband alone first. If that works well, then go ahead with children.

13
Nannies Abroad

Any nanny who has an urge to live and learn from the rest of the world, the nerve to leave home for a time and the desire to earn more money than others in her field of expertise will want to try working abroad for some part of her career. Some girls are employed by English people working abroad, some go with foreigners for whom they have worked in the UK, and others take the biggest plunge and seek employment with the natives who live where they fancy living. As one thriving agency reports 'all our top nannies go abroad'.

Some nannies go abroad to work for Europeans in their respective capitals, but jobs there are more frequently for mother's helps or au pairs, groups who want to improve their language, are not specially qualified to look after children, and who are not there for high wages and glamorous perks. Mrs Baxter, recently retired after twenty-five years as an employment agent, says:

I only send British girls to be au pairs in Europe, not to the USA or Canada, it wouldn't be any good for them. In Europe they gain a language and a different insight.

The British who live on the Continent often choose to employ a British nanny or mother's help. But it is difficult to find a girl who will live abroad successfully. 'Rushing home to mother for the weekend is an expensive and major expedition, friends have to be made from scratch, the basics of a foreign language mastered and understood, and a whole culture grasped and accepted. This is no joke for an English girl,' writes one correspondent from Brussels who has employed trained and untrained British nannies there over five years.

The extent of culture shock depends on the country in question

258

– some countries, like the USA, Australia and Canada, while they may present surprises and challenges, are less of a shock than working in Riyadh, Moscow or Bombay.

Almost everyone wants to go to America, and most will settle for Paris, Rome, Bermuda and places warm. However, if you live in Belgium, Holland, Denmark and Germany, you have to work rather harder to find someone. (Incidentally, some nannies are irritated that whether a girl works a five-hour day with some babysitting or is a trained or experienced nanny – if she is foreign and looks after children in Europe, she will be known to one and all as an au pair. *Rien à faire.*)

What Sort of Girl is Good at Working Abroad?

The kind of girl who employers value when living abroad is a little different from her British-based counterpart. It is just as important to find someone with whom you will get on as someone who is good with the children. The employer, like it or not, is *in loco parentis* for her, ultimately responsible for her behaviour to the community (in which the family are themselves foreigners) and you will be handing out advice and giving help more often than if the job were in the UK.

While the new recruit makes friends and finds things to do, the wise expatriate employer should provide a warm and friendly atmosphere so that the girl does not become homesick and lonely. 'A happy nanny means happy children which means happy parents – something too easily forgotten by many,' says the experienced Brussels employer.

The nannies to avoid are those who want to go 'abroad' just because it is. They are the ones who put Marbella at the top of their list. 'They have a vision of themselves spending every night in a different disco. If they do they will fall asleep the next day while the baby chokes to death on the telephone wire,' informs a jaundiced mum from the Costa del Sol.

The nanny should be able to list positive reasons for working where the employer lives – wants to learn the language, visited the place on holiday, liked it and wants to see more of it (and has some real idea of how it might be out of season), has friends and relatives there (a big plus since she is unlikely to be lonely), is going to settle down in England and wants to do something else in a year's time and to broaden her horizons before doing so. Going abroad just because there is nothing better to do at home is not ideal, but it doesn't necessarily mean that the girl is bad news. Running away from anything is more a recipe for disaster, but you will need to be a canny interviewer to intuit this.

The girl has to be mature, another thing that is hard to tell at once, and preferably with some experience of living away from home. No employer needs the additional worry about a nanny's safety in a strange city when she has still not returned by 4 am. Is she packed and on her way East via Marseilles or smooching with a local lad two blocks away? Willy nilly, the nanny becomes an ambassadress and a flagship for the family in which she works, and she is a reflection on her employers. Foreigners are *always* high profile and in the public eye because the natives are acutely aware of them, at least initially and specially in tight-knit communities.

There is one major drawback for some British nannies working abroad for the locals. They go because they want to improve their grasp of the language of the country, but their employers hire them because they want little Hiro or Jean-Claude or Angelo to speak good English. Actually, not just English but 'pukka English' as one employer requests on the application form. All over the world agencies report that there are families who are rich enough to employ a nanny and choose to do so regardless of the availability of local 'help' – amahs, ayahs etc – and the reason they do? They want their child to be disciplined, well-mannered and speak the Queen's English. The Mary Poppins image is engrained worldwide.

When and How to Find Her

The best time of year to look is, as in the UK, either in the New Year or in June/July/August. This last period coincides with the close of the academic year and is a time when pre-university or post-university girls (who can make bright mother's helps) are looking for work. Newly qualified NNEBs are on the market and nannies, whose charges start school in September and are no longer needed, are looking around for a new post. The chances grow dramatically less good as the year progresses with only a brief upsurge of availability at the year's end.

There are many ways of finding a nanny to work abroad. The well-worn routes are to put an ad in *The Lady*, use a British agency (but you have to reckon with higher fees than for domestic placements), advertise locally or by word of mouth. It is hard for those living abroad to get to England and usually a nanny is found by advertisement, short-listed by letter and interviewed by telephone. The lack of personal interview can make for a high degree of disappointment and discontent on both sides. There is really nothing to recommend it and it is *not* the only way to do it, just the easiest in the short run. An alternative is to ask a friend or relation in your own country to interview for you, although this is never a perfect answer because so much depends on personalities.

Good Business Arrangements and Other Anchors

Once you have ensnared your paragon, consider drawing up a contract (see pages 325–8). Talk it over slowly and carefully. This is particularly necessary if the family or the nanny is not English, since they may have differing interpretations of the same job description.

It is sensible to check local salary rates with friends and other employers and also with one or two English agencies. Salaries must always be fair and will depend on all the usual considerations plus the cost of living adjustment for whichever country you live in. When estimating this, consider the cost of local cinemas, transport, discos, cafés or whatever entertainment is appropriate. If the nanny is not paid the going rate, she will soon discover when she meets local nannies and the combination of finding her feet and thinking that you are being mean may provide the impetus for a swift leavetaking.

Work out with her how she wants to be paid. Half in sterling into an English bank account for saving, and half in local currency in cash for spending, is a popular method.

If the choice is in sterling, agree an exchange rate which you will review according to its fluctuation. Do not forget to take out medical insurance to cover medical and hospitalization costs, find out about the EEC National Health reciprocity agreements, but don't assume they'll be adequate and not bother to find out when an insurance top-up is necessary.

It is doubly important to make an effort with a new nanny if you live abroad and especially so if you are a native of the country. Even buying a bus or train ticket for the first time in a foreign language can be daunting. 'I hardly said a word to my Spanish employers for the first month,' says one nanny who worked in Madrid, 'then the toilet paper ran out and I had to tell them. I couldn't get away with miming it, could I?'

European posts
Brussels

Choosing someone to work in Belgium is hard work. Unless the nanny rejoices in 'O' level geography or, possibly, economics, a predictable number of British girls have hardly heard of it or think of it in terms of the Common Market, or a well-lit autoroute to other more interesting places. Nannies who have worked there like it. Brussels is a small, friendly city and easy to get around. There is an au pair club which is busy and welcomes every nationality. There is the opportunity to learn or improve French (Dutch and German too since these are the other two national languages), but this is by no means necessary since many Belgians speak English.

There is plenty of night-life which is not prohibitively expensive, and an English language magazine, *The Bulletin*, which reports on life in Belgium for both the expatriate and local community. If she wants to travel, it is only an hour to most of Belgium's borders.

Rome

Advertising on the English church notice board or in the one English language bookshop – 'The Lion' – are favourite places for nannies lost and found. There is a bi-weekly English language 'paper' called *Wanted in Rome* which is free and financed by people placing ads in it. Most nannies prefer to be in the centre of Rome, though if enough carrots are dangled – higher pay and use of a car – they will take jobs a bit further afield.

The social life there is boosted by American Marine functions which are frequent and popular, and there is a club called 'Meeting Point', ostensibly for any English speaking person, but usually frequented by nannies, au pairs etc. The English church is quite a good cosy base for new nannies – although nothing is officially organized, cups of coffee after services can lead to friendships or at least a place in the choir!

Most nannies, mother's helps and au pairs go to the Dante Alighieri, the Italian language school, at the start to get a smattering of Italian (important for emergencies, particularly medical). Most British employers keep their girls for the contracted year, but conditions may be attached to a London/Rome/London ticket for a minimum stay of six months. There is a local au pair/nanny agency in Rome, but the British do not use it because it is prohibitively expensive.

There are nannies who stay for years with the English family who recruited them; but on the whole young families seem to prefer either a full-time Filipina, who also babysits, or a part-time daily plus a mother's help or an au pair.

Paris
The unique portrait of a British nanny in France is provided in *The Blessing* by Nancy Mitford and almost nothing was right with the place as far as she was concerned: 'Well, dear, we've had nothing to eat since you saw us, nothing whatever. Course upon course of nasty greasy stuff smelling of garlic – a month's ration of meat, yes, but quite raw you know – shame, really – I wasn't going to touch it let alone give it to Sigi, poor little mite.'

Present-day nannies love working in Paris. Mostly they take sole charge jobs for high-powered French mums. They meet initially at the English church and the vicar's tea parties. There are jobs with the international set here and many nannies jump on a bandwagon which may take them all over the world. Paris, like London, is one of those cities where if you have six houses worldwide you probably have one in each of those capitals. The lyrics of Peter Sarstedt's Sixties hit 'Where do you go to my lovely?' are played out for real for a few.

Oslo, Copenhagen, Stockholm and Amsterdam
The reason that most English nannies and mother's helps like working in these capitals is that there are lots of friendly young people, almost all of whom can speak English. They are also not far away from England.

One Dutch employer says, 'Why do they come? By the time they are about 20 they have been working for four years already as a mother's help in England, so they are glad of a change. They work a 12-hour-day and they are good workers, the English. We have had six of them – one every year for the last six years. No complaints.'

Madrid
A few Spanish aristocrats and British expatriates have nannies in Madrid, but most other employers employ *chicas*, Filipina or Spanish women who provide child care along with housework and cooking. Some English and girls of other nationalities come as au pairs and are usually unhappy because they are treated as maids. Some working mothers in Madrid send their children to private day nurseries – *Jardins*

de l'infancia – and their care is supplemented by relations and friends volunteering to fill the gaps.

Marbella
It is remarkable that so many agencies mention Marbella as a particular nanny favourite. English nannies may be employed there by beach bums and bank robbers. They meet on beaches or at Sinatra's Bar in Puerto Banus. The English-language newspaper called *The Sur* has details of local nanny jobs.

Athens
There are shipping types who employ British nannies but they do not tend to treat their nannies at all as they wish to be treated. Nannies report that they won't stay to be pushed around like skivvies. They are unimpressed by the huge houses and staffs, beautiful islands and big salaries and before long they go.

West Germany
Many British nannies have boyfriends in the British Forces in Germany and want to go and work out there to be near them. This causes a lot of problems for employers because the girls want every weekend off snuggled up with their beloveds, and if either of them gets fed up, they are stuck with each other and often make employers wretched as well.

One colonel's wife in the British Army of the Rhine comments: 'Do not hire a Sloane Ranger type. The number of eligible bachelors will make her the centre of attention and you the employer will trail around with your children in her wake while she is ogled and fêted by every man in the regiment *and* you'll be told how lucky you are to have her.'

Another colonel's wife agrees and adds, 'At least in England there's every chance you will not know the nanny's boyfriend. Here we always do. It is exasperating that instead of scarpering through the window into the night, they insist on facing my husband honourably having been pulled out of the nanny's bedroom. We used to dread going home. All the subalterns were round this one like bees round a honey pot.'

Switzerland
Plenty of nannies go and work for expatriate English and American families, located principally in Geneva and Zurich or some way towards the mountains outside Geneva in picturesque villages like Crans Montana. They have a wonderful time out there, skiing and enjoying the scenery and the opportunity to learn at least one or two languages.

It should be noted that it is illegal for British girls to work in Switzerland, though many do.

Far away
Tokyo

American and British families employ British nannies successfully here. Some hire local girls who are used to being maids but who also help out with the children. Chinese amahs and Filipinas are popular in Japan. The Tokyo locals are not keen on looking after other people's children, and it appears that ex-pats sometimes resort to island girls.

There are a few bad stories about Japanese employers who are sometimes over-strict with the House Rules – 'more like house arrest actually' reports one nanny. 'Even the agency suggested I take refuge in the British embassy with my luggage so that they couldn't get me back. They really behaved horribly to me and I was scared I would never get away. I would recommend anyone doing this kind of trip to make absolutely sure they hang on to their passport for dear life.'

South Africa

'Even Harry Oppenheimer has black nannies, but then he would, wouldn't he?' says one Jo'burg father. 'There is a different tradition in Zimbabwe. In South Africa, almost everyone reckons that if you can hire a local houseboy, nanny and maid all for the price of one English nanny, the choice is simple.'

South America

Nannies have a good time working for the locals in many countries in South America and for expatriates too. In São Paulo, Brazil, there is a small community of British nannies – the older type, 30-plus, working for rich Brazilians and reportedly 'having a ball'.

One British ex-pat in Rio reports, 'There are still maids available all over South America, I never needed a nanny while we lived in Brazil, Chile and Argentina. We just needed babysitters if the maid wasn't there or too busy for any reason. We occasionally hired a European if my husband and I had to go away together and leave the children, just to oversee the household of local staff. The great thing about the beach life in Rio was that everyone took their children to the beach and we all looked after them together.'

Hong Kong

Many expatriates have amahs because they refuse to pay more than £400 a month for British nannies. One employer who was herself raised by an amah says, 'I was in her charge from the moment I came back from the hospital as a baby. She slept in my bedroom until I went to boarding school. I now have an amah in Sussex.' It seems that amahs for ex-pat families are on the decline and Filipina maids are in the ascendant. North Americans cannily advertise for Filipinas in Hong Kong newspapers.

The fact that Hong Kong is an English-speaking colony, glamorous and remote, all appeals to the British nanny or mother's help. But its obvious advantage has traditionally been its century-old attraction for 'the fishing fleet' – English spinsters are reckoned to have a better chance of finding a husband there than back home. There are lots of unattached males and a hectic social life is had by most. Most employers insist a nanny joins the family for a minimum of two years. They usually advertise in *The Lady*, interview in the UK and return with their catch.

One long-time Hong Kong resident says: 'There are one or two agencies here, including the Kally agency and Rent-A-Mum, but they charge vast fees and you wind up having to sift the applicants anyway.' One wistful London agent notes, 'There are about 60 British nannies working there at the moment, I could place hundreds, but there aren't enough British mothers there.'

Nannies meet each other up and down the Peak and also at the English church. 'The amahs spoil the children with too many sweets and fizzy drinks; I want an experienced and well-trained nanny. It is less easy otherwise for children to rejoin their contemporaries in England after a few years here,' says another resident.

Hong Kong is a hard-living, hard-working place and some girls complain that their employers are so busy at work and out so much in the evenings that they don't give their nannies much time to enjoy the night life. 'It's only the nice ones who bother to introduce you to other nannies; sometimes it quite suits them to keep you apart for as long as they can. I left one just like that,' says one experienced nanny there.

Australia

Only a few Antipodean employers want to afford to pay the flight fares for nannies to come and work for them. It is much the best, if a nanny can afford it, for her to pay her own way there and then find an agency. There is quite a lot of work available for nannies, especially in temporary jobs. Sydney and Melbourne seem to be where the greatest number of Australian employers live and occasionally the Brits who are working out there for a year or two take a nanny with them.

Australians cannot hire other Australians to care for their children, any more than they can find cleaners; they have to import them. There are a few rich farmers who live in the outback who hire British governesses rather than send their kids to state schools. 'They are usually nice girls, who probably ride and cook as well as teach,' says one Australian employer.

The Middle East

Regency Nannies agency says: 'Middle East clients collect Norlanders as status symbols. It is nothing for them to collect three or four on their yacht in the south of France. Some of them are offered wonderful presents like £1,000 for a new dress if they are all going out that night.'

Louise Davis of the Norland College says, 'I tell them there is little time off, and it is often very lonely and they may spend a lot of time stuck inside without any opportunity to see the country.'

Sheila Davies of Albemarle Barclay Nannies could be described as *the* agent for the Middle East (see page 284). Even other agencies recommend girls who want to work in Arabia to go to her.

Mrs Davies comments, 'For some girls it is a terrible culture shock. Sometimes they are virtual prisoners, in fact they are much safer than they would be with a family in England. They are shepherded from place to place in limousines and there is no question of them being mugged or raped or whatever.

'However, they are not free to do what they like; they have to be careful what they wear – bikinis are out of the question. Their passports are taken away and they have no exit visas from whatever country they are in.

'I look for much older girls and many Arab families want women in their 40s and 50s. I tell the nannies that if they have a year to spare and want to earn a pile of tax-free cash that is fine as long as they fully understand the drawbacks.' Mrs Davies knows many families personally in the Middle East and puts nannies in touch with their friends and contacts.

One employment agency says: 'It is not worth our while. Without contacts you just don't get paid. Often the nannies don't either. The Arabs flatly refuse to sign contracts and women have no rights under local law. Our biggest debt is from the brother of a bloke who came to London the other day to see the Queen and the Mall was shut for his procession. It just makes it more difficult to collect.'

A Norlander who has worked for a Middle Eastern head of state reports: 'They went abroad a lot and it was extremely lonely and hard work. Lots of money, loads of other staff to cook and clean and transport us. Let no one think that work in this part of the world is a soft option. I have enjoyed my years with the family very much, but I reckon I earned every penny.'

The agencies generally say that their nannies like working in Istanbul and in Cyprus, not surprisingly since there are large numbers of British soldiers stationed there.

Moscow
It seems that many girls who take jobs looking after children in Moscow have hazy, romantic notions of golden onion-shaped spires and snow. The realities of the place for expatriates are different. A limited social life

is the chief drawback for many living in the land of the Soviet Republics. Employers suffer from it themselves and worry endlessly about their child carer's state of mind and whether or not she is having fun. 'Even when the girl's having affairs with US GIs or Russians and therefore, presumably, having a good time, it can be a mixed blessing – it complicates things,' says one mother wearily.

If the lucky man is an American soldier then there is hope that the mother's help marries him, preferably once she has completed her stay with you. If she becomes entangled with a Russian then there can be endless complications. Many Russians regard an affair with an English or American girl as a passport out of the country, so the love knot can be curiously tangled from the start. One erstwhile member of the Moscow diplomatic corps remembers; 'One girl hung about for months trying to help her Russian fiancé achieve his visa. The awful thing was that he had been married before and was trying to get his Russian wife out at the same time!'

Very few trained or experienced nannies get jobs with army, diplomatic or journalist families of any nationality in Moscow. They don't want to go there and they are not paid enough. In fact, most of the child carers there are untrained but have a strong desire to experience Russia for some reason. The most common is that they have a Russian degree or degrees. Often they are highly intelligent, educated souls who know nothing about children.

Mother's helps are paid only pocket money – as little as £30 to £40 a week. They get their return fare home as well. Rates are low because it is virtually impossible to live in Russia under any other circumstances. They tend to be recruited in their country of origin and fly out with the family.

North America
Canada

Many British nannies go to work in Canada. Employers advertise for them locally, use an agency or try putting their need out on the grapevine. 'You can trust the word of your friend or acquaintance more than that of the agency lady,' says one experienced Toronto mother. 'There are more bad agencies than there are good ones and, when I say bad, I mean from the nanny's point of view as well. They don't ask the right questions of either side so they are not satisfactory and a complete waste of time.'

Many people deal with an agency which has contacts abroad who will bring the girls from various countries. They choose a nanny from a file, present an offer by letter and the agency makes all the arrangements (immigration, medicals, visas etc.).

But as one mother says, 'What I have never been able to overcome is that I'm choosing a very important person in my life based on a picture and an application form. There is no opportunity for subjective opinion before the girl is on your doorstep. Also if you need someone in a hurry, it does take 90 days. There are always lots of girls looking who are already here. So probably as many employers pick a girl who is available immediately as get them straight from overseas.'

When girls go to Canada with a job offer from a Canadian family, the air far is usually paid for by the family, though not always. The local agencies in Canada charge one month's salary (some gross, some net), as their fee. It is more expensive for a Canadian employer to hire a nanny through a British agency, but many do it.

The term 'nanny' is used much more loosely than in the UK. In Canada it means more in terms of pay scale than actual duties. Trained British nannies can – and do – do housework in Canada. Unless a girl makes it clear from the start that she is not prepared to do it at all, some housework will be expected of her. The mother's helps, as in the UK, do laundry (including the family's), light housekeeping, cooking, driving and ironing.

The salary seems to be more dependent on age and experience than in the UK. The range is great: from $650 to $1,000 plus (net) a month. The top of the range is a 'nanny housekeeper' who runs the house while mum works full time. She cooks, shops, car pools, does the laundry etc. for two or more school-age children.

There is a Nannies' Friendship and Information Centre in Toronto which is enterprising and well organized. It puts nannies in touch with other nannies and deliberately tackles the usual problem by 'giving each girl a word of advice and reassurance to let them know that they are not alone and to give them a chance to see Toronto and possibly other cities in Canada without the great trauma of homesickness, which is the main reason why girls go home before their contracts are fulfilled,' as its newsletter explains.

The hours of work, time off and living conditions are more specific here than in England. A working week is 50 hours maximum (this is occasionally abused) with a required two days off per week, 36 hours of which should run over Saturday and Sunday (this rule gets elasticized as well).

The Canadian nanny requires private accommodation (own bathroom too) by law. All statutory holidays, two weeks' paid vacation a year and Worker's Compensation paid by the employer and usually health insurance are all the responsibility of the employer.

USA

For the British nanny, the lure of the USA is as much a wish to experience the excitement of a New World as the desire for exceedingly gainful employment. Unlike Arabia, which does bring out the pure materialist in the British nanny, America appeals because there is no language barrier and life there seems larger than life here.

Despite high salaries, American women have stayed away from becoming nannies in droves; the indigenous nanny profession has only just been born and is slowly gaining respect and recognition. Until it does, the cream of nanny-employing Americans import their nannies from England.

The problem is that it is *illegal* to bring a foreign nanny into the USA. The US authorities have always required any alien, including a nanny, coming into the country to work to have a work permit. Before 1987, if an employee was discovered not to have a work permit she was fined and exported. Nothing happened to the employer. As of July 1987 employers of illegals working in the USA have been made responsible by law. The onus is now on them to 'verify' the employment status of anyone hired for a job. This law applies to everyone.

All the papers must be in order within three days of the employee starting work. This precludes an earlier loophole when American employers did the basic minimum necessary to procure a green card and just putting the wheels in motion made the girl legal – a bit like getting a new tax disc for a car here.

Violation can carry a fine for employers of up to $2,000 for each employee who has not got the correct papers to prove the person's identity and employment status. Second offenders can expect higher fines and you hit the jackpot of $10,000 on your third offence. In theory, violators can be sent to jail.

British employment agencies report that their trade has not diminished one whit. Business as usual, meaning that they conspire with American employers to get their nannies past the Immigration Officers (INS) at America's airports.

Many British agencies do a bit of illegitimate work of this kind, if the price is right, though none will go on record as saying so. One agent shows what risks Americans, regardless of their position in public life, will take to hire the English nanny of their choice: 'I have a regular client who works in the White House and this is the second time I have sent him a nanny. If he is not bothered by the threats, who the hell is? Believe it or not I have just placed two nannies in the families of Congressmen in the space of eight weeks.'

An amalgam of many British employment agencies views on the issue runs thus: 'No one, touch wood, has been fined yet; no agency has been put out of business; no employer has had to pay the big max fine; no nanny has yet died under interrogation by an immigration official. Let us get the problem in proportion and not be too hypocritical.

'People go on about how dangerous it is for nannies to go to the States to work illegally, do they have any idea that there are *thousands of them* at it? Many Americans could not care less what they pay, they just want an English nanny. All the old sobersides in London say they bet they have a miserable time there . . . that's hard to do in New York on £500 a week for pocket money.'

British employers or Americans who have been living in the UK for a while (and have employed a nanny for not less than a year) may take nannies with them to the USA legally. The nanny's passport will be stamped specially since she is then designated a member of their staff and a dependant of theirs. She will be bound to work for that family or become an illegal if she leaves them and does not immediately return home. Agencies sometimes backdate contracts so that an employer moving from the UK to the USA can take a nanny with them.

There is a severe nanny shortage in New York, Boston and Washington. 'People are crying out for them and could not care less how they get them,' one Bostonian comments. The risks that people take to procure British nannies are greater now that the immigration authorities have taken this new line of making the employer responsible for, and equally guilty with, the illegal.

All you need is a green card

Are you sitting comfortably? Now the system works like this. A green card is what every nanny wants and is most unlikely to get. It entitles the holder to live and work legally in the USA. Barbara Binswanger and Betsy Ryan explain the process succinctly in their book *Live-in Child Care*: 'There are six preference classes of immigration visas. Domestic workers come in under the lowest, or sixth preference class: the one for skilled and unskilled labour in short supply. Only 10 per cent of all immigration visas can be issued to people in this sixth class, or about 27,000 domestic and other workers per year. If you are trying to bring in a nanny from overseas, she will get no special treatment and be lumped in with this group.'

Doing it legally and getting a green card is a Herculean task, seemingly designed to be frustrating, difficult and complicated. You have to prove that a local unemployed US national is not available to do the job adequately instead and then the red tape and your problems have hardly begun. That process of 'job certification' comes with the need to prove that your nanny has had at least a year's experience of work. Then you have to advertise in your area for three consecutive days and file your job with the local employment office. Then you have to find convincing and legalistic reasons for rejecting the applicants. After *that*, you must wait while the decision is reached on a regional level as to whether your job certification application has been successful.

Still with us. . . ? You won that round and now you have to run the gauntlet of the Immigration and Naturalization Service (INS). They instigate various further checks and procedures and then you wait some more. According to Binswanger and Ryan again: '*It takes about two to three years to get a green card* [our italics].'

Only expatriate Brits need to agonize further over more of the labyrinthine details of this subject – buy Binswanger and Ryan (see Bibliography) if you do. Suffice it to say that it is a bind. *The Lady* and *Nursery World* have refused for ages to allow any mention of America in their ads. No one can any longer pretend that the INS legislation and punishing fines are *really* meant to deter Mexican, Puerto Rican and other foreign workers – the long knives have been pointed directly at nannies and their employers.

What British agencies do about it
Understandably, no agency worth investigation by the authorities admits to sending nannies to America. Almost every one with international contacts and foreign business does place nannies there. A few deal exclusively with the above-board channels – nannies for diplomatic families, bona fide long-term employers moving from England to the US and the legal au pair programmes.

The au pair option
British and English-speaking Europeans between the ages of 18 and 24 can go for a limited time to work in America. The two programmes working at present are The Au Pair in America Program sponsored by the American Institute for Foreign Study Foundation and The Au Pair Homestay USA under the aegis of the Experiment in International Living.

Au pairs go in to America on 'cultural exchange' visas which are valid for a year. There are quite strict rules governing both programmes. The candidates must have had secondary education, some relevant experience or training in child care, hold a driver's licence and be verifiably healthy. The programmes' 'Code of Conduct' prohibits drug use and drunkenness and insists on good notice being given to the host family of any travel plans. Emphasis is placed on politeness and correct behaviour on both sides. Host families apply three months in advance of the date they wish the au pair to start and all applicants are screened in Europe.

The 'au pairs' responsibilities are more onerous than those expected of the au pair arrangement in England (see pages 171–96). They do a 45-hour week and their job description is similar to what a British employer would expect of a mother's help (see page 196). The cost to the host family is about 150 dollars a week.

How was it for you?

Cecil Woodham-Smith in *The Great Hunger* wrote that the Irish who went to America discovered three things. First that the streets were not paved with gold, second that they were not paved at all, and third that *they* were expected to pave them. It is exactly the opposite case with nannies. That is why they risk the huge potential unpleasantness and embarrassment of being found out and deported: the simple fact is that they love it.

Most American employers are generous, considerate, appreciative and determined to keep their nannies and show them a good time. The standard of living is much higher than in Britain and employers are keen to share the luxuries of their lives unstintingly with the angel who cares for their children. The stories of magnanimity are legion:

I didn't just get every weekend off; they used to fly me to wherever I wanted to go in their private plane.

I saw everything there was to see all over America with my employers. They were set on me seeing the sights.

The weather was so great wherever we were. If it got bad we moved to a house somewhere else where it was better!

It is not easy to find the homesick, lonely and exploited comments in that bunch or most others that we heard, though they were not uncritical or without a slight wistfulness for the old country.

But for all her nostalgia, one nanny knows exactly which side her bread is buttered. 'With the favourable exchange rate I'm better off working here and sending money home when I can, than living and working in England. I can imagine a time when constant life in the fast lane of the rat race will wear thin, but it hasn't happened yet.'

Apart from the East Coast market, the nanny scene thrives in the West as well. In Los Angeles, especially Hollywood, the rich and famous have British nannies. The somewhat less rich hire Swedish, French and Swiss au pairs. Anyone else who can afford help has Mexicans, Guatemalans and other Hispanics, who are paid peanuts and do everything. One LA lawyer comments, 'We are both lawyers. We risk a helluva lot each time we hire an English nanny from here on in. It is virtually impossible for us to get them here legally. By the time we succeeded the children would have grown up.'

The Malibu beach set give their nannies a lovely life. They are paid about $250 a week, have nice cars and/or a chauffeur at their disposal, and they socialize in the Tudor Tea Rooms and the King's Head in Santa Monica.

The American Nanny

The nanny profession in America is gearing up and racing away at a terrific pace from a Le Mans start. Deborah Davis, editor of the excellent and provocative *National Nanny Newsletter* in Claremont, California, is one of its most energetic founders. She has organized several nanny conferences and since they began in 1986 many hundreds of nanny agencies have mushroomed, nanny training schools have sprung up and a dozen nanny books have been published. Most recently she has formed the International Nanny Association, and Mrs Louise Davis of Norland is on the Board. It is to be 'a non-profit organization founded to promote and support the development of the professional nanny in America. The larger concern is the quality of child care available to all American families, but the INA will focus particularly on the in-home child care option.'

The market for nannies in the USA is enormous – estimates range from 10 to 250 job orders for every nanny or mother's help available. The big question is will the women of America become nannies in sufficient numbers to supply the domestic market? Recruiting them into child care has been difficult. The main reason that the INS has pushed so aggressively for tighter legislation to support its efforts to exclude aliens may to some extent reflect the current American belief that any idiot can babysit. It must be admitted that the legislation has been a shot in the arm to the US nanny industry.

As Deborah Davis writes: 'Until we perceive that the work of the child care provider is a legitimate profession, our society will continue to reinforce the low status and low pay of the professional nanny. We need to make clear the distinction between babysitter and professional nanny before the career of the in-home child care provider can be viewed as a viable job option for American women.'

The winds of change blow mostly from the West and original American thinking on what has for so long been exclusively the province of the Limeys may provide a much-needed blast of fresh air to uncommunicative employers, training colleges and employment agencies here.

14

What Really Matters

Politics and Crusades

The Americans describe jobs in terms of their 'comparable worth'. The Californian *National Nanny Newsletter* presents the argument thus: 'garbage collectors get good pay and benefits (better than teachers in some communities); they also have uniforms and titles such as 'sanitation engineer'; zoo keepers and janitors receive more pay than nursery school teachers. Judging from the US Department of Labor Statistics, child care is still at the bottom of the list, coming after home nursing aides and maids in the "value to society" scale.'

Scarr and Dunn in *Mother Care/Other Care* (see Bibliography), who have contributed much to the thinking of this book, say:

Many have pondered the low status of work with children and blamed it on the distance of child care from the realms of power and money. We want to propose another explanation. Children belong to women, primarily. Like it or not, we are the sure parent of each child, the parent with the biological connection to the nursing infant. We have come to the conclusion that children, especially babies and young children, are devalued by their close connection with women. In our view it is the low status of women that has tainted work with children, whether done by men or women.

We agree. It is the case that while many battles have been fought and won in the name of women's liberation, crucial battles over what women *and* men should do to make family life run smoothly have scarcely entered the lists. Most of the subjects we raise in this chapter concern these areas. Working mothers, maternity leave, more time off for fathers, tax allowances, day nurseries for everyone – these are just a few of the unresolved issues which affect most women and should concern men too.

275

There is a lot of talk about shared responsibilities, but the fact remains that few men help with the household tasks in a way which genuinely leaves women free to do other things.

Most women are not secure enough in their jobs to say to their colleagues, 'I must go home to my family *now*.' When they do say this they know that it reinforces men's view that women who have children can't be relied on. Many men disapprove of the idea that their employee is working when she has children at home.

Day nurseries

Did you know that less than one per cent of British children under five have council nursery places? Why is 'child care provision for all' of any interest to the comfortably off middle-class mother who has the space and the money to pay for in-home child care? It should be – partly through altruism and partly because, as consumers, there should be a choice. Many middle-class parents would prefer that their children went to a good, clean, well-equipped, happy local-authority day nursery rather than the onus being constantly on the parent to organize other forms of care. Parents rely on relatives and childminders if they haven't got room for a nanny or mother's help. This poverty of choice isn't good enough.

The few state nurseries cater for a desperate minority (page 318). No politician has the gall to claim that these nurseries are adequate or that they meet demand. There are more women voters than men in the UK. Women's, and particularly mothers', votes may be crucial for all the political parties at the next election. It's their turn.

Other European countries make child care a priority. If we do not we will deserve a future in which Two Nations no longer communicate – rich and poor, black and white, educated and uneducated. The nation has focused on child abuse and on horrible instances of cruelty to children in recent years. Social workers have been castigated for not doing their difficult jobs better. But families who have no money *have* no choice.

The mother has to go out to work. She strives to be super-woman with no support – she shops, cleans, washes, feeds and cherishes and may spend 6 to 10 hours a day out of the house working either full or part time. That is the norm for a surprising number of women in Britain today. It might be worse – her husband may walk out on them next week. The children may have to be left in their cots. Sometimes the woman across the hall looks in to see that they are all right. Along comes the social worker and suggests, rightly, that the children should be in care if their mother cannot organize things better.

How can a working mother be blamed for leaving a child alone in a house and at risk of injury, even of death, when she cannot find, or cannot afford, anyone suitable to help out with the children? We have said that nannies make mothers better mothers by giving them some free time and/or the chance to work without worry. Universal day care should provide a similar service for everyone.

Why are there so few child care crusaders? The problem is that those who should be carrying the banners are bogged down with wiping noses and bottoms. Most mothers are too busy to think generally about the difficulties that everyone faces. If they are working they are fretting and angry, knowing that their children are in a bad day nursery but unable to afford any other. *Ad hoc* child care arrangements cause intolerable strain.

When these mothers emerge from their relentless childrearing, understandably they don't want to be involved in any aspect of it ever again. It's someone else's turn to gripe and then *they* are too busy. Still nothing gets done. Parents, local authorities and Westminster have failed to make any radical changes in children's care for the under-fives, for school children or until their parents return from work.

Local councils
Local authorities should require developers to include nursery facilities in new office, industrial and shopping developments. This was done for the first time by City Child, which persuaded Islington to make a large property developer build a nursery as a *quid pro quo* for granting planning consents (see page 321).

Childminders
Local authorities should ensure that registration can be regarded as a mark of ability to provide a *good* standard of child care. They should also require all new childminders to attend pre-

registration training courses and offer training for registered childminders. This could also be made available to nannies and mother's help's. (See also pages 306–18).

Babysitters
In Scotland a law prohibits anyone using a babysitter who is less than 16 years of age. In the rest of the UK there is no such restriction although parents have a 'duty of care'. Legislation is needed urgently. It would not only protect young hired baby-sitters, but also older members of a young family (see also page 202).

The National Nursery Examination Board
Working mothers often say that they feel better leaving their children with someone who is trained. There are sensible arguments for this. No one would want to employ an amateur for the full-time education of their children nowadays; midwives are also professionals. If a childminder is bound by a child's right to have 'a fit person in a fit place', why should the parent reckon to get away with anything less? Training ought to help to make nannies excellent and dedicated. (See chapter 7 on the gripes about the nannies.)

Norland's Mrs Davis says: 'Still too many people see nannying as a second-rate option. But I hope that the NNEB will give greater emphasis in the syllabus to reflect changing patterns in the market – there is not enough emphasis on the fact that half the graduates go into private homes.'

Police records
In the USA employers have access to employees' criminal records, as do the social services departments before they register childminders in Britain. The UK police should provide the same service. In fact the number of nannies or mother's helps who have been convicted is tiny, partly because the police are reluctant to prosecute a nanny for whatever reason, be it theft or child abuse, without strong proof.

Agency black lists
Agencies should co-operate more with each other nationally and agree some form of early warning system when they spot a nanny

who should not look after children. FRES does do this, but too few agencies think it is worth their while to belong to FRES to make its list adequate (see page 341).

Nanny networks

It would make nannying much more enjoyable and satisfying if an organization took responsibility for a nanny's need to share problems and be supported professionally. Nanny networks are commonplace in America; they put nannies in touch with each other in different cities. Employment agencies there are much more willing than in the UK to pool their nanny lists so that nannies can make friends and settle in new jobs regardless of who placed them. The only version in the UK is Lorraine Thompson's Nannies Need Nannies (see Useful Addresses).

Nursery World runs a Nanny Fair annually in London, which is attended by some 800 nannies who are either second-year students committed to nannying or who are practising nannies. Excellent speakers are invited, agencies are well represented and the event encourages new thinking and discussion about every aspect of the profession.

The nanny organizations, PANN or NACNN (see pages 342–3 and 344) should mastermind a proper nanny club and encourage nannies to go on refresher courses. Discontented nanny gripe sessions are rarely attended by fulfilled, busy nannies who might otherwise raise low morale and fire their contemporaries with their enthusiasm for the job. But these happy nannies say that they would welcome going to well-organized evening seminars from time to time. An editorial in *Nursery World* comments, 'Nannies are isolated from their professional colleagues and they are constantly in danger of forgetting what good child care practice is.' This is too true to be good.

More Information: Agencies

Choosing and Using an Agency

An agency should save the employer time, frustration and hassle. Their experience of screening hundreds of applicants a year and talking to hundreds of employers can make them the ideal people to make a good match between the two. They should provide qualified applicants, check references carefully and act as honest brokers if problems arise after the nanny or mother's help has been placed.

Agencies use recruitment methods which are much too expensive for individual families to contemplate. They maintain contact with training colleges all over the country, many visit them and have good relationships with tutors.

An agency is only as good as . . . its last client . . . its last placement . . . its manager . . . . We heard them all, and they are all true. Word of mouth is the most important recommendation an agency can have, so they have good reason to be polite and helpful to you, the employer. And you have some advantage as the writer of the fee cheque as well.

George Bernard Shaw said that theatre goers should not leave their critical faculties outside with their coats; so it is when an employer speaks to an agency. Just because you are paying them to do their job, and probably you will never meet, doesn't mean that it doesn't matter whether you like them or not. Trust your instincts and decide if you react well to the voice on the telephone. If you find it too authoritarian, too stupid, too snobby, too easy-going, ask to speak to the manager, and if you don't like her either, don't use them. If you can't get on with them instinctively before any money has changed hands, you will not respect their services as negotiators and mediators later.

A good agency will ask a lot of questions. Don't be defensive about the number of bathrooms. Don't exaggerate. Sally-Anne Lloyd of The Nanny Connection says that she likes 'employers who sound as though they have thought through all the details before they lift the phone. They describe the nanny's room precisely, and they don't make it sound as though they are doing the nanny a huge favour.' Agencies use the phone all day for screening purposes. They are quick to suss out any sham.

It's bad psychology to tell agencies that you are using several of them simultaneously. It won't make them put you at the head of the queue, rather the reverse.

Agencies have a habit of pretending that no other agency exists. It is not often that agencies are polite about each other without barbed qualification. The main reason for this is that there is a lot of competition nowadays. No one wants to give away any trade secrets or miss a trick. There aren't many reasons for agencies ever to speak to each other and many don't.

Questions to ask an agency

An agency isn't used to being asked many questions by employers, so these will be a good test of keenness to help.

- Where do the applicants come from and how do you find them?
- What does the agency *mean* by the terms 'trained' and/or 'experienced'? Do they have a minimum age?
- How much do its nannies cost to employ per week? (Don't let an agency tell you you can't afford one, that's your business.)
- What is the agency fee, their refund and/or replacement policy and guarantee period?
- How would they describe their interview methods? (You want the Spanish Inquisition and some indication that they do turn down some applicants.)
- Do they check all references properly? By letter or phone or both? How many references do they require and from whom will they accept them? How old can the references be? Do they require a complete record of the girl's working life?
- What aftercare does the agency provide? What are their general attitudes to employers and nannies? (Few agents maintain their balance sitting on that fence.)

Some agents provide excellent aftercare and their intervention, when requested to deal with a problem, can save much misery and difficulty. An agent with 25 years' experience was rung up not long ago by an employer who couldn't stand her nanny loping round the house with bare feet and putting them up on her polished furniture. The nanny said that she thought she could do as she pleased as far as *that* little detail was concerned. The agent was asked to mediate. She spoke to the girl 'Whose house are you working in? Do you think you are at the seaside?'

It was an explosive issue, and if handled badly would have been a surefire case of 'for the want of a shoe . . .', but the nanny respected her agent's view and is still in residence.

If a nanny is unhappy, a good agent should not make a drama out of a crisis. She will be able to tackle the employer unemotionally and tactfully if the girl feels that she is out of her depth. Should a crunch come, the agency should still be around to minimize the fall-out and help both sides part in a civilized manner. Many employers do not realize just how useful an experienced and involved listener may be. It is not beyond price. Hire the one you like and respect.

Beware of:

- One-woman bands working from kitchens or front rooms mushroom and vanish monthly. Aftercare and repayment of registration fees are unlikely.
- Registration fees may be a rip-off unless you receive a list of available nannies by return post.
- Bad agencies attempt to charge the would-be employee. This is illegal.
- Bad agencies are too lazy to check references. The employer should always double check.
- Bad agencies don't offer aftercare for girls they have placed. This is unprofessional. (Good ones will also provide a list of other local nannies, and abroad too.)
- Bad agencies may attempt to lure your nanny to another job once she has been with you for some time.
- Bad agencies do not give an adequate guarantee period. Less than six weeks is silly.
- Bad agencies risk your privacy and security by sending out detailed lists of employers' phone numbers and circumstances.
- Bad agencies send girls abroad without proper instructions, briefing or back-up.
- Bad agencies put pressure on a nanny or employer to accept a match for the sake of their fee.
- Bad agencies crack up jobs to be something they ain't. (Working in a theatrical family *may* be glamorous or *may* involve extra long hours and tension while actors are 'resting'.)
- Bad agencies never see the girls on their books. Personal interviews make happy placements much more likely.

What Employers Say About Agencies

The only employers who have words of praise for the agencies are those with good nannies who feel that the agency fee was well worth her and that the agency saved the employer trouble by doing a good job. Employers are often as resentful about agency fees as they are about their nannies' salaries. Do what you can afford and shop around. If the cost is not the point compared with your aim to find a competent loving professional to care for your children, then you are quids in, in every sense but literally.

There are many agencies who provide an excellent service, but it will be your bad luck, and theirs, if they have not got anyone suitable at that time whom you like. A lot of it is skill. A lot of it is luck, for the agents and the employer.

I can't stand high-handed staff. It never matters how much you can afford, they always say that's not enough.

I don't think they screen the girls or check references properly.

I just call six or seven and hope for the best.

At last I have found a brilliant one. I send so much business their way that they sent me a bunch of roses last month.

I always use agencies so that there is some comeback if the nanny is unsuitable. I don't think I'm a great interviewer and I value their experience.

I like agencies run by ex-employers of nannies best and occasionally those run by really professional ex-nannies. They have the best grasp of the problems.

One agent told me that if she had a ventriloquist's dummy which said it could drive, she would place her twenty times over right away. It's hard to forget that view of agencies.

Agencies Specializing in Nannies

Charlotte Breese comments: the agencies listed below have been generous with their time, not just with this chapter, but with advice for many angles and ideas in the book as a whole. The comments are personal, as is the choice. None of the largest has been excluded, but the list is far from exhaustive. Should readers find that their favourite has been neglected in this edition, we would welcome comments and suggestions.

Fees are classified as 'below average' if less than £350 for a permanent residential nanny, 'average' if between £350 and £700, and 'above average' if more than £700. The same phrases have also been used much more loosely in connection with proxy mothers, babysitters or maternity nurses. To be specific in the Land of the Rising Salary would be to date the book; too many of them tell us that they are reviewing their rates.

Addap Personnel, 3 Melville Street, Falkirk FK1 1H2 Tel: 0324 36101
Fees: well below average

Mrs Adele Pickles runs this delightful agency, which is the only one that anyone recommends in Scotland. She has been dealing with nannies since 1986 and the majority of her clients get NNEB trained nannies from her and occasionally maternity nurses and mother's helps.

'We get lots of calls from London. I send more mature girls there mostly to avoid homesickness problems. We liaise closely with the local NNEB college and everyone is carefully interviewed.'

Albemarle Barclay Ltd, 22 Hans Place, Knightsbridge, London SW1X 0EP Tel: 071 581 3821
Fees: well above average

Mrs Frances Hutchinson runs the UK side of this large new agency, which houses several nanny consultants. They provide experienced and qualified nannies, maternity nurses and temps. It is big business. They also have private tutors and governesses for special needs children. Mrs Sheila Davies is in charge of the overseas department. She has long experience of placing nannies in the Middle East and, as chairman of FRES, sits on the NNEB Board.

'In 12 months we have had a 97 per cent success rate. We go deeply into people's background so we have a real feeling for what they are like.'

Anglo Nannies London, Suite 7, EBC House, Kew Road, Richmond, Surrey TW9 2NA Tel: 081 332 2458/940 8169
Fees: average

In 1989 Mrs Omur Yeginsu started placing nannies in England and abroad. She provides a full menu of daily and live-in nannies, trained and mother's helps, au pairs, maternity nurses, babysitters and temps and also sends English teachers to Turkey.

'We handle business in a professional way in a proper office. We keep careful records and run the show honestly. We know this is a service job and we work very hard to get good results.'

Ask Alice Nanny Agency, 12 Martin's Lane, Exeter, Devon EX1 1EY Tel: 0392 216110
Fees: bottom end of average

Proprietor and founder in 1986: ex-NNEB nanny, Alice May. First choice among employers in Devon as she offers a thorough service for every kind of child care including weekend proxy mothers and babysitters. She expects her nannies not to be over rigid about what they will and won't do.

'They have to be more flexible in the country when there is so much more for everyone to do around the homestead.'

Bees Knees, 296 Sandycombe Road, Kew Gardens, Richmond, Surrey TW9 3NG Tel: 071 876 7039/948 5134
Fees: above average

Mrs Crane started this agency in 1980. Her clients are mainly local, but her nannies and au pairs come from all over the world. She has built up a regular clientèle and provides both daily and live-in nannies, au pairs and babysitters. References are always checked before placement.

'As the mother of two small children, I understand the problems and am a good listener. My success lies in personal service. I never raise false hopes.'

Belgravia Bureau, 35 Brompton Road, London SW3 1DF Tel: 071 584 4343

Fees: above average

Proprietor since 1969, Mrs Andreae-Jones owns the Belgravia Bureau and Ruth Cordeaux runs the nanny section of this big agency. She is very friendly and helpful and an ex-Norlander. Her nannies are principally trained or highly experienced and they work for the rich in the UK and abroad. Excellent interviews and reference checks.

'I think daily nannies are becoming more and more important and we have more working mothers who rightly feel that if they are paying they have a right to a first-class service.'

Bellamy Nannies, The Power House, Alpha Place, off Flood Street, Chelsea, London SW3 5FZ Tel: 071 351 7299

Fees: average

Proprietor since 1984, Mark Rolo runs this agency which provides nannies, mother's helps, babysitters and maternity nurses, Australians and New Zealanders. Business has grown and there are now three assistants and they are astute, helpful, patient and determined to do the job right. Unlike many agencies, this one offers real value for money.

'We seem to be growing slowly and the girls stay in touch because we are always prepared to help.'

Bligh Appointments, 12 New Burlington Street, London W1X 1FF Tel: 071 439 4686

Fees: average but negotiable. If you need a 'follow-on' girl it will cost you a lot less next time around

Since 1988, Jane Sullivan has run this branch of Bligh, which deals with Australian nannies and mother's helps. They have an office in Sydney and they check out each other's references. They interview shrewdly and employers reckon themselves in safe hands and take their advice as gospel.

'I prefer the rural types. I am wary of the second-time jobbers who have become too street-wise to be employable. Some Australians are very unionized in their attitude. The best of the bunch are teachers, nurses and particularly dental technicians. If you can persuade a child to open his mouth in a dentist's chair, you can persuade him to do anything!'

Bunbury Domestic Employment Agency (Everybody Needs Somebody), Foxdale, Bunbury, Tarporley, Cheshire CW6 9PE Tel: 0829 260148

Fees: below average/average.

Proprietor since 1972, Leila Potter is a redoubtable personality whose clients are loyal and admiring. Bunbury is deliberately run as a rather offbeat and extremely personal service. She produces all sorts of staff and every assignment is treated as a challenge. She lectures at NNEB colleges, her service is quick, efficient and always accomplished with style and fun. This all makes using this nanny agency an amusing experience.

'I think our proxy mother service is pretty good, there seem to be less vacancies for nannies at the moment but we have lots of work staffing workplace crèches. We don't like to be too business-like.'

Canonbury Nannies Agency, 6 Northampton Grove, London N1 2PL Tel: 071 704 0639/226 3194
Fees: average

Amanda Drury, a Norlander, has provided a small specialist service since 1982 which supplies trained and experienced nannies for residential and daily work. Everyone is interviewed. Reference checks are exhaustive. Good back-up.

'No nanny over 21 wants to live in. Nannies should act professionally and behave as though they were working in a hospital or nursery. We advise two interviews and a weekend or overnight stay before they take the job.'

Care At Home, 54 Chertsey Street, Guildford, Surrey GU1 4HD Tel: 0483 302275
Fees: above average

Helen Flatt and her team have been working to build this company over the last five years. They have a large team of professional carers whom she does not call nannies. All the managers are trained nurses and the emphasis in this company is on professionalism and total dedication to the children in their care. It is impressive.

'We recruit from all over the country. We provide 24-hour back-up. We try to make it possible for these very dependent children to live to their greatest potential. We are as responsible for that child as if he were our own.'

Carr Nannies, 3 Glebe Road, Barnes, London SW13 0DR Tel: 081 878 8625
Fees: below average/average

Alexandra Carr has run this agency since 1989 and is a worthy new entry. Her office is very busy and she was previously a film production assistant and employed nannies and mother's helps while she was working. She is articulate and keen to help and has nannies, maternity nurses, mother's helps, Australians, New Zealanders, au pairs, temps – the whole gamut of the industry – on offer.

'We have a link with a company in Melbourne and otherwise our business is mostly in London and the rest of England, though we have some international business too.'

Childminders, 9 Paddington Street, London W1M 3LA Tel: 071 935 2049/935 9763
Fees: average

Going since 1968, this agency is under the same ownership as the Nanny Service. The manager is Julia Eason. It provides babysitters *only* from a pool of 1,500 people. This is the largest agency of its kind in England and, they think possibly, in the world. They have 300–500 bookings a week.

'We have masses of student nurses from all the major teaching hospitals on our books and lots of otherwise experienced people and we are very busy every day. We vet everybody thoroughly and they are all over 19.'

Consultus Agency, 17 London Road, Tonbridge, Kent TN10 3AB Tel: 0732 355231

Fees: average

Proprietor since 1963, Mrs Stevens runs a professional service providing nannies, mother's helps and maternity nurses and perhaps most importantly (because they are rare) really competent proxy mothers in an emergency or when parents want or need to be away. She welcomes Australians and New Zealanders.

'Most of our business involves the care of the elderly but 15 per cent is still entirely geared to the young.'

Cotswold Nannies, Stonecroft, High Street, Bisley, Glos GL6 7BS Tel: 0452 770076 also a London branch 081 891 6042

Fees: average

Mrs Kirby, an ex-housemistress at Cheltenham Ladies College, took over this agency in 1987 and works hard to keep it successful and cosier than many London agencies. She provides nannies, mother's helps and maternity nurses. Good interview and back up.

'I'm much more experienced now and find the job so involving I wish I could afford to provide the service without charge.'

Country Cousins, 10A Market Square, Horsham, W. Sussex RH12 1EU Tel: 0403 210415

Fees: below average

Mrs Josephine McGregor, a trained nurse, has run this extremely responsible agency since 1958. She supplies competent and trusted proxy mothers who have mostly been tried and tested over many years. Many employers swear by them.

'There are so many crises in which employers need proxy mothers and they should go to an agency who can vouch for their total reliability.'

Dolly Mixtures, Marlborough Lodge, 11 Springfield Road, Kingston upon Thames KT1 2SA Tel: 081 546 0281

Fees: below average

Proprietor since 1986, Sue Stanley-Davis runs this idiosyncratic and happy agency which often comes up with fresh solutions to old problems. She provides nannies, babysitters, mother's helps and an excellent temp service. Give her 72 hours notice and she can send someone anywhere.

'Kids of the 90s have their mums around much more and people are returning to privacy. Bosses are tougher than they were. But a mum working from home still needs some help with the children while she gets her business underway and we have had lots of experience of providing effective help for short periods at short notice.'

Europairs, The Irish Connection 253a Upper Newtownards Road, Belfast BT4 3JF Tel: 0232 471606
Fees: below average
Susan Shilliday and Rosemary McKee started this agency in 1987 and are exceptionally helpful. They provide nannies, mother's helps and au pairs. Everyone is interviewed. They are also regional organizers for Au Pair in America and their international business is growing.
'I love my London families. We've had very few bad ones and we mostly take references on the families too.'

Fry Staff Consultants, Suite 3, 7 High Street, Aldershot, Hants GU11 1BH Tel: 0252 315369
Fees: below average
Proprietor since 1971, Mrs Eileen Fry knows she prefers professional trained nannies whom she places in the UK and Europe, where she enjoys a high reputation. She also provides mother's helps, au pairs and maternity nurses.
'I like serious girls. I'm always available to help them should they need me. I give them long pep talks, but I pick the nicer ones and they know how to behave.'

Help At Hand, Enterprise House, 113 George Lane, South Woodford, London E18 1AN Tel: 081 530 8464/989 5164
Fees: average
Mrs June Warriner, an SRN, started her agency in 1982. She supplies nannies, mother's helps and au pairs, and has a good working relationship with a Canadian agency. She recently set up a month's training course for nannies within her own training school. This is a unique idea and sounds as though it is working well. The girls do five full days of study learning about safety in the home, good nutrition and play stimulation. They spend 12 days in a family and 12 days in a nursery school.
'It is an ideal taster for girls who may want to do the NNEB and several NNEB courses are sending me their students too.'

Hyde Park Nannies, 33 Southgate Street, Winchester, Hants SO23 9EH Tel: 0962 841234
Fees: average/above average
Tess Archdale has run this large, busy agency since 1982. She provides any private professional staff including nannies and mother's helps in the UK and abroad. She gives a unique 5 year guarantee on the fee and this is a popular agency with London employers.
'We aim to be realistic and positive, treating both employers and nannies courteously. We do not try to persuade either to accept anything that they are not totally happy with.'

Jamie Turner: see **Turner's**

Janet White, 67 Jackson Avenue, Leeds LS8 1NS Tel: 0532 666507
Fees: below average/ average
Janet White is a Canadian who has lived here for 8 years and started her agency in 1978. It provides mother's helps, nannies, maternity nurses and au pairs both in the UK, Europe, Canada and many other places in the world. She is also a regional organizer for Au Pair in America.
'I screen them carefully and always think would I like you to look after my children?'

Kensington Nannies (also Nannies Kensington), 49/53 Kensington High Street, London W8 6ED Tel: 071 937 2333/3299
Fees: above average
Mrs Teeling-Smith and Gilly MacWilliam own this agency and the latter has worked there since 1976. Long established and well respected, this establishment agency provides nannies, mother's helps and maternity nurses. Many Australians and New Zealanders are available through them. This is a perennial favourite with employers and nannies alike.
'We see at least 15–20 girls each day. We interview carefully and welcome nannies with the right attitude.'

Knightsbridge Nannies, 5 Beauchamp Place, London SW3 1NG Tel: 071 584 9323
Fees: above average
This agency has been running for 28 years and has always been reckoned amongst the best. Christine Black is in charge and was trained as a Chiltern nanny. All the staff there have similar qualifications and interview personally and professionally. Nannies, mother's helps, maternity nurses and temps are all available and they provide staff for workplace crèches.
'We deal with all kinds and sorts of nannies. Everyone is suitable somewhere. Flexibility and the right attitude, commitment and loyalty are all vital: nannying isn't like any other job.'

Lady Colwyn's Agency, 65 Drakefield Road, London SW17 8RS Tel: 071 351 9294
Fees: below average
Lady Colwyn started this agency in 1987 and has partners in New Zealand who send nannies and mother's helps to be interviewed and with their references checked. They provide Australians and New Zealanders, and a few British nannies and mother's helps. Employers are very happy with the service they receive.
'We get good bunches of girls who spend ten days getting to know London before interviewing with anyone. It's a good system which gives them ready-made friends.'

Lifesavers, 4 Binns Road, Chiswick, London W4 2BS Tel: 081 995 7235/ 747 8517
Fees: below average
This tiny agency started life as a babysitting agency and has become a source of experienced or trained nannies, temps, weekend nannies, nanny shares and part-time permanent nannies – a boon for flexi-time working mums. Jeditte Hocking is a very friendly efficient person who is well capable of handling many different queries and putting together successful combinations. She nannied for 10 years so has a clear view of everyone's points of view. An excellent, cheap new agency.
'I am often asked to organize the more complicated arrangements like nanny shares for my clients and then there is lots of more straightforward work. I enjoy it all very much.'

Mrs Lines Employment Agency, 25A Kensington Church Street, London W8 4LL Tel: 071 937 4165/8505
Fees: average
This agency has been around for 95 years and about one-third of its business is nannies, mother's help and au pairs who are placed in the UK and abroad. Mrs Patel is the manager and Mrs Hurst has worked there since 1971. She has a faithful clientèle.
'It is really a domestic agency. We have a small number of nannies and a large number of au pairs. Most of our clients are ex-directory.'

Little Things, 8 Gorst Road, London SW11 6JE Tel: 071 223 3281
Fees: below average
Sarah Robinson provides nannies, mother's helps and a babysitting service in Clapham, Wandsworth and Tooting. She visits clients before placing residential nannies in their home. Good back up.
'We are busier and bigger than we were, but I still make time to meet both employers and nannies.'

Looking Glass Nannies, 5 Boringdon Villas, Plympton, Devon PL7 4DY Tel: 0752 348694
Fees: below average
Founded by still very young experienced nanny Kate Hodgkins in 1990, this small agency has all the makings of an excellent service for seekers of nannies and mother's helps west of Exeter. Kate visits both nannies and clients all over Cornwall and Devon and tries hard to make a perfect match. She only interviews a girl at home after receiving a strong response from referees.
'If a girl doesn't get many referees bothering to confirm I'm afraid she goes to the bottom of the pile.'

Monroe Nannies, 18 South Molton Street, London W1Y 1DD Tel: 071 499 8867
Fees: above average
Jane Street has run this agency since 1984. It has trained and experienced nannies, mother's helps and maternity nurses available for work in London, Europe and

the Middle and Far East. Over 50 per cent of its work is now international. They recruit only half their applicants. This is an up-market and professional business. 'Bad placements are bad advertisements. Vocational nannies are happy to have the mother around. We like our nannies to have a high sense of ethics and responsibility.'

The Nanny Company (incorporates Kensington and Chelsea Nurses and Nannies and Tempo agencies), 168 Sloane Street, London SW1X 9QF Tel: 071 581 5454
Fees: above average
Harri, who owns this company, takes great care of his clients and nannies alike. He provides nannies, mother's helps, babysitters and maternity nurses in the UK and abroad alongside a huge number of other services, which range from ladies maids and footmen to music masters and dog walkers. The reason that they are all just mad about Harri is obvious; he treats everyone as though they represent the only job he really minds about. All staff interviewed and references checked in unusual detail. A top people's agency.
'We want nannies who look the part. I see myself as being on their side. Ours are professional and take their job seriously.'

Nannies Incorporated, 63/64 Margaret Street, London W1N 7FJ Tel: 071 323 3338
Fees: above average
Annie Martin owns this company and is mostly to be found in their branches in Paris or Brussels, but Janet Maher runs the nanny section in the London office. This is a swish set-up started in 1989. Janet is capable and sympathetic and was an NNEB nanny and then worked at Regency Nannies for some time.
'The UK office deals principally with maternity nurses – they are about 70 per cent of our business, but we have nannies, mother's helps and temps as well.'

The Nanny Connection, Stern House, 85 Gloucester Road, London SW7 4SS Tel: 071 835 2277
Fees: average/above average
Sally-Anne Lloyd worked as a nanny and then at The Nanny Service for five years before setting up this agency in 1987. She has attracted a lot of Australians and New Zealanders on to her books, along with NNEB nannies and a few mother's helps and temps. The agency reflects the owner's bubbly, bright, practical nature, continuing to maintain high standards and remaining a great favourite with employers and nannies alike.
'It has been really hard work in the last couple of years, but we have new premises and all goes well.'

The Nanny Service, 9 Paddington Street, London W1M 3LA Tel: 071 935 3515
Fees: above average
Paul Rendle owns this agency, which has been going since 1976. Izzy Blanchard and Nikki Cameron provide nannies, mother's helps and maternity nurses and have lots of reliable temps, a boon in emergencies. References are checked and

girls always interviewed. This is a good place to inquire for Australians and New Zealanders.

'We aim to be polite, friendly and efficient.'

Nash Nannies, 53 Church Road, Hove, Sussex BN3 2BD Tel: 0403 711436
Fees: average

Mrs Patricia Newland runs a long-established busy agency which specializes exclusively in placing nannies and mother's helps abroad worldwide. She interviews thoroughly and provides good aftercare. The agency has an excellent reputation.

'I recommend giving a kind, friendly but tough interview as it is preferable to deter the weaker applicants. They would never last in the job.'

Newbury Nannies, Rye Cottage, Peasemore, Newbury, Berks RG16 0JN Tel: 0635 248091
Fees: average

Susan Mitcalfe and Nicola Walters and Anne Collins run this confident agency and provide nannies, maternity nurses, mother's helps, temps and babysitters. Norlanders are often available. They interview everyone and take up references.

'The wages remain exorbitant but employers expect really good value for money. It takes a lot of time and trouble to place people correctly.'

Nightingale Nannies, 2 Downs Villas, Park Road, Tring, Herts HP23 6BW Tel: 0442 890714
Fees: well below average

Sue Tomkys is an accountant with four children who works from home and now owns this agency and can help you find nannies, mother's helps and maternity nurses. She covers Beds, Bucks, Herts, Oxon and London.

'We have contacts with five agencies in other parts of the country and visit all the local colleges. We are strong on conciliation if there is a problem and we listen hard to what people say.'

The Norland Register, Norland Nursery Training College, Denford Park, Hungerford, Berks RG17 0PQ Tel: 0488 682252
Fees: There is a non-returnable deposit of £25 which is deductible from the engagement of a Probationary Nurse, who can be engaged for 10 per cent of her first 9 months' gross earnings. Otherwise qualified Norlanders cost 10 per cent of their first year's gross earning to a maximum of £750 (heart-warming for an agency to recognize the top line!)

Mrs Jenkinson runs the Norland Register and prospective employers are advised to write or telephone and will then be sent a registration form. They fill in their requirements and it is a good idea to send a detailed job description with a covering letter and some photographs too. The details are then circulated and the Register seeks to match employers' requirements to nurses' capabilities and wants. Norlanders contact the Register for many years after qualification for long-term and temporary situations, where they are often wanted for maternity work or as proxy mothers. Even those with school-age children often ring up requesting short-term posts.

Probationers are guided by the Principal and the Nursery Matron in their choice of post but 'their learning is fresh in their minds and they are very keen to make a success of their first job in order to qualify for the full diploma.' The College provides excellent back-up.

Norfolk Agency, 19 London Road, Downham Market, Norfolk P38 9BP
Tel: 0366 384448
Fees: below average
Mrs Parker is an SRN and health visitor who provides experienced and trained nannies, 'new' nannies, mother's helps and au pairs. She enjoys a high reputation as does her agency, which has been going since 1985.
'I look for nannies who really love children and are safe, kind and caring.'

North London Nannies, 92 Creighton Avenue, London N10 1NT Tel: 081 444 4911
Fees: average
Jackie Lewis has run this agency since 1983 and has four children herself. She supplies trained nannies and mother's helps both in the UK and abroad. Occasionally she also deals in au pairs 'as a concession to my old clients who have grown out of nannies'. Interviews and aftercare are good and there are lots of appreciative noises made by satisfied customers. She is fond of Australians and New Zealanders.
'I advise that employers don't spring things on nannies after the interview stage when everything should be openly discussed.'

Occasional and Permanent Nannies, 2 Cromwell Place, London SW7 2JE Tel: 071 225 1555
Fees: above average
Angela Hovey is a Norlander who worked in a nursery in South Africa and then for Knightsbridge Nannies before she took over this long-established, big agency in 1973. She is resourceful, approachable and efficient and has qualified staff who also provide thorough interviews and good back-up. They supply nannies, mother's helps and maternity nurses in the UK, Europe and abroad. The agency is renowned for its good temps.
'Clients are choosy and at the moment we have more girls than jobs, so employers are getting a good deal. It is their turn.'

Oxford Aunts, 2 George Street, Oxford OX1 2AF Tel: 0865 249784
Fees: average
Mrs Josephine McDougall started this agency in 1967 and Mrs Ann Robinson runs the nanny section. They supply nannies, babysitters, mother's helps and a few maternity nurses largely locally but occasionally abroad. Everyone is interviewed and confidential character references are taken.
'We have expanded lately, but both clients and nannies are poorer so the au pair business is assuming more importance.'

probably for locals only (handwritten annotation)

Pembroke Maternity Service, P.O. Box 449, London W8 4RX Tel: 071 727 5058
Fees: average.

293

Patsy Smith has run this specialized agency, which provides maternity nurses of every kind, since 1986. She has exacting standards, befitting an ex-Great Ormond Street trained nurse, where she held responsible positions for many years before becoming a maternity nurse herself. She is reassuring, direct and kind. Interviews are excellent and advice and aftercare constantly available. Many agencies who find maternity work a nuisance hand on their clients' enquiries to her.

'It's hard to get proper professional maternity nurses these days, but I have several on my books. I always need more.'

The Princess Christian College Register, 26 Wilbraham Road, Fallowfield, Manchester M14 6JX Tel: 061 224 4560

Mrs Rigby is still inundated with inquiries at her small college.

'It is quite impossible to meet demands.' Although people take it rather personally when they fail to make the top of the list, many go on trying.

Quick Help Agency, 307A Finchley Road, London NW3 6EH Tel: 071 794 8666

Fees: just above average

Mrs Norma Cutner, the proprietor of this agency since 1971, speaks French and her assistant is German. Although Mrs Cutner has some local nannies, she specializes in Australians and New Zealanders. They are interviewed in their home countries and arrive to work in pre-selected jobs. Mrs Cutner reckons on an 85 per cent success rate.

'Most of my clients want the nanny/mother's help/housekeeper type and these young women have a practical approach to domestic life.'

Regency Nannies, 50 Hans Crescent, London SW1X 0NA Tel: 071 584 7265/581 4544

Fees: above average

Mr and Mrs Wright have owned this big thriving agency since 1982. They supply nannies, mother's helps, excellent temps, proxy mothers and are particularly known for a large pool of maternity nurses both in the UK and abroad. This is a thoroughly professional outfit.

'We are setting up a separate division for the international placements which will be my baby. We have had a very busy time lately, but are always pleased to provide the exceptions, like a special nurse for a sick baby.'

Rockinghorse, 44 Amerland Street, London SW18 1PZ Tel: 081 874 1884 and also at 1 Alfred Street, Oxford OX1 4EH Tel: 0865 794224

Fees: below average

Sarah Cook started the London Rockinghorse in 1989 and can supply nannies, mother's helps, maternity nurses and babysitters.

'I think experienced girls are often just as good as the trained ones, it really is personality and aptitude which count.'

Grainne (pronounced Grania) Lamphee runs the very busy agency in Oxford which sounds extremely friendly and good.

'We have an amazing mixture of nannies available to our clients: Chiltern girls from the nearby college, prospective Oxford students who want to fill in a year before they start at the university, NNEBs and NAMCW students from Abingdon.'

Solve Your Problems Ltd, 5 Vale Road North, Surbiton, Surrey KT6 5AG Tel: 081 974 2449

Fees: average

Employers will remember this agency from their youth and it has been run since 1988 by Caroline Kolbe-Booysen, who offers many solutions to domestic problems which include nannies, mother's helps, babysitters, proxy mothers and temps.

'I aim to provide every sphere of help with children and the home.'

Spectrum, 119 George V Avenue, Worthing, Sussex BN11 5SA Tel: 0903 506127

Fees: below average

Mrs Atkinson has been providing nannies and mother's helps from this agency since 1986. She runs a country-wide introductory service and doesn't interview. She has many girls from the North and the Midlands on her list.

'We are keen on a contract of employment and like girls with commonsense.'

Swansons, 12 Thornton Avenue, London W4 1QD Tel: 081 994 5275

Fees: below average

Anne Babb has provided nannies and mother's helps since 1983. She is a delightful person to deal with and interviews everyone 'eventually' and issues weekly lists. She also rings up if a possible match appears between lists. References are always checked and good, reliable aftercare is offered. Clients are mostly local, though nannies come from all over the country. Employers recommend this agency highly.

'Smaller agencies often take greater care than big ones. They may have a larger selection of girls, but they don't often take as much trouble as they should.'

Tinies, The Stable House, Lammas Lane, Esher, Surrey KT10 8PN Tel: 0372 467447 and many other branches

Fees: average

Janet Trethewy, an SRN, started this agency in 1975 and has sold franchises all round the M25. There are now twelve branches, mostly round the M25, linked by their owners being trained by the franchisors, Janet Trethewy and Susan Boothroyd, and using a common operational manual. They all set aside one room as an office and work from home. They provide nannies, mother's helps, temps, maternity nurses and proxy mothers.

'One of our strengths is that girls are passed from office to office, so we can be very useful if a temp is needed desperately.'

Treasures, 2 Cowley Way, Sutton Benger, Chippenham, Wilts SN15 4SD Tel: 0249 720647

Fees: below average

This is a small agency which employers regard as a great treat and well guarded secret. It is run by Jacqueline May, who provides nannies, mother's helps, temps and proxy mums in the UK, Europe and Canada. It is particularly friendly and helpful.

'We run a very active local nanny circle and try to make sure that the service everyone receives is equally personal.'

Turner's Nannies and Mother's Helps Ltd, 2/4 Kenway Road, Earls Court, London SW5 0RR Tel: 071 370 7333
Fees: average
Jamie Turner has been uncrowned king of the Australian and New Zealand nanny market for a long time now. His able assistant, Wendy Anderson, was a nanny and hauls in trained recruits from a Brisbane nanny college called Charlton Brown and also from a contact in New Zealand. Employers love this agency and so do the nannies. They have a great knack of being dead straight with both sides.
'We really understand where they are coming from. Both of us have lived there and not much gets past us. For teachers, nurses and girls who have done office work, it is a great temporary job for six months.'

Universal Care, Chester House, 9 Windsor End, Beaconsfield, Bucks HP9 2JJ Tel: 04946 78811
Fees: below average
Peter and Gillian Cullimore have been running this agency since 1987 and provide maternity nurses, nannies, mother's helps, au pairs and proxy mothers. Their staff includes an NNEB and an SRN and they have close contacts with their local NNEB colleges where they hand out Universal Care awards to the best students.
'Our aim is to give a complete service from a professional office with excellent organization.'

Vanessa Bancroft, 24 Broomhill Road, Orpington, Kent BR6 0EN Tel: 0689 831701 and also 19/23 Prospect Street, Bridlington, North Humberside Tel: 0262 400214
Fees: average
Vanessa Bancroft worked for the Belgravia Bureau for 5 years before setting up her own agency outside London. She provides nannies, mother's helps and au pairs in the UK and abroad. Interviews and aftercare are good. She is friendly, relaxed and efficient.
'I find the work very satisfying and thoroughly enjoy it. I now live in the north and ship girls south and I hold interview days in Kent.'

Wealden Nannies, Ringle Crouch, Sandhurst, Cranbrook, Kent TN18 5PA Tel: 0580 850585
Fees: below average
Rosemary Broadbent, an SRN, set up in 1985 and provides mother's helps and nannies. They come from 'excellent local colleges'. She runs a personal and reliable service. She interviews, checks references and provides excellent after-care.
'I don't like employers who just want to use country agencies because we are cheaper. Those ones tend to treat their nannies as skivvies. I don't want nannies who are butterflies on my books, they are no good for my reputation. The girls are often young and gullible and there are very bad employers in rough areas.'

Mrs Wigginton's Family Help, 33 Ritherdon Road, London SW17 8QE
Tel: 081 767 4851
Fees: below average/average
Mrs Wigginton worked at the Brompton Bureau for 8 years before setting up on her own in 1985. She provides nannies (NNEB and Norland), mother's helps and sends pre-university English students abroad to families as au pairs. Everyone is thoroughly interviewed and references checked. She likes New Zealanders and Australians.
'There are more good girls around than previously. I really try to help and place people carefully.'

Wizard, 3 Station Approach, Chorleywood, Herts WD3 5NE Tel: 0923 285418/260096 (24 hour answerphone)
Fees: average
Suzanne Lazenbury started this agency in 1984 and offers a thorough range of domestic help including nannies, mother's helps, babysitters, maternity 'nannies' (doesn't call them nurses, *they* are only necessary for a sick baby), temps and proxy mothers. Genuinely interviews everybody, takes up references, however hard to trace and introduces staff to clients personally. Warmly recommended by employers and, exceptionally, other agents.
'We work for our money and the nannies do too. I don't think the money is that good for all the hours they put in. Some clients are very careless with their children. I worry more about who I leave my dogs with. It's all wrong.'

Agencies Specializing in Au Pairs and Mother's Helps

Hilaire Gomer comments: like the agencies that concentrate on nannies, when you ask an au pair agency how it places its au pairs it puts great emphasis on 'recommendation', i.e. one mother has used it and tells her best friend it is marvellous; or perhaps just, that of the six she rang, this agency came up with someone, although she felt it was more luck than effort on their part. Agencies don't dwell on the second, common reason why they were 'recommended'.

They also find many au pairs from commercial agencies (and several state ones) in Europe. Agencies often have as many as 20 or 30 such agents scattered about the Continent who recruit the girls and organize their papers. The European agent receives a fee from the girl for getting her a job in the UK; it receives nothing from the UK agent.

Agents also talk about 'contacts', which can mean anybody – their aunt, a friend, school and university teachers, embassies, the British Council – or au pairs they have placed in the past find them suitable girls.

Many zone in on two or three countries where they have a special link, and gather the majority of their September and December harvest there.

Some also advertise in foreign papers and periodicals. In the UK a great many advertise in *The Lady* magazine and in local papers, but most of them favour British Telecom's Yellow Pages. Some are proud to say they *never* advertise. They say this is because they don't need to. Many of the one-woman bands that are au pair agencies are comfortably placing 100 to 200 au pairs a year and have built up the business to an extent that makes advertising superfluous. The bigger agencies recruit more girls – 400 to 600 plus – and are more likely to advertise. One big agent comments, 'I never believe these agents who say they don't need advertising – what they mean is they can't afford it.'

References

Most agencies say they ask for at least two written references from the au pairs recruited from abroad. The 'walk-in' au pair girls already in this country don't have, often, references from abroad with them. No agency checks an au pair's references. They say flatly that they cannot afford the time or money given their fees to make overseas phone calls to check references, which is fair enough. Others say that references are checked 'where possible' by the European agency involved; some will have actually interviewed the girls in person. Others, often the smaller agencies, say they talk to some of the girls on the telephone if they have any doubts or queries.

A few agencies ask for a registration fee or deposit which has to be sent with the agency's completed questionnaire about the client's requirements and information about her family. This fee may be deducted from the final bill once an au pair has been found for the client, or it may be an unrecoverable, once-only fee. Most others work on a 'no au pair no fee' basis. Many agencies want their full fee, once you have agreed on a particular au pair, before divulging the girl's address and telephone number.

Most agencies say that they will replace a girl who doesn't work out after about two to three weeks. A lot won't refund; some have a sliding scale. It isn't a problem with many agencies as they give the employer two weeks' grace to make up her mind about the girl before expecting payment. If a girl leaves early, for example after four months, because of some crisis at home, good agencies will come to some arrangement to compensate for the lost months. A few replace completely free of charge if the girl lets the family down and leaves before she is meant to.

Rates of pay for au pairs vary enormously. The average in London is about £1 an hour, though many au pairs receive a higher rate than this, and out of town many receive much less. Don't be intimidated by strong-minded agents (and they tend to be) who may well think top London prices and expect you to pay top whack. If you can afford it and/or if you reckon she has a tougher job than other au pairs – like several small children to handle, plenty of housework, quite a lot of sole charge, or she has to walk miles to the nearest bus – then pay above the local going rate. A litmus test is to say, 'Would I do this job for this pocket money if I was an au pair in a foreign country?' Otherwise pay her what you think is *reasonable*, rather than exploitative, given her duties.

Many agencies, particularly around London, can arrange au pair plus. Others say they won't as it causes friction and their girls don't want to do more than 30 hours usually.

Most of the agents interviewed for the following pages were helpful and gave the impression they were responsible, offering everything you would expect from a good agency, like an 'aftercare' service for employers and girls if they had problems, some sort of replacement deal if things didn't jell. They all say they require two references, a medical certificate and two colour photographs.

Whatever they tell you when you ring them, it is wise to be sceptical and watch out for irresponsible behaviour. Some may send you just anyone without making much of an attempt at a match. One London agency with a good reputation comments:

I can't give you the names of the cowboy agents but, believe me, there are loads of them. The number of girls I get in here in tears because the job wasn't what she thought it would be. One au pair the other day was thrown out because she smoked 40 cigarettes a day. It seems that the employer said she didn't want a smoker and the girl claims she said she smoked on her form. These agents aren't doing their homework.

Summer Au Pairs

Summer au pairs are growing more popular, reckon some agents, as more families are cottoning on to their usefulness. Many agents place around 40 to 50 summer au pairs a year. For once there are usually more girls seeking summer jobs than families wanting them. Many families only learn about this type of au pair through friends. One agent comments:

It's quite a different deal. There are no classes to go to so the girls spend a lot of time with the families and they are much more flexible about the number of paid hours they are prepared to be on duty. Because they stay only for the summer holidays I only take on girls with good English. A lot are teachers on holiday or girls who are about to go to college.

Living Abroad

Many of the agents listed below also place British girls as au pairs, and would be delighted to help anyone planning to live abroad who wants part-time help. Within the EEC there are no restrictions about taking a British mother's help either. See page 173 for which foreign nationals are allowed to be au pairs in this country. All Eastern bloc countries, with the exception of Yugoslavia, are excluded from the Home Office's au pair arrangement.

Nationality of Agents
Where possible the au pair agency list below highlights the non-British origins of the agents and/or whether they have been au pairs or have ever hired them. Being of foreign extraction is a plus in the au pair business, not least because the agent probably speaks at least one other language fluently and is likely to have good contacts with agencies and girls back home. It is a good idea to ask the agent if she speaks any other language and go for the girls that the agent knows most about. i.e. she speaks the same language or was born in the same country.

Fees
On the whole, agencies either concentrate on nannies or on au pairs. Mother's helps fall between the two and neither type of agency majors in them. It is usually cheaper to recruit a nanny or a British mother's help from a mainly au pair agency because the bulk of its overheads – and time and expertise – goes on its au pair business. The smaller number of mother's helps or nannies, who perhaps live locally, are windfall placements.
Fees listed below are rated below average if £60–£75 per au pair six-month placement; average if £76–£90; and above average if more than £90. Several agencies charge £120 up to £160. Nanny and MH fees are rated as for the nanny agencies (see page 283).

MHs = Mother's helps

The Adam Agency, 139 North Hill, London N6 4DP Tel: 081 348 4004
Fees: above average
Proprietor since 1982: Swedish-born Mrs Kerstin Adams. Medium-sized au pair agency, Swedish girls only. Mrs A comes to visit clients in their homes in London so she can get an idea of the sort of girl they will like.

Au Pair Agency Bournemouth, 23 Richmond Park Avenue, Bournemouth BH8 9DL Tel: 0202 532600
Fees: below average, but above average registration fee
Proprietor since she founded it in 1977: Mrs Heidi Rose. A big, long established au pair only agency, which places girls all over the south west as far as Bristol and into West Sussex.

Au Pairs of Surrey, England, Buddenbrook, 15 Steward's Green Road, Epping, Essex CM16 7BX Tel: 0378 560180
Fees: above average

Established au pair only agency, now owned by David and Christine Martin. FRES member.

Avalon Agency, Thursley House, 55 Station Road, Shalford, Guildford, Surrey GU4 8HA Tel: 0483 63640. Also has a Brighton office: Tel: 0273 421600
Fees: above average
Avalon is owned by Philip Scattergood of Scattergood Catering.

Bees Knees Agency, 296 Sandycombe Road, Kew Gardens, Richmond, Surrey TW9 3NB Tel: 081 876 7039/948 5134
Fees: expensive, way above average
Proprietor since 1980: Mrs S Crane. She specializes in nannies, MHs, and UK and overseas au pairs. She is French and so does a lot of work with France. She also places British girls in nanny and MH jobs abroad.

C.A.R.E. Agency, 1A Chepstow Villas, London W11 3EE Tel: 071 229 0095
Fees: below average
Proprietor since 1965: Mrs A Alfandary. Au pair only agency which specializes in Austrians and the Swiss (all girls from Switzerland are interviewed over there). Above average sized agency. Never advertises. Extensive aftercare service, gets girls in touch with their country's clubs, and they are asked to come and see her if there are any problems. Mrs A concentrates on matching personalities: 'If I feel that their personalities are going to click, the girl's ability at housework, or experience with children is not so important.'

Capital Girl, Bishop's Court, 17A The Broadway, Old Hatfield, Herts AL9 5HZ Tel: 0707 271864
Fees: above average
Proprietor since 1973: Mrs Wynn. One of the biggest agencies for au pairs and some MHs, placing over 1,000 girls a year; covers the 'M25 circle' around London and environs. The agency has partnerships abroad in France, Italy, Spain, Turkey and Switzerland, so should provide a better than average service.

Daylies Agency, 7 Richmond Road, St Anne's, Lancashire FY8 1PE Tel: 0253 729739
Fees: au pair: above average. MHs and nannies: below average
Proprietor since 1983: Mrs Lesley Adams. Nannies, MHs, au pairs and all domestic staff.

Edgware Au Pair Agency, 19 Manor Park Crescent, Edgware, Middlesex HA8 7NH Tel: 081 952 5522
Fees: average
Founder and proprietor since 1963: Lorraine Bass, who speaks five languages. Big au pair, demi au pair and au pair plus agency. Also does au pair in the USA and specializes in placing girls with Canadian families. Also owns the Solihull Au Pair and Nanny Agency (see page 305).

English Home Holidays, 4 Albert Terrace, High Street, Bognor Regis, Sussex PO21 1SS Tel: 0242 865793
Fees: below average
Proprietor since 1968: Michael Bordier. This is a Paris company with an office in Bognor. It runs a big agency placing French-only au pairs, holiday family assistants (where, in return for board and lodging but no pocket money, the 'assistant' does three hours work a day during the holidays), as well as paying guests. Its bread and butter is its English language courses for French students.

The system operates very differently from an ordinary agency because the French girls pay a sizeable fee to EHH in France for finding them a pleasant family. EHH hires representatives around the country, including Scotland and Wales, who visit each prospective family personally. The result has to be a much higher success rate than with an ordinary agency. EHH interviews nearly all its girls in person through its reps in France. With its French reputation at stake, EHH only sends a girl to a family if it is confident that the match will work.

Euro Employment Centre, 47 Upper Union Arcade, Bury, Greater Manchester BL9 0QF Tel: 061 7976400
Fees: just above average
Established mostly au pair agency. Proprietor since 1988: Mrs Helen Verby. Places girls all over the country, including Scotland.

Euroyouth Ltd, Educational Holidays, Paying Guests and Au Pairs, 301 Westborough Road, Westcliff-on-Sea SS0 9PT Tel: 0702 341434
Fees: below average
Proprietor since 1961: Austrian-born Mrs Hancock. Au pairs only. A well-established agency which never advertises.

Fiola Agency Pinner, Mayfield Drive, Pinner, Middx HA5 5QT Tel: 081 866 4505
Fees: average
Proprietor since 1965: Mrs H Budd. Au pair only. Will refund. Doesn't advertise. FRES member.

The German Catholic Social Centre, Lioba House, 40 Exeter Road, London NW2 4SB Tel: 081 452 8566
Fees: the Centre asks for a donation equivalent to one week of the au pair's pocket money.
Run by Miss A von Oy since 1971. A non-profit making organization for young German-speaking men and women staying in London which organizes trips and outings. German girls can stay at the hostel for a few days on arrival and the Centre finds them a family.

All employers have to call in person and meet the manageress to help successful matching.

The German YWCA/Verein fur Internationale Jugendarbeit e.V, 39 Craven Road, London W2 3BX Tel: 071 723 0216
Fees: there aren't any, but the YWCA asks for a donation and pitches its suggested figure a bit lower than the cheapest agency.

Part of a worldwide non-commercial organization, which has been going in London since 1978. It is not a hostel and it recruits direct from Germany with excellent access to girls wishing to be au pairs. It has a thorough aftercare service with organized trips and events – employers of German au pairs recruited elsewhere can ring the agency for details.

The YWCA asks all employers to come for an interview.

Handihelps Ltd, 30 Rushgrove Avenue, Colindale, London NW9 6QR
Tel: 081 200 6331
Fees: above average for au pairs and well below average for MHs and nannies
Founded in 1981. Proprietors since 1989: Mrs Maureen Green and Mrs Joy Russell, both former employers of au pairs. This agency's speciality is *daily* domestic help of every kind as well as residential nannies and MHs and babysitters. It also provides au pairs, with supplies of Turkish, French and Spanish girls.

Helping Hands – Au Pair and Domestic Agency, 10 Hertford Road, Newbury Park, Ilford, Essex IG2 7HQ Tel: 081 597 3138
Fees: below average
Proprietor since 1981: Mrs R Glass. A small au pair agency which provides plenty of summer au pairs.

Ianda Au Pair Agency, 501A Walmar House, 296 Regent Street, London W1 5HB Tel: 071 580 1949
Fees: average
Proprietor since 1982: Mrs Suzanne Aarons. Quite large au pair agency, which also does MHs and nannies.

International Au Pair Agency, EBC House, Richmond Station, Richmond, Surrey TW9 2NA Tel: 081 332 1404
Fees: way, way above average and a small registration fee
This reasonably sized au pair only agency, which places British girls abroad too, is owned and run by Jane Oram, who with her husband also owns the long established Britannia Agency (see nanny Directory) in Chelsea, London.

Jackson's Au Pairs, Eden Lodge, Tilford, Farnham, Surrey GU10 2EB
Tel: 0251 252163
Fees: just above average
Founded in 1985. Now run by Mrs Zan Ward, who has hired au pairs herself and speaks French. Medium sized, au pairs only agency placing all round the country. Locally placed girls are put in touch with a good language school which organizes outings.

Jolaine Agency, 18 Escot Way, Barnet, Herts EN5 3AN Tel: 081 449 1334
Fees: average
Proprietor since 1975: Mrs Irene Rendlick. A big au pair agency which also does all other domestic staff and paying guests.

Key Personnel, 12A Market Place, Braintree, Essex CM7 6HG Tel: 0376 41330
Fees: way above average
Proprietor and founder in 1982: Mrs Jenny Stoneman. Mrs Stoneman and Rebecca McKinnie always tell potential clients that they charge the highest fees for au pair placement in the country. There is a registration fee, introduction fee and then a weekly fee. But it's a popular agency, placing girls throughout England, the 24-hour aftercare service is terrific and if the girl leaves early the client stops paying the weekly fee, which could make the cost the same as a less expensive agency. Mrs Stoneman speaks Spanish and specializes in Spanish au pairs. Her former au pairs recruit for her in Germany and Holland.

Linden Bureau, 68 Deanecroft Road, Eastcote, Pinner, Middx HA5 1SP Tel: 081 866 5435
Fees: average
Proprietor since 1966: Mrs Binnie Perez. Big agency mostly for au pairs and specializes in Finns and Norwegians.

London Au Pair & Nanny Agency, 23 Fitzjohn's Avenue, London NW3 5JY Tel: 071 435 3891
Fees: Au pairs and nannies: four times weekly net salary
Proprietor since 1985 when set up by her: Polish-born Mrs Mariola Innes. Small agency provides all domestic staff, more nannies than au pairs.

Millrace Agency, Old Mill House, Shoreham, Kent TN14 7RP Tel: 0959 4745
Fees: above average. Way, way below average for nannies and MHs
Proprietor since founding the agency in 1985: Hilary Burdis and Karen Smart. Small, well-run agency split between nannies and MHs (speciality Australians and New Zealanders) as well as au pairs including demi and au pair plus. Its area is the south coast and London fringes. Proud of its successful match rate and knowledge of clients.

Mondial Agency, 32 Links Road, West Wickham, Kent BR4 0QW Tel: 081 777 6271
Fees: below average
Mr Talbot set up this au pair and paying guest agency in 1949, now his widow, Mrs J Talbot, runs it. Places many summer au pairs. Caters primarily for the south east, but also for an increasing number of London families in areas like Wandsworth, Clapham and Kensington, 'thanks to word of mouth'.

The Personal Au Pair Service, 273 Eversholt, London NW1 1BA Tel: 071 383 5581
Fees: above average
Proprietor since 1985: Ms Teresa Godbold, speaks several languages. Above-average sized au pair agency specializing in Swedish and Danish girls. Half of her au pairs are already in London and she interviews them all. The other half she brings over from abroad. 'I used to visit all the families, but it took so much time, I

found it doesn't help particularly. My role model has been Sister Sheelah at St Patrick's. She is so caring. She taught me about matching family and girl; it's so important.'

Problems Unlimited Agency, 86 Alexandra Road, Windsor, Berks SL4 1HU Tel: 0753 830101
Fees: above average
Founder and proprietor since 1980: Mrs Hilli Matthews, who speaks French, Italian and some German. Recruits from these countries, also Spain, Yugoslavia and Turkey. Also places British girls abroad. 10 per cent discount to long-term clients.

Quick Help Agency, 307A Finchley Road, London NW3 6EH Tel: 071 435 7671
Fees: just above average
Proprietor since 1971: Mrs Norma Cutner who speaks French. One of the biggest au pair agencies.

St Patrick's International Centre, St Patrick's School, 24 Great Chapel Street, London W1V 3AF Tel: 071 734 2156/439 0116 Telex: 295929
Fees: below average
Manageress since 1984: Sister Sheelah Clarke. St Patrick's runs Catholic youth activities, the language school and a non-profit-making average-sized agency. Mostly au pairs, some MHs.

Solihull Au Pair and Nanny Agency, 87 Warwick Road, Olton, Solihull, West Midlands B92 7HP Tel: 021 7070179
Fees: average. Nannies and MHs: below average
Proprietor and founded by Mrs Lorraine Bass in 1990, owner of the Edgware Au Pair Agency (see page 301). More emphasis on MHs and nannies because of the good source of girls.

Stanmore Introduction Agency, 7 Spring Lake, Stanmore, Middx HA7 3BX Tel: 081 954 0666
Fees: below average
Proprietor since 1968: Mrs Ruth Abrahams. Very experienced au pair and au pair plus only agency. Specializes in Spaniards.

Students Abroad, Elm House, 21b The Avenue, Hatch End, Middx HA5 4EN Tel: 081 428 5823
Fees: just above average
Proprietor since 1976: Mrs Lilian Hildebrand, who had au pairs herself 'a long time ago' and has been an au pair agent for over 20 years. Mostly au pair and some MHs. Places au pairs abroad. Offers au pair in USA.

Weigan Services Ltd, Priory Manor, Kington St Michael, Chippenham, Wilts SN14 6JR Tel: 0249 758196
Fees: average
Lady Cottenham took over this agency, which has been running for 46 years in

1988. She specializes in Swiss au pairs and New Zealand MHs. 'Most of my jobs come from London and the Home Counties, but I'd be very glad to help anyone who asks me.'

Other useful places to contact

Your local Catholic priest and/or convents. Many convents in London put up foreign Catholic girls. The best known is the Convent of Mary Immaculate, 16 Southwell Gardens, London SW7 4NR Tel: 071 373 7007. Sister Valentina will try to help anyone who rings. There is no fee but a donation is appreciated, as with all convents. Resourceful employers also put notices up in the churches and clubs of the various nationalities like the Swedish Church and the Danish Club (see Useful Addresses).

Childminders, Nurseries and Other Day Care

There are over 5.6 million children in the UK under five and the overwhelming majority are cared for by their parents. Where the mother still works, relatives outstrip by far any other form of child care. In-home care accounts for as little as 1–2 per cent of the children. After relations, childminders are the second most popular form of child care, looking after just over 5 per cent of the children of mothers in full-time employment.

State day nurseries for the under fives are run by local council social services departments (under the overall control of the Department of Health and Social Security) and have on offer nearly 29,000 places. There is a great demand for these few places and they are taken mostly by children who are considered 'at risk' in some way, who are referred to the nursery by social workers.

In the UK the number of private day nurseries has grown enormously, and with workplace nurseries (which have increased at a much slower pace) they now total about 1,750 and have places for nearly 47,000 children.

Most private day nursery care and nannies are expensive, though there are a number, usually in cities, which are competitive with childminders (see below). Generally speaking, day nurseries and nannies are not an option for the majority of working parents, because of the cost. Consequently, most children with parents who work are cared for either by relatives, by friends (who are, strictly speaking, un-registered childminders), or by childminders.

Childminders

There are 84,000 *registered* childminders, and there is an unquantifiable number of unregistered childminders. The guestimate used to be that about one in three to four childminders were registered. But Peter Moss, of the Thomas Coram Research Unit in his *Review of Childminding Research* concludes that the bad old days of thousands of illegal childminders are over; unregistered childminders are now a minority.

The rise in the number of registered childminders has been enormous. In 1982 there were 44,000. This, coupled with a decline in the number of women taking in children for a few hours and not bothering to register, has come about because local councils have become more responsible and because they have made efforts to promote registration. The campaigning work of the National Childminding Association (NCMA) has also had a considerable impact (see page 342).

The definition of a childminder from the Nursery and Childminders' Act 1948 is 'anyone who in his or her own home for reward looks after a child under compulsory school age for any period, or aggregate of periods, of more than two hours in any six days'. Close relatives are exempt from this rule. Local authorities keep by law a register of their childminders. The law on childminding is open to interpretation by each local authority, hence the maximum number of children and the screening of childminders varies around the country. Commonly, the maximum number of children allowed per childminder is a total of three under fives (*including* the minder's own children). Only one of this number may be under a year old. Since the 1989 Children's Act it has become law for childminders to register if they care for children up to and including 8 years old. There is also to be a limit on the number of 5 to 8 year olds a childminder may have.

A few authorities allow four children under five. An important thing to remember when choosing a childminder is that there is no limit to the number of children of school age that a childminder may take as well.

It is *illegal* for any childminder not to register with a local authority and she can be prosecuted for failing to do so. Strangely, the parents of the children she minds can't be prosecuted for using her. This anomaly is something that the NCMA has questioned.

There are many positive reasons for a minder to make the effort to register with the local council. Once registered, the council should put her in touch with other minders who may be organizing activities in the area. She should have recourse to the social services officials, like Under Fives Officers, Childminder Advisers and Day Care Officers, who are responsible for all aspects of childminding.

The local authority may well be able to offer help and support to registered childminders in the form of 'drop-in centres', toy libraries, pre- and post-registering training courses, and the loan of equipment, such as fire guards and double buggies. The Department of Health and Social Security provides a free third of a pint of milk per child per day.

Councils vary enormously in how much effort and resources they allocate to childminding. Some do the absolute minimum, but the vast majority now have some element of support service. Many provide lots of back-up in terms of toys and pre-registration courses for interested mums. They work closely with the NCMA. If you are thinking of employing a childminder send an s.a.e. to the NCMA (see Useful Addresses) ask for information about it in your area; it may also give useful information about your council's and neighbouring councils' (useful if you live on the border) links with the NCMA.

Thankfully, the image of the illiterate, scruffy, fag-smoking minder with hordes of children around her is now a rarity.

The Registered Childminder

It cannot be stressed enough that new mothers and fathers, intending to leave their offspring with someone else must go for the best they can afford in whichever field of child care they choose. The highest common factor in childminding is the registered childminder. People who will not register and want to be paid to look after children are beyond the pale; they are breaking the law and cannot be expected to be adequately responsible nor to have a professional approach.

Registration does not mean that the minder has received any sort of seal of approval from the council about her ability to provide a high standard of child care. Registration may simply mean that the childminder has been asked to buy a fire guard for the sitting-room fire which the children use as a playroom and a guard for her cooker hob. But it is no guarantee that either will be used every day.

At the moment, because of the wording of the legislation, all comers have a good chance of being able to register. Councils do turn down applicants and do strike minders off their registered list; and some are a lot more choosy about whom they register, and keep on the register, than others. Although a council does not have to give reasons why a candidate has been rejected, the candidate may appeal. So the reasons for rejection have to be ones that will stand up in court, should it go that far.

It is tough to deny someone access to legal earnings. Thus officials are under some pressure not to turn down a person who meets the basic negative criteria to do the job, like not being a criminal, not having some illness or physical disability and having adequate, hygienic surroundings for the children to live and play in. She may well not have many shining positive characteristics that give the register a gut feeling that she would make a first class carer of children. Under the present legislation he can't allow himself to make the sort of value judgement which might lead to her being denied her registration.

There is much criticism of the vagueness of the 'fit person' clause in the childminding legislation. The consensus among those working in this field is that the law must change so that registration 'should be recognized as a mark of the *ability* [our italics] to provide a good standard of overall child care,' according to the NCMA study.

Why Do Childminders Do the Job?

Many mothers do not want to go out to work or cannot find work, or if they can, it does not pay enough to have something over after paying the child care costs. So some turn to childminding. They enjoy looking after children and are pleased that their own have some company. They like to feel wanted and they want to do more than be a housewife. Many feel that if they are looking after one or two of their own anyway, the more the merrier. Last, but most important, the job does bring in cash each week. If a childminder is taking in the maximum number of children under five permitted, not to mention any over fives she may have as well, she will probably be taking over £120 a week. From this she has to deduct expenses – heat, food, disposables etc. Childminders pay their own tax and National Insurance as self-employed, and might be able to claim up to two-thirds of their income as expenses against tax.

Who Uses Childminders?

It is a popular myth that childminding is forged for the poor by the poorer. This is out of date. Today relatively few parents who use childminders are semi-skilled or unskilled manual workers; more are in professional or managerial jobs. They are paid enough to be able to afford a childminder and often this type of care is the only option for them if they have no relations living locally. With the upwardly mobile 'nuclear family' this happens as they have often moved away from their parents' neighbourhood and so they cannot benefit from the children's grandmother helping out. The less well-off tend to use relatives and friends if they work.

The women who use childminders tend to be younger, in their late 20s and likely to be in an early stage of parenthood with only one child, according to Peter Moss in his *Review of Childminding Research*. He goes on: 'Mothers are likely to have had more education and have more qualifications than the minders they use . . . there is little evidence about the "match" of mothers and minders in terms of colour or ethnicity . . . childminders are more likely to be have been born in the British Isles than are the mothers of the minded children.'

A growing proportion of the professional middle class use childminders. A small but significant number of childminders are popular among this group in inner cities, and particularly in London where more mothers with young children continue to work. Many houses and flats in London do not have a spare room for a living-in nanny or mother's help. Where the artisan cottages of Fulham, Balham and Kensal Green have been gentrified, the next-door neighbour may double as the cleaning lady or the childminder, or even both.

The NCMA comments: 'Childminders are popular with teachers, doctors, health visitors and social workers – curiously all community-based professions. There are no statistics yet, but they may come across childminders in their professional life, see how they operate, like it and decide it could work for their children.'

Many working parents do not wish to label themselves as employers of what they feel is, in effect, a servant, or they will not make the psychological adjustments necessary to having someone living with them permanently, so they choose childminders.

The Pros and Cons of Using Childminders

Apart from the obvious advantage of childminding being a comparatively cheap option for the care of one child, there are many others. The minder is almost always a mother herself, so will be experienced in child care. You can tell quite a lot about the quality of care by watching the minder's own children, her home, and the toys and activities she provides.

The child is likely to be one of several, to enjoy the company and learn to be sociable and share the toys. It is good for children to have the experience of another environment in which they feel at home. The consistency of the care is an advantage – the minder has probably lived in the area for some time, is unlikely to move and so the child may benefit from several years of uninterrupted care from one person. This is in marked contrast to the day nursery option and to the living-in or daily nanny.

One mother quoted in the Working Mothers' Association Handbook says that she is 'now in a position to compare the relative merits of childminders and nannies and I have to say that, for me, the childminder wins hands down. What I have come to appreciate is the sheer lack of organization involved when employing a childminder.'

Childminding is a bit more flexible than a nursery or a crèche, although, quite rightly, childminders resent parents being continually late in picking up their children. How can a childminder broach the ticklish matter of over-time pay?

Many people associate a childminder's home with homeliness. They feel that their child is receiving a more personal and 'normal' upbringing than in a larger group with several staff in a nursery.

One of the major, insurmountable drawbacks of childminding is the fact that a mother is more of a client than an employer of a childminder. She must go along largely with the minder's views on, and standards of, child care.

Moreover, the minded child (or for that matter the child at a nursery), cannot ask a friend home to lunch, or visit a friend's house for tea easily. This form of socializing can be a most enjoyable pastime for many children aged three upwards.

There are plenty of examples of good and bad childminding experiences by working mothers. To generalize, it could probably be said that most mothers are content with their childminder. But just as with live-in care, there is a natural tendency for the parents to accept the status quo and to want to believe everything is fine. As long as the child isn't in tears at the end of each day, and greets mum and dad with a great big kiss, the parents feel with relief that the child care is OK. All too often there is no alternative anyway, or the work-weary parents haven't the interest, or time or energy to search for something better.

It is a good idea to talk to mothers who have used childminders for some time to get an idea of what to expect, be aware of and what to look out for. One mother tells us, 'When I went to meet the childminder, everything was sweetness and light and there were lots of toys and games around. Over the next few weeks I kept thinking that maybe they had been put away before I went to collect Jason, because I didn't see them again. So I asked Maggie to show me where she kept them. There was some blustering and rudeness, but it became clear that they had not been hers; she must have borrowed them for our meeting. I took him away; how could I trust her after that?'

Many childminders see their role as caring for children. They don't see themselves as educators: they don't see themselves as the home version of the Montessori teacher, or even the NNEB who knows about child development in all its manifestations. There is more chance that the minder will take a somewhat *laissez faire* approach to the child's play and enthusiasms. If she has three children under five to look after, feed and take to the lavatory, it is not surprising that she may have little time to sit on the floor and play with them. It is even less likely if she is fitting in her washing, ironing and cooking the evening meal for her family. You can't expect her to be a Superwoman.

311

As one ex-childminder put it: 'There is the good, the bad and, occasionally, the ugly in childminding.' There is also the mediocre. A mediocre childminder is not good enough for your child and it may not be at all easy to detect one at the outset. The onus is on mothers to be vigilant, and expect the best rather than accept the indifferent.

The NCMA advises: 'There are lots of excellent childminders with modern ideals and ideas. But I do recommend that mothers shop around a bit and do not take the first childminder on offer.'

What Childminding Costs

Childminding is attractive to all those who use it because it is cheap in comparison with nurseries and daily nannies. Whether or not it can also be considered good value depends on the quality of the minder. Childminding is better paid now than in the past, as parents and minders have grown to expect more from each other. Childminders offer a better service and parents are glad to pay properly for it.

The range of weekly earnings for a childminder per child varies widely, but the NCMA recommends a minimum of £50 a week for full-time care and a minimum of £1.30 an hour. The NCMA continues to work for higher wages. It has managed to get some of its members living in a particular area to form a cartel and fix a set rate. Rates may depend on the demand for childminding in the area, or on geographic location and even on the size of the parent's own income, as some minders will charge an individual more or less, depending on what they can afford.

A childminder may charge extra for certain sorts of food, nappy washing, disposables, museum, zoo and playgroup fees, special baby needs (zinc and castor oil cream, bibs etc), fares or, rarely, petrol for special outings.

Where to Find Your Childminder

Research shows that most mothers seeking childminders do not 'shop around', and they tend not to interview more than one candidate. She is often recommended on the grapevine or is someone they or a friend know. 'Hauling around lots of addresses with a small child is daunting, especially for women who in any case often feel anxious or guilty about leaving their child,' says Peter Moss.

Some mothers who have made the decision to return to work after a baby feel vulnerable, and, in a curious way, actually resist finding out all about various sorts of child care. It is as if, by opening more than one door, they may be overwhelmed by a whole range of options and choices which they haven't got the energy, time or resilience to think through and deal with. Some are plain lazy; others too sensitive; some are aggressive and some are just foolish. Whatever the reason many cannot cope initially with the effort required to seek out a really good minder.

Even with the best will in the world, in some areas there are very few childminders available and a mother may be stuck with someone less than ideal.

Childminders make themselves known by: advertisements in the local paper (it is a good sign if they quote their registration number), newsagents, laundromats, one o'clock clubs, schools, clinics and local shops. They also leave their names with staff at the local clinic and tell the health visitor they are looking for children to mind. Any local NCMA group probably operates a vacancy list.

Also it is a good idea to place your own advertisements in all these places locally. As with all ads in public places, it is advisable not to give your name, just the telephone number and as many details of your needs as can be fitted on to a postcard.

Lists of registered childminders are available from your local authority offices. Write to the NCMA asking for a list of local groups, remembering to enclose an s.a.e. (see Useful Addresses). Ask your health visitor for help. Remember if you live near a borough boundary it is worth consulting the neighbourhood authority as well.

How to Choose a Childminder

Parents should leave no stone unturned when interviewing a registered childminder. Scepticism, albeit heavily camouflaged, should be uppermost when you interview a childminder. After all, when did the council officers last check that all is just as it should be in the childminder's home? This, incidentally, is something a prospective client can ask the childminder herself. If she has nothing to hide, and wishes that an inspector would call so she can show off her new plastic slide in the garden, she won't be put out by *any* prying questions.

The first thing to do is to acquaint yourself thoroughly with the tasks involved in childminding and the qualities and skills that you reckon she will need to perform them. Only by knowing quite a lot about what the job involves is a mother able to make a choice which she will respect in a few months' time.

A childminder needs to be a capable organizer. If she is not, the routine of running her house and family, personal shopping and other arrangements will not allow her time to play and attend to the needs of another child or children fully. She has to juggle her house, her children, her time, her husband and her job – just like any other woman, but she is being paid so the least you can expect is that she does it well.

A childminder needs to be able to communicate with both parents and children. She must be able to tell a parent about any problems with their child or deal with a parent who takes her for granted without souring the

313

atmosphere for weeks. She must also support the whole idea of a working mother. She should co-operate with other childminders and the authorities as well.

A childminder must also be good at looking after her own emotional and physical needs if she is to provide a secure and reliable service. You don't want anyone who strikes you as unstable, or a ditherer who is unable to care for children with calm, firm, cheerful affection. Be wary of someone who is anxious to be all things to all parents, she may end up pleasing none of them or at least aggravating you with her half-baked, never-followed-through ideas about discipline, play and manners. She should have the confidence to be able to explain to parents how she organizes her day and how she expects the children in her house to behave.

The NCMA reports: 'Childminding can involve providing: love, play, security, food, time, warmth, attention, outings, routine, stimulation, sympathy and protection.

'What qualities and skills does a minder need? To be able to listen, a sense of humour, "broad shoulders", "thick skin", to stand up for herself, to think of others, to be understanding, to be sympathetic, to be business-like, [to have] good health, tons of energy, tolerance, kindness, to be unflappable and to be clear thinking.'

The Interview
Depending on what sort of person you are, either interview the childminder alone or take your child with you. If you don't take the child then he can visit at a later date. This second meeting may help you make up your mind about the childminder and give you a chance to see whether she gains points by the way she handles your little darling. If you intend to interview two or three childminders (and this is thoroughly recommended), maybe the simplest thing is to give them all a preliminary interview and take the child with you to see the favourite again.

The interview will vary depending on the personality you encounter. The childminder will ask you a lot of questions too. You will both be hoping that your priorities and wishes coincide well enough for a successful partnership. You will not necessarily see much of each other during this relationship, but that makes it all the more vital that everyone concerned is entirely happy with it.

Apart from looking to see that the child's physical needs will be well taken care of in terms of enough space, light, adequate toys and a garden or whatever you decide you most want for your child, there are other areas which are just as important to investigate.

Right at the beginning of the interview ask her if she is registered, whether she is a member of the National Childminding Association, and if not why not? If she is, is she a member of a local NCMA group? Ask her to tell you about it. Ask her how much she will charge per week. Is she keen on taking the children to playgroups, local activities? Ask her about her previous work experience. Does she have any qualifications, like nursing or NNEB, that would make her particularly suitable for childminding? How long has she been childminding? Does she intend to do it indefinitely or does she intend to go out to work soon?

A childminder ought to agree with the parents' views on child rearing – discipline, potty training, nutrition, safety etc. You also need to ascertain that the childminder is not going to give your child the benefit of any prejudices which you do not tolerate – racism, xenophobia or sexism for example. It will be far from ideal if the child has to witness anti-social habits like smoking, swearing and blaspheming. In other words, if you care about the *quality* of the care, you have to try to find someone as like you as possible, whose views coincide with yours.

Many minders respond to, and are keen to comply with as much as possible, individual theories about child rearing if the mother takes time and finds the courage to explain to her. If, having spent an hour in the childminder's company, you are not entirely at home with her and her ideas, resist the temptation to compromise. Say that you have other minders to see, leave and do not go back.

No mother can *make* a childminder do anything she doesn't want to do, that is not the nature of the job. Some minders do exactly what they like. The conscientious ones try to be amenable but even the cream may end up doing in practice what is easiest, given that she has three children round her feet. Alternatively, she may end up doing what she thinks is best for the child, not the mother. The mother has to check out *what* the minder does at the very least, and preferably that it is of benefit to the child.

One of the first things to ask her if not known already is whether she takes in more children apart from her own for after-school care? If she does, think seriously before going any further. The NCMA comments, 'Often a child that was minded by one of our members before going to school comes back after school is over each day until his mother returns from work. This can work well for everyone. The school age child enjoys being with his minder and can help out with the younger ones. We wouldn't recommend that a mother reject a minder who takes in one or two school children for a couple of hours in the afternoon. But it is something that she should know about and it would be a good idea to discuss the matter with the council's Under Fives officer.'

Ask the council officer concerned whether she knows if the child-minders she has available do take in older children after school and get her to find out if she doesn't know.

Talk around some of the following: Does she smoke? (Don't forget children inhaling expelled cigarette smoke are more likely to get colds and chest infections, not to mention the long-term effects.) Does she practise any religion? (Always interesting this one.) What are her views on TV, sweets, discipline and manners at table and generally? What about vegetarian or ethnic food? When does she do her shopping? What about her housework, washing and ironing? The ideal correct answer to this one is when every other person who works and doesn't have a cleaner does it – at the weekend or before or after work.

What hours do her children and/or husband keep? Will any of them be around the house during childminding hours? How old are they and what do they do? Try to meet all the house inmates and have a chat to see what they are like. Is there a dog? (Not ideal with small children around) or a cat? (A cat can suffocate a small baby.)

Does her home look clean and safe? Are there lots of toys around? Does the garden have any play equipment and, if not, how often, when and where does she propose to take your child out? How old are the other children that she minds? Where will your child be changed/rest/go to the lavatory? What are her views on manners/exercise/reading stories/playdough/painting/puzzles? Is there a First Aid box? What is her emergency drill in the case of fire, or one of the children having an accident? Does she know she can get cheap public liability insurance if she is an NCMA member? Does she have insurance if any of her charges are injured or killed or damage property? Does she seem to be intrigued by the stages of child development? Observe how she takes to your child. How does she handle him? Is her interest superficial? Do you feel that he means not much more to her than another £50 a week in her pocket?

There are many ace childminders and just as many who would be better if mothers made the effort to persuade them of children's needs, such as the above. She should have answers to all these queries. It helps if she has overt characteristics that you like, such as being cuddly, warm, showing obvious affection for children, being stimulating, humorous, intelligent, informed, wise, efficient. Turn to page 56 for a list of adjectives describing the ideal nanny. They are just as relevant to the ideal childminder.

Ask lots of questions about the other children she is minding at the moment. Don't forget you may like her but find her charges far from appealing. Have her describe a typical day and figure out how much time your child will spend with her picking up other children from schools or playgroups, and accompanying her to shops and on other errands.

Watch closely the other children who are being minded. Do they look clean and tidy? What are their manners like? Do they have snotty noses? What are they doing? Are they happy and occupied? If they are lying on the floor watching TV, ask them how long they've been watching. Are they wandering around listlessly or making a great deal of noise and bouncing off the walls with pent-up energy? Are they fond of their minder and do they come and sit on her knee? How is the minder reacting to the children's mood whatever it is?

Remember to find out what the childminder's rules are when she, or one of the children, is sick. What arrangements does she make for her holidays? Will you be paying her throughout the year? May you pop in when you can? What will you both do if the child has an accident? Check that the minder is not doing an evening job as well; many do and their childminding can be affected. Tell her of any illnesses, abnormalities, any special diet or allergies, fears or particular favourites that your child might have.

Here is the NCMA/Open University list of things which children do that some childminders say they find hard to tolerate:

makes a mess with the toys
gets dirty
refuses to stop and look before crossing the road
excludes another child from play because of skin colour or sex
teases other children
is rude to me after being told off
refuses to tidy toys away
hurts another child
breaks someone else's special toys/object/book
won't walk on the pavement when out shopping
calls a black child names
runs around indoors
takes food without asking
bangs on windows
teases or hurts an animal
tells lies
constantly tries to get attention
fights with other children

Think about the implications of this list. Is your child guilty of much of this irritating behaviour? Warn the childminder about his peccadilloes if you know he is badly behaved and/or always getting into scrapes. Talk about a few of your childminder's likes and dislikes as well as making your preferences and expectations clear. Talk to her about the ways in which she disciplines the children in her care.

A good minder will ask for the following information from the mother: the child's full name, date of birth, phone number and address and details of the child's doctor and health clinic, a record of infectious diseases and immunizations, both mother's and father's names and work phone numbers. Work out a contingency plan in an emergency – tell her whom to contact in an emergency and where they are likely to be.

She should want to know as much as possible about your child – his personality, what he likes doing, his habits and his stage of development. With any luck she will encourage you to send the odd toy and comfort objects along with him. She should assure you that she will make it easy for you to talk to her about problems and encourage you to express any worries you may have. Don't forget that it is possible a childminder can turn you down, probably because she doesn't think you and she see eye to eye sufficiently. If she does, don't persuade her otherwise; respect her judgement!

Many minders and mothers favour contracts nowadays. It does not have to be a complicated document, but should mention the hours and the pay. As with in-home child care, a contract can cut out a lot of resentment at a later stage. Peter Moss of the Thomas Coram Institute reports that: 'The pleasures of minding centre around the children and the dissatisfactions around the parents . . . major sources of friction are money, hours, feelings of being used and differences of opinion about child care . . . in general parents appear less critical of minders than minders are of parents.'

To summarize, babies and toddlers may spend happy days with an involved, well-balanced, conscientious childminder and it can be a most successful form of care. Contact and communication between mother and minder must be energetically maintained by both. Parents and childminder must be sensitive and sympathetic to a child's need to settle in gently to the new routine. It is a good idea, as soon as the child is old enough, to arrange for him to go to a playgroup or nursery school. This enables both minder and minded to get away from each other for two to three hours during a long day. It will break the routine for the child and may mean that some parents need be less concerned about the amount of varied entertainment and stimulation their adored offspring receives week after week.

Day Nurseries: State Day Nurseries

In this country the majority of state day nurseries, especially in cities, are used by local authorities to provide care for children who are on the 'At Risk' Register. These children are so described because their family background and circumstances are such that they may be physically or emotionally 'at risk'. This means that social workers decide that it is best for the child to spend most of his day in a nursery and away from his parents. There are long waiting lists for the remaining places which are usually filled by the next children 'in most need', or who are considered to be 'high priority' cases.

These euphemisms carry a certain stigma for the parents who use state day nurseries. In fact, not every child at a day nursery is *necessarily* in danger at home. Some gain a place because they are living in poor housing, have working single parents, or have parents on social security, or because their parents simply cannot cope for a whole variety of reasons. In the rougher areas of inner cities there is almost no chance that 'normal' children will be admitted. Nor would most caring parents wish them to be if there are other options. Some parents cannot afford the alternatives – and state day nursery charges for child care are minimal.

One mother, a Yugoslav who emigrated to the UK fifteen years ago, says, 'I could have put my daughter in a day nursery because I am alone and in a small flat. I would never put my child in such a place. I pay £60 a week for her to go to a good local private nursery in West London.'

Another working mother in Camberwell says, 'I managed to get my daughter into a day nursery. It was all right when she wasn't walking but then the competition with the other children was too much. She kept coming home scratched and was knocked about a bit. She was always getting infections and they wouldn't take her when she was ill. I took her away and sent her to a childminder.'

Another mother got a place for her little boy in a Marylebone day nursery because he 'hadn't slept at night for two years. Me and my husband were going spare. The social worker was very sympathetic. Both of us work and getting her a place at the nursery was such a break.'

State day nurseries are usually open between 8am and 6pm including school holidays. Some take children from six weeks to school age. Coote and Gill in their book *Women's Rights* comment bleakly, 'Some try to provide good educational facilities, but many are over-worked and under-staffed.' The percentage of pre-school children in state day nurseries has declined from 17 per cent in 1948 to less than one per cent today. The number of working mothers during this period has risen enormously, so too has the number of single parents with no one at home to help them look after the children.

The growth of part-time working mothers has boosted the women's work force statistics and it is explicable by the nature of an often poorly paid and part-time job that mothers fail to make child care arrangements. Astonishingly, 17 per cent of part-time working mothers leave their children unattended at home; 7 per cent of mothers at work full time do the same.

State day nurseries are mostly staffed by NNEBs and officially the ratio of staff to children is meant to be always one per three children under a year and one to five over 18 months. Standards vary enormously and the morale of the staff is variable too. 'It is hard sometimes to keep everyone idealistic about working hard and trying new things with the children,' says one nursery officer. 'Most of the time my job is challenging and rewarding, but we badly need more modern equipment and more toys and books. At times gloom is as contagious as the infections which spread so quickly. After three days of rain and too many streaming noses, it's not surprising. The staff do get tired and sick too.'

It is difficult to argue that there is much benefit to the children in being solely in the company of others with problems. 'Many of them are at risk of not developing properly – they don't talk or behave like kids of their age. They often have very poor concentration spans. They all need a rest in the afternoons; most are very familiar with the little dot on the TV screen at closedown,' says another nursery officer.

The state day nursery is not the only form of state-aided child care. Anxious to find alternatives to the low status day nurseries, working parents on their own or with charities have set up day care nurseries, community day nurseries, workplace crèches and the like. In many cases local authorities have been persuaded to help, and contribute for example, a quarter or half of a centre's running costs.

Community Nurseries

These have often been set up by a community – like those living in a group of tower blocks – and their aim is often to provide an alternative to existing care in a specific way. Many community nursery organizers feel strongly about racist and/or sexist bias and some challenge traditional organizational methods by working together as a collective. All the staff are paid the same and there is no hierarchy.

Children attending a community nursery live close by. One of its attractions to parents is that it doesn't carry the stigma of the state nursery where some parents feel criticized by staff. They resent also the minimal link between them and staff in many state nurseries. The community nurseries are trying to change all that. Parents are treated as partners with the staff in the care of their children. They are on the management committee and can influence decisions about the way the nursery is organized.

The committee decides on wages and these can vary enormously but are competitive with childminders' fees. They can be based on a percentage of the parents' income so that the better off pay more.

Alternative forms of care like community nurseries mean a great deal of hard work for staff and parents. Time has to be spent organizing, campaigning and approaching charities, businesses, parents and local authorities for funds to keep the nursery solvent.

Workplace Nurseries

These are in their infancy, but many parents welcome the chance of seeing their children during the working day. Its disadvantage, as with all out-of-home care, is not only the sweat of the early morning rush, but the trip into work accompanied by a child or two instead of parking them with a childminder round the corner. And they come home with you in the evening rush hour.

The workplace crèche pioneers in this country during the 1970s included the Kingsway Children's Nursery and the Chandos Place Nursery, both in central London. Today they are in effect private nurseries, though some of their places are subsidized by up to two thirds by the parents' employers. Bigger companies tend to be, and can afford to be, more philanthropic, though Walker Books, a small but successful publisher of children's books, has its own nursery at its offices.

The City Child Nursery broke new ground when it opened in 1988. It remains a rare collaboration between the Corporation of London's social services department, Islington Council and property developers. The developers were granted planning permission for a Barbican site, so long as they included a 30 place nursery and agreed to underwrite it for 10 years. The tenants of the property are American bankers Merrill Lynch, who agreed to pay two thirds of the cost of a nursery place for any of their staff who wanted to place their children in it.

'One Euro-bond dealer married to another Euro-bond dealer asked me if the crèche could be open 24 hours? I replied that we aim to supply high quality *day* care facilities. Just think of that poor child's routine. They obviously need a live-in nanny. We are only providing one option; it won't suit everyone. But it is one way of sharing domestic and work responsibilities peacefully and we welcome as much parental involvement as parents want' comments Susan Hay, a funder of City Child.

Although the City Child would like to help employers open other nurseries (Spitalfields and the Docklands have been mooted), the fantastic expense of real estate in these places and the high running costs of a nursery, not to mention a firm's subsidizing of children's places, militate against companies wanting to become involved.

Institutions with plenty of space, like universities and hospitals have been particularly generous. For example, St George's Hospital in Tooting, south London, has a nursery for all its staff which caters for shift work.

A much simpler and cheaper solution has been developed by the National Childminding Association and the insurance group Allied Dunbar in Swindon. Childminding in Business liaises with 40 local childminders who reserve places for the children of Allied Dunbar staff. The NCMA hopes that there will be many other such arrangements in the future.

It is always worth checking out a workplace nursery. The standards are often high and the staff well motivated. If it has a vacancy or two, a local child may be eligible.

Workplace nurseries received a boost when the tax which employees had to pay on their employer's contribution to the cost of the nursery place was abolished. At a stroke this reduced the cost of childcare for employees and cut the administrative red tape for employers too. Sadly, it is just because there are so few workplace nurseries, and a belief that it will be a long time before there are many more, that the government felt able to waive this tax. Another problem with the whole scheme is that it is not always easy to work with a perk which ties the user to the job so closely. It may be possible, however, to arrange to keep the nursery place for your child should you decide to change jobs.

The National Childcare Campaign, the Workplace Nurseries Campaign, City Child and the Working Mothers Association (WMA) all campaign and lobby to increase workplace nurseries. See Useful Addresses.

Private Day Nurseries

Private day nurseries have grown enormously in popularity. They have sprouted everywhere: in cities and towns. They are useful to the full or part-time working mother who can choose to leave her child a whole or half day or even for a few hours a day once or twice a week. Now that there is more choice the quality of nurseries has risen. But they are expensive to run, needing high staff-to-child ratios, so they are a more expensive option than childminding but are often competitive compared with daily nannies. A few nurseries are subsidized by local authorities and will therefore charge less. A drawback, which is not confined to state day nurseries, is the prevalence of infection. One mother who is a doctor says, 'There are higher instances of respiratory and gastro-intestinal problems wherever there are large groups of small children, unless hygiene is scrupulous.'

The cost of a nursery varies, but expect to pay £100 and more for a full week's child care. One mother says: 'My son goes to our excellent local private nursery in Fulham – we are incredibly lucky; there are two that are equally good there in the Fulham Palace Road and one in Moore Park Road. Hilary runs my son's in a converted flat and she really brings the children on. There are about ten children. They charge £23 a day, so I send him whenever it suits me – about once or twice a week, and he is as happy as a sandboy.'

One of the reasons for the growing popularity of good private day nurseries is that there is every chance that their properly qualified staff will provide responsible, stimulating child care in pleasant surroundings. Private day nurseries can be an excellent option for working mothers who can afford it. With a child at a good day nursery she shouldn't have to worry. She can relax, knowing that her child's minders are themselves supervised. There is no risk of young Freddie having to endure his nanny's rock music tapes, cooped up inside all day, for all the busy mum knows.

Checking Out the Private Nursery

As with all types of child care, do not vet just one nursery; compare several, then you will be more likely to be happy with your final choice. There will probably be only one that is close to home, so the choice will be minimal. However, try not to plump for the nearest one if there is something better further away; at the very least check others to highlight what you are getting with the nursery that is the favourite because it is the nearest.

The only way to judge a nursery's quality is to see it in action. Keep your eyes wide open and chat to all the staff. Be sure to visit when all the children are *in situ*.

Staff should be qualified – NNEB, Montessori and possibly playgroup leaders. Ask about the staff to child ratio. Consider the size, shape, light, safety and airiness of the room. As you survey the premises ask yourself the following questions: Does this place have a happy atmosphere? Are the children full of life? How much time do babies spend in their cots and playpens? Do they receive well-balanced meals when they should? Are they getting enough rest? Is there a rest area that is quiet and conducive to a zizz? Are bottles propped up, or are babies cuddled and fed?

Are the children reasonably clean? Are there too many of them with green, streaming noses? How does the nursery clean toys, changing mats, mugs etc? Are there enough toys/games/books/tricycles and other equipment? Do they paint and draw and model in plasticine and playdough? What does the nursery offer in the way of exercise? Can the children go swimming or do ballet? Is there somewhere for them to play outside?

'Is it better than I could do? Are the walls crammed with "artwork" and is the room humming with an activity which I could not possibly match?' says one mother. 'Those are the things I always think about.'

It is vital to chat to every member of staff and get a clear picture of lines of command. Who really runs the place and directs what will happen next? Is there a common policy on discipline, potty training, manners, and do they encourage the children to enjoy letters and numbers? Ask if the child will get one-to-one attention? Is there a small room where a child can do something alone and quietly or with a nursery nurse? How structured will the child's day be? Are there specific times when the children are read to, go outside, listen to music, enjoy 'free play'?

What happens to a child who is taken ill? Is there a bed in a peaceful corner? What does the nursery do when one or more of its staff are ill?

Nobble other mothers on the subject of how they are treated by the nursery. Are they kept at arm's length and their input ignored? Do parents and staff meet and discuss the child now and again? Sally Provence, a professor of paediatrics at Yale, writes from her own experience of managing a day care centre for babies and young children about the requisites for their good care. Her list, quoted in *Mother Care Other Care*, includes 'opportunities for the child to act on his environment: materials and opportunities to hammer, paste, colour, cut, sweep, dress, wash, build, mash, throw, kick, mix, stir, beat, pedal, run, dance, strum, jump, skip, button, zip and spit. Young children need these to feel effective and competent.

'[Also] an enriching emotional atmosphere: good relationships with caregivers who are consistently available, affectionate, patient, good listeners, good talkers and enthusiastic about the child's achievements. Every child deserves somebody to be excited about the first time he walks and the first time he rides a tricycle.

'[And] limits, prohibitions, and expectations for conformity: just as children need opportunities to express themselves, they also need to learn limits on their behaviour which will make themselves acceptable members of their society. Children do not come into the world knowing the social rules; adults must teach them. Firmly enforced guidelines for behaviour, especially those aspects which affect safety and others' rights, are essential in any child-care situation.'

If these requirements coincide with yours and the place seems to be running pretty much along these lines, this may be the nursery for you. One full-time working mother took her little son from six months to 3 years to a private nursery and says: 'He had a wonderful time every day. He loved his carers and they became fond of him. He did so much creative play and enjoyed his peers' company tremendously. As my only child at the time, I was certain that he had a much better time there than he would have done with me or with a super-duper nanny or childminder.'

After School and Holiday Care

One of the biggest problems for working women is what to do with their children when school finishes while they are still at work for at least another couple of hours. A few councils provide year-round playcentres but they are not open much after 6.30 pm. There are schemes around the country which organize entertainment and supervision of after-school kids (see Useful Addresses: Kids Club Network). Charities like the WMA and the National Out of School Alliance work untiringly to better the lot of this group.

Rather like community centres, out of school and school holiday schemes can be found anywhere – school buildings and village halls – and they are funded hand to mouth in a host of different ways.

324

The Contract

Why Bother?

By the 1990s employers were beginning to realize that the more professional they were in their dealings with their nannies, and indeed, their mother's helps, the less stress, trouble, misunderstanding, guilt and resentment everybody had to suffer. Until recently it would have seemed too like litigious America to be so pompous as to commit a nanny's duties to paper – surely everyone knew what they ought to be doing, didn't they?

The Americans have recently started to create training for nannies, but already employers' attitudes there are way ahead of their British counterparts. Contracts are the norm in the USA. Barbara Binswanger and Betsy Ryan in their useful book *Live-in Child Care* say: 'Many parents – even those who negotiate office contracts with ease – find ironing out similar agreements with their live-in helper time-consuming, embarrassing, or even trifling. But don't allow yourself to fall into that trap. A clear financial arrangement made at the outset . . . will pave the way for a smooth relationship . . . you and your prospective live-in helper can negotiate an equitable salary arrangement with a minimum of hidden upsets later on.'

The UK pioneer in nannies' conditions of employment statements was the Norland College. It protected its probationers from exploitation in their first jobs by drawing up its own neat and formal contract. Also, the Federation of Recruitment and Employment Services (FRES, page 341) have adapted its domestics' 'statements of employment' for a nanny. (Send an s.a.e. to FRES to receive a copy, see Useful Addresses).

A few conscientious employment agencies have created their own, like Birmingham's Pre-Select agency and Occasional & Permanent in London. Some agents still don't like contracts. An agent says, 'It's a two-edged sword; both sides can get too specific and rigid, and flexibility and common sense is jeopardized.'

Most British employers have not yet adopted the written statement of employment. The new converts now swear by them. The point about it seems to be that with any luck no one ever refers to it again, but the niggly points which may eventually cause friction have at least been considered and discussed before any contretemps has blown up. Apart from anything else, it forces employers to think through the whole business of having an employee in the house and helps to make them behave professionally towards the nanny. Likewise it will also bring home to the carer that she is doing a proper job with responsibilities and duties to which she has agreed. Both parties have had to focus on their expectations of the job. A contract provides a psychological rein on thoughtless behaviour on both sides.

It should be mentioned that several nannies say that they think nannies choose this profession because of their love of children and dislike of red tape and routine. Some employers reckon that they want their relationship with their nanny to be warm and informal and they are disturbed by the formality of a contract.

The contract that one employer draws up with a nanny or a mother's help may be extremely long or very brief. It would be absurd to detail every little preference and minutiae of the routine, but just as silly to omit salient detail. There is a golden mean dictated by common sense and how much the job is shared with the employer.

Working mothers are well served by having a contract and drafting it carefully and fully. The nannies of working mothers say that it helps them a lot to have a written routine and clear guidelines about the mother's expectations of their child's day. You might as well extend a written routine to a contract.

Under the Employment Protection (Consolidated) Act 1978, after 13 weeks in any job employers must give their staff a 'statement of employment'. It is binding in law but is more a statement of intent by both parties. In other words, there is no reason for either side to be scared of it. The idea of the statement is to give the employee some protection against his employer so it has to contain certain basic terms and conditions of the job.

However, it is toothless as far as the law and the outside world is concerned in the sense that you can still sack the nanny without *any* notice within the first year. After a year the maximum she can claim in law is a week's pay in lieu of notice. Unfair Dismissal legislation is not relevant to nannies unless they are part of a staff of over ten. The statement of employment is not chiselled in granite and unchangeable: an employer in consultation with the nanny can discuss changes.

Nannies and mother's helps should not be asked to commit themselves to more than one year with the family. Miserable nannies, anxious to leave but bound by their contract, should be released from it and let go for the children's sake.

Try not to reject the whole scheme as a time-consuming bore. Think of a contract as an aid, a useful tool for both employer and employee. Contracts should not be considered the sole preserve of the pukka nanny, as they are at present in this country. The good reasons for having one apply for any kind of child carer who comes to your home. This is a proven way of reducing friction and gives you a better chance of a long-stay nanny. It does not have to be typed. It need not extend beyond one page – a list or long note will do fine. All the details should be discussed with the nanny by the employer before being written out neatly, and then both parties sign it.

The Contract

What the shortest statement of terms of employment might include
(All those asterisked must be included by law)
- Names of employer and employee*
- The employee's job title*
- The date the employee starts work and her expected length of stay*
- Hours of work* (you don't have to be specific about this one; 'variable' would do)
- Period of probation
- The salary: amount, how and when it is to be paid*
- National insurance and tax
- Sick pay arrangements
- Time off: the number of days and weekends off in a month
- Paid and/or unpaid holiday and bank holidays*
- Pension* (this must appear in the statement by law even if there is no pension and there is unlikely to be; with 99 per cent of nanny jobs the employer writes 'no pension')
- Notice on both sides*
- House rules
- Sackable Offences, discipline and grievance procedure*
- The date
- The employee's signature confirming that she has received her statement of employment*

Some employers include additional items like:

- Overtime or additional payments, if any
- Salary review (when and the amount)
- Oral and written warnings before dismissal
- Dress (if uniformed, the employer pays for the upkeep and replacement)
- Description of the girl's accommodation
- Which appliances she may use in the house
- Car arrangements (who pays for what)
- Telephone (who pays for what)
- Entertainment of guests (boyfriends, girlfriends)
- A list of duties (especially outlining anything other than child care like feeding animals, housework, shopping, doing accounts etc)
- Availability for travelling (for long periods away from the family's home)
- No holiday to be taken until she has worked for three months
- Joint referral of disputes to the agency who placed the carer and agreement to abide by its arbitration
- Babysitting (not more than two friends to accompany or whatever)

The statement can be amended by both employer and nanny at any time. Since our research shows that a high proportion of employers do not pay full tax and national insurance on behalf of their nanny and thereby break the law (see page 338), spelling out these details on paper is not sensible. If a nanny agrees that only part of her salary is declared to the Revenue, presumably these details will also be fudged in the contract.

The clause about Sackable Offences is a Pandora's box. Quite a lot of this area can be chatted about rather than written down. But if you know perfectly well that if your nanny ill-treated a child/lied to you/stole from you/brought a man into the house without your permission, you would have her out on the street within the hour, it may save a lot of fuss to put it in the contract.

A Specimen Contract

Joanne Marden's contract as living-in nanny employed by Hugh and Emma Blackwell of 27 Ashley Gardens, London SW1.

Joanne starts work on 30 April 1988. She agrees to stay for a year, which is renewable because Emma would prefer a 2-year contract. There is to be a 4-week probationary period. Joanne will do the usual nanny duties looking after Tom (5) and Martin (15 months) and she will keep the children's hours.

The salary is £. . . gross a week. Joanne's NIC is £. . . a week and her tax is £. . . a week. Emma pays this £. . . a week on Joanne's behalf. After tax and NIC, Joanne gets £. . . a week. (Emma also has to pay £. . . towards Joanne's NIC.) Emma will pay Joanne £ . . . a week in cash. The remainder will be paid once a month by standing order into Joanne's account at the Nat West. Emma will give Joanne 4 weeks' sick pay a year from when she arrives. Joanne will have alternate weekends off and 2 extra days each month i.e. a total of 6 days off each month. Joanne will get 3 weeks paid holiday a year including Christmas and New Year, but excluding Bank Holidays. Both sides agree to give each other one month's notice.

Our House Rules are: no boyfriends in the house; girlfriends to stay by permission only; telephone used after 6 pm except in emergency; home at midnight if working the next day; no gossiping about our business; no high heels on duty; no smoking at all.

Instant Sackable Offences: stealing or lying, neglect or cruelty to the children, boyfriends in the house. We would sack for these things without notice.

Joanne will help Tom look after his hamster. We need her to come with us to the US annually for 6 weeks in the summer. We will go on holiday for 2 weeks a year alone and for a few weekends – Joanne and the children will mostly go to Granny in Bath.

Insurance and Suing

Is Your Carer Insured?

Motor

If the nanny or mother's help is under 25 and has no 'no claims discount', and/or has a conviction for a driving offence, an employer is likely to have to pay more to insure her to drive his car. The odds increase sharply if she is to drive in a city. Do not assume that if you have 'any driver' insurance she can jump in the car and drive it. Always check with your insurer whether she is covered. An au pair with no UK driving experience will elicit an extra premium.

Accidents and Disasters at Home

Suppose your nanny or mother's help was in a room in your house and the ceiling collapsed, or shelves avalanched down on top of her, or she was electrocuted by one of your appliances. Who would pay her compensation for her accidental bodily injury (including death, disease or illness)?

You will be pleased to know that anyone who has home contents and building insurance is usually covered for accidental injury for an *unlimited* amount for anyone who is not of his immediate family, like a nanny or any other domestic staff.

It is sensible to check exactly what your own insurance cover is if you are not quite certain.

You should also be covered for an unlimited amount under the same policy if a slate fell off the roof of your house on to your nanny's head, or a tree in your garden came crashing down on her. If a visitor to your home (like another nanny) is injured as a result of your slate or tree falling on her, you should also be covered usually for up to £1 million.

For a claim to be successful, it must prove that the accident happened as a result of your negligence – for example, if the shelves weren't fixed properly or if the flex on the iron had loose wires. If the nanny tripped down the stairs because of a carpet tack and, for example, broke her leg, then you could be liable to pay her compensation. If she was just clumsy she would probably receive nothing, unless she has personal accident insurance.

A nanny can take out individual 'personal accident' insurance or her employer can for her, which will cover her for any accidental injury resulting in death or permanent disablement. Some policies also provide cover for temporary instead of, or in addition to, permanent disablement.

If the employer has house contents cover which includes 'accidental damage' insurance, then if the nanny damages an ornament, spills bleach on the carpet or, burns a hole in the sofa with her cigarette, he can claim for replacement or repair of the item. Incidentally if a nanny's, mother's help's or au pair's cigarette burned the house down, it would be treated the same as if your cigarette was the culprit.

An employer can arrange extra cover – either standard contents or 'accidental damage' cover – for the nanny's possessions in his home.

Check Your Daily Nanny Is Insured Properly

A daily or temporary nanny's car must be insured and reflect the fact that she is using it for 'business purposes' rather than for pleasure, if she drives your children in it. Temporary nannies should have taken out professional negligence insurance (see below). She is likely to be handling several different families in a year which could expose her to greater risk of accidents than a living-in nanny who is intimate with all the house and garden hazards.

The Nanny's Professional Negligence Insurance

Employers' liability, public liability and personal accident insurance should not be confused with 'professional negligence' cover.

If an employer believes that his nanny has been negligent, he may take her to court for damages. For example, if a child trips, falls and injures himself because of an untied shoelace while in a nanny's charge, she could be sued for negligence. If a pram being pushed by a nanny plunges down a hill, crashes into a car and damages it, and injures the child, the nanny could be sued for negligence.

Robert Burrows plc, a long established Lloyd's broker, handles most of the employment agencies' insurance business. As part of its service to these agencies, many of whom place nannies and mother's helps, it offers the UK's only professional indemnity policy for nannies. It costs £50 per year and buys £1 million of cover arranged with a major insurance company. The policy also includes personal liability cover for the nanny. She will be likely to be covered under her employer's policy for this, but having her own cover, should she accidentally burn a hole in the sofa, is a bonus as her employer may not want to make a claim on his own policy for some reason.

Many people have heard of the ancient aphorism 'a master may not sue his servant' and think that it is therefore a waste of time for a nanny to take out insurance as an employer would not get far in a court pursuing his claim.

Although there are not many cases of a master suing his servant, the law is quite clear that an employer can sue his servant for carrying out duties negligently. Incidentally, for the legal world 'master and servant' and 'employer and employee' are synonymous.

A nanny, like any employee, is contracted to perform her duties with proper care and reasonable skill. If an employer can show that she has failed to do this, then he has a chance of winning a court case. Thus she could be sued under a contractual claim. In *any* job, the employee has to carry out his or her duties with reasonable efficiency and care. This is implicit in all arrangements where one person works for another for payment and it prevails whether it is written into a formal contract or not.

The long and the short of it for the nanny, or indeed mother's help, is that the risk of a nanny being taken to court for negligence, or for breach of contract is more theoretical than actual at the moment.

Suing

As far as we know there has been no case of an employer taking his nanny to court in the UK, though it has happened, reportedly, in the USA. Apart from anything else, there would be no point in an employer suing if his nanny had no money to pay damages should they be awarded him. Ironically, it is only when a nanny has professional negligence insurance that suing becomes worthwhile.

The subject of suing is not one on which anyone wants to dwell – employer and employee alike. Most employers in the UK haven't given it much thought yet as something to which they might resort in extreme circumstances when they felt that sacking a nanny was insufficient punishment and/or recompense for professional negligence on her part.

Most mothers are adamant that they would never consider suing. They say the reason for this is that they feel they must take the ultimate responsibility for anything a nanny does and so suing would be inappropriate. Others squeak with indignation, 'Would you sue a member of your family?' Some say, 'It's a risk you take'; others chime, 'Accidents will happen and I think it's bad luck when the children have them with the nanny.' A few think differently:

I would sue if she had been blatantly careless and irresponsible.

I don't know. My husband and I are both lawyers and rather overprone to suing and threatening it.

I might sue if there was an accident in the car and the girl was breathalysed and it proved positive and one of my children was badly hurt and she was using the car without my permission – God, I can't bear to think of it.

Employers Suing Employment Agencies

Good employment agencies have substantial professional negligence insurance. If an employer takes on a girl from an agency and she steals the T'ang horse and is found to have a criminal record, her employers could sue the agency that placed her with them for not screening her thoroughly.

Temporary nannies are often covered by their agency. To date there have not been many claims made against an employment agency as a result of the behaviour of one of their nanny placements.

Income Tax, National Insurance and Sick Pay

Ask most parents about tax and National Insurance contributions (NICs) for the nanny or mother's help and they groan. If anyone is doing it, it is usually the wife, though some husbands do help.

The most painless solution is to hand over the whole thing to the accountant. The best thing about the accountant is that he has to remember to ask for key documents, which is better than you having to remember them, usually just after you've posted the nanny's quarterly returns.

In virtually all cases, people who employ nannies are indeed 'employers' and have a duty in law to organize the employee's tax and NICs if they are paying them a minimum sum or more each week. The minimum usually changes each year, so one of the first things you need to do is to find out from your local tax office what the current threshold is.

You have to inquire from the local social security office the current pay threshold for National Insurance. This changes most years and it is set lower than the one for tax. An employee has to pay the state's National Insurance contributions (NICs) to ensure she is eligible to receive maternity and unemployment pay. It is the employer who has by law to deduct the girl's contributions from her gross pay each week. Also, the employer has to contribute from his own pocket towards his employee's total National Insurance payment. Whatever she has to pay, the employer has to match, and remember it is on top of the nanny's *gross* pay.

The Importance of the Distinction Between 'Gross' and 'Net' Pay

It is important to get absolutely clear with the nanny whether you are paying her 'gross' or 'net'. 'Gross' means *before* tax and NICs have been deducted; 'net' means *after* they have been deducted.

Many employers make the mistake of talking about their nanny's pay in net terms. For example they say, 'She's earning £100 a week.' Often they mean this is what she 'takes home', i.e. net. Some employers are deliberately vague if they are not paying NICs and tax, or only some of it. A giveaway is if the nanny's net pay is a neat figure like £80 or £100 a week. The odds are that the employer isn't paying her tax and NICs as the net figure never comes out neatly to a round sum once you have deducted tax and NICs.

Talking 'net' pay is not a good idea. It is dismissive of tax and NICs, and the nanny should not be encouraged to think in these terms. It underplays the fact that the employer has taken time and trouble on the nanny's behalf to make sure her tax and NICs are paid. Thinking net allows the nanny to think only in terms of take-home pay. In an ordinary PAYE job she would know her gross wage or salary and how much had been deducted and why.

Talking 'net' is very common among nannies and indeed their trainers. Even heads of residential training colleges still talk about so many pounds a week 'clear' rather than encouraging their girls to think in terms of a gross salary.

In order to give the nanny or mother's help some idea about how her wages compare with 'the real world', it is worth considering talking about an 'annual' salary at the interview, and again when you offer an applicant the job. For example, you could say: 'I intend to pay you £5,460 a year which works out at £105 a week (for 52 weeks) before tax and National Insurance. I give four weeks a year sick leave, four week's holiday pay, and you will have bank holidays as well, or another day off in the week.' Don't forget to tell her that you are paying *your* contribution to her National Insurance each week as well.

The Mechanics of Paying the Nanny's Tax and National Insurance

Under the Pay As You Earn (PAYE) scheme, employers have to deduct tax from their employee's pay. The Inland Revenue accepts payment from a nanny's employer each quarter. At the same time, the employer must pay over her contribution to the nanny's total NICs and also the nanny's contribution. If the nanny has paid a minimum amount of NICs each year, she is entitled to statutory sick pay, unemployment benefit and state maternity pay, as well as getting one year closer to qualifying for her state pension.

When you have decided to pay a living-in nanny or mother's help a taxable wage, contact your local tax office and ask for the name, address and telephone number of the PAYE tax office responsible for the area in which you live. The local office can also tell you the current minimum lower earnings limit for National Insurance contributions (NICs) and the current pay threshold at which point tax must start to be paid. Both items differ and change most years. Next, telephone the PAYE tax office, say you are hiring a nanny or mother's help and ask them to set up a Simplified Deduction Scheme for you straight away. Ask for an official's name so that you can ask for him or her again, and make sure they have your telephone number.

It helps the tax man if the employer can give him the girl's P45, the form that her last employers should have given her on leaving, stating her paid tax to date, her tax code and other bits of information. A nanny who had a nanny job immediately before joining your family won't have a P45. In fact nannies and mother's helps are always on 'emergency tax'. This means her taxable pay is constant throughout the year, to make it easier for the employer to work out her tax and NICs. Thus the tax office doesn't have to know previous tax details immediately, though he may send a P15 form for the nanny to fill in, so he can allocate the nanny a tax code.

The tax office should send you a new employer's 'starter pack' containing:

- a card headed 'How to operate the Simplified Deduction Scheme (ref: P16). This will include a very simple tax table for you to use.
- a form P16A, which every employer completes when taking on a new employee.
- Booklet CF7, which gives a simple outline of the National Insurance system and what contributions you make on your own behalf as an employer and the ones you make on your nanny's behalf.
- a red booklet of current Statutory Sick Pay tables and an SSP guide (see SSP on page 340).

Payslips to fill and return to the Inland Revenue with your quarterly tax and NIC cheque will be sent separately and will show a specific Accounts Office reference number.

Do not let a zealous tax officer bog you down with *any* other additional material like the 'Employers Guide to Income Tax'. The above mentioned should be all you need for the job.

The tax officer will also give you two reference numbers: the tax district number and a 'Q' reference (this appears at the top of the Deductions Card), and an accounts office reference which you use when filling in the quarterly pay slip.

At the top of the Deduction Card the tax officer will have filled in the nanny's tax code and the amount of tax-free pay she receives, as well as the Tax District number and a reference number, both of which you need to quote in all correspondence. The card looks more daunting than it is. If you find you are sitting too long at the kitchen table trying to fathom out the information, take all the papers to a local tax office or Tax Inquiry

Centre and let them sort it out. Once you know the nanny's gross pay each week and how much 'free pay' (as the card calls the nanny's tax-free pay) she has each week, working out and logging her net pay is not difficult. Nor is selecting her NI contributions from the relevant booklet.

Although you will probably fill in the Simplified Deductions Card once a quarter just before the cheque to the Revenue is due, it will make things much easier if you do your computations on a *weekly* basis, rather than once a month. There is less room for error with this method and this is how you probably think in terms of the nanny's pay anyway.

Once you have done this, completing the Simplified Deductions Card should take 10 minutes once a quarter. Work out the figures before she arrives, and then set up a standing order to be paid into the nanny's bank account each month.

Many nannies ask sensibly for a payslip stating the details of their earnings each month and it is a considerate thing to do. Mrs Davis insists that the employers of her Norlanders do so. 'It is illegal not to,' she says, 'and it is the only tangible proof they have that they have paid their NICs and tax.'

At the End of the Tax Year

The tax year ends on 5 April each year. The employer fills in a P37 form (which the tax office should have sent him) which is a declaration of the employee's total tax NICs and sick pay paid in the last tax year. Then he sends the P37 and the Simplified Deductions Card at the end of the week in which 5 April occurs. He sends the tax and NIC cheque to the Revenue at the same time. The tax office will send him a new Card.

Each time a new tax code for the nanny is issued (usually at the end of each tax year), the tax office will send a new Simplified Deductions Card. Whenever an employer receives a new Card, he must start using this and send the old one to the tax office.

When She Leaves

As soon as the nanny or mother's help starts to serve her notice, inform the tax office that she is leaving. When you have paid her last wages, send the tax office her Simplified Deductions Card when she leaves and a cheque for any outstanding tax and NICs.

Some employers have been confused when their nanny has asked if they could fib and confirm, when the social security officer rings, that she was fired for, say, incompetence, even if she left quite amicably having served her notice. If she doesn't join another family straight away, it is only if she has been *sacked* that she can receive social security instantly. If she left a job of her own accord she then has to wait several weeks for unemployment pay.

Incidentally, make quite sure that an unscrupulous mother's help whether British or from the EEC or an au pair who is an EEC national is not claiming social security while working for you. One employer was most taken back when her German au pair asked innocently, 'Do you mind if I go on collecting social security?'

'Girls from Overseas Don't have to Pay Tax and National Insurance.' True or False?

Many parents think, quite mistakenly, that to employ a girl from overseas, say from Europe and for some odd reason more particularly a girl from Australia or New Zealand, exempts them from having to pay tax. It is remarkable how often the happy employer of a Kiwi will say with a smile, 'And of course, because she is from New Zealand, we don't have to worry about tax.' Total poppycock.

Just for the record, no overseas visitor, including an Australasian or a Canadian, has a special tax arrangement with the UK which exempts them, miraculously, from PAYE and NI. Certainly, there are reciprocal tax arrangements between Britain and many countries whereby a person resident in this country *and* paying tax will not be asked to pay tax in his homeland. But that is something quite different.

The myth has grown up partly because foreign mother's helps are often not employed for a full year, and sometimes with Australians and New Zealanders it is as little as four months. So in practice many foreign visitors just don't pay tax and their employers are happy to go along with the fact that the Revenue is unlikely ever to catch up with them. Although in an ideal world the Revenue would love to make sure tax dodgers paid up, in practice, as far as mother's helps are concerned, a tax inspector has got more pressing problems than to chase back tax from an itinerant Australian.

The chances of detection are even smaller than when an employer skips paying an English girl's tax and NICs. Before you can say The Taxman Cometh, these mother's helps are off on their travels again or have returned home, or come back to the UK after a spin round Europe three months later.

The Single Person's Tax Allowance is another reason why few employers pay a foreign girl's tax. The allowance means that the mother's help, like everyone who has to be on PAYE, earns a proportion of her salary *free of tax*. If she doesn't work part of the year by leaving the country after a few months, she should get that tax-free part of her wages back at the end of the tax year. Getting this tax rebate may be difficult if the girl has gone back to Australia.

Many employers feel that if the girl is no longer with them, there is no chance of the Revenue knocking on their door chasing back tax. But be warned, the tax man has statutory powers to collect tax and NICs from the employer, even if the girl in question has left the family.

Even though the Inland Revenue would prefer the authors to drop any reference to employers' illegal behaviour in failing to pay tax and NICs for nannies from overseas, the purpose of the book is to explain the facts, though we in no way condone what is practised.

Not paying NICs for an overseas girl is not the immoral act that it is for a British girl. If she is a Commonwealth national she is allowed into the country under The Holidaymaker Scheme, provided she is self-supporting and doesn't apply for state benefits like social security and unemployment benefit.

Different Types of Employer: How They Deal with Tax

There are three types of employer when it comes to the nanny's and mother's help's tax.

1 Those who pay tax and National Insurance in full. This is the minority. They know their local tax officer well, or their accountant does, and they pay the lot. We need spend no more time on them except to award them a rosette.

2 Those that do the total fiddle. This is the type who have such a phobia of red tape and resent handling the taxman a penny more than they have to, duck out of the whole business, and do a total fiddle, i.e. they don't pay their nanny's tax and NICs at all and pay her cash. It is surprising that many families who pay nannies around £100 a week risk the total fiddle. It is less surprising with mother's helps who are paid less than nannies. Many mother's helps are paid just below the minimum earnings level to avoid the tax hassle. This may mean that she is eligible to pay NICs where the minimum earnings level is a few pounds lower. Conscientious employers may play it straight on NICs, and pay their contribution and deduct the girl's from her wages, so that she has access to state benefits.

3 Those who semi-fiddle. We believe these are the majority of nanny hirers. They feel unhappy about the total fiddle, and so arrange a part declared/part undeclared tax system for their nanny. This can mean declaring, say £60 a week for tax purposes and giving the rest, say, £40 a week in cash. Often the employer pitches the declared level just above the minimum earnings level. The rest is paid in cash.

Some parents argue that it is absurd for anyone earning around £100 a week, as most nannies and mother's help do, to have to pay tax. They are keener that she should pay her NICs, but unfortunately you can't dodge one and not the other.

So they say with enlightened self-interest that the *least* that they can do to improve the nanny's lot is not to declare *all* her wages and they give her the extra five or ten pounds they have 'saved' her by keeping quiet. Thus they set up her salary so that her employ is less expensive for them.

The 'semi-fiddle' is a popular tack as the nanny has all her NICs paid as well as a small amount of tax. Thus she doesn't lose out on any of the DHSS benefits like maternity pay, sick pay, and her pension rights. An advantage of this is that the nanny receives full National Insurance cover at, in effect, a reduced rate. NICs are much more expensive than tax for low wage earners; the two come more into line at around £100 gross a week. So while a nanny may earn £100 a week gross, if her employers declare only half of this, she pays NICs at a third of the rate they should be. Her employers also have the bonus of paying their NI contributions at the same 'reduced' rate. It is straightforward Black Economy stuff and is popular with all concerned.

A Nation of Nanny Tax Fiddlers

Many parents just don't want to think about, or indeed want to know about, their living-in child carer's tax and NICs at all, on the 'live now, pay later' principle. In fact they want to know as little about it as possible because then they feel in some way they are not breaking the law to the same extent if they don't know their obligations.

Many try to avoid the subject. If the nanny or mother's help brings up the dreaded topic, as she ought to, then with a sigh the employer might start making enquiries. When they have found out more they are so appalled by the Inland Revenue paraphernalia, the gobbledygook, the endless, 'dos' and don'ts', that a high proportion of them put the whole thing off again, or quite simply tax evade.

Most employers shy away from crude words like 'evade'. It is not something they talk about much in mixed company anyway (who knows if the man at the next table is a tax inspector?). They don't talk about 'fiddling' the nanny's tax either, but in effect this is what the vast majority of employers do.

No nanny should be fobbed off by lazy employers' mutterings about 'self-employment', which means that she is responsible for paying her own tax and NICs. Nor should employers accept a nanny's statement that she regards herself as self-employed. It is very rare that a tax inspector accepts a residential nanny as self-employed, though it is *always* worth asking.

Why It Is Important to Organize Tax and NICs

Although the temptation to forget about tax and NICs by both employer and nanny is understandable, neither are treating the job professionally and it shouldn't be shirked. One of the secrets of the successful employer/nanny relationship is that they treat each other with respect and the business of caring for the children is looked upon by both as a serious, professional job, with proper pay and conditions, including tackling the boring old PAYE.

It has been reiterated throughout this book that the employer is wise to keep in mind that the nanny's job description should bear some resemblance to a 'real' job. Failing to pay tax and NICs would not be acceptable in most jobs.

Christine Little, head of FRES, comments: 'We feel strongly that employers should pay their nanny's tax and NICs. The nanny loses out in the long run. Just because it is cheaper not to pay tax and NICs, doesn't mean it is right.'

Sick Pay: Statutory and Otherwise

A person's right to receive sick pay is based on his or her average earnings eight weeks before making the claim. State sick pay goes a good deal of the way to making up the nanny's salary when ill and may be paid for up to 28 weeks in any period of sickness.

The nanny only becomes eligible for SSP after four consecutive days of absence from work. There are no DHSS rules about producing a sick note, but remember that a doctor won't produce one for an illness under seven days' duration.

The Importance of An Employer Making a Sick Pay Arrangement

Many employers fudge the issue of sick pay. They don't like to think about the possibility of the nanny becoming ill, and when she does they often resent it a great deal because it inconveniences them and they loathe the girl for lying in bed while they have to drop everything to take over the child care.

As usual it is best to make quite clear what you are prepared to offer in the way of sick pay at the interview. If an employer doesn't mention it, the nanny should once she has been offered the job and the nitty gritty about pay and conditions is discussed. Sick pay details can be spelt out in the contract of employment (see page 327), so there is no doubt on either side.

An employer should think about the unfortunate eventuality of the nanny falling sick, and should work out the necessary contingency plans, including how long the sick pay is to last and how much it will be each week.

It is reasonable for a living-in nanny or mother's help to expect four weeks' full pay while she is sick (though many employers don't offer this), if she is intending to stay with the family a year. The longer she has been with them, the longer caring employers are likely to carry her until she is well and back with the children.

When Is She Eligible to Claim State Sick Pay?

A nanny on a contract of less than three months is excluded from SSP. A temporary nanny is likely to have arranged with her tax officer to be self-employed, so the temporary employer has no obligations in law to her when she falls sick.

SSP is earnings related and unfortunately the rate is set each year. Find out from your local DHSS office the current rate. As far as the employee is concerned, SSP is treated as pay by the Inland Revenue, so the employer has to deduct tax and NICs from it as he would from the nanny's salary, and the employee receives it net in the same way.

The red tape when sorting out her sick pay is not as straightforwward as it is when paying a nanny's tax and NICs. This is largely because your friendly tax office does not become involved. Any cries for help should be directed at the local Social Security (SS) office.

Those wishing to claim SSP will find they have been sent by the Inland Revenue in its 'starter pack' (see page 334) a yellow booklet N1268, *Quick Guide for Employers*. It is thoughtful to get from the local DHSS office a *Check Your Rights to Statutory Sick Pay* for the nanny.

There is a column in the Simplified Deduction Card where the gross amount of SSP has to be logged if it has been paid during the completed quarter. If an employer pays out SSP during the quarter, most of it can be reclaimed from the NICs of the same quarter. In other words, at the end of the quarter the employer adds up the *gross* amount of any SSP the nanny has received in that quarter and deducts it from the usual total tax and insurance cheque that she pays to the Revenue each quarter.

An employer must by law keep records of SSP in a form comprehensible to a DHSS officer for at least three years after the end of the relevant tax year.

Untrained British and Foreign Mother's Helps and Au Pairs

If trained professional nannies have difficulties when it comes to sick pay, the grey area develops into a thick fog with the untrained mother's help with not much experience, foreign mother's helps and au pairs.

Quite unfairly, an employer feels under less pressure to do the decent thing when she is employing someone untrained and less well paid. Any girl working full time for a family should have some sort of sick pay deal, and if staying for a year should receive four weeks on full pay as the pukka nanny expects.

The case of the au pair is again slightly different because she is there for a short time and works part time, and the issue of sick pay rarely crosses the employer's mind. In practice an au pair who is with a family for six months and is off sick for a week within weeks of arriving may not get paid at all for that week, or she may be expected to make up the lost half days or some of them once she has recovered.

An employer might insist that a mediocre au pair, who is limping through her six months with no laurels, make up the time lost. The same employer might ignore a few days' sickness in an excellent au pair who did more in a day than some do in two.

Ideally, it is always best to err on the generous side, it makes everyone feel cheerful.

Trade and Professional Associations and Unions

The Federation of Recruitment and Employment Services Ltd (FRES)

FRES is the trade association for private recruitment agencies of every kind in the UK, including those who specialize in providing nannies, mother's help and au pairs. It was founded in 1930 and aims to 'represent its members to government and opinion-forming bodies and helps to raise standards by which agencies operate'. FRES has a seat on the NNEB representing the interests of private sector employers.

It is a good sign if an agency has taken the trouble (and expense) to become a member of FRES. The FRES booklet states clearly the minimum requirements expected of its members.

They are all laudable ones that should indeed be met by any self-respecting, reputable agency. But there's the rub. FRES lists 51 member agencies nationwide, many of which are very small. Of the two to three hundred in existence, many are long-established good agencies who choose not to be members of FRES, believing that it has nothing to offer them.

However, FRES, run by Christine Little and her staff, does provide a useful service in informing agencies about contracts of employment, tax and National Insurance, setting up an agency and a mass of legal technicalities. (See Useful Addresses.)

The National Association of Certificated Nursery Nurses (NACNN)

NACNN is the NNEB's professional association. It has about a thousand members who pay a small membership fee each year. It holds a conference once a year and an annual seminar. There are branches throughout the country which are formed wherever people have the energy and find the time to run them. They organize social and educational meetings.

The idea is 'to encourage nursery nurses to keep in touch with modern methods of child care and to stimulate interest by postgraduate lectures and conferences.' The sort of topics discussed include children with special needs, parents as professional partners, and new government legislation on child care.

The Association is geared almost entirely to the nursery nurse in the public sector. It has very few nanny members and does not really cater for them, but wishes it did. There is, however, a leaflet issued giving guildelines on a nanny's pay, duties, holidays, hours of work etc. It is run by committed nursery nurses with full-time jobs who have little time even to keep it ticking over. It falls far short of being a proper support group, but any working nanny can contact NACNN (see Useful Addresses) and discover if there is a local branch.

The National Childminding Association (NCMA)

It was partly to counteract childminding's appalling public image that back in 1977 the NCMA was started by a group of childminders, parents and interested organizations.

The NCMA objectives are: 'To promote the provision of day care, recreation and education of young children; to promote good standards of childminding; to advance the education and training of childminders and to conduct research into all aspects of care, recreation and education of children under five.'

Its membership has gathered momentum impressively in recent years and now totals 45,000. It is partly funded by the DHSS but its contribution is declining, and the NCMA relies more and more on the support of its members who pay just a few pounds a year. NCMA members have access to cheap public liability insurance cover. This means they have insurance if, for example, their clients' children were injured or even killed while under their care and they are sued. It also insures their charges' property (like prams and buggies if they are lost, stolen or damaged).

Members receive a bi-monthly newsletter called *Who Minds?* This excellent publication keeps members in touch with the latest news and opportunities in childminding nationwide, and through it they can get in touch with each other. Members can receive free Tips Packs, a *Minding to Music* book and a First Aid Manual. They can also buy the Open University childminding pack which is popular in group discussion among committed childminders.

Unions

Employers may be unaware that nannies can belong to unions. There are very few nanny members as yet, but it is important that employers know about nanny unions. The unions' idea of promoting professional standards and good pay and conditions should not put off a good employer. Union membership does not automatically turn your nanny into a red under the bed. She may just be taking the job seriously and every employer can be glad of that.

As the Professional Association of Nursery Nurses (PANN) states: 'Employees have responsibilities to do the job for which they have been employed. If they fail to do the job or breach their employer's trust in any way then their employer may take disciplinary action against them.'

The best bet for the nanny in constant employment in the private sector is PANN, but since it has no negotiating clout because it is an anathema to the TUC, NALGO or NUPE is the sensible choice for a public sector employee.

PANN

More and more nannies are joining PANN. This is the newest of the trade unions in this field. It is not affiliated to the TUC and it does not believe in strikes, but it is the first union to attract the residential qualified nanny. Its membership consists mostly of nursery nurses in the public sector, though its nanny contingent is growing. Its total membership hovers around the 4,000 mark. Graduates of the NNEB, NAMCW's two-year diploma and B/Tec's nursery nurse diploma can all become members. It looks after and protects its members entirely out of its own subscription income. PANN is proud to say that 'it is the only union that is run by nursery nurses for nursery nurses.'

Like NACNN (page 342), it issues guidelines on pay and conditions. It is keen to promote the necessity for a contract for the nanny. It has its own lawyer to give free advice to members. There is a sliding scale of inexpensive union fees, depending on when a nanny joins during the year. PANN believes in solving problems by discussion and provides a 24-hour telephone service to give advice on problems (see Useful

Addresses). Members receive union support in the event of a dispute with employers.

PANN says: 'The care of young children is a very demanding job. Nursery nurses will only improve their pay and conditions when they can demonstrate that they are fully qualified professionals.'

NUPE and NALGO

The traditional unions for nursery nurses in day nurseries are the National Union of Public Employees (NUPE) and the National Association of Local Government Officers (NALGO). NUPE has the lion's share of nursery nurse membership. They both loathe PANN, and they remind all concerned that PANN has 'not even an outside chance of winning national negotiating rights' as it is not a member of the TUC.

NUPE and NALGO are represented on the NNEB Board.

Useful Addresses

Advisory Group for Au Pairs, c/o St Patrick's International Centre, 24 Great Chapel Street, London W1V 3AF Tel: 071 734 2156/439 0116 Contact: Sister Sheelah Clarke
(The group is a refuge for all au pairs; it helps to solve difficulties, disseminates information, introduces girls to each other. In early October each year it organizes an Au Pair Day when 700 au pairs gather in Leicester Square.)

Au Pair in America, 37 Queen's Gate, London SW7 5HR Tel: 071 581 2730

Robert Barrow plc, Robert Barrow House, 24–6 Minories, London EC3N 1BY Tel: 071 709 9611
(Nanny professional negligence insurance.)

The Business & Technician Education Council (B/TEC), Tavistock House (South), Tavistock Square, London WC1H 9LG Tel: 071 387 4141
(B/TEC runs a Nursery Nursing National Diploma.)

Chiltern Nursery Training College, Peppard Road, Caversham, Reading, Berks RG4 8JZ Tel: 0734 471131

City and Guilds of London Institute, 46 Britannia Street, London WC1X 9RG Tel: 071 278 2468

The Danish Church, 5 St Katherine's Precinct, Regent's Park, London NW1 4HH Tel: 071 935 7585

The Danish Club, 62 Knightsbridge, London SW1Y 7JX Tel: 071 235 5121

The Dutch Church, 7 Austin Friars, London EC2N 2EJ Tel: 071 588 1684

The Federation of Recruitment and Employment Services Ltd (FRES), 36–8 Mortimer Street, London W1N 7RB Tel: 071 323 4300

The Kensington Committee of Friendship for Overseas Students, Basement, 13 Prince's Gardens, London SW7 1NE Tel: 071 584 3989 between 10.30 am and 5.30 pm weekdays only.
(Excellent social introductions for an au pair who may enjoy this charity's full programme of events for small membership fee.)

The International Catholic Girls Society, 24 Great Chapel Street London W1V 3AS Tel: 071 734 2156

The Isle College, Ramneth Road, Wisbech, Cambs PE13 2JE Tel: 0945 582561

The Kids Club Network (until recently known as the National Out of School Alliance), 279 Whitechapel Road, London E1 1BY Tel: 071 247 3009

The Lady, 39–40 Bedford Street, London WC2 9ER Tel: 071 836 8705

The London Montessori Centre, 18 Balderton Street, London W1Y 1TG Tel: 071 493 0165

Maternity Instincts, 35 Beryl Road, London W6 8JS Tel: 081 741 8819 (Run by Alice Lewes: safety and play courses, see page 132.)

Maternity Alliance, 15 Britannia Street, London WC1X 9JP Tel: 071 837 1265
(Provides information on maternity rights and services, send an s.a.e. with request.)

The Nannies Need Nannies Association, Co-ordinator: Lorraine Thompson c/o 28 May Street, South Shields, Tyne & Wear, NE33 3AJ Tel: 091 454 2617

National Association of Certified Nursery Nurses (NACNN), 162 Langdale Road, Thornton Heath, Surrey CR4 7PR

The National Association for Maternal and Child Welfare (NAMCW), Strode House, Suite 25, 46–8 Osnaburgh Street, London NW1 3ND Tel: 071 383 4541

The National Childbirth Trust, Alexandra House, Oldham Terrace, London W3 6NH Tel: 081 992 8637

The National Childminding Association, 8 Mason's Hill, Bromley, Kent BR2 9EY Tel: 081 464 6164

Nannies Friendship and Information Centre, Co-ordinator: Linda Downes, 3 Rosedale Road, Toronto, Ontario, Canada M4W 2P1 Tel: 416 920 3409

Useful Addresses

The National Nanny Newsletter, 976 West Foothill Boulevard, Suite 591, Claremont, California 91711, USA

National Nursery Examination Board, 8 Chequer Street, St Albans, Herts AL1 3XZ Tel: 0727 867333 *28p stamps + A4 envelop.*

Norland Nursery Training College, Denford Park, Hungerford, Berks RG17 0PQ Tel: 0488 682252

The Norwegian Club, 21–4 Cockspur Street, London SW1Y 5BN Tel: 071 930 3632 Secretary: 071 930 4084

The Norwegian (Seamen's) Church, 1 Albion Street, London SE16 1JB Tel: 071 237 5587/5588

The Norwegian YWCA, 52 Holland Park, London W11 3RS Tel: 071 727 9897/9346

Nursery World, The Schoolhouse Workshop, 51 Calthorpe Street, London WC1X 0HH Tel: 071 837 7224

Pre-school Playgroups Association, Alford House, Aveline Street, London SE11 5DJ Tel: 071 582 8871 *JAN Chapronière* *" 828-2417 081-368-3575*

The Professional Association of Nursery Nurses (PANN), 99 Friar Gate, Derby DE1 1EZ Tel: 0332 43029

The Princess Christian College, 26 Wilbraham Road, Fallowfield, Manchester M14 6JX Tel: 061 224 4560

Toy Libraries Association, Seabrook House, Wyllyotts Manor, Darkes Lane, Potters Bar, Herts EN6 5HL Tel: 0707 44571 *Moved*

Working Mother's Association, 77 Holloway Road, London N7 8JZ Tel: 071 700 5771
(Open Monday–Thursday 9am–1pm)

The Young Women's Christian Association, Clarendon House, 52 Cornmarket Street, Oxford, OX1 3EJ Tel: 0865 726110

Diploma £240. per year.

Secondary proposal from Government Now

Brent Mon–Wed. Classes Tues–Thurs.

347

Bibliography

Baby Travel, St John's Wood Press, 1987

Binswanger, Barbara and Ryan, Betsy, *Live-in Child Care*, Dolphin, Doubleday and Co, 1986

Conran, S., *Superwoman*, Sidgwick & Jackson, 1975

Cooper, Jilly, *Class*, Corgi, 1985

Coote, A. and Gill, T., *Women's Rights*, Penguin, 1974

Cullum, M., *Becoming a Nursery Nurse*, Batsford, 1986

Gathorne-Hardy, J., *The Rise and Fall of the British Nanny*, Weidenfeld & Nicolson, 1972

Gostelow, M., *The Complete Woman's Handbook*, Penguin, 1986

Hodgkinson, L., *The Working Woman's Guide*, Thorsons Publishers, 1985

Marianne Mulder von. H., *Das Au-Pair-Buch*, Althenaeum, 1986

Martin, J. and Roberts, C., *Women and Employment: A Lifelong Perspective*, HMSO, 1984

Metzroth, Jane P., *Picking the Perfect Nanny*, Pocket Books, 1984

Moss, P., *A Review of Childminding Research*, Thomas Coram Institute, 1987

Moss, P. and Brennan, Julia, *Managing Mothers*, Hyman, 1990

New, Caroline and David, Miriam, *For the Children's Sake*, Pelican, 1987

Purves, L., *How Not To Be a Perfect Mother*, Fontana, 1986

Rice, R., *The American Nanny*, TAN Press, 1985

Scarr, S. and Dunn, J., *Mother Care/Other Care*, Pelican, 1987

Slaughter, A., ed., *The Working Woman's Handbook*, Century, 1986

Solomon, J., *Green Parenting*, Optima, 1990

Solomon, J., *Holding the Reins*, Fontana, 1987

Thompson, M., *A Handbook For Nannies*, Batsford, 1986

Travers, P. L., *Mary Poppins*, Puffin, 1962

Velmans, M. and Litvinoff, S., *Working Mother*, Corgi, 1987

Whitehorn, Katharine, *How to Survive Children*, Methuen, 1975

The Working Mothers' Handbook, (constantly updated by WMA), 1981

INDEX

Index